**Handbooks of
Archaeology and Antiquities**

A HANDBOOK

OF

GREEK CONSTITUTIONAL HISTORY

MACMILLAN AND CO., Limited
LONDON · BOMBAY · CALCUTTA · MADRAS
MELBOURNE

THE MACMILLAN COMPANY
NEW YORK · BOSTON · CHICAGO
DALLAS · SAN FRANCISCO

THE MACMILLAN CO. OF CANADA, Ltd.
TORONTO

A HANDBOOK OF

GREEK

CONSTITUTIONAL HISTORY

BY

A. H. J. GREENIDGE, M.A.

LATE LECTURER AND FELLOW OF HERTFORD COLLEGE, AND
LECTURER IN ANCIENT HISTORY AT BRASENOSE COLLEGE, OXFORD

MACMILLAN AND CO., LIMITED
ST. MARTIN'S STREET, LONDON

1928

COPYRIGHT

First Edition 1896
Reprinted 1902, 1911, 1914, 1920, 1928

PRINTED IN GREAT BRITAIN
BY R. & R. CLARK, LIMITED, EDINBURGH

PREFACE

THIS little book is meant to be of assistance to those who find difficulty in mastering what I have often found regarded as the least attractive, probably because it is the least understood, portion of Greek history. The merest glance at its pages will be sufficient to show how little it attempts to compete with such standard works on Greek Political Antiquities as some of those mentioned in the brief bibliography which I have given on page xv. My debt to the works of Hermann, Schömann, Gilbert, and to the scholars who have written in Handbooks or in Dictionaries of Antiquities, is very great indeed; for no one can move a step in Greek Constitutional Law without consulting authorities as remarkable for the fulness as for the accuracy of their detail. But, apart from the obviously smaller compass of this treatise, my object has been somewhat different from that of most of these writers. Completeness of detail could not be aimed at in a work of this size; such an attempt would have changed what professes to be a History into a too concise, and therefore almost unintelligible, Manual of Political Antiquities. My purpose has been to give in a brief narrative form the main lines of development of Greek Public Law, to represent the different types of states in the order of their development, and to pay more attention to the working than to the mere structure of constitutions. I have attempted, in the introductory chapter of this work, to offer some considerations which justify a separate study of Greek political institutions, so rarely attempted in this country; consequently it is needless to anticipate at this point the reasons for a procedure which, perhaps, does not need defence.

Throughout the work I have cited the original passages from ancient authors on which every fact or assertion of any degree of importance is based. Considerations of space forbade more ample quotations from the texts of the original authorities or a fuller discussion of passages which have given rise to differences of interpretation. In citing inscriptions references have been given to the Handbooks which I believed to be most easily accessible to students. In no case have I referred to the *Corpus Inscriptionum Graecarum* or the *Corpus Inscriptionum Atticarum* where I knew that the inscription was to be found in the Manuals of Hicks, Dittenberger, and Cauer.

My thanks are due to my wife for valuable suggestions in the correction of the proofs, for a great share of the labour in preparing the Index, and for the map which accompanies this volume.

A. H. J. G.

OXFORD, *June* 1896.

CONTENTS

(The references are to the pages)

CHAPTER I

INTRODUCTORY

SECT.
The constitutional aspect of Greek History, 1. Primary political conceptions, 4; the State and the Constitution, 4; political office, 6; the Citizen, 7; the Law, 8; public and private law, 9; authoritative character of law, 10.

CHAPTER II

EARLY DEVELOPMENT OF THE GREEK CONSTITUTIONS THROUGH MONARCHY, ARISTOCRACY, AND TYRANNY TO CONSTITUTIONAL GOVERNMENT

Origin of the city-state; the tribe and the clan, 12. Origin of Greek monarchy, 14; character of the heroic monarchy, 15; downfall of this monarchy, 17. Transfer of government to the clans, 19; nature of the clan, 20. The early aristocracies, 21; tendency to oligarchic government, 22. Impulse to colonisation, 24. Early Greek tyranny, 25; its origin, 25; the tyrants, 27; character of their government, 30; how far was it constitutional, 31; political and social consequences of their rule, 32; downfall of tyranny, 33. Rise of constitutional government, 34.

CHAPTER III

COLONISATION—INTERNATIONAL LAW

COLONISATION

1. Causes of colonisation as affecting the form of the colony, 36. Settlements due to the migrations; characteristics of the Asiatic colonies, 37.

Colonies due to political and commercial causes, 38. Military colonies, 39. Cleruchies, 40. The act of colonisation and colonial charters, 40. Relations between the colony and the mother city, 42. Political history of the colonies; characteristics of the Western settlements, 44.

INTERNATIONAL LAW

2. The unity of Hellas, 45. International obligations based on religion, 46. The amphictyonies and games, 48. Tribal amphictyonies, 49. Intertribal or interpolitical unions, 50. The amphictyony of Delphi, 51. Secular relations between Greek states, 53; interchange of civic rights, 54. Commercial relations, 54. Arbitration, 55. Treaties, 55.

CHAPTER IV

CLASSIFICATION OF CONSTITUTIONS—OLIGARCHY

THE DIFFERENT FORMS OF GOVERNMENT

1. Principles of classification, 56. Tendencies of development and causes of variation in constitutions, 57. Classification of constitutions with reference to their form, 58. States in Greece that were not cities, 59. The three main forms of constitution, 60.

OLIGARCHY

2. Conception of oligarchy, 60. Instability of this form of government, 62. The more permanent types of oligarchy, 62. The cities of Thessaly, 62. The Malians, 64. The Opuntian Locrians, 65. The Ozolian Locrians, 66. Thebes, 66. Megara, 68. Sicyon and Corinth, 70. Sicyon, 71. Corinth, 71. Causes of our ignorance of the details of oligarchic governments; probable simplicity of the type, 73.

CHAPTER V

MIXED CONSTITUTIONS

Meaning of mixed constitution, 74. Characteristics of governments of this type, 76.

SPARTA—THE CLASSES, THE CITIZENS, AND THE LAND

1. Sparta's position in Laconia, 78. Origin of the Perioeci, 78. Ethnic elements in Sparta, 79. Condition of the Perioeci and their relations to the ruling city, 80. The Helots, 83. The Neodamodeis, 86. The Mothaces, 86. The Spartiatae, 87; "peers" and "inferiors," 87. The common meals, 88. Nobles and commons at Sparta, 89. Tenure of land at Sparta, 90. Economic evils of the constitution, 91.

THE POLITICAL CONSTITUTION

3 Meaning of rhetra, 92. Constitution of Lycurgus, 93. Rhetra of Lycurgus, 94. The obes and the tribes, 94. Character of the early constitution, 96. The later constitution, 97. The Kings, 97. The Council of Elders, 100. The Ephors, 102. Character of the developed constitution, 106.

THE PELOPONNESIAN CONFEDERACY

3. Origin of the confederacy, 108 ; its legal basis, 108. Means by which Spartan influence was secured, 109. Relations of the states to one another, 110 ; their relations to Sparta, 111. The Council of the Confederacy, 112. Elements of weakness in Sparta's hegemony, 113 ; her imperial system, 114. Decline of the Spartan state, 114.

THE CITIES OF CRETE

4. Origin of the Cretan constitutions, 115. Relations of the Cretan cities to one another, 116. The classes in the states, 117. Social institutions, 118. Political constitution, 118. General character of this constitution, 120. Change to democracy, 120.

CHAPTER VI

DEMOCRACY

Evolution of the power of the people ; the principle of democracy, 122. Degrees in this principle ; modified forms of democracy determined by intention or accident, 123.

ATHENS—THE CLASSES AND THE STATE-DIVISIONS

1. Elements in the population of Attica, 124. Early political condition of Attica, 125. The συνοικισμός of Theseus, 126. The four Ionic tribes, 127. The clans, 128. The phratries, 129. The Eupatrids, 129. Citizenship at Athens, 131. The slaves, 132. The resident aliens, 133. The trittyes and the naucraries, 134.

THE POLITICAL DEVELOPMENT OF ATHENS—THE MAGISTRACY AND THE COUNCIL

2. Decline of the monarchy and early history of the archonship, 135. "The Archon" as the president of the state, 136 ; Damasias, 137. Decline of the power of the archonship, 137. Early modes of appointment to office, 138 ; modified use of the lot, 138. Meaning of appointment by lot, 139. Justification of this mode of appointment, 140. Qualification for office, 141. The original council at Athens, 142. The Ephetae, 143. The Areiopagus ; history of this council, 145 ; downfall of this council, 147. Powerlessness of the original elements in the constitution, 148.

xii   OUTLINES OF GREEK CONSTITUTIONAL HISTORY
SECT.
EPOCHS OF CONSTITUTIONAL REFORM AT ATHENS

3. Early movements towards reform; the constitution of Draco, 149. Reforms of Solon: social, 150; political, 151. Institution of the heliaea; democratic tendency of this reform, 153. General view of the Solonian constitution, 155. Dangers which threatened this constitution, 156. Reforms of Cleisthenes, 157. General estimate of the work of Cleisthenes, 162. Reforms effected by Pericles and his successors, 162.

THE WORKING OF THE DEMOCRATIC CONSTITUTION OF ATHENS

4. The council of five hundred; its structure and powers, 166. The ecclesia, 169; limitations on its powers, 170. The safeguards of the constitution, 170. Legislation at Athens, 172. Administrative powers of the ecclesia, 173. The heliaea: its organisation, 175; its powers, character, and place in the constitution, 176. Administrative offices held by individuals, 178. Great power of individuals at Athens, 179. Offices which furnished a basis for such power: the strategia, 180; position and powers of the strategi, 180; finance offices, 183; administration of finance in the fifth century, 183; the great finance offices of the fourth century; ὁ ἐπὶ τῇ διοικήσει and ὁ ἐπὶ τὸ θεωρικόν, 185. Unofficial influence exercised by individuals; the προστάτης τοῦ δήμου, 187.

THE ATHENIAN EMPIRE

5. Origin of the Athenian Empire, 189. The confederacy of Delos, 190, change in the character of the confederacy, 190. The Empire, 192. The autonomous allies, 193. Legal basis of the Empire, 193; charters of Erythrae and Chalcis, 194. Duties of the allies to Athens, 196. History of the tribute, 196. Modes of assessment of tribute, 197; the tribute-lists, 198. Imperial jurisdiction, 199. Character of the imperial administration of Athens, 200. The cleruchies, 201. Theories of imperial government, 202. Religious unity of the Empire, 202. Political unity of the Empire as a great democratic alliance, 203; its influence on the constitutional history of the East.

THE ATHENIAN CONFEDERACY

6. Origin of the second Athenian confederacy, 204. Conditions of the league; relations of the states to Athens, 205. Relation of the synedrion to the Athenian ecclesia, 206. Dissolution of the confederacy, 207.

DISTURBANCES IN THE ATHENIAN CONSTITUTION—THE CLOSING SCENE

7. Opposition to the democracy; the moderates and the oligarchs, 208. Motives of oligarchic reaction, 209. The political clubs, 209; their character at the close of the Peloponnesian war, 210. The Four Hundred, 211. The Five Thousand, 211. Proposed reform in archonship of

Eucleides, 212. Athens a timocracy after the Lamian war, 212. Athens under Roman rule, 212.

OTHER DEMOCRACIES—ELIS, ARGOS, SYRACUSE, RHODES

8. Elis, 213. Argos, 214. Syracuse, 216. Rhodes, 218.

CHAPTER VII

FEDERAL GOVERNMENTS

What constitutes a federal government, 220. Federations of cities and of cantons, 221. Types of federal government, 222. Thessaly : the monarchy and the early federal constitution, 222 ; the tageia and the second federation, 223 ; federal system under Macedonian and Roman rule. Boeotia : the religious league, 224 ; the oligarchic federation, 225 ; the democratic federation, 226. Acarnania : early international union and later federation, 227. Olynthus : attempt at federal government, 228. Arcadia : early religious union and later federation ; the federal system of Arcadia, 229. Federalism becomes the normal type of polity, 231. Aetolia : early cantonal union ; extension of the federal system, 232 ; constitution of the Aetolian league, 233. Achaea : early federal union ; dissolution, revival, and extension of the league, 236. Constitution of the Achaean league, 237. Lycian league, 241 ; peculiarities of the Lycian federal system, 242. Representation in Greek federal governments, 243.

CHAPTER VIII

HELLENISM AND THE FATE OF THE GREEK CONSTITUTIONS

Meaning of Hellenism, 244. Modes in which Greek political civilisation was extended to the barbarian world, 245. Hellenism beyond the limits of the Roman Empire, 246 ; in the Parthian Empire ; in Asia Minor and the Asiatic provinces of Rome, 247. The Roman province of Achaea, 248. Greek political civilisation in Macedonia and Thrace, 249. Latin political civilisation replaces Greek in Southern Italy and Sicily, 250 ; in Africa, Spain, and Gaul, 251. The Latin West and the Greek East, 251. Greek constitutions preserved under the Roman Republic, 251 ; destroyed under the Empire by the centralised system of government and the application of Roman administrative law, 252.

APPENDIX

The President of the College of Strategi, 253.

INDEX

	PAGE
(i) of subjects	257
(ii) of Greek words	266
(iii) of passages from ancient authors referred to in the text	271

MAP

POLITICAL MAP OF GREECE, CIRC. 430 B.C. . . . *Frontispiece*

SELECT BIBLIOGRAPHY

1. GREEK CONSTITUTIONAL HISTORY AND LAW

BUSOLT, G.—" Die griechischen Staats- und Rechtsaltertümer," 2te. Aufl. (*Handbuch der klassischen Altertums-Wissenschaft*, herausg. von dr. Iwan von Müller, Bd. iv.) München, 1892.

GILBERT, G.—*Handbuch der griechischen Staatsalterthümer*, 2 Bde. Leipzig, 1881-85.

HERMANN, C. F.—*A Manual of the Political Antiquities of Greece, historically considered.* Oxford, 1836.

JEVONS, F. B.—*Constitutional and legal Antiquities* (Book vi. of *A Manual of Greek Antiquities*, by Gardner and Jevons). London, 1895.

SCHOEMANN, G. F.—*Antiquitates Juris publici Graecorum.* 1838.

Griechische Alterthümer, 4te. Aufl. neu bearbeitet von J. H. Lipsius. Bd. I., "das Staatswesen." Berlin, 1897.

The Antiquities of Greece; translated from the German by E. G. Hardy and J. S. Mann. London, 1880.

THUEMSER, V.—*Lehrbuch der griechischen Staatsaltertümer*, 6te. vermehrte und verbesserte Aufl. (K. F. Hermann's *Lehrbuch der griechischen Antiquitäten*, Bd. i.) Freiburg, 1889.

2. CONSTITUTIONS OF SPARTA AND ATHENS

GILBERT, G.—*The constitutional Antiquities of Sparta and Athens;* translated by E. J. Brooks and T. Nicklin, with an introductory note by J. E. Sandys. London and New York, 1895.

3. CONSTITUTION OF SPARTA

ARNOLD'S *Thucydides*, vol. i. App. 2, "On the Constitution of Sparta" (reviewed by Sir G. C. Lewis in the Philological Museum, vol. ii. p. 39).

GILBERT, G.—*Studien zur altspartanischen Geschichte.* Göttingen, 1872.

HERMANN, C. F.—*Antiquitatum Laconicarum libelli quatuor.* Marburg, 1841.

MUELLER (C. O.), *Die Dorier.* Breslau, 1824.

translated into English by Henry Tufnell and G. C. Lewis. 2 vols. Oxford, 1830.

KOPSTADT, A.—*De rerum Laconicarum constitutionis Lycurgeae origine et indole dissertatio.* 1849.

4. CONSTITUTION OF ATHENS

BELOCH, J.—*Die attische Politik seit Pericles.* Leipzig, 1884.
GILBERT, G.—*Beiträge zur innern Geschichte Athens im Zeitalter des Peloponnesischen Krieges.* Leipzig, 1877.
HEADLAM, J. W.—*Election by lot at Athens.* Cambridge University Press, 1891.
WHIBLEY, L.—*Political Parties in Athens during the Peloponnesian War.* Cambridge University Press, 1889.

Popular Assemblies.

SCHOEMANN, G. F.—*De comitiis Atheniensium libri tres.* 1819.

Jurisdiction.

FRAENKEL, M.—*Die attischen Geschworenengerichte: ein Beitrag zum attischen Staatsrecht.* Berlin, 1877.
MEIER (H. E.) und Schömann (G. F.)—*Der attische Process;* neu bearbeitet von J. H. Lipsius. Berlin, 1883.

Public Economy.

BOECKH, A.—*Die Staatshaushaltung der Athener;* 3te. Aufl. herausg. und mit Anmerkungen begleitet von Max Fränkel; 2 Bde. Berlin, 1886.
    The public Economy of Athens; translated from the German. London, 1828.

5. HOMERIC TIMES

FANTA, A.—*Der Staat in der Ilias und Odyssee; ein Beitrag zur Beurtheilung der homerischen Verfassung.* Innsbruck, 1882.

6. TYRANNIES

PLASS, H. G.—*Die Tyrannis in ihren beiden Perioden bei den alten Griechen;* 2 Theile. Bremen, 1852.

7. OLIGARCHIES

WHIBLEY, L.—*Greek Oligarchies.* London, 1896.

8. FEDERAL GOVERNMENTS

FREEMAN, E. A.—*History of Federal Government in Greece and Italy;* edited by J. B. Bury. London, 1893.
DUBOIS, M.—*Les ligues étolienne et achéenne.* Paris, 1885.

9. PROPERTY AND LAND TENURE

COULANGES, F. de—"Recherches sur le droit de propriété chez les Grecs," in *Nouvelles Recherches sur quelques problèmes d'histoire.* Paris, 1891.
GUIRAUD, P.—*La propriété foncière en Grèce jusqu'à la conquête romaine.* Paris, 1893.

10. DICTIONARIES OF ANTIQUITIES CONTAINING ARTICLES ON GREEK CONSTITUTIONAL LAW

DAREMBERG-SAGLIO, *Dictionnaire des antiquités grecques et romaines* (A to Med). 1875-1902.
PAULY, F.—*Real-Encyclopädie der classischen Alterthumswissenschaft;* in 6 Bde. Stuttgart, 1839.
PAULY-WISSOWA, *Real-Encyclopädie, etc.* (new edition of the above, A to Di). 1893-1902.
SMITH, *Dictionary of Greek and Roman Antiquities* (third edition, edited by W. Smith, W. Wayte, and G. E. Marindin). London, 1890.

11. GENERAL HISTORIES OF GREECE

ABBOTT, E.—*A History of Greece.* London, 1888-1900.
BUSOLT, G.—*Griechische Geschichte.* Gotha, 1893-1897.
CURTIUS, E.—*Griechische Geschichte,* 6te. Aufl., 3 Bde. Berlin, 1887-1889.
The History of Greece, translated by A. W. Ward, 5 vols. London, 1868-1873.
DUNCKER, M.—*History of Greece;* translated by S. F. Alleyne and E. Abbott. Vols. i. and ii. (containing the history of the earliest period). London, 1883.
GROTE, G.—*History of Greece,* 10 vols. London (Aberdeen), 1888, 8vo.
HOLM, A.—*History of Greece.* London, 1894-98.

CHAPTER I

INTRODUCTORY

THE central idea and what may be called the spirit of Greek history is its constitutionalism. "The constitution," says Isocrates, "is the soul of the state"; "the constitution," says Aristotle, "is the state."[1] Here at any rate we get a coincidence between the common-sense and the philosophic view which ought to be decisive. But this is far from being the impression left on our minds by the Greek historians. It cannot be denied that Greek history is rendered incoherent, sometimes almost grotesque, by the brilliant personalities that stalk across the stage and blot out the constitution. They are stage characters without a setting, and the fault of such representations is to be found, not in the characteristics of Greek history, but in the mental attitude of those who have handed Greek history down to us. The student of constitutional history is glad to be freed from these oppressive personalities that seem so completely to overshadow their own creations. For in Greece, as everywhere in the civilised world, the creation was greater than the creator. The tyranny of law in history was at least as great as the tyranny of abstract ideas in philosophy; but the former can be severed from personality even more easily than the latter, and the rule of law can be fully appreciated only if we abstract the "material" from the "form."

A further danger to the student is one threatened by Greek philosophy. To regard the political speculations of Plato and Aristotle as fully representing the tone of political thought in

[1] Isocr. *Areop.* § 14; Arist. *Pol.* iii. 3.

Greece is like regarding the odes of Pindar as a fair expression of the waves of emotion that swayed the mixed rabble at the Olympian and Isthmian games. Such speculations are the highest expression of political thought, and for this reason they are not the truest for the historian of constitutional law. The most difficult of his tasks is the careful analysis of these political speculations—the attempt to distinguish history from theory, the opinions of the writer from the opinions of the average Greek, of which they are an exaggerated development. The humbler the source the better the information. A political view of Isocrates is worth more for our purpose than one of Aristotle, a judgment of Xenophon is more valuable than a page of Plato.

How much is gained or lost by such procedure is a question that will be answered differently by different minds; but the chances are that to the genuine student of legal history the unrivalled beauty of the Greek constitutions will never appeal so forcibly as when released from the trammels both of science and of personality. They then appear as symmetrical creations, delicate and often fragile in their artistic completeness. But the completeness was given them by nations rather than by lawgivers, and their symmetry is not rendered more perfect by the airy castles raised on them by Greek scientific thinkers. The lawgiver *as a creator* is himself to a large extent a fiction of the philosophers; and perhaps the most striking fact in Greek political development is that real logical coherence was obtained by growth, that development led to a real system of law, not to a system of political conventions which, as in Rome or in England, patch up the rents made by adding new cloth to old garments. This fact alone is sufficient to establish the truth that constitutional law can be found in no more perfect form than in the states of the old Greek world. It is also the key to the strange fact noticed above—that Greek historians, sometimes more by their silence than by their statements, have given at least an inadequate, if not a false picture of the great political movements in Greece. Symmetry is a dangerous thing in politics, more especially if it be due to the genius of a nation and not of a man, and one of its dangers is the lack of attention it induces in those who are accustomed to such a system. Thucydides tells us that Pericles was monarch of Athens, but gives no hint as to the basis on which his power rested; he speaks of the δῆμος without specifying which of the opposite poles of the constitution he means,—the executive body called the "ecclesia," or the supreme court and legislative sovereign called the "heliaea"; he has written the history of the Athenian Empire and told us almost nothing of its organisation. And this lack of attention was, it must be admitted, accompanied by a corresponding lack of reverence. In few Greek states was there an unbroken chain of political tradition; the citizen of the democracy could not look back with pleasure or with pride to the age of oligarchies or of tyrannies. And the changes had been so rapid in the past that none could tell what might be in store for the future. From a state of bondage worse than the feudal system of mediæval Europe, Athens under Solon had stepped forth into the full blaze of democracy, and the people were not blinded. The new *régime* seemed as natural as the old. But in a country where such miracles as this could happen the unexpected did not exist. Hence the restlessness and the fever of Greek political life. It was not always a low political ambition which made the great traitors of Greece, whose brilliance almost redeems their treason. It was their imagination—the restless desire to plunge into the unknown in politics as in science—which led Aristotle to regard as the greatest potential criminal, not the footpad or the housebreaker, but the refined young man of boundless energy and leisure.[1]

The even flow of Greek constitutionalism was thus ruffled by many a storm; it was not often that the storm took the violent and extreme form of the τυραννίς. Sometimes it was due to waves of sentiment, which would lead in modern states to a change of government, which led in Greece to a change of constitution. Such changes, often prompted from without, might disturb our view as to the continuity of Greek political life, did we not see that they are merely temporary, that there are tendencies stronger than those of a changing sentimentality and the will of the few strong men who are capable of availing themselves of it, and that underneath these fluctuations there runs a coherence which developed types of states both normal and abnormal.

The normal type of the free Greek state attracts us on account of the universality which it was destined to attain.

[1] Arist. *Pol.* ii. 7.

The more abnormal type attracts us from its very singularity. Political work strangely wrought out meets us at every turn, and sometimes the constitution is the only valuable product of a country. The glories of Athens rest but partly on her constitution, which must have been singularly uninteresting when compared with those of other communities of which we catch but glimpses; and we are at times almost forced to regret the fate which has handed down so many petty details about the typical democracy, and has told us so little of the singular forms which political life took in Sparta and in Crete, and the still more fantastic shapes which it assumed in some of the western colonies. To the historian of constitutions the part which a state has played in the history of the world matters little, except in so far as this accidentally determines the amount which is known about its history. If the constitutions about which most is known are treated at disproportionate length in these pages, it must be remembered that this is the result of accident, not of design.

Before entering on an historical sketch of Greek political development it will be necessary to give some idea of the fundamental political conceptions which we shall express by the words "state," "constitution," "citizen," and "law." This order is necessary if we would express the logical sequence of the terms. A political is often the reverse of an historical series; and, whatever may be our view as to the origin of law and government, from the standpoint of a developed society where alone constitutional law can exist, man is only a citizen through the state and its constitution, while law itself although an invariable is not a strictly necessary complement of the ideas either of state or citizenship.

With respect to the first two terms, "state" and "constitution," it will be observed that where we possess two abstract or semi-abstract terms the Greeks had only one. This is not an accidental difference. To us the "state" is an abstraction which should, when used in its strict sense, express the whole of the national life, the "constitution" expressing but a part of it. To the Greek the constitution (πολιτεία) is the city itself (πόλις) from an abstract point of view; it professes, therefore, to express the *whole* of the national life. This idea, which underlies the constructive theories of Plato and Aristotle, and which has given rise in modern times to the strange notion that

Greek society "subordinated the individual to the state," is only a fiction in the sense that it was a theory which did not always square with the facts of political life. As a genuine theory, the realisation of which was consistently pursued by philosophers if not by legislators, it runs through the whole of Greek political thought. It is the ground for Aristotle's statement that the constitution is the "form of the state" (εἶδος τῆς πόλεως), and of his seeming paradox that the identity of a state is the identity of its constitution.[1] The justification for this paradox is found in his definition of a πολιτεία, which, unlike some of the other definitions of political terms found in his *Politics*, is only a formal expression of the current Greek view. The constitution he defines as an ordered arrangement (τάξις) which specifies three things—(1) the ethical end of the city, which is itself the means by which the state has decided to attain good life, (2) the distribution of offices, and (3) the sovereign body of the state, by what individual or class of individuals supreme office is to be held.[2] It is this third element (the most obvious from the point of view of practical politics) which is dwelt on in another definition, where the constitution is said to be a τάξις of magistracies in general, and especially of the sovereign one, and where it is finally identified with the governing body of a state (πολίτευμα δέ ἐστιν ἡ πολιτεία).[3] An important aspect of this definition is the question it raises as to the connection between the sovereign body (τὸ κύριον) and the laws in Greek communities. This we shall consider later; but the reason for the identification may at once be seen if we take yet another statement of Aristotle's, to the effect that the constitution is "a life" of the state.[4] It is an expression of some particular life that the state has elected to live, some particular theory of existence which it has determined to put into force. But different theories of life are represented invariably by different classes of society, and thus, when a new theory is adopted, it means that a new class has risen to the top in political affairs. This class will be τὸ πολίτευμα, *the* privileged class for the time being; and hence the question "What is the πολιτεία?" will be answered when we can reply to the question "What is the πολίτευμα?" The second problem is the simpler; when it is extremely difficult, if not impossible,

[1] *Pol.* iii. 3.
[2] *ib.* iv. 1 = p. 1289 a.
[3] *ib.* iii. 6.
[4] *ib.* iv. 11 = p. 1295 b.

to give a direct answer to this latter question, one has the puzzling phenomenon of a "mixed constitution" (μικτὴ πολιτεία), a state in a permanent condition of suspended revolution.

πολιτεία, therefore, meant to the Greek something more than "constitution" or "government" means to us. It was not merely a convenient form of organisation under which men lived. Aristotle, as an historian, realised, as perhaps only a Greek could realise, that with every change of constitution the balance of power was entirely shifted. Classes of individuals which had been kept in the background now came forward and showed themselves sovereign; the beliefs and interests of one class had given place to the beliefs and interests of another; a change of constitution was a change of creed, and the sovereign class could force its subjects to bow down to the political creed of the day. In most Greek states there was little or nothing of the compromise, the principle of mutual political concession, which is such a striking feature in Roman history and in that of our own country. When the balance of power had swung over, everything went with it, and the change was thorough and radical. Thus Greece has given us no code of laws, and but few examples of gradual political development. She substituted the lawgiver for the code, and the lawgiver was the creature of the revolution. It is a significant recognition of this truth that the constitution is the governing class, that Aristotle, in place of a full discussion of the modes in which constitutions may alter in obedience to social changes, has, in a book of his *Politics*, given us a treatise on the art of avoiding revolutions.

From the conception of the constitution we naturally pass to the Greek idea of political office. The assertion that the constitution has to deal with the assignment of magistracies in the city implies that the state is a distributer. The conception of distributive justice, so fully worked out by Aristotle, is contained in germ in the most inchoate political society. Every association distributes burdens and rewards; but it is only with the former, in the shape of political offices, that we are here concerned. The state assigns provinces of rule (ἀρχαί) to its members, and by ἀρχή Aristotle understands every possible kind of administrative activity: we can hardly add legislative activity, for this, as we shall see, was not contemplated as a regular function of government in Greek states. He includes under the term the duties of a member of a senate or popular assembly, or even those of a juryman.¹ Here he confessedly goes beyond the limits of current terminology, for the Greeks tended to confine the word ἀρχή, like our "office," to the individual magistracies of a state. But Aristotle is justified in employing a common term to express a common conception. When the primitive notion of the magistracy as a unity of power, which was derived from the prehistoric kingship and was never lost at Rome, had been broken down in Greece, no fundamental distinction existed between the branches of the executive that were shared amongst the people. The distinction that continued to exist was merely one based on the conveniences of the state. It was held that some functions could better be exercised collectively by bodies of men, while others could be better performed by individuals. It is true that the tendency was to subordinate individual to collective control, but even this subordination did not imply the *de jure* sovereignty of popular bodies. At Athens the assembly, the law-courts, the generals, the archons, and other individual officials are all alike branches of the executive, carrying out the law which is not the mandate of any one of these bodies or of all of them collectively.

These executive functions are distributed amongst some or all of the members of the community. As the πολιτεία is the basis of distribution, we should naturally conclude that the recipients of these functions were the only πολῖται. It is the logical conclusion to which Aristotle is led when he defines a citizen as "one who is capable of ruling and being ruled in turn."² But this was not a conclusion accepted by the average Greek mind, and Aristotle himself feels that it does not fit the facts of Greek history. It was an ideal of citizenship pitched far too high for many a Greek state wrestling with poverty and seeking only for protection. It is a definition true only of democracy,³ the ideal πόλις with all the corollaries which accompany the attainment of its ideal end—leisure, universal education, and the possession of a large slave class. Since the inevitable tendency of nearly all Greek states was towards democracy, and most succeed, at some period of their history, in at least a temporary attainment of the ideal goal, the definition has some historical

¹ *Pol.* ii. 12; iii. 1. ² *ib.* i. 2; vii. 14 = p. 1332 b.
³ *ib.* iii. 1; vi. 2 = p. 1317 b.

justification. But by all cities in the early stages of development, and by many who at a later period still lagged behind, other criteria had to be accepted. There were two definitions of citizenship current in the Greek world which Aristotle set aside as incomplete. These were "the protection of private rights" and "descent from original citizens." The possession of neither of these alone would have been sufficient to make a man a πολίτης, but both together would probably have furnished a satisfactory claim to the position in an oligarchy like that of Corinth, where political privileges were not distributed beyond a narrow circle, but where political duties—such as military service—equally demanded a clear definition of citizenship. The first of these factors is insufficient, as Aristotle remarks, because in some Greek states the resident alien (μέτοικος) could enforce his private rights in his own name;[1] the second is rather a test than a definition, but in practical politics traditional tests are of considerable importance, especially when they are connected with the two most powerful bonds of union, the family and religion. Hence what we may call the "phratric" conception of citizenship, its dependence on birth and consequently on membership of the "phratry" or the clan, completely overshadowed all others in the eyes of Greece. We shall have occasion to discuss the conception in connection with the history of Athens, where the conditions of citizenship are best known to us; and so we need not dwell on it here. We need only notice its importance as the connecting link between the family and the state, as one of the many signs that in the Greek world the claims of the family, in politics as well as in religion, continued to control the activity of its own great offspring, which had grown great enough to absorb its parent, but not strong or wilful enough to neglect its claims.

Lastly, we must consider the Greek conception of law, its relation to the constitution and to the governing class. Law is not regarded as a primary factor in Greek political life; it is but secondary to the constitution, the support of the structure. As the constitution is the whole expression of the life of the

---

[1] *Pol.* iii. 1. This was probably the case in great commercial oligarchies, such as Corinth, where the ideal of citizenship was low, χειροτέχναι were cultivated, and foreigners consequently welcomed. In such states the usual requirement of representation by a προστάτης would not have been insisted on. Such metoecs would have resembled the *cives sine suffragio* of Rome.

state, there is no adequate ground for a distinction between public and private law; and, in fact, this distinction does not exist in its pure form, in spite of the marked differences between public and private procedure which we shall have to trace at Athens and elsewhere in Greece. Yet it was felt that some laws were universal, while others were peculiar to particular societies. Hence the distinction between κοινὸς νόμος and ἴδιος νόμος,[1] and amongst the ἴδιοι νόμοι would certainly fall the laws protecting the structure of the state. The further distinction within these between ordinances protecting society and those which protect the government could hardly be drawn in states where, as for instance in Sparta and in the cities of Crete, a peculiar structure of society was so closely interwoven with government that the two could not be separated even in thought. Law, in its relation to the constitution, has clearly a protective character, and this agrees with the common Greek notion, so different from that which we gather from the philosophers, that law is prohibitive rather than positive.[2] The general idea of Greek political organisation is that of a structure framed on a certain principle of life, with rules ordained to protect it and to prevent its being destroyed. The constitution has the force of the community on its side, and this must be used by the magistrates to carry out the laws.

While, therefore, by "public law" we generally mean the actual constitutional arrangements of a country, the Greek would have understood by it the protective measures by which the permanence of these arrangements is secured, and the Greek νομοθέτης is a creator before he is a legislator. The necessity of law to a constitution depends entirely on the idea of the imperfection of human nature and on the probability of resistance by certain individuals or classes to the ideal set up by the state. But the "state" and the "law" are both mere abstractions: how, it may be asked, can one impersonal entity support another? In facing this question the Greek showed more courage and consistency than his modern successors have done. He did not fall back on the theory of a personal sovereign; to him laws are enforced by, but are in no sense

---

[1] Arist. *Rhet.* i. 10, 3 νόμος δ' ἐστίν, ὁ μὲν ἴδιος, ὁ δὲ κοινός. λέγω δὲ ἴδιον μὲν καθ' ὃν γεγραμμένον πολιτεύονται· κοινὸν δὲ ὅσα ἄγραφα παρὰ πᾶσιν ὁμολογεῖσθαι δοκεῖ.

[2] Lycurg. *c. Leocr.* § 4 ὁ μὲν γὰρ νόμος πέφυκε προλέγει ἃ μὴ δεῖ πράττειν: cf. Aesch. *c. Timarch.* § 13.

the product of a government; he only faintly appealed to the gods, and, while giving law a divine character, rarely in the historical period gave it a directly divine origin.

The charge that Greek law lacked an authoritative character is therefore not unnatural; but it is wrongly stated when it is implied that the Greek looked on his state as an "oracle of spiritual truth," as a "parochial Sinai," as a Pope who could not be "ecumenical."[1] It is true that spiritual life based on divine authority is not an idea wholly unknown to the Greeks. We find the idea in acts such as the purification of Athens by Epimenides, in ceremonies such as the Eleusinian mysteries, celebrated by a privileged race which has received its authority from God. The laws of Minos have a divine origin; all those of Sparta are Πυθόχρηστοι νόμοι. But nowhere is the state the sanction; to the Greek mind generally the only authority on which a revelation rests is the authority of nature and reason. Plato embodies this doctrine when he would have his laws couched in a persuasive form, not merely command or threaten.[2] In a sense every state was regarded by its citizens as "ecumenical"—that is, as teaching and enforcing a doctrine which ought to be valid for all the world. This will become more apparent if we cull some definitions of law from two very different sources. Law has a divine origin as the "discovery and gift of the gods"; it expresses human reason, and is a "covenant" between man and man.[3] It is order, the passionless reason, the rule of God and of reason, and derives its force from habit.[4] Law is, therefore, a covenant between men dictated by the divine reason; it is the fixing of the best custom or habit in a generalised form; it comprises those rules of life which ought to have absolute validity; and, as comprising them, it may be, and ought to be, itself sovereign. It was not supposed that all that was understood by law would find its way into the statute-book. There were unwritten laws, more important and powerful than the written laws of a land.[5] Amongst them was a body of rules directly supporting the structure of the state in the mixed governments of Greece, such as we now call the "custom of the constitution." Their

---

[1] Newman *Politics of Aristotle* vol. i. pp. 81, 82.
[2] Plato *Laws* p. 859 a.
[3] [Dem.] *c. Aristag.* i. § 16.
[4] Arist. *Pol.* ii. 8; iii. 16; vii. 4 = p. 1326 a.
[5] *ib.* iii. 16.

sanction was simply the consciousness that the state would become unworkable, and a revolution result, if they were violated.

Yet, in spite of the universal character of law, it is equally true that with every revolution that part of the ἴδιοι νόμοι which directly supports the constitution, and which we should call "public law," must necessarily change. The legislator will have to find those rules of reason which defend the interests of the class which has entrusted him with the task of reconstruction. If he is an arbitrator, like Solon, he may seek the interest of more than one, and, like Solon again, he may not aim at finality. If his work is an advance in the direction of the unknown, he may believe himself one step nearer an indefinitely distant goal, or he may hark back again, like the Athenian reactionaries of 411 B.C., to a supposed bright period in the history of the past. But in either case, so far as his work does not merely appeal to the interest of a class, so far as it wins general acceptance from the community, its validity rests on its reasonableness alone, on its peculiar suitability to the moral and social conditions of the nation and of the time.

When the work has been done, the privileged class, armed with its code, proceeds to enforce it and to defend it with all its might. As long as there is a code there is a constitution; where there is none, as in the great upheaval caused by tyranny, there no constitution exists. It is in this modified sense that we must interpret the two apparently conflicting maxims of Aristotle that the "constitution is the governing class," and that "where the laws do not rule there is no constitution."[1]

[1] *Pol.* iii. 6; iv. 4 = p. 1292 a.

CHAPTER II

EARLY DEVELOPMENT OF THE GREEK CONSTITUTIONS THROUGH MONARCHY, ARISTOCRACY, AND TYRANNY TO CONSTITUTIONAL GOVERNMENT.

THE city-state was a late development of common life in Greece, and sprang from the looser aggregate of the tribe (φυλή).[1] Although contemporary literary records are not lacking of political units lower than the πόλις, a description of Greece in these tribal days can be based only on the guesses of writers who, like Thucydides and Aristotle, try to get behind the history of the city-state. Their accounts, though mainly reconstructions, can yet be shown to contain a large element of truth.

Thucydides[2] argues from survivals of this tribal life, and from such survivals attempts to depict the primitive condition of the whole Greek world. Hellas, he thinks, was not originally inhabited by any fixed population. There were frequent movements of races and no settled life or freedom of intercourse. Greece was occupied by a number of small communities seeking little more than the provision of their daily wants. Traces of such communities were found in his own time in Ozolian Locris[3] and in Aetolia.[4] A treaty of alliance between Elis and the Heraeans of Arcadia of the middle of the sixth century speaks of both these communities as "districts" (δῆμοι),[5] while portions of Arcadia, even in the

---

[1] φυλή, according to Dicaearchus, a contemporary of Aristotle, meant originally a union of individuals into a community or state, not a unity within the state (Steph. Byzant. s.v. πάτρα).

[2] Thuc. i. 2.
[3] ib. iii. 101, 102.
[4] ib. iii. 94 κατὰ κώμας ἀτειχίστους.
[5] Hicks n. 8.

fifth century, had not risen above such tribal associations. The unit of political life in such societies is described as the κώμη or village community; whether this was ever the highest unit we cannot say, but the belief that it was at least an independent unit underlies Aristotle's sketch of the origin of the πόλις.[1] He builds up the state from two constituent elements, —the village community, and behind this the household (οἰκία)— and traces an ascending scale of development. Since he regards the village community as identical with the γένος, he bases the earliest forms of association on family life and on this widest of family units, the clan.

This is not the mere abstract speculation of a philosopher: it is a view based on survivals; for, although it is true that the household and the clan are nowhere found in history as entirely independent organisations, yet the notion of ultimate family connection in the larger units which made up the πόλις is engrained in Greek life. The clan continues to play an important part in the inner life of the state, and even furnishes the type for later modes of union; for the symbol of relationship, the eponymous ancestor, is borrowed from the clan to be applied to purely artificial forms of association such as the "deme" and the "tribe." Its influence on the religious life of the state is yet more strongly marked, and we shall find that the public worship of a community is often but a recognition of the private "cultus" of the clan.[2] It has left its trace on political institutions in the use of the word γέροντες or elders, which is applied in the Homeric poems to the councillors of the king.[3] As the Latin word *patres* applied to the Roman Senate was probably derived from *patres-familias*, so γέροντες may mean "heads of families," the elders of the tribe. The councillors of Sparta preserved this name into historic times, and it can be proved that the γερουσία of that state ever continued to represent the noble clans of the community.

Although the influence of the clans may be thus clearly demonstrated, what their precise relation was to the early

---

[1] *Pol.* i. 2.
[2] See the article "Genos" in Smith's *Dict. of Greek and Roman Antiquities* (3rd ed.) A curious instance of the claim to a public priesthood basing itself on descent is to be found in Herodotus vii. 153. The family of Gelo became ἱροφάνται τῶν χθονίων θεῶν on the foundation of the city of Gela, because an ancestor Telines had brought the ἱρά of these goddesses with him.
[3] *Il.* ii. 404; iv. 344.

tribal unions cannot be determined. The φυλή may have been sometimes an extended family, sometimes an aggregate of families. In any case it is the most primitive form of association known to us, and the πόλις grew up with the union of various tribes just as at a later stage still the central city, such as Athens or Elis, grew up with the "housing together" (συνοίκισις) of various smaller πόλεις. And the district or the city, when first known to us, is under the rule of a king.

The accounts of the kingly power given by the philosophers, and particularly by Aristotle, are attempts to solve what was to the Greeks of historic times a very difficult problem—the origin of monarchy, an institution alien both to their experience and to their sympathies. At one time Aristotle suggests that the earliest monarchy was patriarchal, that it was the rule of the eldest agnate of the family, and that the "common hearth" was the source of the kingly honour.[1] Elsewhere he gives a different explanation. The first chiefs, he thinks, must have been benefactors of the people in arts or in war.[2] He explains their position by the fact that they were the fittest, and he is doubtless right in saying that the monarchy of the heroic times originated with the settlement of a community or the acquisition of territory. The monarchy of the heroic times, like most others, originated with conquest; and, if the earliest Greek kingship was patriarchal, this peaceful and paternal monarch must have been superseded, when the time for movement and action came, by the one strong man who could win territory for his people, protect their persons, and avenge their death. The very etymology of the word βασιλεύς has been thought to show a military power,[3] and the kingly titles which were preserved in historic Greece tell the same tale. At Sparta they were leaders (βαγοί) and rulers of the people (ἀρχαγέται), and one of the titles borne by the king of Thessaly is the military one of ταγός. Vague as are the descriptions found in the Epos of the relations between the king and his nobles or people, yet even

---

[1] *Pol.* i. 2; cf. vi. 8 = p. 1322 b ἀπὸ τῆς κοινῆς ἑστίας ἔχουσι τὴν τιμήν· καλοῦσι δ' οἱ μὲν ἄρχοντας τούτους οἱ δὲ βασιλεῖς οἱ δὲ πρυτάνεις. Charon of Lampsacus—*circa* 470 B.C.—gave to his treatise on the Spartan kings the title Ἄρχοντες καὶ πρυτάνεις Λακεδαιμονίων.

[2] *ib.* iii. 14.

[3] βασιλεύς is derived by G. Curtius from the root βα and λευ (= λαο, cf. Λευτυχίδης). It would thus be equivalent to the German "Herzog," and not dissimilar to the Latin *praetor* (*prae-itor*), one of the original appellations of the king of Rome and the title of the earlier consuls.

here we find traces of a military past. The notion of fealty to the chief is very strongly marked; the duty of the ἑταῖροι to the βασιλεύς is the duty of a retinue, a *cohors amicorum* to its general.[1] On the other hand, the king owes duties to his nobles and to his people; he is bound to protect them and to avenge their death. The monarchy at this early period was, to use Maine's expression, rather a matter of status than of contract; but where the monarchy was preserved in later times we find that, in some cases, the tacit had become an expressed covenant. At Sparta a monthly oath was interchanged between the king and the ephors. The king swore on his own behalf that he would rule in accordance with the existing ordinances of the state, and they on behalf of the city that as long as he kept his oath his monarchy should remain unimpaired. A similar custom is recorded of the Molossians. After a sacrifice to Zeus Areius the king swears to rule in accordance with the laws, and the people to preserve his kingly power.[2]

These evidences point rather to the selection of a king as a leader in war, and to a mutual understanding between king and people for their own protection, than to a monarchy based merely on right of birth. Perhaps, as in the Germanic kingdoms, personal fitness and descent were both recognised; perhaps the military power, when long established, tended to be transmitted within a certain clan. In any case, this chieftainship developed into the stereotyped monarchy of the Epos, which is described by Aristotle as hereditary and legal.[3] The idea of heredity, which we now meet for the first time, is a characteristic Greek conception. It exercised an influence even in the most democratic states, and its importance is fully recognised by the philosophers.[4] It is based on the notion of an actual transmission of excellence (ἀρετή) from father to son, and also on the idea that the acquisition of this excellence is dependent on the fact of being born in a certain station.[5] In the time of the monarchies, and of the aristocracies which

---

[1] *Il.* iv. 266, 267 Ἀτρείδη, μάλα μέν τοι ἐγὼν ἐρίηρος ἑταῖρος ἔσσομαι, ὡς τὸ πρῶτον ὑπέστην καὶ κατένευσα. Cf. *Il.* xvi. 269 ff.

[2] Xen. *Resp. Lac.* 15, 7; Plut. *Pyrrh.* 5.

[3] *Pol.* iii. 4; cf. Thuc. i. 13 ἐπὶ ῥητοῖς γέρασι πατρικαὶ βασιλεῖαι.

[4] Plato *Crat.* p. 394 A ἔσται γάρ ποτ' ἐκ βασιλέως βασιλεὺς καὶ ἐξ ἀγαθοῦ ἀγαθός καὶ ἐκ καλοῦ καλός, καὶ τἄλλα πάντα οὕτως, ἐξ ἑκάστου γένους ἕτερον τοιοῦτον ἔκγονον, ἐὰν μὴ τέρας γίγνηται.

[5] Aristotle (*Pol.* v. 1 = p. 1301 b) defines εὐγένεια as προγόνων ἀρετὴ καὶ πλοῦτος. Cf. iv. 8, p. 1294 a ἡ γὰρ εὐγένιά ἐστιν ἀρετὴ καὶ πλοῦτος ἀρχαῖος.

succeeded them, ἀρετή is equivalent to good birth, and the word ἀριστίνδην, meaning "by right of birth," becomes almost a technical legal term.[1] In the Epos it is the kingly race which is thus chiefly honoured—the race within which the royal sceptre must descend. We find also the idea that the kingly honour (τιμή) springs from Zeus, but a divine right to pre-eminence, if not to rule, is shared by others than the king; the other princes (βασιλεῖς) are under the protection of the gods from whom they draw their race; they too are "heaven-born" and "heaven-reared." The growing power of the nobles is, in fact, very apparent. The monarchy described in the Epos, probably of the ninth and eighth centuries B.C., is by no means a great power, and unfortunately we have no record of the strongest period of kingly rule in Greece. If we could regard the discoveries at Tiryns, Mycenae, and on the east coast of Greece generally as representing a purely Hellenic civilisation, we should indeed have evidence of a period of despotism, of a difference of life between king and subjects, and of a command over their persons and manual labour which find their counterparts only in the East. But the differences between the civilisation of Mycenae and that portrayed in the epic poems are more fundamental than the resemblances. We can see in the former only the traces of an immigrant oriental despotism, and for the Greek βασιλεύς we must turn to the Homeric poems, which show us a power approaching dissolution. This weakening of his position may be best exemplified by a rapid review of his powers. As we should expect, his military authority in the field is of all his prerogatives the least impaired. He has the supreme command, with the power of life and death. Besides being general the king is priest, and in a certain sense priest of the community. The Homeric king sacrifices to all or any of the gods, and he may have sacrificed for the δῆμος as the house-father sacrifices for the family; but he is priest chiefly as the representative of the greatest family in the state, and therefore the maintainer of its hereditary worship and sacrifices.[2] For this very reason his priesthood is limited. Aristotle says that he was "lord of the sacrifices

---

[1] As in one of Draco's laws (Hicks n. 59). By the τριακόσιοι ἀριστίνδην δικά-ζοντες who tried those guilty of the death of the Cylonian conspirators Plutarch means three hundred Eupatrids (Sol. 12).

[2] As in Agamemnon's offering to Zeus (Il. ii. 402 ff.), and Alcinous' to Poseidon (Od. xiii. 181).

so far as they did not belong to special priests."[1] There were, therefore, other ἱερατικαὶ θυσίαι which belonged to representatives of other families who held the hereditary priesthoods of their clan. Thus we find that, when the monarchy comes to an end, the various cults of the state are in the hands of a close corporation of nobles, whose position is strengthened by their being the sole depositaries of religion.

Again, the king is judge, as the keeper of the ordinances of Zeus, the interpreter of the unwritten law of the community. The sceptre and the ordinances go together.[2] But he is not the only judge. Even in the oldest parts of the *Iliad* more than one judge is mentioned, and there are many δικασπόλοι in a single δῆμος.[3] Thus others of the nobles have the θέμιστες from Zeus, and even when the king judges, the nobles are there to aid him with their knowledge of δίκη, which expressed the customary law.[4]

Laws as yet are only θέμιστες, "institutions" or single adjudications. Justice itself appears in a semi-abstract form as δίκη, "straightness" or "rightness"; but if language be a test of thought, there was as yet no notion of customary law (νόμος), for there was no name for it, although we must believe with Plato that its presence was felt in the heroic period, and that it was believed to regulate the ordinances of the king.[5] The idea of νόμος grew up, no doubt, in the time of the succeeding aristocracies, which become the depositaries and expounders of traditional law, and it became fixed in the codifications effected by the great lawgivers of the seventh century—Zaleucus, Charondas, and Draco.

The pictures we possess of the heroic monarchy point, therefore, to a power approaching decline; and this is natural enough if these pictures date from the ninth and eighth centuries B.C., for about the middle of the eighth century the monarchies fell throughout the Greek world. In Athens, in 752, the rule of the Melanthidae was limited to a ten years' presidency. The same tendencies are found in Asia Minor;

---

[1] *Pol.* iii. 14 κύριος τῶν θυσιῶν ὅσαι μὴ ἱερατικαί.
[2] *Il.* ii. 206.
[3] δικασπόλοι οἵ τε θέμιστας πρὸς Διὸς εἰρύαται, *Il.* i. 238.
[4] In the trial scene on the shield of Achilles (*Il.* xviii. 497), the ἵστωρ is probably the judge, *i.e.* the king, who, after taking advice of the γέροντες, pronounced the sentence (Fanta *der Staat in d. Ilias u. Odyssee* pp. 82 ff.)
[5] Plato *Laws* iii. p. 680 A ἀλλ' ἔθεσι καὶ τοῖς λεγομένοις πατρίοις νόμοις ἑπόμενοι ζῶσιν.

monarchy gave place to aristocracy in Ephesus, Cyme, and Lesbos. In Corinth, at about the same period, the monarchical rule of the Bacchiadae was replaced by a δυναστεία of the same family. The movement spread through Peloponnese. In Messenia, soon after 750, the monarchy was weakened. We have many general references to an early state of anarchy in this district, and from these it is evident that the kings of Messenia tried to maintain their royal prerogative, but without success.[1] In Argos, though the monarchy was preserved and is found as late as 480,[2] the influences of the time were shown in the abandonment of the hereditary principle. The power was taken from the Heracleidae and given to another house—that of Aegon. In Sparta the monarchy had been saved by the readjustment of the constitution at the end of the ninth century. Order was restored, but at the expense of the kingly power.

So little is known about the details of this startling change that historians, in their attempts to account for it, have been reduced mainly to conjecture. The movement was so widely spread that it is safe to assert that very general causes must have been at work, and these are more easily discovered than the details of each particular revolution. The storm of the great migrations, during which the guidance of an able king had been invaluable, had left behind it a period of comparative calm, and there was less need for the continuance of a great military leader. The nobles possessed definite power, their council-board (γερουσία) was organised, and they could easily take over the duties that the monarch had once fulfilled. In the states affected by the migrations conquest had meant an increase of material power to the nobility. Many of the noble families had shared in the fruits of victory, and had received allotments (τεμένη) in the conquered territory, comparable to those of the early kings.[3] They had grown to wealth and power, and were placed in a position almost independent of the reigning house. It has also been thought that the very isolation of the nobles in the conquered provinces, in face of the

---

[1] Plato (*Laws* iii. p. 691 E) says that the kings of Argos and Messenia ruined themselves and Greek power by not knowing that the half was better than the whole. Plutarch (*Lyc.* 7) speaks of the δήμων καὶ βασιλέων στάσεις καὶ κακοπολιτεῖαι.

[2] Her. vii. 149.

[3] It is possible that the rights of the king and nobles extended beyond their private τεμένη, and that they had the power of collecting dues from the small settlers on the common land.

subdued populations and of their own turbulent δῆμος, made them more ready to trust to their own mutual assistance, less willing to trust in a king appointed from their midst. We are told that the Dorians of Messenia quarrelled with their leader, Cresphontes, on account of the privileges which he gave to the conquered race;[1] and tradition says that it was a revolt of the Dorian nobles against their own δῆμος and the native "perioeci" which brought about the foundation of historic Sparta.[2] If we add to these considerations the fact that, as the result of conquest, new cities had been formed, that the bonds of civic life had everywhere been drawn closer, and that the Greek πόλις, with its restricted area and public life, was eminently unsuited to a kingly form of government, the dignity of which requires for its support a certain degree of seclusion, we shall have ample reasons of a general kind for the almost simultaneous downfall of the monarchies of Greece.

The consequence of the downfall of the monarchies, in Greece and in Asia Minor, was the transfer of government to the clans. This transfer might assume either of two forms. In some cases the government lapsed from the royal clan to the many noble clans of a community. At other times it was kept within the ruling clan, but, instead of being reserved for one individual, was vested in the members generally. The government of a union of clans is perhaps exemplified by that of the Eupatridae at Athens, for although the title "Eupatrid" in historical times designated only a very small section of the community, it was probably applied originally to all the noble families.[3] Of the second form of clan government a great many instances were preserved even in historic times. The great Thessalian clans, the Aleuadae of Larisa, the Scopadae of Cranon (both claiming, like the Spartan kings, descent from Heracles), and the Creondae of Pharsalus, still continued to rule their respective cities. The Bacchiadae, also of the conquering race of the Heracleidae, who formed a close corporation, marrying only within the clan,[4] took over the government of Corinth. The Penthelidae are found in Mitylene, and some-

---

[1] Ephorus ap. Strab. p. 361.
[2] ib. p. 364.
[3] The Eupatridae, as described by Plutarch (Thes. 25), (i.) had the knowledge of sacred things and were the instructors of the other citizens in things sacred and profane, (ii.) they were the expounders of the laws and so possessed all jurisdiction, and (iii.) they filled the offices of state.
[4] Her. v. 92 ἐδίδοσαν καὶ ἤγοντο ἐξ ἀλλήλων.

times in Asia Minor the name of the clan reflects its royal origin. Thus the Basileidae held sway in Ephesus[1] and Erythrae.[2] An inscription found at Arkesine, in the island of Amorgus, bears the tribe-name Βασιλεῖται.[3]

An appreciation of the character of this government can be formed only by some knowledge of the nature of the clan. The γένος was a close corporation, the individual members of which believed themselves to be ultimately connected by blood; and it was a corporation that for this reason always remained inexpansive. It might be recruited by adoption, but by no other means. The most democratic legislator in the most democratic state could not increase its numbers: Cleisthenes of Athens created new citizens; he enrolled them in the tribes and phratries; but he could not add them to the clan. The members of this body, the γεννῆται, recognised in common some mythical ancestor, who was generally suggested by the patronymic ending of the clan-name, which expressed the belief of the members in their ultimate relationship. They possessed a common worship, which was closely dependent on their common ancestry, and was the only living evidence of it, the clan-name borne by the individual, which was preserved in Rome, having been early lost in Greece.[4] The ancestor who gave his name to the clan might be a god himself, or some hero whose descent connected it with a god.[5] Thus the Spartan kings were priests of Zeus, under his two titles Λακεδαίμων and Οὐράνιος. They were the link by which the whole state was

Bound by gold chains about the feet of God;

and this was partly the secret of the maintenance of their power.[6] The statement of Hecataeus that his sixteenth ancestor was a god[7] is probably not an exaggerated expression of the current Greek belief in the possibility of divine descent.

[1] Strabo p. 63.
[2] Arist. *Pol.* v. 6.
[3] Gilbert *Staatsalt.* ii. p. 273.
[4] Herodotus (v. 66), speaking of Isagoras, the opponent of Cleisthenes, says of him οἰκίης μὲν ἐὼν δοκίμου· ἀτὰρ τὰ ἀνέκαθεν οὐκ ἔχω φράσαι· θύουσι δὲ οἱ συγγενέες αὐτοῦ Διὶ Καρίῳ. Compare with this the simpler Roman test, *gentiles mei sunt qui meo nomine appellantur* (Cincius ap. Fest. p. 94).
[5] This is the idea expressed in the *Iliad* by the epithets διοτρεφής and διογενής, which are applied, not only to the βασιλεύς or king, but also to the βασιλεῖς or princes (*Il.* i. 337; xi. 823, etc.) See Fanta *op. cit.* p. 33; cf. *Od.* iv. 63 γένος διοτρεφέων βασιλήων.
[6] Cf. the story of the restoration of Pleistoanax (Thuc. v. 16). The oracle bids the Spartans, under penalties, to restore "the seed of the demigod son of Zeus."
[7] Her. ii. 143.

Often, however, a family traced its origin, not directly to a god, but to some seer or priest intrusted with his worship; and in such families a hereditary craft or gift was not infrequently associated with the hereditary cult. The Talthybiadae at Sparta owed their position as state-heralds to their being descendants of Talthybius,[1] and it was by this right that the great prophetic families of Elis, the Tellidae and Iamidae, exercised their hereditary gift.[2] Sometimes a peculiarity in worship was thought to mark a radical difference of race. Thus in Attica the Eumolpidae were considered, probably on grounds of ritual alone, to be of Thracian origin; the Gephyraei, whom Herodotus considers to be Phoenician, had their separate shrines and worship, in which the rest of the people had no share, and were in turn excluded from certain religious festivals of the Athenians.[3]

We may now form some idea of the power of this nobility of birth. In most cases its members had won their territory by the right of conquest, and were the large landowners in the states; their special claims to honour were the exclusive possession of the sacrifices and higher religious rites of the state, the exclusive knowledge of its laws, and the sole possession of that citizen ἀρετή which resulted from higher birth and from inherited wealth and culture. This was the rule of the best (ἄριστοι), and for a time these governments may well have been the truest aristocracies that the Greek world ever saw. It was not merely the position, it was still more the qualities which made these men at once priests, judges, and soldiers that seemed unattainable by the common herd. Their rule had a divine sanction, but the theocratic element was not oppressively present; it was less obvious than at Rome, for the clan-worship, exclusive as it was, was less baneful than the inscrutable knowledge of the priestly colleges of the Roman Patriciate, which created a strong tie of interest between all the families of the privileged class, and professed to give rules for all things human and divine. In Greece the lay functions overshadowed the priestly character, and that *status* and merit were thought to be coincident is shown by the growth of a characteristic Greek conception, which in after days was barely eradicated from the most democratic states. This was the idea of βαναυσία,

---

[1] ἀπόγονοι Ταλθυβίου, Her. vii. 134.   [2] *ib.* v. 44; ix. 33, 37.   [3] *ib.* v. 57.

primarily a military conception,[1] dependent for its origin on the obvious fact that certain modes of life and the exercise of certain trades disqualify from prowess in the field. The artist and the artisan are equally exposed to the charge; agriculture is comparatively exempt; for, even when the master works on his own field, the life is one of greater leisure and of healthy influences. Even in these early days the word may also have implied the absence of leisure for the higher arts of peace, ritual, and law, and thus have formed the basis for the complex philosophic notion of a life that debars from all pursuit of the higher arts, politics and philosophy,[2] by its continuous drudgery, its fixed boundaries, and the professionalism which drags the mind along a single narrow groove.

The purely aristocratic character of these governments was, it is true, tempered by the accompaniment, perhaps in some cases by the introduction, of the oligarchic element of wealth. For wealth must from an early time have had an important influence in determining the character of the government, chiefly as supplying the means for the military equipment in vogue. Aristotle lays special stress on this element as determining the form of an oligarchy. He states that, after the time of the monarchies, the earliest privileged class (ἡ πρώτη πολιτεία) was chosen from the warriors, and at first from the "charioteers" or "knights" (ἱππεῖς). It was only later, as cities grew larger and the hoplite formed the main strength of the army, that governments became more liberal.[3] A type of this first form of aristocracy, which was dependent on wealth, is furnished by the rule of the ἱπποβόται of Chalcis, on whose lands the Athenians established a cleruchy in 507. It is described by Strabo as an aristocratic government based on a property qualification.[4] In governments of this type the

---

[1] Herodotus (ii. 167) rightly assigns it this origin, and remarks on its presence in the most warlike of the barbarian nations. He adds that in Greece the commercial town of Corinth showed the least contempt for χειροτέχναι.

[2] Arist. Pol. vii. 2 = p. 1324 a.

[3] ib. iv. 5 = p. 1292 b. It must have depended entirely on the character of the country whether ἱππεῖς meant charioteers or horsemen. The rule of ὁπλῖται Thucydides and Aristotle regard as that of a liberal oligarchy, since the ὁπλῖται are εὔποροι (Thuc. viii. 97; Arist. Pol. iv. 13 = p. 1297 b). Extreme democracy consists in the admission of the ψιλοί and the ναυτικὸς ὄχλος to government.

[4] Strabo p. 447 ἀπὸ τιμημάτων ἄνδρες ἀριστοκρατικῶς ἄρχοντες. Herodotus (v. 77) calls them οἱ παχέες. A similar form of government existed in Eretria (Arist. Pol. iv. 3 = p. 1289 b).

poorer members of the noble clans must have been excluded from all share in power; but as a rule, especially in countries such as Attica, where wealth depended almost wholly on landed possessions, the aristocracy of wealth and birth must generally have coincided. Such, however, could not have been the case in the maritime states of Asia Minor which were given up to trade, and yet it is here that the aristocracies of the "knights" are especially prominent. Such governments were found at Magnesia on the Maeander, at Colophon, and at Cyme. Another kind of government that hovers between an aristocratic and an oligarchic character deserves some mention here; for, although it belongs to a later stage of political development, some instances of it are as old as the eighth century. It is the aristocracy of the colonies, where the original possession of landed property has created a *status* which may in some cases have become fixed enough to exist without its original support. The privileged class is formed by the γαμόροι or γεωμόροι, round which the later δῆμος gathers. Instances of such governments are found at Samos, and at Leontini and Syracuse in Sicily.

The last stage is marked by more artificial forms of oligarchy, where the aristocratic element is thrust still further into the background. Such governments are mentioned here because, although they are found chiefly in the western colonies, they may in certain cases be a reflection of an earlier state of things in Greece. Even, however, if they be regarded as pure political experiments, such as are found earliest in colonial settlements, the work of the legislator who created them is but an expression of the tentative spirit which at the close of this epoch was seeking to find some other basis for power than that of birth. Sometimes these governments depend on a fixed property-qualification, sometimes they admit only a certain number of citizens to power.[1] The government of "the thousand" (οἱ χίλιοι) is so widely spread in Italy that it may well have owed its origin to some master-mind. At Locri[2] it was probably the work of Zaleucus, and to this influence its presence at Croton[3] and Rhegium[4] may also have been due.

---

[1] If we are to believe the *Ath. Pol.* (c. 4), a constitution of the first kind was found at Athens by Draco when he began his work of organisation; but this is probably an anachronism.
[2] Polyb. xii. 16.
[3] Jambl. *Vit. Pythag.* 35, 260.
[4] Heracleid *Fragm.* 25.

The precise forms assumed by the early aristocracies of the Greek world can very rarely be determined. They depended on the supremacy of caste or of wealth combined with caste, and they may rightly be termed "constitutions," in so far as the power of these governments, like that of the monarchies which had preceded them, was supposed to be limited by the observance of traditional law. There is only one extreme form, which, if it is rightly interpreted by Aristotle, hardly deserves the name of constitution. This is the δυναστεία or hereditary oligarchy, in which "son succeeds father, and personality and not the law is the governing force."[1] The government of the Thessalian clans in later times furnishes instances of at least the relics of such a system; but the best example of such a "dynasty" which we possess is the rule of the Bacchiadae of Corinth, where the caste system was more marked, and the government apparently more tyrannical, than elsewhere in the states of Greece.

The administrative character of these aristocracies is as obscure as their form, and the little that we know about the nature of their rule is confined to the period of their decline. If we fix our attention on the primitive states of Greece proper, and neglect for the moment the later colonial developments on which we have touched, the chief characteristics which we find noted may be summed up in two points : their almost universal oppression of the lower classes, and the extraordinary impulse which they consequently gave to colonisation. The varied and sometimes minute causes which led to the planting of colonies belong to the general history of Greece and not to the history of her institutions; it is sufficient to remark here that, after the period of the migrations, the latter part of the eighth and the first part of the seventh century were the great periods of the expansion of Hellas; and for this fact certain general causes can be assigned. One, it is true, was purely physical: the movement set on foot by the migrations was not yet over, and Greece possessed teeming populations with no room to settle on the mainland. But a great political cause is to be found in the discontent of the δῆμος at home under oligarchical government; for that this was the chief stimulus to emigration is proved by the fact that with the rise of democracy and settled government colonisation on a great scale ceases. Proximate

[1] Arist. *Pol.* iv. 5 = p. 1292 b.

causes were often furnished by quarrels in the ruling houses. Young and noble adventurers, whom crime or revolution had driven from home, went with bands of retainers to seek new settlements. Such were Archias, the Heracleid founder of Syracuse,[1] and the Spartan Partheniae, founders of Tarentum.[2] In later times some of the wiser despots, and later still some of the constitutional ministers of Greece, revived colonisation as a political measure. They often succeeded in their immediate objects, but were never able to give colonisation a history such as it had in this age. This was to a greater degree than others the age of chivalry and enterprise in Greece; for it was the age of discontent, which is the basis of enterprise. And the dissatisfaction with the existing order of things which produced colonisation was soon destined to give birth to a product whose influence was to be as great on the political development of Greece. This was tyranny.

The cities of Greece ever showed a remarkable tendency to accept personal rule, for universal subjection was at least one of the modes in which true democratic equality might be secured. We shall find that from the close of the fourth century, at a time when almost every political experiment had been tried and had seemed to fail in turn, tyranny, which at that time usually meant the protection of Macedon or of Persia, was again resorted to and became almost the normal type of government. But, in the earlier period that we are considering, the phenomenon is not complicated by external influences. It was a spontaneous development, and but a passing symptom of the growth of some new and powerful organ. Fortunately the new factors which created it and determined its character can be discovered with some success.

The origin of Greek tyranny was in the main commercial, and Thucydides is only reflecting this truth when he makes the somewhat enigmatic statement that it was due to the growing wealth of Hellas.[3] It is true that tyrannies sometimes arose in states, such as Athens, which had no claims to commercial greatness; wherever there was a discontented class —whether this were formed of merchants or peasants—there was a latent possibility of its growth. But the earliest, strongest, and most permanent despotisms certainly sprang

[1] Thuc. vi. 3; Plut. *Amat. Narr.* ii. p. 944 Didot.
[2] Paus. x. 10, 6; Strabo p. 426.
[3] Thuc. i. 13.

from a sudden assertion of their claims by the rich and unprivileged classes—the commercial folk who were outside the pale, and who were not only excluded from all share in the government, but found their properties exposed to the plunder of the dynasties which ruled the towns. These were the conditions which gave birth to the tyrant in Corinth, the rich manufacturing and shipping town which commanded the trade of the Isthmus,[1] and in Sicyon, renowned only next to Corinth for its commercial enterprise.[2] Both were ripe for revolution. In the former city a violent reaction against the Bacchiadae, who had grossly abused their power and appropriated to their own use the profits of the commercial class,[3] upset the dynastic government; in the latter the social movement was complicated by an ethnic question. At Sicyon both the tyrant and his supporters belonged to the weaker Ionian element in the state —the tribe of the Aegialeis—and the revolution took the form of a reaction against an oppressive Dorian nationality [4] and the assertion of the freedom of the state from Argive influence. Perhaps in this respect Sicyon did not stand alone. The effect of the Dorian migration had been to make social coincide with national distinctions, and tyranny may elsewhere have been the assertion of external freedom for the state as well as of internal liberty for the masses. More than a century later we find the same social causes that had affected Corinth at work in the western colonies. The tyrannies that sprang up during the close of the sixth century in Sicily and Southern Italy, at Leontini, Gela, and Rhegium, developed out of oligarchies,[5] and were probably due to the same assertion of their claims by the rich and unprivileged classes. In other states, where a commercial had not yet replaced a wholly agricultural civilisation, it was the championship of the poorest class on which the despot based his claim to power. It was thus that Peisistratus of Athens led the poor hill-men of the uplands of Attica, the Diacrii, against the rich men of the plain.[6]

Throughout Greece the difficulties, whether national or social, that called for settlement, could admit of but one solution—a personal ascendency of some kind that could lead

[1] Κόρινθος ἡ εὐδαίμων, Her. iii. 52.
[2] Strabo p. 382.
[3] Ael. *Var. Hist.* i. 19; Strabo p. 325.
[4] Her. v. 68.
[5] Arist. *Pol.* v. 12 = p. 1316 a.
[6] Her. i. 59; Arist. *Pol.* v. 5 = p. 1305 a.

to the readjustment of the conflicting claims of the rival parties in the state and the framing of a constitution. But the nature of this personal ascendency varied. In some rare cases it took the form of a constitutional dictatorship. At times the contending factions were fortunate or reasonable enough to come to an arrangement, and to agree in appointing an individual for a settlement of their difficulties who bore the title of αἰσυμνήτης. Such an office was held by Pittacus in Mitylene, by Zaleucus in Locri, and we may even say by Solon in Athens, for, although nominally sole archon, he was practically dictator. It was the only constitutional form of despotism in the Greek world, and is described by Aristotle as an "elective tyranny," and as combining the characteristics of monarchy and *tyrannis*.[1] The aesymnete was given a body-guard of sufficient force to enable him to carry out his work of organisation,[2] and, with respect to the length of his tenure of power, three forms of the office are described.[3] It was held either for life, or for a fixed term of years, or until certain duties had been performed.[4] But in most cities faction was too intense to admit the recognition of such a temporary and legitimised despotism. More frequently the reins of government were seized by a man who constituted himself champion of a section of the community, and by its help rose to be tyrant.

Normal and inevitable as we have seen the development of tyranny to be, it is yet possible that even in its earliest forms it was to some extent a conscious imitation of oriental despotism. At least the word τύραννος, which cannot be explained as Greek, seems to have come from Lydia and Phrygia, where it is found frequently on inscriptions, both as a title and as a proper name.[5] The meaning conveyed by the word to the Greek mind of a later age was that of a man who wielded an absolute authority, which was not sanctioned by the ordinances of the state in

---

[1] Arist. *Pol.* iii. 14; iv. 10 = p. 1295 a. "They are royal in so far as the monarch rules according to law and over willing subjects; but they are tyrannical in so far as he is despotic and rules according to his own fancy" (Jowett).
[2] *ib.* iii. 15.
[3] *ib.* iii. 14.
[4] The *aesymnesia*, though it belongs particularly to this period, never died out in Greece; and there is an instance, in a later period, of an aesymnete, Iphiades of Abydos, who made himself despot (Arist. *Pol.* v. 6 = p. 1306 a). In some states, such as Teos, Cyme, Naxos, and Megara, the title is found as that of a standing office.
[5] See Böckh's comment on *C.I.G.* n. 3438, where the title is applied to Zeus (κατ' ἐπιταγὴν τοῦ κυρίου τυράννου Διὸς Μασφαλατηνοῦ κ.τ.λ.)

which it was exercised. Absolutism and irresponsibility are the chief connotations of the word. To the citizen of a later age the tyrant was an outlaw in a threefold sense. He had placed himself outside the pale of positive law; for this reason he seemed exempt from all moral control, and, as an equally necessary consequence, was outside the protection of the law. It was this idea of "irresponsibility," of being above the ordinances of the state, which above all shocked Greek sentiment, and gave rise to the gloomy generalisations as to the character and conduct befitting such a position with which the readers of Herodotus are familiar.[1] We need only note in passing the gratuitous addition to this conception developed by the later philosophic thought of Greece, viz. that the rule of the tyrant was exercised not in the interest of the subject, but in that of the ruler. It forms the chief ground for Aristotle's distinction between monarchy and tyranny,[2] and was a natural consequence of the idea that the latter government was outside the pale of law; but it was a deduction not always justified by the facts. Historians must judge by results and not by motives; and few governments in Greece betrayed such a keen interest in the welfare of their cities as these unauthorised monarchs.[3]

The portraits of these pretenders who rose to power in the seventh and sixth centuries are drawn invariably in the same broad outlines.[4] They were demagogues who united military prowess, and sometimes, like Peisistratus, a past record for good service in the field, with a zeal, real or pretended, for the popular welfare. They were men who, in later Greece, would have been constitutional "champions of the people" (προστάται

---

[1] Her. iii. 80 κῶς δ' ἂν εἴη χρῆμα κατηρτημένον μοναρχίη, τῇ ἔξεστι ἀνευθύνῳ ποιέειν τὰ βούλεται; Here we get the key-note to the Greek prejudice against *tyrannis*. The internal state of the despot soon became the subject of debate in the philosophic schools; and this speculation, assisted perhaps by the experience of the inferior tyrants of the fourth century, formed the basis for the ideal pictures of Plato and Xenophon (Plat. *Rep.* p. 580; Xen. *Hiero, passim*), and for such a monstrous creation as the Periander of Herodotus (v. 92).

[2] Arist. *Eth.* viii. 10, 2; *Pol.* iii. 7, 5.

[3] The treatment of the vigorous external policy of the tyrants, which raised their cities to a greater height of power than was ever attained in their former, and sometimes in their subsequent history, and of the magnificence of their courts—the natural result of peace and prosperity—which is so strangely misconstrued by Aristotle (*Pol.* v. 11 = p. 1313 b), does not belong to constitutional history. I have attempted a sketch of these points in the art. "Tyrannus" in Smith's *Dict. of Greek and Roman Antiq.* (3rd ed.)

[4] Plato *Rep.* viii. p. 565 D; Arist. *Pol.* v. 10 = p. 1310 b; Dionys. vi. 60.

τοῦ δήμου); but they lived at a time when the sword was a keener weapon than the tongue, and when there was no organised assembly of the people to be swayed by their eloquence, but only a rabble to be led to the acropolis. The best-known types for this early period are Orthagoras of Sicyon, Cypselus of Corinth, Theagenes of Megara, and Peisistratus of Athens. But this type was very constant, and perpetuated itself even in the fourth century. At a time when there was no further political principle left to be fought for, we find Dionysius reaching the throne in Syracuse by a championship of social in default of political rights, and he is cited as one of the great historical instances of the demagogue despot.[1] It was naturally in the earlier tyrannies that this phenomenon was of most importance, for, as Aristotle was the first of Greeks to see, their holders were everywhere the precursors of a new phase of political life. The immediate effect of their rule may be summed up by saying that everywhere they found distraction in their cities, and everywhere they left something approaching unity. We extract from Herodotus,[2] an unwilling witness, the fact that at Athens the rule of the Peisistratidae first created a national spirit. It is after their overthrow that the δῆμος emerges as a united whole, by alliance with which Cleisthenes created the democracy. As unifiers of their cities they were the precursors of popular government, which requires a collective will. It is true that a democratic form of government did not everywhere follow their overthrow; but even in these cases a constitution of any kind was an improvement on the old dynastic rule. Corinth, the city most grievously chastened, and perhaps the most improved by tyranny, still remained an oligarchy, but an oligarchy of a constitutional type, which rested on, if it did not express, the popular will.

The social position of the individual demagogues who made their way to the throne is of some importance for constitutional history, since sometimes it shows a connecting link between the new *régime* and the old. In some cases, it is true, the tyrants sprang from the oppressed classes which they championed; Orthagoras, for instance, the founder of the dynasty of Sicyon, belonged to the weaker Ionian element of the state, and is said to have been a cook.[3] But more frequently they illustrate the truth that the best democrats spring from the ranks of the

---

[1] Arist. *Pol.* v. 5 = p. 1305 a.   [2] v. 66.   [3] Diodor. viii. 24.

nobility. They were often members of the oligarchies they overthrew, and sometimes even executive officials of these governments, who made the great powers which they possessed as magistrates a stepping-stone to the crown. According to one account,[1] Cypselus of Corinth was enabled to found his dynasty by the mode in which he exercised the office of "polemarch," or chief military commander of the city. It was by the straining of the powers of a magistracy that Phalaris rose to be tyrant of Agrigentum,[2] while at Miletus a tyranny arose out of the office of president ($\pi\rho\acute{u}\tau\alpha\nu\iota\varsigma$) of the state.[3] Peisistratus of Athens was of the royal family of Codrus,[4] and Lygdamis, whom he established in Naxos, belonged to the old nobility.[5] In cases where a magistracy had been held the transition to power was easier: a fragment of the constitution still remained, and the chief change was that popular now replaced dynastic support. At times this popular support was sufficient to maintain the government which it had established. Thus we are told that Cypselus remained a popular hero, and during the whole period of his rule at Corinth never required a body-guard.[6] But as a rule the despot could not hold his position by popular support alone. It was perhaps not so much a distrust of the loyalty of the masses as of their efficiency to protect their leaders against the attacks of the hostile clans, that led to the almost universal employment of bands of mercenaries, for the support of which the subjects were taxed.[7] This unfortunate accompaniment of their rule deepened, if it did not in some cases create, the idea of its unconstitutional character. The maintenance of the tyrant's rule was often typical of its beginning; for the throne that was supported by force had been in many cases won by violence. A *coup d'état* was the necessary supplement to popular favour in the case of Peisistratus; in other cases it seems to have been a substitute for popular support. It was thus that Polycrates gained the throne in Samos,[8] that Aristodemus made himself despot of

---

[1] That of Nicolaus of Damascus, p. 58.
[2] Arist. *Pol.* v. 10 = p. 1310 b.
[3] *ib.* v. 5 = p. 1305 a.
[4] Her. v. 65.
[5] Arist. *Pol.* v. 6 = p. 1305 b.
[6] *ib.* v. 12 = p. 1315 b. The Corinthians whom he slew, robbed, and banished (Her. v. 92), must have been members of the hostile oligarchy.

[7] *ib.* iii. 14; v. 10 = p. 1311 a. Herodotus (i. 61) speaks of the Argive mercenaries of Peisistratus.
[8] Yet, if it is true that he seized the acropolis with only fifteen hoplites (Her. iii. 120), he must have relied on the discontent of the $\delta\hat{\eta}\mu o\varsigma$, and believed that it would accept the result of the *coup d'état*.

Cumae in Italy,[1] and that Cylon attempted to occupy the same position at Athens.[2]

The first exercise of the tyrant's power was naturally a work of clearance. The most powerful members of the clans, which it was their declared object to resist, had to be disposed of; and we are not surprised to find that the Bacchiadae were expelled from Corinth by Cypselus,[3] and that even Peisistratus, in spite of the mildness of his rule, found it necessary to banish some of the nobles.[4] But by the wiser despots no violent change seems to have been made in the machinery of government where such machinery existed. The Peisistratidae, we are told, ruled in accordance with the κείμενοι νόμοι, only taking the precaution of having the great offices of state filled by members of their own family.[5] The Greek mind, it is true, would eliminate tyranny altogether from constitutional history; but the position of the Peisistratidae suggests the question whether the early Greek tyrannies were so unconstitutional either in theory or in practice as they are generally represented to have been. Unfortunately the case which we know best can scarcely be taken as typical, for despotism at Athens was a comparatively late development, and followed a thorough reconstruction of the state by Solon. There was a machinery to hand which the new ruler might use, and Peisistratus, while as absolute as the Roman *princeps*, posed like him as an executive authority and as a part of the constitution. In the earlier tyrannies this chance was hardly offered, for with the overthrow of the dynasty the whole machinery of government went with it. Yet in those cases where the exercise of a magistracy was made a stepping-stone to tyranny, some shadow of legality might have been preserved by the maintenance of this office. The case of Gelo of Syracuse proves how even the greater tyrants craved legal recognition,[6] and how sometimes

---

[1] Dionys. vii. 2-11.
[2] Her. v. 71; Thuc. i. 126. His failure was largely due to the fatal mistake he made in relying on foreign, in this case Megarian, aid. See W. Fowler *The City State* p. 127.
[3] Dionys. iii. 46; cf. Her. v. 92.
[4] *ib.* vi. 103.
[5] *ib.* i. 59; Thuc. vi. 54. In the *Ath. Pol.* (c. 16) Peisistratus is said to have ruled μᾶλλον πολιτικῶς ἢ τυραννικῶς, and his reign was called the age of Cronus. For his observance of constitutional forms see Arist. *Pol.* v. 12 = p. 1315 b.
[6] The rulers of Sicily are exempted by Thucydides (i. 17) from his general condemnation of the pettiness of the tyrant's aims. In Herodotus (vii. 163; cf. 157) Gelo is despot, not of Syracuse, but of Sicily.

this might be won. The lofty ambition of Gelo more than redeems his tyranny; it was nothing less than the defence of western civilisation against its deadly foe the Semite, by a union of the Sicilian Greeks to resist the Carthaginians. The union was effected, and by the battle of Himera in 480 the victory was won. Then it was that Gelo was acclaimed by the Syracusans as their saviour, their benefactor, and their *king*.[1]

The true evil of *tyrannis* was supposed to be most clearly shown by the necessities of its internal administration. To create a slavish feeling in the subjects, to sow mistrust amongst them, to allow no prominent men in the state, to encourage flatterers, parasites, and espionage, are said to be the characteristics of the despots;[2] elsewhere stress is laid on the bloodstained character of their rule.[3] It is impossible to say whether these criticisms are really applicable to the earlier tyrannies, and they are largely due to the later Greek sentiment that irresponsible must mean evil rule. We hear nothing of general oppression of the citizens; if we may judge from the case of the Peisistratidae, taxation seems to have been light: they collected only one-twentieth of the products of the soil;[4] and there are many typical stories which show that it was to the interest of the tyrants to keep the lower classes contented and employed.[5]

More important are the social changes with which they are credited. The scattered notices of these deserve examination since, whether consciously pursued with this motive or not, these reforms had a decidedly political tendency. An inevitable object of their policy was to raise the depressed portion of the population at the expense of the dominant section. This change, probably universal, was most marked where the distinction between classes was a national one. Hence the fame of Cleisthenes's reforms at Sicyon. His hatred of the memory of Adrastus, the Dorian hero, his suppression of the Homeric recitals, and his alteration of the tribe-names,[6] were

---

[1] Diodor. xi. 26 εὐεργέτης, σωτήρ, καὶ βασιλεύς. See Freeman *Hist. of Sicily* ii. p. 501. Even before this Athenian envoys are represented as addressing him as ὦ βασιλεῦ Συρηκοσίων (Her. vii. 161). This was a courtesy title, and in fact the only mode of address possible to a tyrant from envoys of a friendly state.

[2] Arist. *Pol.* v. 11 = p. 1313 b.

[3] Her. iii. 80; v. 92.

[4] Thuc. vi. 54. The *Ath. Pol.* (c. 16), probably wrongly, makes Peisistratus himself exact a tithe.

[5] *Ath. Pol.* 16; Ael. *Var. Hist.* ix 25.

[6] Her. v. 67, 68.

all meant to elevate the Ionian element in the state at the expense of the Dorian. National unity was to the interest of the tyrant, since his power was equally threatened by clan feuds and by local factions. For this purpose religious festivals were instituted, and Peisistratus's establishment of the greater Panathenaea [1] is typical of the mode in which pageantry might be employed in the interest of order. A third element in their reforms was, characteristically for this period of Greek history, also religious. It can hardly be an accident that the names of Periander, Cleisthenes, and Peisistratus are all associated with the cultivation of the Dionysiac worship;[2] for by the encouragement given to these festivals they were substituting universal and popular cults for the aristocratic and exclusive worship of the nobles. The Dionysiac-Orphic ritual is of great importance in the history of the democracy. It is not a primitive cult in Greece; even at Eleusis it replaced an older native worship of Poseidon. With its advent from Thrace two popular movements began—the drama and the mysteries. The mysteries were above all anti-aristocratic; they were part of a spiritual cult, to which any one might be admitted; they had, it is true, their special priests, such as the Eumolpidae and Ceryces at Athens, but noble and commoner were on a level amongst the initiated. In all the states the Dionysiac worship was a new thing, connected with no traditional ancestry, appealing to no particular clan. Its tendency was thus unifying and levelling, and for this reason it was encouraged by the tyrants.

It was not in the nature of tyranny to last long, however powerful the individual ruler might make himself. We do indeed meet with despotisms of a duration which rivalled that of the ordinary constitutional governments in Greece: the Orthagoridae ruled at Sicyon for a hundred years, the Cypselidae at Corinth for seventy-three years, the Peisistratidae at Athens, exclusive of the period during which Peisistratus was banished, for thirty-five; but these periods were exceptional. The tyrants were, as a rule, ministers of the people irregularly appointed to perform a special work, and when the work was done and there was no further reason for their continuance, they fell. Their government was brought to an end sometimes through the

---

[1] *Schol. Aristeidis* p. 323.
[2] Periander (Her. i. 23), Cleisthenes (Her. v. 67); for Peisistratus the evidence, though more abundant, is less direct. It is collected and examined by Dyer *The Gods in Greece* pp. 125, 126.

degeneracy of the successors to the original usurper, as in the case of the Peisistratidae; sometimes through conspiracies inspired by private motives—a cause of ruin which Aristotle illustrates by the downfall of the earlier and later despotisms at Syracuse.[1] But not infrequently their overthrow was effected by external force, and the earliest crusades undertaken in support of a political idea were the expeditions made by certain cities for the destruction of tyranny in others. In early times Sparta gained the greatest name as a liberator, and is said to have put down *most* of the tyrannies in Greece.[2] The other great instance is that of a city which had itself suffered: Syracuse, after the death of Thrasybulus, and after that of the younger Dionysius, vigorously undertook the liberation of the other Sicilian states.[3]

Such in the main are the faint glimpses we get of early Greek tyranny through the haze of false tradition and real fear. For it was fear that moulded the later Greek conception of this rule. The law-abiding Greek of the fifth and fourth centuries had ever in his mind the haunting fear of a possible despotism such as seemed threatened by men of the type of Alcibiades of Athens—men unwilling to submit to the equality of a democratic constitution, whose chief characteristic was a covetous ambition ($\pi\lambda\epsilon ov\epsilon\xi i\alpha$), and whose rise to power meant the negation of all political principle. It was difficult for him, with such a vision before his eyes, to look back to a time when tyranny had represented a principle, and when it had helped to secure rights for the common folk.

With the close of Greek tyranny the ancient history of Greece is left behind us. The rest is modern, in the sense now so familiar to us of history that is modern in its characteristics. If, as has been said, the history of civilisation is the passage from *status* to contract,[4] we may say that *status* in Greece had now been left behind, and that the basis of the contract on which society rests was to be examined and criticised. The most definite answers to the question appear in the various forms of constitution which were now to spring up. Conscious political thought soon followed these creations, with varying results. One day the respective merits of these forms was to be

---

[1] *Pol.* v. 10 = p. 1312 b.
[2] Thuc. i. 18; cf. Arist. *l.c.*, Her. v. 92.
[3] Arist. *l.c.*; Diod. xi. 68; xvi. 82.
[4] Maine *Ancient Law* c. 5.

settled by an appeal to the sword in the great political struggle of the Peloponnesian War; and meanwhile the more peaceful discussion of these claims, which appears already in Herodotus and grows more subtle in Thucydides, had been handed down to the still colder judgment of philosophy, to find at length its grandest exposition in Aristotle's *Politics*. It was Greek tyranny which, by breaking down all artificial barriers, prepared the way for the "bazaar of constitutions" exhibited there.

CHAPTER III

COLONISATION—INTERNATIONAL LAW

THE differences of political development which followed the downfall of tyranny are too great to allow us to treat Greek history collectively from this point onwards. Henceforth we shall have to examine distinct types of development; but, before entering on this more minute phase of the work, it will be convenient to touch here on two political factors which are common more or less to the whole Greek world, to that Hellas which is the name not of a territory, but of a people. These are colonisation and the tendencies which led to such unification as Hellas as a whole attained.

§ 1 *Colonisation*

We have already noticed that the period of the aristocracies was the great epoch of the expansion of Greece, and we have seen the general political tendencies to which this movement was due. The particular causes which led to the planting of colonies at this or at any other time are of importance for constitutional history only in so far as the motive for the foundation of the new state may have affected its form or its relation to the mother city. The differences of the periods in which colonies were founded must have been equally important in both these respects; but of these we can say but little. It is difficult, in a comprehensive treatment of colonisation, to separate the old from the new, the later deliberate organisation which we know so well from the earlier and more spontaneous movement of which we hear so little.

The causes may be summed up generally as being migration

and the movement of peoples, political faction, agricultural and commercial enterprise, and, lastly, the motives of military and agrarian settlement in the interest of the colonising state. Settlements due to the migrations—such as were, according to current Greek opinion, the Aeolian, Ionian, and Doric cities on the coast of Asia Minor, which some have thought to have had an independent origin and to be as old, at least in germ, as the cities of Greece proper itself—are, if the story of their settlement or reinforcement by the migrations be accepted, rather the result of spontaneous national movement than of conscious colonial enterprise.[1] It is possible that the movements of these emigrants may have been to some extent guided by prominent cities on the mainland of Greece; but later historical reflection, which strove to connect the traditions of East and West, and to attach them to the great working hypothesis of the Dorian migration, was of itself sufficient to float such a theory as that which represents certain of these Ionian cities as having taken their sacred fire from the court-house of the Athenians.[2] The theory was assisted by, and made the excuse for later political connections; it established a claim on Athenian protection,[3] and formed the basis of the counter claim which Athens made, in the period of her Empire, that she was only ruling over her natural dependencies. Otherwise its political importance is slight, and the peculiarities of the political history of the Greeks in Asia are due to other causes. The antiquity of these settlements led to their pursuing the normal lines of Greek constitutional development, with the exception that the element of wealth seems to have been more strongly marked in their period of aristocratic development.[4] Some, such as Miletus, developed tyrannies of the spontaneous type;[5] but their political growth was soon arrested by foreign conquest. Herodotus[6] mentions a crop of so-called "tyrants" of the Greek cities of Asia Minor of the sixth and fifth centuries, such as Daphnis of Abydos, Aeaces of Samos, Aristagoras of Cyme,

---

[1] Later settlements were due to a similar cause—movement caused by the pressure of enemies. To this was due the emigration of the Phocaeans, under pressure from the Persians, to Velia in Italy and Alalia in Corsica (Her. i. 167), and of the Teians to Abdera (*ib.* i. 168). Similarly the Byzantines and Chalcedonians, after the Ionic revolt, fled from the Persians and settled at Mesembria on the Euxine (*ib.* vi. 33).

[2] Her. i. 146.

[3] *ib.* xi. 106; Thuc. i. 95.

[4] See p. 23.

[5] See p. 30.

[6] iv. 138.

and others. But these cannot be classed with the despots of the early period in Greece proper, Italy, and Sicily, for they were merely native princes who governed the Greek dependencies of Persia, and who were kept in their position by Persian support. Subsequently the Persian government learnt that democracy was a better basis for loyalty than tyranny;[1] but henceforth these Greeks of Asia have scarcely any independent political history: they are the slaves of Athenian, Spartan, and Persian caprice; whatever form of government they possess is imposed, or at least tolerated, by a foreign power; yet they perform their function in the world's history none the worse for this. It was to be the Hellenism of the East, the beginning of which may be traced in the uniform system of the Athenian Empire, while the end is to be found in the municipal administration of the eastern half of the Roman Empire.

Political faction, as a ground for colonisation,[2] is in no sense a determinant as regards either the nature of the colony or its relation to the parent state. The autonomy enjoyed by such settlements is simply a result of the normal theory of colonisation, not of the special circumstances of their departure. Such a colony is not a chance aggregate moving off in anger from the mother city. It parts with it in a friendly spirit; the parent, though relieved at the departure, gives the blessing and authorisation necessary to make the offspring a colony; and the ties of sentimental allegiance between the two are at least as close as those consequent on other motives.

When, on the other hand, we turn to the commercial motive, we find many points that demand attention. That it was the most constant of the inspiring causes is shown by the "Greek fringe woven round the coast of the barbarian," noticed by Cicero;[3] but the stability of Greek political institutions is largely due to the fact that the Greek settlement was rarely, like the Phoenician, a mere factory. The agricultural element, so prominent in the cities of Sicily and the eighty Milesian colonies on the Black Sea, was almost invariably present; and agriculture implies a permanent settlement and attachment to the soil. Sometimes, indeed, trade might be the only motive; a Greek "emporium," to which rights had been granted by the people with whom it traded, might grow into a city. It was

---

[1] Her. vi. 43.   [2] See p. 24.   *agris quasi attexta quaedam videtur*
[3] *de Rep.* ii. 4, 9 *ita barbarorum*   *ora esse Graeciae.*

thus that Amasis of Egypt recognised the existence of Naucratis, composed of a society of Greeks of various cities who had long been trading at the Canobic mouth of the Nile. It remained a thoroughly Greek settlement; its manners and laws were Hellenic, and its constitution appears to have been modelled on that of one of the founding states.[1] Yet it was hardly a colony (ἀποικία) in the ordinary Greek sense, for it lacked the two characteristics of a mother city and a founder (οἰκιστής). But Naucratis is probably an exceptional case. Many of the early commercial settlements may have had a similarly unconscious growth; the πόλις may have been a late development from the factory, yet there is every reason to believe that when it became an organised community it received a sanction from a founding state, and became in the strict sense a colony, but with no further political connection with the mother city than that contained in treaties which were the result of community of commercial interest. The tie was sometimes closer when, in place of this unconscious growth, a powerful commercial city founded settlements along its own trade-routes. Corinth attempted a direct control of her western colonies on the coasts of Illyria, Epirus, and Acarnania, and we have a passing reference to the presence of certain Corinthian officials called ἐπιδημιουργοί in Potidaea.[2]

The political connection was necessarily closer still between colonies founded to serve a military purpose and the states which sent them out. Such settlements were artificial creations of a later age, merely attempts to hold distant dependencies or to create a sphere of military influence near an enemy's territory. They are peculiarly interesting to the student of constitutional history, since the two colonial charters which have been preserved—that of the Periclean colony sent to Brea in Thrace, and that regulating the settlement of Naupactus by the Opuntian Locrians[3]—are concerned with foundations the main object, at least, of which was military. From the nature of the case the dependence of such a colony on the mother city is very close, and hence the relations between the two are far

[1] τιμοῦχοι are magistrates of Naucratis as of Teos. The other founding states were—Chios, Phocaea, Clazomenae (Ionian); Rhodes, Cnidus, Halicarnassus, Phaselis (Dorian); and Mitylene (Aeolian). These appointed the Board of Trade (προστάται τοῦ ἐμπορίου). Her. ii. 178.

[2] Thuc. i. 56.

[3] Hicks nn. 29, 63. The respective dates of these foundations are approximately 440 and 460.

from typical. Amphipolis and the other Periclean colonies in Thrace, which may be taken as types of such settlements, were founded within the empire of Athens, and therefore within the sphere of her direct military influence. The Spartan colony of Heraclea in Trachis,[1] a bold enterprise undertaken during the Peloponnesian War for the purpose of commanding the northern dependencies of Athens, was a mere military outpost under the immediate command of Spartan governors.

One step further in history and we find the central control becoming still more definite. The κληρουχία, the last stage in the development of the colonial theory in Greece, is merely an outlying fragment of the central πόλις with some municipal organisation of its own. Technically it belongs rather to the history of agrarian legislation than to that of colonisation, although military might be combined with social objects in its creation. The cleruchies are known to us almost entirely as one of the modes in which Athens employed her control of subject territory to further the interests of her own state,[2] and their treatment consequently belongs more properly to that division of our work which deals with the Athenian system of imperial administration.

The questions we have touched on have already illustrated the fact that colonisation was always regarded as a public act in Greece; no settlement was regarded as quite legitimate unless this act of state had been performed by some city, which was then regarded as the metropolis, and might afterwards become the grandmother of the offshoots of its own colony, since ancient custom directed that the latter, in founding a fresh settlement, should seek a leader (οἰκιστής) from its own parent state.[3] The act of colonisation was preceded by certain formalities. A religious sanction was obtained by the consultation of an oracle,[4] generally that of Delphi, which appears to have had the fullest information of the places best suited for settlement. Next came the charter of incorporation (τὰ

---

[1] Founded in 426 (Thuc. iii. 92).

[2] The cleruchies were not, however, confined to Athens. Some of the Milesian settlements on the islands (Strabo p. 635), e.g. at Leros, seem to have been of this nature.

[3] Thuc. i. 24.

[4] Cic. de Div. i. 1, 3 quam vero Graecia coloniam misit in Aeoliam, Ioniam, Asiam, Siciliam, Italiam sine Pythio aut Dodonaeo aut Hammonio oraculo? The tendency to consult the Pythian oracle gave rise to the worship, so frequent in the colonies, of Apollo Archegetes.

ἀποίκια) given by the government of the founding state. This charter set forth the conditions under which the colony was to be founded, and sometimes the relations, whether religious or political, which were to be maintained between it and the parent state. The fortunate preservation of the decree establishing the colony of Brea gives us a vivid insight into the contents of such documents. This decree (1) specifies the social condition of the intending colonists: they were to be chosen from the "Zeugitae" and the "Thetes," the two lower classes in the Solonian census. Such a clause, though characteristic of the state-directed colonies of the Periclean age, must have been extremely unusual, if not unknown, at an earlier period: since emigration, though directed by the state, was as a rule a voluntary act and a matter of private enterprise. (2) It appoints a certain Democleides to be the oecist, the guide and leader, of the new enterprise, and gives him the fullest power over the details of the "establishment" of the colony.[1] We can hardly understand by this a free permission to frame constitutional details at his pleasure, although at an earlier period the influence of the oecist on the structure of the new constitution must have been immense. (3) Here follows a clause which is the most remarkable instance we possess of the recognition of absolute religious obligations by constitutional law. It enacts that the religious enclosures (τεμένη) in the territory destined for the settlement should be left as they are and no others be enclosed.[2] This can only be an injunction to worship the native gods,[3] a provision of Greek international custom to maintain the religious observances of a conquered district, which here finds expression in the public law of Athens. It is probable that universal legal recognition accompanied a sentiment which we know to be typically Greek, and which widened the native Pantheon by the absorption of the cults of Asia Minor and of Thrace, and even of the strange worships left by Sicel or Sican in the West.[4] (4) Next comes the mention of the

---

[1] Hicks n. 29, A l. 8 Δημοκλείδην καταστῆσαι αὐτοκράτορα.

[2] l. 9 τὰ δὲ τεμένη τὰ ἐξῃρημένα ἐᾶν καθάπερ ἔστι καὶ ἄλλα μὴ τεμενίζειν.

[3] Gilbert *Staatsalt.* ii. p. 400.

[4] The absorption of oriental worships by colonists is not so striking, since it was but a fresh recognition of an influence early felt by Greek religion. More remarkable is the assumption by Greek settlers of such wholly non-Hellenic worships as those of Hadranus and the Palici in Sicily. See Freeman *History of Sicily* vol. i. pp. 517 ff.

supply of money granted by the state to set the colony on its way (ἐφόδιον); this was generally accompanied by the equally necessary provision of a supply of arms.[1] (5) Land-commissioners (γεωνόμοι) are appointed to divide the territory into allotments. The lots would probably be equal, and the recipients would form the "Gamori," who would remain the chiefly, and in some cases the solely, privileged aristocracy as the settlement grew with the influx of new residents.[2] So fully was it recognised by this class that the maintenance of its privileges depended on its remaining a landed aristocracy that sometimes, as in Locri,[3] laws appear to have been made to prevent alienation of the lots. (6) Finally, provision is made for sacred offerings, symbols of a religious allegiance, to be sent to the festivals of the mother state. In some cases the latter sent sacred envoys to colonial festivals, where special honours were accorded them.[4] Another generally observed custom, not mentioned here, was the taking of the sacred fire from the prytaneium of the founding state.

Some of the clauses in colonial charters may have been dictated by circumstances and have varied from time to time; but most of them—the appointment of the oecist, the injunctions as to religious duties, and perhaps the ἐφόδιον, if asked for—were, like the consultation of the oracle, "customary observances," the neglect of which was likely to entail disaster on the settlement.[5] The whole procedure is an expression of the Greek sentiment which pictured the act as that of a mother who sends her child out into the world.[6]

The relation between a colony and its mother city was as a rule merely sentimental and religious, and was emphasised by the worship of the personal founder as a hero after his death.[7] Sometimes, indeed, it was difficult to preserve even this sentimental relationship. Although directed by a single city, colonies were sometimes composed of very mixed elements, and in this case little attachment to the founders was to be looked for. It

---

[1] Argt. to Demosthenes *On the Chersonese* καὶ ἐλάμβανον πεμπόμενοι ὅπλα ἐκ τοῦ δημοσίου καὶ ἐφόδια.
[2] See p. 23.
[3] Arist. *Pol.* ii. 7, 6.
[4] Thuc. i. 25.
[5] τὰ νομιζόμενα they are called by Herodotus (v. 52). Here he relates the dreadful fate which overtook Dorieus the Spartan for not obeying these customary rules.
[6] cf. Plato *Laws* p. 754.
[7] For the worship of the οἰκιστής see Her. vi. 38, Thuc. v. 11.

was an aggregate of races of this kind, planted by the Athenians at Thurii in 443, that declined to worship a founder of more limited nationality than Apollo Archegetes himself.[1] But community of commercial and political interests often bound the two states closely together, and sometimes this community found expression in a fixed agreement included in the charter. A clause such as that in the charter given by the Locrians to Naupactus about 460—that the colonists should swear not to quit alliance with the mother city, and that thirty years later each state might call on the other to renew the oath[2]—was, in spite of the late date of this document, probably not unusual. We have noticed the actual attempt at government of her colonies made by Corinth. Elsewhere we find tokens of dependence given by the colony, but on reasonable grounds. Cotyora, Trapezus, and Cerasus, colonies of Sinope, had to pay to the mother state a yearly tribute. It was merely, however, a sign of the precarious tenure of their soil, for these colonies had been founded on land which Sinope had taken from the barbarians.[3]

But dependence of any kind was rare; and although the slight bonds of Greek international law were here reinforced by the tie of sentiment, and it was considered impious to bear arms against the mother state,[4] the general feeling in Greece seems to have been that all political interference on the part of the latter was sufficient to dissolve the bonds of sentimental allegiance.[5] The chief reason for this independence of the colony is no doubt to be sought simply in the idea of the autonomy of the πόλις, the foundation of Greek political life. Modern practice takes a different view of these relations because modern colonisation is based on the theory of territorial sovereignty, which implies that any territory settled on and claimed by members of a state is by right of occupation a part of that community—an easy conception when the basis of civilisation is ethnic, but impossible where, as in Greece, the city was regarded as the highest political unit. But there were practical reasons which rendered colonial dependence impossible. The distance of some of these settlements from the colonising state, as of Massilia from Phocaea, would have prevented close supervision. The mixture of population—a characteristic even

[1] Diod. xii. 10.
[2] Hicks n. 63 i. A.
[3] Xen. *Anab.* v. 5, 10.
[4] Her. iii. 19 ; viii. 22.
[5] Thuc. i. 34.

of the early colonies,[1] and still more strongly marked in the joint settlements which were in vogue in the fifth century [2]—combined with a difference in the conditions of life that could evolve "gay Tarentum" from sombre Sparta, resulted frequently in a complete difference of civilisation. Lastly, colonies often became more powerful than their mother cities; and it was fortunate that no such fiction existed as that which would have asserted a supremacy of Corinth over Syracuse, or of Megara over Byzantium.

The rigorous theory of the independence of the colony would, if strictly carried out, have led to a dissolution of all family ties and to an abandonment of all legal family claims between the members of the respective states. But this was not in accordance with Greek sentiment, and is provided against by certain clauses in the charter of Naupactus. Provision is there made for the next of kin in the mother state claiming intestate succession to a colonist, for a Naupactian taking his share of his deceased brother's property in Locris, and for a colonist who leaves a father behind him being entitled to his share at his father's death.[3] Easy conditions are even made for the resumption of citizenship in the mother city;[4] and, though the document that contains these clauses is of late date, still there is every reason to believe that here, as elsewhere in Greece, the family and religion created ties that even the dissolution of those of the city could not break.

The political history of the colonies was marked by a rapidity of development and a comprehensive grasp of social problems which found no parallel in the states of Greece proper, at least until the beginning of the sixth century. The arrested development of the East furnishes few examples of their political progress. In the West it was different. Here ingenious political experiments were tried, such as the timocracies, which sprang up in Locri, Rhegium, Croton, and probably in Sybaris. The struggle between classes assumed a new and interesting phase,

---

[1] *e.g.* of the Ionian cities of Asia (Her. i. 146) and of Cyrene (*ib.* iv. 161); the Milesian colonies on the Black Sea must also have been mixed settlements.

[2] Diod. xii. 10 (Thurii); Thuc. iii. 92 (Heraclea); cf. i. 27.

[3] Hicks n. 63, A, *F*, and H.

[4] "If a colonist returns, leaving an adult son or brother in his place, he may be enrolled in the E. Locrian registers without entrance-sacrifice." The conditions are almost precisely the same as those which regulated the *jus exsulandi* at Rome, between *socii* and *Latini* and between *Latini* and Roman citizens.

and revolution, the product of material rather than of artificial distinctions, began earlier than in the older states of Greece. The first clear glimpse which we catch of the history of Syracuse shows us the Gamori exiled by their own demos and the serf population.[1] The tyrannies which we have already noticed in other Sicilian states came later indeed in time than those of the mother country, but earlier in the political history of the cities they affected. The same tendencies are visible in Magna Graecia; in Rhegium the aristocratic government was overthrown by Anaxilas; and Telys of Sybaris is called indifferently demagogue and tyrant.[2] The application of scientific thought to practical life finds ample illustration in these western civilisations. In 532 the school of the Pythagoreans with its aristocratic tendencies sprang up at Croton, only to be driven out by a democracy whose wants were more powerful than the theories of its opponents. More than a century earlier legislation, the product of mixed populations, who are as susceptible to new laws as to new impressions,[3] had begun. Zaleucus of Locri (662) must have been more than a codifier, for he created a type of constitution and fixed the penalties of the criminal law, which had hitherto rested on the discretion of the judge.[4] The legislation of Charondas of Catana (*circ.* 650) must have been less political than that of his predecessor, and of a very universal type, since it was extended to the other Chalcidian cities of Sicily and Italy. We know nothing of the tenor of his laws; but that its chief characteristic was accuracy of expression ($\dot{a}\kappa\rho\iota\beta\epsilon\iota a$)[5] is a sign of a new spirit in Greece—a spirit that would accept nothing that it could not explain, and would realise only what it believed it understood.

§ 2 *International Law*

The tendency to disintegration, which had been born with the tribal unions of the Greeks, had been still further increased by the expansion effected by the period of colonisation. Yet it was always possible to say where Hellas was, and the tests that could be applied to discover its existence are summed up by Herodotus

[1] Her. vii. 155.
[2] Diod. xii. 9 δημαγωγός : Her. v. 44 τύραννος or βασιλεύς.
[3] Plato *Laws* p. 708.
[4] Ephorus ap. Strab. p. 260.
[5] Arist. *Pol.* ii. 12.

as community of blood, language, religion, and manners.[1] Ultimate community in the first two factors the Greeks did not care to trace, and community of race had little meaning for them apart from an obvious resemblance in language, tradition, and type of political civilisation. In reality language and religion are the most tangible symbols of unity to an early people, for they mean a tendency to community of worship (which is the basis of such international law as they possess), common literature and art, and to a large extent community even in the forces of morality and social life. From the earliest time these last are inextricably interwoven with religion, although the power of a common language is even here not to be ignored. We have in modern times to a large extent outgrown the tyranny of words; but to the Greek the common word was the common thing. Expressions such as δίκη, νόμος, ξένος, which appealed in the same way to every Greek, were binding as terms long before they became valid as concepts.

Externally, at least, religion was the most important influence in effecting the unity of Greece; for so far as there was community of worship there was a common international law. It was, it is true, rather a negative than a positive law—a mild protest of religion against the entire absence of order. For Greek society practically assumed a wholesale denial of international relations other than those based on interest or convenience, and carried out with the utmost strictness the theory that there are no rights of man other than those conferred by membership of the city-state. It never evolved a secular basis for international law such as the *jus gentium* or the *lex naturae;* but there was just a minimum of common morality which a common religion enjoined on all Greeks alike, and it was this which formed the basis of the "law common to the Greeks." This law often appears unsupported by any institution that could enforce it, but its validity is not impaired by its purely impersonal sanction. One form it assumed was the duty of hospitality to the stranger (ξενία), which developed on the one hand into the institution of προξενία, the representation of the interests of one state by a citizen resident in another, who undertook this duty either voluntarily or by commission;[2] on the other hand, into the rules regulating the *status* of a stranger in any community. An alien from a foreign city had

---

[1] viii. 144.   [2] Hence the distinction between πρόξενος and ἐθελοπρόξενος.

as a rule[1] no legal personality, and could, therefore, exercise his rights as a resident alien (μέτοικος) only through a duly qualified citizen whom he took as patron (προστάτης). Hence in some states[2] the principle was observed that a stranger could not reside more than thirty days in the city without enrolling himself as a metoec and attaching himself to a patron. It was only thus that the alien could cease to be an enemy and become a guest. But even as an enemy religion invested him with certain rights, and it was in the sphere of war that its influence was most clearly seen. The herald was sacrosanct for the state to which he journeyed, if not for the states through which he passed;[3] and this sanctity spread beyond the sphere of influence of the Greek gods to invest even the herald of the barbarian.[4] Duties were owed to the bodies of the slain in battle; they might not be mutilated,[5] and the victors were bound to give them up for burial. Shrines and temples in conquered countries were to be preserved, and the religious ceremonial continued;[6] and rules were even framed to modify that most repulsive aspect of Greek civilisation, the treatment of prisoners of war. According to Greek ideas prisoners passed wholly into the hands of the conqueror; they might be kept or sold as slaves, or put to death. But three modifying principles came finally to prevail. A fixed ransom of two minae might be offered for a captive soldier, although it is doubtful whether, in the time of the citizen armies at least, there was any obligation on the victor to accept it;[7] it was claimed that unconditional but voluntary surrender should carry with it the preservation of life,[8] while in conditional surrender the condition must be

---

[1] The rule was not quite universal; see p. 8.

[2] This principle is found in a commercial treaty concluded between Oeanthia and Chaleion, two towns on the Corinthian Gulf. Hicks n. 31. l. 8; cf. Hicks n. 63 Z.

[3] The execution of Aristeus, a Corinthian envoy to the Persians, by the Athenians (Thuc. ii. 67) makes it doubtful whether the herald was sacrosanct for the whole Greek world.

[4] cf. the story of the wrath of Talthybius in Her. vii. 134 ff.

[5] Mutilation is conduct worthy only of a βάρβαρος (Her. ix. 79). This word, the primary meaning of which is "rude," "strange," and which was applied to nations of the highest degree of civilisation, has come here, and in other passages of Herodotus and Thucydides, to mean "unworthy of a Greek."

[6] For these last two duties see the curious discussion between the Athenians and Boeotians after the battle of Delium in 424 (Thuc. iv. 98).

[7] For this ransom see Her. v. 77; vi. 79. Aristotle (*Ethics* v. 7, 1) makes it a universal rule; but then he is writing in the time of mercenary armies.

[8] It is a νόμος τοῖς Ἕλλησι (Thuc. iii. 58).

observed, but only if it had been ratified by an oath. The oath might create a wholly new series of international relations, temporary or permanent, between two states; but the most solemn form of promise, unaccompanied by a religious formula, had no binding force.[1] It is not surprising that this belief sometimes made the literal performance of an oath override the fulfilment of the spirit of an agreement.[2]

The sanction of such rules is that their violator exposes himself to the vengeance of the common gods of Greece, or, in the case of a covenant, of his native gods by whom he has sworn. But sometimes these rules rested partly on a human institution—that of the "amphictyonies" of Greece—partly on the sworn compact on which these organisations themselves reposed; and the divine and human sanction were here closely interwoven. The amphictyony was a body of representatives of different tribes or cities meeting at stated intervals round some common religious centre.[3] The object of their meeting was, primarily, to preserve the temple and its worship and to defend the territory of the god against aggression; secondarily, to mitigate excess of rancour in wars between the states of this religious league, and to preserve that minimum of international morality which a common religion enjoined.[4] Often the principles they professed to maintain were formulated and ratified by oath, but many questions appear to have been discussed at these meetings the answers to which were not contained in any written code.[5] These religious meetings were identical in origin with the great games, which through their more popular character eventually overshadowed them. Friendly contests of various kinds (ἀγῶνες) are mentioned in connection with all the chief amphictyonies. They are found at Onchestus in Boeotia,[6] in Delos,[7] at Mycale,[8] and at Triopium[9]; and down to the latest times one of the four great games, the Pythian, was never a festival of all Greece, but was confined to the

[1] Thuc. ii. 5.
[2] ib. iii. 34.
[3] ἀμφικτίονες = περικτίονες "dwellers around" (so used in Her. vii. 148). The form ἀμφικτύονες is found also in inscriptions.
[4] Dionys. iv. 25 νόμους καταστησάμενος ἔξω τῶν ἰδίων, ὧν ἑκάστη πόλις εἶχε, τοὺς κοινοὺς ἅπασιν.
[5] e.g. the request made by the citizens of Delos in 345 or 344 for freedom from the Athenian hegemony, which was referred to the amphictyony of Delphi, had no connection with the ordinary functions of this body.
[6] Hom. Hymn. in Ap. Pyth. 52 ff.
[7] Thuc. iii. 104.
[8] Her. i. 148.
[9] ib. i. 144.

members of the amphictyony of Delphi. The sacred truce (ἱεραὶ σπονδαί or ἐκεχειρία) is common to both; but these associations, originally the same, branched off into two distinct lines of development. Sometimes the games outgrew the amphictyony—as at Olympia, where there had originally been a meeting of the Pisatans, and afterwards of the Aetolians of Elis, for the worship of Zeus and Here. The Nemean games were similarly a festival of Cleonae, which afterwards fell under the direction of Argos, and the Isthmian were at first a Corinthian festival in honour of Melcarth. When this was the tendency of the meeting the chief direction of the festival came again to be vested in the hands of a single state, and the council of the league tended to disappear. In other cases the association itself continued to be of chief importance. Then it remained an amphictyony, in which any individual city ceased to have an undue preponderance. It is at least an association of the cities of a tribe, but more usually it is an association of tribes or of different cities of different tribes.

The tendency of these societies was to change from being a union of one tribe into becoming a union of many, but in some this development was arrested, and amphictyonies may consequently be divided into two classes—those that remained tribal and strictly national associations, and those that were unions of many different nationalities.

Amongst tribal unions that of Delos, re-established by Athens in 426,[1] was of high antiquity. It was an ancient association of "Ionians and neighbouring islanders," who celebrated contests, gymnastic and musical, in honour of Apollo. An inscription of the early part of the fourth century (377-374) shows that it was still composed of Ionians of the islands under the presidency of Athens,[2] and that the Athenian presidents of the temple are still called Ἀμφικτύονες, and share this office with members from the other states.[3] The chief historic interest of this society is its revival by Athens for the purpose of effecting the religious unity of her empire. Two national amphictyonies were formed by the Greeks of Asia Minor: the one Ionian, which met at the Panionium on the promontory of Mycale for the worship of Poseidon,[4] and for one moment,

---

[1] Thuc. iii. 104.
[2] Hicks n. 82.
[3] Thus Ἀμφικτύονες from Andros are found. *C.I.A.* ii. n. 814.
[4] Her. i. 148.

during the heat of the Ionic revolt against Persia, became almost a federal government;[1] the other a gathering of the six Dorian cities of the South, which worshipped Apollo at the promontory of Triopium.[2] In Argolis we find a religious association, also strictly national, but of a slightly different character. For Argos had once possessed a political hegemony over the members of the league, the surrounding cities of the Argolid, founded as she claimed by herself, which met to worship Apollo Pythaeus on her own acropolis. Traces of her political hegemony survive into historic times,[3] but at the close of the fifth century her coercive power seems to have been confined exclusively to religious matters.[4] At the extreme west of Peloponnese the Triphylian townships kept the memory of their Minyan nationality alive by a gathering at the promontory of Samicum for the worship of Poseidon Samios;[5] but any political importance which it possessed must have been lost in the early part of the fifth century on the conquest of the country by the Eleans.[6]

Once at least in Greek history an association of this kind seems to have paved the way for real national unity. The gathering of the Boeotian cities at Onchestus probably dates back to a time before the hegemony of Thebes was fully established, and when the union of Boeotia was mainly religious.[7] The cities met in the territory of Haliartus to worship at the temple of Poseidon. The amphictyony doubtless prepared the way for the federal government, for the archon of Onchestus is identical with the archon of united Boeotia,[8] and even in the third century B.C. this district is still the centre of the Boeotian alliance.

Amongst amphictyonies which were composed of a number of cities of different nationality, the most prominent in early times must have been that which met in the island of Calauria, where seven cities gathered to sacrifice in the temple of Poseidon. These cities were Hermione, Epidaurus, Aegina, Athens, Prasiae, Nauplia, and Orchomenus in Boeotia.[9] Later the place of Nauplia was taken by Argos, and that of Prasiae

---

[1] Her. vi. 7. [2] *ib.* i. 144. [7] Strabo p. 412.
[3] *ib.* vi. 92. [4] Thuc. v. 53.
[5] Strabo p. 343.
[6] For the Minyan nationality of the Triphylians and their conquest by the Eleans see Her. iv. 148.
[8] In inscriptions the formula ἄρχοντος ἐν Ὀγχήστῳ appears side by side with the formula ἄρχοντος Βοιωτοῖς. See Gilbert *Staatsalt.* ii. p. 53 n. 3.
[9] Strabo p. 374.

by Lacedaemon. Commerce was probably a leading motive for this powerful association, before the relations of the chief trading states became disturbed and Athens and Aegina drifted apart. Its religious influence must have paled before that of the amphictyony of Delphi, which, owing to the repute gained by its oracle, was ever growing into greater importance.

The accident of the tragic part played by this Delphian association in the downfall of Greek liberty before Macedon has raised it into greater prominence than it deserves. Historically it is of little importance; it played a feeble part in the great struggle with the Persian, and it sat passively by to watch the horrors of the Peloponnesian War. To the student of ethnology it is interesting, because its advance from Thermopylae to Delphi seems to keep pace with the spread of Dorian influence and of the Hellenic name; but to the student of institutions it is invaluable, for it tells of a time when the Greeks possessed a common religious organisation before they dwelt in cities, and it displays institutions which must have suggested federal unity to any race less blind to such an allurement than the Greeks. Its great antiquity is proved by the fact that it was a union, not of cities, but of twelve tribes or nationalities ($\ddot{\epsilon}\theta\nu\eta$),[1] and also by the names of some of the tribes included in the list. The Perrhaebi, Magnetes, and Phthiotian Achaeans, all in historic times subject to the Thessalians, appear by the side of the Ionians and Dorians—a fact which shows that its date precedes the time when Thessaly was conquered from Epirus. The association included all the colonies of these tribes;[2] but though sometimes called the common assemblage of the Greeks ($\tau\grave{o}$ $\kappa o\iota\nu\grave{o}\nu$ ‘$E\lambda\lambda\acute{\eta}\nu\omega\nu$ $\sigma\nu\nu\acute{\epsilon}\delta\rho\iota o\nu$), it was really not representative of the whole of Hellas, the Aetolians, Arcadians, Dryopians, and (apparently) the Achaeans of Peloponnese being excluded.

The object of the association was the twofold purpose characteristic of all amphictyonies, and was clearly expressed in the oath which forbade the members to cut off water from any amphictyonic city or to raze it to the ground, enjoined them all to defend to the utmost the territory of the Delphian god, and bound them to march against the transgressors and destroy

---

[1] Thessalians, Boeotians, Dorians, Ionians, Perrhaebi, Magnetes, Locrians, Oeteans, Phthiotian Achaeans, Malians, Phocians, and Dolopes.

[2] Aeschines *de Falsa Legatione* § 115.

their city.[1] Its practice was even wider than the professions of this oath, for the history of the league in the latter half of the fourth century shows that, with skilful manipulation, almost any charge of a violation of international right in religious matters might be brought before the body, to be enforced only when political enmity or interest prompted aggression against the offender. The two sacred wars in which it engaged (596-586 and 355-346) were both undertaken professedly in defence of its narrower object of defending the privileges of Delphi.[2]

The council met twice a year, at Delphi in the autumn and at Thermopylae in the spring. There were twenty-four votes in all, each of the tribes (ἔθνη) possessing two, and all the votes being of equal value. It is clear that these tribal votes must have been in some way taken over by cities, although how this was effected can only be a matter of conjecture. In some cases a single πόλις may have been chosen as the permanent representative of a nation, in others cities may have undertaken the duty in rotation. An inscription of Roman times shows us that when at this period an ἔθνος was divided into two regions, each took a single vote. Thus the vote of the Dorians was divided between those of the metropolis and of Peloponnese, that of the Ionians between those of Attica and Euboea; but there is no authority for transferring this arrangement to an earlier period, and it does not solve the difficulty of election by cities.

The duties of representation were performed by two classes of officers, the ἱερομνήμονες and the πυλαγόραι. The evidence on their respective functions is vague and conflicting, but it is generally believed now that the hieromnemones were the official representatives of the tribes, who therefore formed a council of twenty-four members, and were the authoritative assembly, the pylagorae being the informal representatives of the various cities. It is possible that we have here an instance of the double system of representation, which we shall find to be characteristic of the Greek federal system. The votes of a tribe—which could never be more than two—were probably determined by the hieromnemones and the pylagorae of that

---

[1] Aeschines *de Fals. Leg.* § 109.
[2] With the ἱερὸς πόλεμος of 448 (Thuc. i. 112) the amphictyons had nothing to do. The Lacedaemonians put the temple into the hands of the Delphians, and the Athenians after their departure restored it to the Phocians; but the council remained passive spectators of this transference.

tribe acting together, the former being more permanent officials meant to represent the minimum of voting power that must be present, the latter being an indefinite number of added representatives whose presence was advisable but not necessary.[1] Besides these two bodies, the general mass of votaries and worshippers present formed a kind of ecclesia or assembly,[2] which was only summoned on special occasions. From Aeschines we should gather that debate was allowed in this body, but that it could pass no formal or binding resolution. This could come only from the two official boards, and it is unlikely that they were in any way bound by the decisions of the assembly.

A council that represents nations and cities naturally assumes something of a federal character. But the resemblance fades away entirely when we glance from the bare outlines of the organisation to the motives of the league, the duties with which the members were entrusted, and even to the character of their constituencies. The amphictyony of Delphi was a purely religious body, composed of laymen invested for a time with a sacred character, who may have performed their functions as curators of the temple efficiently, but who failed in enforcing even the minimum of international law which it was their duty to enjoin. It did not represent the whole Greek world, and the absurd distribution of votes would have rendered its political activity ineffective even for that portion which it did include. Its ineffectiveness unfortunately did not render it harmless, and its cumbrous machinery proved an engine of destruction in the hands of an able man like Philip. It is characteristic of Greek political sentiment that no reform in its organisation was ever contemplated which might have made it a possible means of salvation.

Principles so vague and so inefficiently enforced as the early international customs of the Greeks could not long remain the only ties between developed societies. We find, therefore, a series of relations springing up, the real basis of which was the

---

[1] That the ἱερομνήμονες were the authoritative assembly seems shown by Aesch. c. Ctes. § 124 τέλος δὲ ψηφίζονται ἥκειν τοὺς ἱερομνήμονας ἔχοντας δόγμα κτλ. From which it appears that they drew up the resolutions. It is these officers, too, who mark out the ἱερὰ χώρα (C.I.G. n. 1171). On the other hand, "resolved by the Pylagorae" occurs in the decree in Dem. de Cor. § 197. Harpocration makes both the Hieromnemones and Pylagorae representatives of cities (s. vv. ἱερομνήμωσι and πύλαι).

[2] Aeschines l.c.

secular motive of interest or convenience, although the religious element still remains in so far as they were specified in agreements ratified by oath.[1] International courtesy, springing from political or commercial interests, sometimes prompted an extension, which was usually accompanied by an interchange, of certain civic rights, either by the decree of one of the states or, in the more usual case of the conferment being reciprocal, by a sworn treaty concluded between the two. The relation thus established usually assumed the form of a mutual interchange of the private rights of citizenship (ἰσοπολιτεία). The chief of these rights were that of intermarriage between the citizens of the two states (ἐπιγαμία) and that of holding landed property (γῆς καὶ οἰκίας ἔγκτησις) in their respective domains; and these rights might be conferred or interchanged either separately or in combination.[2] Much rarer is the institution of συμπολιτεία, or the reciprocal conferment of full political rights. It did not imply a complete amalgamation of the two states which entered into this relation, nor a diminution of the civic independence of either; it was only a voluntary contract, capable of dissolution, which gave each of the members of these communities a double citizenship.[3]

Commerce also created a series of new relations, and treaties (σύμβολα) were drawn up which regulated the manner in which suits should be tried which were brought by individual citizens of different states against one another, by an individual against a foreign state, or by a foreign state against an individual. The general principle regulating these δίκαι ἀπὸ συμβόλων seems to have been that the case should be tried in the court of the defendant.[4] This was at times, however, only a court of first instance, and the plaintiff was allowed an appeal to the courts of a third city (ἔκκλητος πόλις). Where no commercial treaty existed between two states and a contract had been violated, the party wronged was entitled by an act of justifiable piracy (hence called συλᾶν) to seize as a pledge the person or property

---

[1] It appears also in the occasional sanction of the payment of a fine to a temple by the party who breaks the treaty (Hicks n. 8).

[2] Cauer n. 119 (treaty between Hierapytna and Priansus in Crete) ἦμεν παρ' ἀλλάλοις ἰσοπολιτείαν καὶ ἐπιγαμίας καὶ ἔνκτησιν καὶ μετοχὰν καὶ θείων καὶ ἀνθρωπίνων πάντων.

[3] Hicks n. 176 l. 35 ff. Here the people of Magnesia are made full citizens of Smyrna.

[4] The *forum rei* of Roman law. But the practice of the Athenian Empire seems to show that sometimes the *forum contractus*—the place where the contract was concluded — was adopted.

of the wrong-doer, either before or after a judicial decision in his own court, and by means of this security, if justified by the verdict, to gain satisfaction for his wrong.

Arbitration was as fully recognised, if not as frequently resorted to, in matters of international dispute as in private commercial relations between two cities. A state or individual was appointed by consent of the parties; to this the contending cities sent their advocates, and bound themselves to accept the decision of the commissioners.[1]

The attitude of latent hostility which, according to Greek notions, was the juristic condition of independent states towards one another, was frequently turned into one of temporary toleration by military alliances, offensive and defensive. In the treaties which contain these alliances are found detailed specifications of the *casus belli* which was to call the partners to action, and often minute regulations as to the amount of assistance to be rendered and as to the furnishing of support for the contingents supplied.[2] Their religious sanction was an oath, their temporal an immediate dissolution of the alliance on the breach of its conditions. Minor questions in dispute were sometimes, by the terms of the treaty, referred to arbitration.[3]

Some of these alliances were concluded in the hopeful spirit that they would be perpetual;[4] but as a rule peace was only concluded for a term of years—thirty, fifty, or a hundred, as the case might be.[5] With the close of this period there is a resumption of the state of war—the normal state *de jure*, and too often *de facto*, of the independent cities of Greece.

---

[1] Offers of arbitration, Thuc. i. 28; v. 41. The Spartans arbitrate between Athens and Megara for the possession of Salamis (Plut. *Sol.* 10).

[2] Thuc. v. 47.

[3] *ib.* v. 79.

[4] Dittenberger n. 85 συμμαχία (between Athens and Thessaly) εἰς τὸν ἀεὶ χρόνον. By the charter given to Naupactus by the Opuntian Locrians (Hicks n. 63) each state might call on the other to renew the oath after an interval of thirty years.

[5] Thuc. i. 115; v. 18; iii. 114.

CHAPTER IV

CLASSIFICATION OF CONSTITUTIONS—OLIGARCHY

§ 1 *The different Forms of Government*

HITHERTO we have been content to trace in parallel lines the political growth of some of the more important types of the city-state in Greece—a treatment to some extent justified by the paucity of our materials for the history of this earlier period. But this treatment will no longer suffice. Information now becomes more ample, and political creation more complex, and the difficult question arises, "On what principle are we to classify the myriad forms of constitution which now sprang up in Greece?" It is obvious that in a work of this compass any attempt to grasp the details of these varied forms would be idle and fruitless; even in works of a larger scope the reproduction of the scanty details which have been preserved about most of the Greek constitutions present but scattered bones of skeletons, which the historian can clothe with flesh and blood only by analogy with the structure of those organisms whose life is known from history. It is to these better known types that we shall in the main confine ourselves; but still the question remains, "On what principle shall the types be classified?"

The leading principle is presented to us by the continuity which Aristotle was fortunate enough to be able to trace in the history of the Greek constitutions amidst their manifold forms of development. Although like most Greek thinkers he sometimes inclines to the theory of the omnipotence of the legislator, he recognises fully that this creator is limited by the material

CLASSIFICATION OF CONSTITUTIONS

with which he has to deal,[1] and he sees that there has been a historical development in Greece which no legislator can be said definitely to have controlled.[2] The rule of the one able man—a single rule, because such men are a rare product of a primitive age—was followed by a stage when many of equal merit arose, sought a "commune" (κοινόν τι), and set up a constitution. Then these governments began to enrich themselves at the expense of the state, and degenerated into oligarchies. The narrowness of the oligarchies and their abuse of power strengthened the people; they were followed by tyrannies, and then by democracies, and in the final stage of the history of the Greek *city* the *inevitable tendency was towards democracy*. Here, therefore, he recognised a tendency which was almost beyond control, and, accepting the lesson, we shall proceed immediately to discuss those oligarchies which survived the shock of tyranny, and reserve to the last the democratic as the culminating type of Greek city life. Beyond the city and the Hellene Aristotle did not care to pass; but the Greek genius went further both in its creative power and in its influence. We shall have to consider the history of federal governments (really a stage in the history of democracy), and to touch on Hellenism, the political legacy which the Greek left to the barbarian.

We must bear in mind, however, that a general tendency, though it may be a good guide to discussion, is never a sufficient explanation of particular cases. The government of a people may be profoundly influenced by an event which is so far out of the reach of human control that it may be called an accident.[3] Aristotle recognised that the battle of Salamis hurried on the democracy at Athens,[4] that at Argos it was not merely Spartan intervention, but the distinction gained by the young nobles at Mantineia which led to the overthrow of the democracy in 418, and that it was the victory over the Athenians which changed the government of Syracuse from a moderate to an extreme democracy.[5] Social conditions, which depend on geographical and other data, are still more powerful in moulding the form

---

[1] *Pol.* iv. 11 = p. 1295 a.

[2] *ib.* iii. 15. It ran parallel with a corresponding development in education and culture (*ib.* viii. 6 = p. 1341 a). The military aspects of this evolution are also traced (*ib.* iv. 13 = p. 1297 b).

[3] *ib.* ii. 12 φαίνεται δ' οὐ κατὰ τὴν Σόλωνος γενέσθαι τοῦτο (the democracy) προαίρεσιν, ἀλλὰ μᾶλλον ἀπὸ συμπτώματος.

[4] *l.c.*

[5] *ib.* v. 4 = p. 1304 a.

of a nation's life; and it is on these, as well as on its ethical characteristics, that a constitution is based.[1] The state is composed of households and based on professions, and it is the different combinations of classes and lives that give us the different forms of the state, as it is the variation in the combination of organs which gives us the different forms of animal life.[2] Political science was aiming high, and yet reflecting an obvious truth, when it asserted that the same form of maritime democracy (one only among many forms) was not suited to the fishermen of Tarentum and Byzantium, the crews of the triremes at Athens, the merchant sailors of Aegina and Chios, and the ferrymen of Tenedos.[3] Closely allied to these determinants are what we vaguely call national characteristics —the genius and the needs of peoples, such as their relative capacity to produce a dominant race or a mass of citizens endowed with the sense of legal rule,[4] tendencies which might be explained by such a knowledge of their history as we rarely possess, but which are not readily analysable into distinct social conditions. But such factors, powerful as they were, led rather to the acceptance than to the existence of a constitution in the developed Greek states. There are no blind forces at work, except occasionally that of strong external pressure from a neighbouring state. The multiplicity of changes almost conceals the strong undercurrent of public opinion, without the support of which, Aristotle suggests, no government in Greece stood a chance of permanence. The ethical spirit which determined it might be represented only by a class, but it must be one accepted by the masses, whose power in the last resort decided the fate of the constitution.[5]

It has been necessary to give this brief summary of the possible causes—social, ethnic, and even geographical—of the various forms of constitution, because, except in those rare cases where our authorities enable us to trace a continuity of development, we cannot use any or all of them as a basis for classifying forms of government. As a rule we know too little of the social distinctions between one state and another to make

---

[1] Arist. *Pol.* iv. 3 = p. 1289 b.
[2] *ib.* iv. 4 = p. 1290 b.
[3] *ib.* iv. 4 = p. 1291 b.
[4] *ib.* iii. 7.
[5] This may be illustrated by Aristotle's appeal to education as a support to the constitution, and by his recognition of the force of customary law; cf. *Pol.* iv. 12 = p. 1296 b δεῖ γὰρ κρεῖττον εἶναι τὸ βουλόμενον μέρος τῆς πόλεως τοῦ μὴ βουλομένου μένειν τὴν πολιτείαν.

these our guide. Ethnic distinctions are too little marked in Greece to be a sufficient ground for classification, and geographical circumstances are not a sufficiently powerful determinant. An arrangement of the constitutions of Greek states by nationalities or districts is therefore somewhat meaningless. The difficulty which besets the alternative which we shall adopt —the consideration of states with reference to the *form* which their constitutions assumed—is that this form is not unalterable. There may be a strong tendency in one direction, but there is an ebb as well as a flow in Greek political life, and what seems like reaction often sets in to impede apparent progress. But these changes need not prevent us from assuming—what a study of the particular state is in most cases sufficient to prove —that there is as a rule one final or at least most permanent form which a city's life assumes, and that all its deflections from this type may be looked on as aberrations.

It is true that at times we shall not be treating the πόλις simply. The constitutional history of Athens leads us on to empire, that of Sparta to a military league; and both the league and the empire are (in spite of the protests of Plato and Aristotle) of the essence of the city-state. It is in Greece proper that the highest forms of political life were in the main attained;[1] and the πόλις as a *wholly independent* political unit in this portion of Hellas is something of a fiction. If we take the middle of the fifth century B.C. as representing the acme of Greek political civilisation, and think of the distribution of races and cities during that period, we find no less than five systems of federal or tribal government in existence, in Thessaly, Boeotia, Achaea, Acarnania, and Aetolia; one compact nation composed of many cities, that of the East Locrians; and some smaller ἔθνη, such as the Malians and Oeteans. Sparta exercises a so-called "hegemony" over most of the cities of the Peloponnese, which means that she controls the politics of the stronger ones by diplomacy, of the weaker ones by force of arms; while Argos hovers between an attempt to govern and an effort to destroy the cities of her own domain. Athens, Sparta, Corinth, Argos, and perhaps Elis—these are the really independent city-states of the period;[2] the rest are merged in

---

[1] The one great exception is the constitution of the Dorian cities in Crete; but they have a very close parallel in Sparta.

[2] Phocis probably formed a league; Doris was under Spartan protectorate; in the small predatory communes of West Locris independence was the result of a low degree of civilisation.

larger units or dwell in an indefinable region somewhere between nominal sovereignty and municipal self-government. To treat Athens without her empire would be to ignore the power which gave democracy to the Eastern world; to describe Sparta apart from her confederacy would be to shut our eyes to the only moral and material force that was able to stem the tide of democracy in Greece.

The classification of forms of government for historical purposes is simple. It is better to avail ourselves of the limited phraseology adopted by the average Greek, and which has survived through all time, than to adopt the subtle refinements of Aristotle. The average Greek divided ordinary forms of government into oligarchy and democracy; he regarded aristocracy as a form of the one, "polity" or moderate democracy as a form of the other.[1] He was equally conscious that there were some forms of constitution which would not fit these simple types, for they seemed in a manner to combine the elements both of democracy and of oligarchy. These he called mixed governments. Later on we may have to resort to minuter differentiation; but for the present oligarchy, mixed government, and democracy give us a classification of governments sufficiently comprehensive for practical purposes, now that monarchy, the early aristocracy of *status*, and tyranny have been left behind.

§ 2 *Oligarchy*

Oligarchy is described both as the rule of the few and as the rule of the rich. As the two classes invariably coincided in Greek states, we need not pause to discuss with Aristotle the question whether the qualitative or the quantitative element be of more importance in the definition of the term.[2] To the average Greek mind they were inseparably associated; but there is historical justification for the belief that wealth was conceived to be the main "principle" (ὅρος) of such a constitution—the chief, though not the only, claim of the few to rule. It was natural that this should be so; for it is material goods which on a shallow analysis of the needs of government must seem to contribute most directly to the preservation of the state, and it

---

[1] Arist. *Pol.* iv. 3 = p. 1290 a.   [2] *ib.* iv. 4 = p. 1291 b.

is on the obvious ground of the possession and use of such goods that the demand for recompense, in the shape of political influence and honour, can most readily be made. We have already seen the aristocracies of birth admitting the principle of wealth in early Greek societies;[1] the theory that the rule of the few was the rule of the richer class was made still more apparent in the brilliant commercial life of the colonies, and was finally stamped for ever on Greek thought by the great social struggle of the Peloponnesian War, which was everywhere a contest between the rich and the poor—the only two classes which can never overlap in the same community.[2] The rude and shallow claim of the oligarch for a superiority of political power in virtue of his "stake in the country" may even have originated the theory of distributive justice, of men receiving from the state in proportion to their desert; for wealth is the primary symbol of this joint-stock conception of political life. But it would be a mistake to suppose that this is the only claim of oligarchy, and that the pride of the oligarch rested on his money-bags alone. To him the rule is aristocratic, at least in a single, possibly in a twofold sense. The possession of wealth was taken to mean respectability, as implying education and freedom from temptation to crime.[3] Hence such names as καλοὶ κἀγαθοί and γνώριμοι, which were usurped by the wealthier classes even in democratic states, and the contemptuous πονηροί, which they applied to the masses. And the claim of birth was never extinguished—that "good birth" (εὐγένεια) which, as we saw, was defined in terms of inherited wealth and culture.[4]

But general acceptance is necessary for the stablishing of shadowy claims like these; and this general acceptance was rarely forthcoming. To the average consciousness the oligarch was a covetous man (πλεονέκτης), who had more than his fair share of the goods of the state already, and whose iniquity was aggravated by his impudence in demanding more. To the ordinary Greek the claim of wealth overrode all others, and oligarchy therefore appealed to him as the straining of the narrowest of political principles to its utmost limits. It might be tolerable in certain commercial states such as Corinth or Sicyon, for there the wealthiest men ought to be the "directors"; in cities with wider views of life and nobler aims it was intolerable.

[1] p. 22.
[2] Arist. *Pol.* iv. 4 = p. 1291 b.
[3] *ib.* iv. 8 = p. 1293 b; cf. iii. 13.
[4] p. 16.

The later oligarchies of Greece are in fact, like the earlier ones whose structure we have discussed, transitional forms of government. It was seldom that they could stand alone unaided by some foreign power. The oligarchies in Peloponnese were largely due to Spartan influence; and at a later period, from the close of the fourth century onwards, we find Macedon adopting the same device to hold nations such as Thessaly and Achaea in subjection. Sometimes, indeed, they spring up, like the Four Hundred at Athens in 411, in reaction against democratic excesses, but as a rule only to disappear again if the state be isolated.

Oligarchy was unstable because it rested or appeared to rest on a single principle which was in itself little justification for good government, and which, except under unusual circumstances, was not likely to win the tacit support of the masses, without which no government could continue to exist. In Greece the best chance for the permanence of such a constitution was its admission of some alien principle which changed it into a mixed form of government; and it is, therefore, not surprising that the state which was the real centre of oligarchic influence in Greece was itself not an oligarchy. In dealing with the Peloponnesian league we shall be treating of a crop of oligarchic governments whose main support was Sparta, itself a harmonious balance of opposing principles. The mainspring was perfectly adjusted, and was sufficient to keep intact the outer works of the machine, which, without this regulation, would have hopelessly collapsed. The consideration of this influence will come later; meanwhile we shall confine ourselves to the few clear instances of oligarchies proper which were able to exist for a time unsupported, or only partially supported, by external influence.

Northern Greece presents us with some curious instances of oligarchies of an aristocratic type. In some of these districts commerce had not flourished, and the course of years had brought little change in their primitive agricultural societies. It had given them a πολιτεία and a fixed conception of citizenship, but the claim to rule was based, as in early Greece, on birth, landed possessions, or military service. The states of THESSALY furnish instances of aristocracies of the ancient type. The history of the whole district hardly prepares us for this, for it is one of monarchy, followed in the course of the fifth century by a kind of democratic federation. But the character of the government of the towns is dynastic in the extreme, and a comparison of the condition of the towns with the tendencies of the central government makes it difficult to believe that the influence of the noble Thessalian clans was everywhere, or even in the majority of cases, recognised by law. Many of the cities may have been *de facto* rather than *de jure* oligarchies: they may have possessed a professedly liberal constitution and yet have had their chief offices, and especially the military leadership of the state, monopolised by the noble clans; in other states, perhaps, the dynastic influence enjoyed a fuller legal recognition. In spite of the existence of the federal council, which succeeded the monarchy perhaps as early as the middle of the fifth century,[1] the different states seem largely independent of one another; and though the foreign policy of the whole country was to some extent directed by the central government, the details even of this were entirely under the control of the separate hereditary oligarchies. Thus we find that, when Thessaly sent help to Athens in 431 at the commencement of the Peloponnesian War, each of the cities appointed its own commander. Larisa appears to have had the misfortune to possess two great families instead of one, and consequently its forces were led by two generals, each chosen from a separate clan or faction in the city.[2] Sometimes we find the nobles arming their retainers, the Penestae, and taking an independent part in the wars of foreign nations.[3] Occasionally the states encroached on one another's liberties—the powerful city of Pharsalus, for example, extended its rule over some of its smaller neighbours;[4] but the larger states seem to have been practically independent, or were connected only through the ramifications of the great family of the Aleuadae of Larisa, which established dynasties in many towns.[5] Other clans who controlled their respective cities were the Creondae of Pharsalus and the Scopadae of Cranon.[6] These families were enabled to maintain their ascendency largely through the preponderance of cavalry amongst the Thessalians; the character of the country

---

[1] See ch. vii., where Thessaly is treated as a federal government.

[2] ἀπὸ τῆς στάσεως ἑκάτερος (Thuc. ii. 22).

[3] As Menon of Pharsalus in 364 B.C. (Dem. *c. Aristocr.* § 238).

[4] Xen. *Hell.* vi. 1, 8.

[5] Pind. *Pyth.* 10 *ad fin.* ἐν δ' ἀγαθοῖσι κεῖται πατρώϊαι κεδναὶ πολίων κυβερνάσιες.

[6] On these families see Her. vi. 127, vii. 6, ix. 58; Diod. xv. 61, xvi. 14; Schol. in Theocr. xvi. 34.

and the numbers of their retainers enabled the nobles to support large bands of horsemen, while the hoplite force, the backbone of constitutional government, was comparatively unimportant.[1] The cities of Thessaly, where we find almost the sole survival of the old feudal nobility, are, with short intervals of unity and peace, a scene of political confusion unparalleled in the Greek world down to the time of their conquest by Philip of Macedon in 344. The democracy aimed at centralisation, the nobles at isolation, whilst in the individual states the struggle of faction raged, sometimes between the members of the clans, sometimes between the clans and the popular party. In some cities a compromise was for a time effected; at Larisa a mediator ($ἄρχων$ $μεσίδιος$) was called in to allay the feuds of the ruling clan, while magistrates of a popular character ($πολιτοφύλακες$ and $δημιουργοί$) were set up as a concession to democratic claims.[2] At last the $δῆμος$ threw off the rule of the clan in the most effective, and perhaps the only possible way. In 404 a tyranny was established at Pherae, which for a time became a constitutional government of the whole of Thessaly. This in turn led to a federal system, the fortunes of which we shall follow elsewhere.

As we go south from Thessaly we pass from the most violent type of oligarchy to its mildest form. The little people of the MALIANS possessed a constitution such as Aristotle calls a "politeia" or constitutional government, but which more closely resembled a moderate oligarchy than a modified democracy. The privileged class ($πολίτευμα$) was composed of those citizens who had served as hoplites, the magistrates being chosen from those actually on service.[3] The latter provision seems to show that the whole organisation of the state was military; but as the hoplite was in Greek society equivalent to the middle-class citizen, and as it was in the $μέσος$ $πολίτης$ that true political virtue was supposed by certain Greek theorists to reside, it is curious to find a backward Greek tribe realising so easily a political ideal which Athens tried in vain to attain,[4] and which many great thinkers regarded as the best practical form of government for any state.

---

[1] Arist. *Pol.* iv. 3 = p. 1289 b; Thuc. ii. 22; Her. v. 63; Dem. *contra Aristocr.* § 238.

[2] Arist. *Pol.* v. 6 = p. 1305 b; iii. 2; *Etym. M. s.v.* $δημιουργός$.

[3] Arist. *Pol.* iv. 13 = p. 1297 b. The $πολιτεία$ was composed $ἐκ$ $τῶν$ $ὡπλιτευκότων$: the magistrates were chosen $ἐκ$ $τῶν$ $στρατευομένων$.

[4] See ch. vi. § 7.

A tribal oligarchy of narrower type, and one that seems clearly to be a persistent survival of the early aristocracies of Greece, is found in the wider territory of the EAST or OPUNTIAN LOCRIANS. This people did not form a city but a nation. From the fifth century onwards the independence of the separate towns seems to have been lost, and Opus became the capital of the tribe. The Locrians might perhaps have described the central government as a "commune" (κοινόν) of the various cities[1]—an expression which is generally used in Greece to denote federal association, but which in this case seems to express something more akin to a common national life. There are traces of something like community of citizenship and of a common taxation, but on the other hand of a variation in the local laws,[2] which seem to point to an extensive municipal autonomy enjoyed by the several cities that had resigned their sovereign independence. The government was an oligarchy of a thousand men,[3] chosen, as has been conjectured with much probability, from the hundred most prominent and richest clans of the Locrians, which we know were singled out in some special way from amongst the families scattered through the territory.[4] It was a landed aristocracy, and that every effort was made to preserve its numbers intact may be concluded from a law which forbade the possessors to alienate their land except on proof of stringent necessity.[5] It is a form of government that so far finds its parallels in the early aristocracy of Thebes, in the landed interest that we shall find Sparta supporting at Mantineia, and perhaps in the narrow oligarchy of a hundred and eighty which ruled in Epidaurus; for although these were members of the city, and were distinguished from the country δῆμος,[6] they probably represented the noble clans who were the large landed proprietors in the district. But the commune of the Eastern Locrians differs from all these in being something wider than a city, and presents us, in the selection of the round number of a hundred families

[1] After the Roman conquest we meet with the κοινὸν τῶν Λοκρῶν τῶν Ἑοίων.

[2] Hicks n. 63.

[3] *ib.* n. 63 Θ ὅ τι κα μὴ δοκέῃ Ὀποντίων τε χιλίων πλήθᾳ.

[4] Polybius (xii. 5), in treating of the Epizephyrian Locrians, speaks of εὐγενεῖς from the ἑκατὸν οἰκίαι, and continues ταύτας δ' εἶναι τὰς ἑκατὸν οἰκίας τὰς προκριθείσας ὑπὸ τῶν Λοκρῶν πρὶν ἢ τὴν ἀποικίαν ἐξελθεῖν. The words *may* mean only "singled out for the purpose of the colony."

[5] Arist. *Pol.* ii. 7, 6 (if this passage does not refer only to the Locrians of Italy; see p. 42).

[6] Plut. *Quaest. Graec.* 1.

from the surrounding cantons, with a more striking instance than we elsewhere possess of the boldness with which a purely natural association like the clan might be manipulated for the purposes of political representation. No such union appears to be found amongst their less civilised kinsmen of WEST or OZOLIAN LOCRIS. The independence of their petty states was perhaps more suited to the freebooting habits of the people, although commercial treaties sometimes restrained their tendencies to mutual plunder. One of these treaties, concluded between Oeanthia and Chaleion, furnishes some slight evidence that the government of these towns was of an aristocratic character.[1]

In some of the more developed societies of Southern Greece, whose wealth or position entitled them to be ranked amongst the great powers of the political world, we sometimes find an astonishing persistence of oligarchic government, the reasons for which, so far as they were social, are almost entirely hidden from our view, but which can sometimes be explained by the external relations of these communities with other powers. Degrees of permanence of oligarchic rule may be illustrated by the histories of Thebes, Megara, and Corinth, with the last of which the neighbouring town of Sicyon may be associated.

THEBES is the only city in Greece which seems to have no fixed political characteristics at all. Its transitions from a narrow to a liberal form of government and back again are violent without being rapid; it runs a successful course of oligarchy during the Peloponnesian War, to pursue a still more successful democratic career during the period of that ascendency in Greece which it secured in the year 379, and it is successively at the head of an oligarchic and a democratic league. These changes cannot be explained as an illustration of the normal development in Greek states, for the two parties within the city seem at all times to be fairly evenly balanced, and the tendency in either direction is determined by considerations of foreign policy and by the city's one paramount object of ambition—the maintenance of her position as head of the Boeotian league. In the earlier part of her history she had to face the rampant democracy of Athens, which was sowing

---

[1] Hicks n. 31. l. 15 δαμιωργὼς ἐλέσται τοὺς ὀρκωμότας ἀριστίνδαν. The Demiurgi are the magistrates, and ἀριστίνδαν means "by right of birth." See p. 16.

disaffection amongst her cities, in the later she was meeting the oligarchic hostility of Sparta. Thebes is a remarkable instance of the sacrifice of political proclivities to one great national object, and her polity is but a means of securing her hegemony. The nature of her popular government, both earlier and later, is unknown; probably in its developed form it resembled that of the typical democratic state, Athens, with the modifications necessary to suit it to a federal system; but of the oligarchic phases of her constitution some traces have been preserved, which show that they exhibited at different periods three separate forms, two of which are easily recognisable.

The downfall of the monarchy was followed by the type of oligarchy with which we are now familiar—that of a privileged class who were the owners of the land. The "laws of adoption" (νόμοι θετικοί) of the legislator Philolaus at the end of the eighth century, by regulating the adjustment of the lots (κλῆροι) with reference to population,[1] attempted to secure the permanence of this government; whilst its exclusiveness is exhibited by an enactment, perhaps due to the same legislator, which prohibited any one from sharing in political privileges who had not retired from trade for ten years.[2] This landed aristocracy, which excluded the class actually engaged in trade, and was therefore not quite a pure oligarchy, had by the year 480 dwindled into a very narrow δυναστεία.[3] The unpatriotic part played by this family clique during the Persian wars strengthened the hands of the anti-Medising or popular party after Plataea; and doubtless a more liberal form of government followed the expulsion of the Mede. It is impossible, however, to say when Thebes became an actual democracy, whether before or after the battle of Oenophyta (456), which asserted the Athenian influence in Boeotia. The only certain fact is that the Athenian protection thus secured gave to the infant democracy a security which led to its degeneration and its fall.[4] The oligarchic was now the patriotic party, and a reaction set in which reached its height when the battle of Coroneia (447) freed Boeotia from the Athenians. The reaction was justified by its results; the supremacy of Thebes over the states of

---

[1] They are laws περὶ τῆς παιδοποιίας, Arist. Pol. ii. 12.
[2] Arist. Pol. iii. 5.
[3] Thuc. iii. 62 δυναστεία ὀλίγων ἀνδρῶν εἶχε τὰ πράγματα.
[4] Arist. Pol. v. 3 = p. 1302 b.

Boeotia was secured, and an oligarchic type of federal government established, the details of which we shall examine elsewhere. The government of the states was necessarily modelled on that of the central city, the municipal organisation of which, as distinct from its share in the federal constitution, is almost wholly unknown. The peace of Antalcidas in 387, by robbing Thebes of her hegemony and strengthening the oligarchic governments, which she herself had encouraged, of the now liberated cities of Boeotia, prepared the way for the subsequent reaction;[1] and this was rendered inevitable by an occurrence which for a time seemed to strengthen the oligarchic influence in the city. The seizure of the Cadmeia, the citadel of Thebes, by the Spartans in 383 showed that democracy was the only chance of securing freedom from foreign control and a renewed ascendency over Boeotia. In 379 the Spartans were driven out, and the re-establishment of the democracy was followed by a campaign against the oligarchic cities of Boeotia. The federal association was revived, but now on a democratic basis; and this condition continued until 338, when Chaeroneia gave the Thebans a Macedonian garrison and an oligarchic government, and robbed them of their hegemony. Thebes is not a great nation politically, for its politics were swayed too much by those of the neighbouring powers; but we must remember the prize that it had at stake, and its glorious inconsistencies—the product of a rare self-restraint—are due to a nobler motive than the selfish interests of classes or individuals which led to revolution in other states.

The political history of MEGARA is in some respects a parallel, in others a contrast, to that of Thebes. Both experience alternations of democracy and oligarchy; but the changes in Megara, though not unassisted by external influences, seem to be the direct outcome of social revolution; her democratic fervour awoke earlier and burnt more fiercely than that ever kindled in Thebes, or perhaps in any Greek city before the time of the Peloponnesian War, while the period of her oligarchic repose was for a long time undisturbed by questions of political expediency. Here the struggle of classes which gave rise to tyranny was not ended by the rule of the tyrant, and the social question awaited another and a more violent settlement. It is

---

[1] Xen. *Hell.* v. 4, 46 (378 B.C.) ἐν πάσαις γὰρ ταῖς πόλεσι δυναστεῖαι καθειστήκεσαν ὥσπερ ἐν Θήβαις.

true that the close of the rule of Theagenes was at first marked by a compromise. Probably it was the relief of all parties at being rid of despotism that led to the temporary establishment of a moderate constitution,[1] of the details of which we are wholly uninformed, but which was probably some kind of timocracy or liberal oligarchy. This was followed by a democracy of the most reckless type. The people, led on by demagogues of communistic views,[2] proceeded to insult and plunder the wealthier classes, to call back interest, and finally to banish the notables and to confiscate their goods. This promising beginning was checked by the return of an army of banished nobles, who were successful in getting possession of the state.[3] In the new oligarchy that was established exile was taken as the test of political orthodoxy, and offices were held by the *émigrés* alone.[4] So far Megara had been left to its own devices; now external influences come into play, and the little state becomes the shuttle-cock of Athens and Sparta, but changes its constitution as often in reaction against as in obedience to the claims of these two cities. The democracy which we find during the earlier part of the Peloponnesian War was probably the result of the alliance concluded with Athens in 455; but the independence of the state was the guarantee of the permanence of the democracy. The Megarians preferred the loss of their individual rights to the loss of their national autonomy, and an attempt made by a section of the demos in 424 to betray the liberties of the state to Athens, led to an oligarchic reaction and the establishment of a very narrow and singularly permanent form of government. Thucydides remarks with wonder that a change effected by such a small party should have been so lasting.[5] Whether the new government won the confidence of the people, or whether the national fear that prompted the revolution continued to secure the permanence of its results, we do not know; but the oligarchy continued down to the fourth century. Perhaps it was the fear of Spartan hegemony that in its turn prompted the state to become again a democracy. It appears as such in 375, a year marked by an attempt

[1] Plut. *Quaest. Graec.* 18 Μεγαρεῖς Θεαγένη τὸν τύραννον ἐκβαλόντες, ὀλίγον χρόνον ἐσωφρόνησαν κατὰ τὴν πολιτείαν.
[2] Arist. *Pol.* v. 5 = p. 1304 b οἱ γὰρ δημαγωγοί, ἵνα χρήματα ἔχωσι δημεύειν,
ἐξέβαλλον πολλοὺς τῶν γνωρίμων κτλ.
[3] Plut., Arist., *ll. cc.*
[4] Arist. *Pol.* iv. 15 = p. 1300 a.
[5] Thuc. iv. 74 καὶ πλεῖστον δὴ χρόνον αὕτη ὑπ' ἐλαχίστων γενομένη ἐκ στάσεως μετάστασις ξυνέμεινεν.

of the oligarchs on the constitution which resulted in complete failure.[1] Democracy seems to have flourished in Megara from that time to the close of its existence as an independent state. Such scanty details of its civic organisation as have been preserved refer, unfortunately, entirely to this period of democratic rule, and tell us nothing of the earlier oligarchic organisation.[2]

It is a relief to turn from these changing governments to the more stable oligarchies of Corinth and Sicyon. There were no cities in Greece where the duration of tyranny was longer and its work more complete; and perhaps this purification of the state may have assisted the stability of any government subsequently established; but another reason for the permanence of these constitutions is to be sought in their freedom from any foreign influences of a democratic kind. Both were at an early period members of the Peloponnesian confederacy, and therefore within the sphere of Sparta's influence. Corinth was too strong and too isolated in her naval and commercial supremacy ever to be touched by Athenian influence, which her rival interests alone would have urged her to repel; while Sicyon had early shaken off the hegemony of Argos, and thus obtained security from the democratic propaganda which that state spread through Peloponnese. The absence of disturbing causes explains not only the preservation but to some extent the existence of these oligarchies, which, certainly at Sicyon and probably at Corinth, were of a liberal type. For at the time when they were founded hardly any other form of government was possible, especially in cities that remained mainly Dorian and had the Dorian tenacity for old customs and ancient forms. The commercial character of both these states, while it may have assisted the permanence of these governments, is also a striking testimony to their justice. There are no blanks in Greek history that are more to be regretted than the absence of information on the social conditions and the political structure of these two commercial oligarchies. Neither, as will be seen, ended its days in peace; but both had a tenure of power remarkable for any government in Greece, and one which proves that they were valuable creations, a knowledge

---

[1] Diod. xv. 40.
[2] Gilbert *Staatsalt.* ii. p. 71. During the democracy the inevitable βουλὰ καὶ δᾶμος (Cauer n. 108) appear at the head of the state. It is possible that the "aesymnetes" who introduce business (Cauer *l.c.*) may be a modified survival of some oligarchic office. See p. 27.

of whose details would have added in no mean degree to
the political wisdom of the world. Unhappily a few lines are
sufficient to sum up so much of the constitutional history of these
states as has been handed down to us. At SICYON the ethnic
changes introduced by the tyrant Cleisthenes [1] continued in
force for sixty years after his death; then the state was united
by a friendly agreement, a sign of which was the reversion to
the old Dorian tribe-names.[2] The constitution which followed
was an oligarchy which Plutarch regards as a type of the pure
Dorian aristocracy,[3] and which must have been of a moderate
kind, for the Spartans, in the panic caused by the democratic
reaction in Peloponnese which led up to the battle of Mantineia,
found it necessary in 418[4] to narrow the circle of qualified
citizens. Whether this change was permanent is not known; but
that the government during its later stages must have been to
some extent dependent on foreign support seems proved by the
fact that the date of its overthrow by Euphron,[5] 369, is
coincident with the decline of Spartan power in the Peloponnese.
Democracy during the lifetime of Euphron meant little more
than the personal ascendency of its creator; but the work
seems to have survived its author, and a popular form of
government to have prevailed in Sicyon during the short
interval which elapsed between his death and the Macedonian
supremacy. Then a succession of tyrants of the later dependent
type sprang up, and Sicyon only regained a constitution by a
partial surrender of its autonomy when Aratus united it to the
Achaean league.

CORINTH possesses a still less varied history. The consistency
of its foreign relations was based on the stability of its government, and the narrowness of both is remarkable. The tenacity
of purpose with which this city pursued its definite commercial
objects at any cost, even at the risk of affronting Sparta, the
acknowledged leader of its foreign policy up to the close of the
Peloponnesian War, shows oligarchy at its best in Greece, and
exhibits the truth that the narrower and more permanent the
executive of a state, the greater is the gain in consistency and
concentration of purpose, and the greater the power of carrying
this purpose into effect, if other circumstances favour a com-

---

[1] p. 32.
[2] Her. v. 68.
[3] Plut. *Arat.* 2 ἐκ τῆς ἀκράτου καὶ Δωρικῆς ἀριστοκρατίας ὥσπερ ἁρμονίας συγχυθείσης κτλ.
[4] Thuc. v. 81.
[5] Xen. *Hell.* vii. 1, 44; vii. 3, 4.

munity of interest between the ruler and the ruled. Of the executive which guided Corinth all that we know is that it consisted of a council of unknown numbers, at the head of which stood eight πρόβουλοι.[1] In the scope of its powers this council probably preserved the characteristics of the old γερουσία;[2] but its constitution could not have depended on birth, since a passing remark of Herodotus shows us that every trace of the aristocratic conception of βαναυσία had been eliminated from this commercial state.[3] Probably admission depended on a high franchise, but on one attainable by all. Merit, as it is understood in commercial life, must have been the road to office and was reflected in the exercise of rule. Rights were rigorously protected, the material advantages of all the citizens consistently pursued,[4] and, like the "refined aristocracy" of Tarentum,[5] the rulers of Corinth seem to have learnt the lesson that "the poor have no passions, only wants," and to have checked the growth of ambition by satisfying the demands of necessity. Where the masses were prosperous there was little chance of a social revolution, which would have meant democracy and possibly tyranny, the fear of which, as a menace to life and property, seems to have been ardently fostered by the oligarchic rulers.[6] External causes may also have contributed in a less degree to the permanence of this government. Corinth, though really isolated through the greater part of her history, was yet in such violent antagonism to the rival commercial power of Athens that she naturally favoured the coalition headed by Sparta, which represented a political principle hostile to democracy. From the time of the downfall of the Cypselidae to the beginning of the fourth century her oligarchic constitution remained unshaken. When the change came it was in one of those subtle forms of foreign aggression which meet us everywhere in Greece. In 392 Argos supported a rising of the democrats and the oligarchy fell.[7] But with it the state fell too. It is not often that a social

---

[1] Nicol. Damasc. *Frag.* 60.

[2] Diodorus (xvi. 65) speaks of a γερουσία with criminal jurisdiction which must have been identical with the council.

[3] Her. ii. 167 ἥκιστα δὲ Κορίνθιοι ὄνονται τοὺς χειροτέχνας. See p. 22.

[4] Pind. *Ol.* 13, 6 ff.

[5] Arist. *Pol.* vi. 5 = p. 1320 b.

[6] See the speech of Sosicles the Corinthian against the restoration of the Peisistratidae in Her. v. 92; cf. iii. 48. It was from Corinth that the stories of the cruelties of its tyrants, Cypselus and Periander, came. See p. 28.

[7] Diod. xiv. 92. Xen. *Hell.* iv. 4, 6; v. 1, 36.

movement is powerful enough to annihilate a nation; but, like most extreme tendencies in politics, even this is illustrated in Greek history by the union of Corinth and Argos from 392 to 387. Strictly speaking Corinth, from the age of the tyrants, ever remained an oligarchy; for the restoration of this government in 387 meant the renewed independence of the state. When democracy did come it was in the modified form which admission to the Achaean league necessitated.

If these few instances of the more or less permanent rule of the few give us most of the information on oligarchic rule with which we are acquainted, we are tempted to ask why most of the details of this form of government have been suppressed, and why so little of the constitutional arrangements of oligarchies appears, not only in philosophical writings, but in inscriptions. The transitoriness of these governments may account for much, the secrecy of their administration for more; but the main reason for this silence seems to be the comparative simplicity of the type. The forms were few, the details of organisation limited. It is true that this limitation is not inherent in oligarchy: there is as ample room for variety here as in governments of the most democratic kind, for both the growth and the combination of the necessary elements of government are as possible in the narrowest as in the widest sphere. Proofs of this are found in the early constitutional arrangements of Athens, in the permanence of monarchy at Argos, in the survival of a double council in the democracy of Elis, in the antiquity of the lot as a mode of appointment to office. But we may believe that in the most permanent oligarchies, even where the constitution was a survival, variations of this kind tended to be swept away; that a unity of administration, such as the combination of judicial and executive power which we observe in the council of Corinth, was generally possessed by the deliberative assembly; and that all individual magistracies proceeded from and were directly responsible to this body. Here there could be none of the distribution and of the conflict of authority which arrest attention and lead to investigation of the exact structure and working of a government. Political research quitted the simple forms, after briefly noticing the variety of principles on which they rested, to concentrate its attention on the truly abnormal phenomenon of constitutions of the mixed type.

CHAPTER V

MIXED CONSTITUTIONS

It has often been denied that such a thing as a "mixed constitution" is possible. This denial is based on the two assumptions that the character of the constitution of a state is determined by the nature of its sovereign, and that the sovereign is always an individual or a determinate number of individuals. From these assumptions it inevitably follows that but three types of state are possible—which we call monarchy, oligarchy or aristocracy, and democracy respectively, according as the supreme power is held by the one, the few, or the many. As the holders of the supreme power are always determinate, the constitutions which they define must be always simple; and the "mixed constitution," to which Greek thinkers devoted such minute attention, is but the product of a shallow and superficial analysis, a confusion of the semblance with the reality of the thing, a confession of incapacity to pierce beneath the apparent working of a constitution to the one central fact of sovereignty.

If this position were tenable, the conclusions of political science might indeed be accurate, but could hardly be considered valuable. If we enumerate a sufficient number of elements in a state, we can generally discover (although, it must be admitted, with considerable difficulty) something approaching to a determinate sovereign—that is, we can generally find an aggregate of individuals who, taken collectively, seem to hold the supreme power in the state. But a discovery, though true, may be of very limited value, and such a discovery as this tells us exactly what we do not desire to know. What we really wish to discover is not what men or bodies of men hold power in the state, but how the supreme power is distributed between such individuals or bodies; for it is this that constitutes the nature and the working of a constitution. It may, indeed, be denied that the supreme power can be distributed, for by the "supreme" is usually meant the legislative power, and the unity of the legislative sovereign is a postulate of modern political thought. As a matter of fact it can easily be shown that there have been states, such as Rome or England, where through the accidents of growth even legislative functions have been divided, and where the only supreme or regulative power has been the tacit recognition of customary law. But, apart from these instances, the objection of the impossibility of the division of legislative authority, which appeals with such force to the modern inquirer, did not appeal at all to the Greek, for the simple reason that, as we have shown,[1] he did not recognise a legislative sovereign. His sovereign (τὸ κύριον) was merely vested with executive functions; and as it is far easier to conceive the distribution of executive than of legislative power, the idea of a μικτὴ πολιτεία was a far more natural conception to a Greek than that of a "mixed constitution" can ever be to us. Theoretically it seems that, from this point of view, even a purely quantitative analysis of governments, if classes rather than mere aggregates be taken into account, might justify the use of the term. But its main justification is to be found in that qualitative analysis of constitutions which, to Aristotle's view, far outweighed in scientific as in practical importance any mere appeal to quantitative distinctions.[2] In regarding the basis of government as qualitative we assume certain simple forms of constitution to be dependent on certain simple principles—*e.g.* democracy to be based on the idea of numerical equality, oligarchy or timocracy on the idea of what Aristotle calls "proportional" equality regulated by wealth, aristocracy on the same idea regulated by ἀρετή. When these principles, as represented by the power given to certain corresponding classes in the state, are found not singly, but in combination, then the government may be called a "mixed government." Such a government is, in the first instance, a balance of principles. But principles are mere abstractions of which practical politics can take no account unless they are embodied in classes of the population; and from

---

[1] p. 10.
[2] *Pol.* iv. 12 = p. 1296 b ἔστι δὲ πᾶσα πόλις ἔκ τε τοῦ ποιοῦ καὶ ποσοῦ. But the numbers of the sovereign are mere accidents (συμβεβηκότα); the quality is the true determinant.

this second point of view a mixed constitution implies a balance of power between classes, which may be vaguely or accurately defined according to the social conditions of the country. For the "normal" state (the ὀρθὴ πολιτεία of Aristotle) this might be a sufficient account; in such a state several distinct classes, on which political power has been conferred, embody principles, each of which can be proved to tend in some way to the interest of the community. But we must also consider the peculiar *interests* of the classes themselves; for it requires a very superficial acquaintance with Greek history to convince us that bodies of men who strive for power are seeking their own as well as the common good; and, from this third point of view, a mixed constitution secures a balance of interests. What, it may be asked, was gained by this harmony or balance of principle, class-power, and interest? The Greek thinker answered "permanence"; but his experience taught him that it was a permanence secured by growth, and no thinker seems seriously to have believed that a successful mixed government could be the work of conscious creation. It is, indeed, too delicate a mechanism to be other than a product of nature, and, as in the case of other abnormal products, its existence is its justification; for so strange a growth must be the fittest expression of the wants and capacities of the nation which gives it birth. History has shown that such forms of government are suited to a common-sense non-idealistic people: the Phoenicians of Carthage, the Dorians of Greece, Romans, and Englishmen have all developed this type of polity. It is one which shows a lack of political genius, which is a genius for "revolution" in the sense of "radical change" (μεταβολή); and, though the permanence of such governments is often secured by the crudity of minds which decline to seek symmetry in politics as in art, yet they have their own attendant dangers. The paradox of Tacitus [1] that a mixed constitution "can rarely be realised, and, if realised, cannot be lasting," contains more than one element of truth. Besides the acknowledged difficulty of the creation of such a system, besides the friction necessarily entailed by the war of jarring elements, so amply illustrated by the histories of Sparta, Rome, and England—a friction

---

[1] *Ann.* iv. 33 *nam cunctas nationes et urbes populus aut primores aut singuli regunt: delecta ex iis et consociata rei publicae forma laudari facilius quam evenire, vel si evenit haud diuturna esse potest.*

which sometimes paralyses action, and always retards reform—
there is the element of revolution, which, though infrequently
displayed amongst such peoples, assumes a curiously easy
because a legal form in this type of government. A peculiarity
of such states is that the central power comes often to be vested
in the hands of some body not contemplated in the strict theory
of the constitution. The Ephors at Sparta, the Senate of
Rome, to a less extent the Cabinet in England, furnish familiar
illustrations of this tendency. Its result is not infrequently a
questioning of the rights of the actually controlling power by
a sudden assertion of the claims of some part of the *de jure*
sovereign which has long been slumbering. It is to the credit
of these types in Greece that they show no parallel to the complete overthrowal of the Roman constitution by the struggle
between senate and people. The nearest approaches which can
be shown are the conflicts between kings and ephors at Sparta,
culminating in the suppression of the social revolution which
Agis IV. sought to effect in the third century; probably the
Cretan ἀκοσμία,[1] the temporary abolition by the nobles of the
supreme judicial power; and the later democratising tendency
which we shall trace in the cities of this island, which perhaps
belonged to the same class of revolutions. But the historian
has to face what to him is a more serious consequence of the
non-correspondence of the theoretical with the actual sovereign.
The working of the constitution is hopelessly obscured, and he
has in the main to reconstruct it from his knowledge of the
powers possessed by the different elements in the state. We
shall try to illustrate the working of a mixed constitution in
Greece from the histories of Sparta and the cities of Crete, the
Dorian states which developed this form of polity; but the
product can be understood only by some acquaintance with
the social conditions and the early history of these states.
Fortunately the evidence for these primary factors in national
life is more abundant for these countries than for any which
we have hitherto discussed.

§ 1 *Sparta, the Classes, the Citizens, and the Land*

Conquest and amalgamation were the means by which large
states were founded in Greece; it was of the first of these two

[1] Arist. *Pol.* ii. 7.

movements that Sparta was a product, although, as we shall see, the phenomenon of the συνοικισμός was even here not quite unknown. In the historic period Sparta represents the district of Laconia; it is the "city of the Lacedaemonians" (ἡ τῶν Λακεδαιμονίων πόλις)—a title which is somewhat misleading, for the word "Lacedaemonians" is used indiscriminately to describe the Spartiatae and the non-Spartan perioeci, and the latter were, as we shall see, not strictly members of the Spartan state. There was, however, almost certainly a time when Sparta no more represented Laconia than Rome originally represented Latium—a time, that is, *succeeding* the Dorian migration, when she was only one out of many cities holding a dominant position in the district. This truth underlies both the accounts which we possess of the effects of the original Dorian conquest of Laconia and of the origin of the subject race of the perioeci—accounts which are in other respects perplexing, for they differ both in the causes which they assign for the subjection of this people, and in the statement as to its original nationality. Ephorus [1] says that they were the original Achaean inhabitants of the country which the Dorians had invaded, that during the first generation after the invasion they not only remained possessed of all private rights, but shared in the political franchise of the invaders, but that in the next generation these political privileges were taken from them, they were reduced to a condition of subjection, and even made to pay tribute to the dominant Dorians. The story told by Isocrates [2] differs considerably from that of his pupil Ephorus. He draws no such distinction of race between the Spartans and the perioeci; on the contrary, he represents the latter as having been originally the demos of the Spartan state, which, expelled after a period of faction, was reduced to the grade of a subject population by the victorious oligarchy and scattered through the many small townships of Laconia. The chief point of agreement in these accounts is that they both represent the political condition of the perioeci as having been originally better than it was in historic times; but the guesses as to the nationality of this people are valuable, because they exhibit the important fact that in historic times there was no recognisable difference between the nationality of the perioeci and that of the Spartans themselves. Both together are Λακεδαιμόνιοι:

[1] ap. Strab. vii. p. 364.   [2] *Panath.* p. 270.

the word Σπαρτιᾶται conveys the idea of a higher political status more distinctly than the idea of a different race. Yet it is certain that the perioecic population was to a large degree tinged with the old Achaean element; and a theory which takes account of all these facts and guesses must, like that stated by Curtius and others,[1] recognise two distinct stages in the Dorian occupation of Laconia. The first stage was marked, as in the contemporary histories of Messenia[2] and Elis,[3] by amalgamation with the native inhabitants, the original circle of dominant states established in Laconia not being peculiarly Dorian.[4] The second stage is marked, as in Messenia, by a reaction against this intermixture. The scattered Dorian elements are collected at a single central point by the influence of the noble clans, amongst which the two families which afterwards gave Sparta her kings must have been prominent. This central point was Sparta, which was naturally chosen as having been originally the nucleus for the spread of Dorian influence in Laconia, as Stenyclerus was in Messenia. It is for this reason that the Achaeo-Dorian towns of Amyclae, Pharis, and Geronthrae are called her colonies; these so-called colonies were conquered about 800 B.C. by the mother state,[5] when she had assumed the form of that historic Sparta with whose history we are concerned.

The foundation of the city was, therefore, partly the effect of conquest, partly of amalgamation; and it seems that in this amalgamation certain non-Dorian elements must have crept into this mainly Dorian state. One of the royal houses, the Agidae, claimed Achaean descent;[6] of the nationality of the other royal house, the Eurypontidae, we know nothing. It was possibly Dorian; although if the tradition that the kings were the descendants of the twin sons of Aristodemus was the official Spartan legend, there can be no doubt that this Dorian community was professedly governed by two Achaean kings. A third element is represented by the "great tribe" of the

---

[1] E. Curtius *Hist. of Greece* Bk. ii. ch. i.; Guirard *La Propriété foncière en Grèce* pp. 43, 160.
[2] Ephorus ap. Strab. vii. p. 361.
[3] Strabo viii. p. 354.
[4] Curtius speaks of an original "hexapolis." The six most prominent states may have been Amyclae, Pharis, and Geronthrae (said to have been colonies from Sparta), Oenus, Boeae (the latter said to have been founded by a Heracleid chief), and Sparta itself.
[5] Paus. iii. 2, 6.
[6] Her. v. 72.

Aegeidae.[1] The importance of this tribe is better established than its origin; it is connected traditionally with the wandering race of the Minyans,[2] and legend says that it came from Boeotia, where was the great Minyan town of Orchemenus.[3] The Achaean element in Sparta is probably something of a fiction, meant to connect their ruling houses with the ancient name of the Atreidae, and the Aegeidae were probably later comers who swelled the Spartan demos. This συνοικισμός, which must have occurred not long before the year 800, did little to modify the purely Dorian character of the state.

The nationality of the perioeci, on the other hand, was much more decidedly mixed. They might be described roughly as an Achaeo-Dorian race, to which other elements were subsequently added, such as the Ionians of Cynuria and the Sciritae, the inhabitants of the wolds of South Arcadia. But Dorism must here, as in Argos,[4] have imprinted its stamp on the mixed nationality, and the ethnic difference between Spartans and perioeci came to be but a slight one. Politically, however, by the close of the ninth century at latest, the distinction was firmly established between the rulers and subjects; and we may now proceed to consider what the relations created between them were.

After the reduction of the perioeci we are told that they were forced to pay tribute to Sparta.[5] Two views have been entertained as to the nature of this tax. We are told of property-taxes (εἰσφοραί) which existed for the whole of Laconia, including the Spartan territory, but which in course of time came not to be paid by the Spartiatae;[6] and it has been thought that the tax paid by the perioeci was of this nature—a land-tax to the state, understood to affect the Spartans as well, but evaded by them,[7] and not a tribute paid in token of subjection. The more probable view is that it was a tax based on the theory of territorial sovereignty, the land being supposed

---

[1] Her. iv. 149 φυλὴ μεγάλη ἐν Σπάρτῃ. It is possible that φυλή here may not be used in the sense of one of the political subdivisions of the state; but that it means more than a γένος or φρατρία (Stein *in loc.*) seems shown by Pindar *Pyth.* v. 101.

[2] Her. iv. 148.

[3] Strab. pp. 346, 401.

[4] Herodotus (viii. 73) says of the Cynurians ἐκδεδωρίευνται δὲ ὑπό τε Ἀργείων ἀρχόμενοι καὶ τοῦ χρόνου.

[5] συντελεῖν τῇ Σπάρτῃ, Ephorus ap. Strab. p. 364.

[6] Arist. *Pol.* ii. 9 διὰ γὰρ τὸ τῶν Σπαρτιατῶν εἶναι τὴν πλείστην γῆν οὐκ ἐξετάζουσιν ἀλλήλων τὰς εἰσφοράς.

[7] Grote *Hist. of Greece* pt. ii. ch. vi.

to belong to the Spartans by right of conquest, and the perioeci paying a revenue to them for the right of possession.[1] Other tokens of dependence were the absence of all civic privileges—which, if Isocrates is right in saying that the ephors could put the perioeci to death without trial,[2] was pushed to the extreme of denying them all rights of protection against the state—and the absence of the right of intermarriage with Spartans. But, in spite of these disabilities, the perioeci do not appear to have been an oppressed people, and show little discontent with their position. In the great revolt of the helots in 464 only two perioecic townships joined the insurgents,[3] and it is not until the time of the conspiracy of Cinadon in 398 that we find any traces of general disaffection amongst them.[4] Their loyalty was believed in, for we find them serving as hoplites in the Spartan army,[5] and their nobles (καλοὶ κἀγαθοί) voluntarily enlisting in the Spartan service.[6] We occasionally find a perioecus in very high command both in the diplomatic[7] and in the naval[8] service, although, as we should expect, never in a position which subordinates a Spartan to his control.

In her relations with this people Sparta, like Rome, adopted the principle of division as the basis of her rule; for it is clear that all national life was stamped out of the inhabitants of Laconia, and from the vague accounts of our authorities there is room for conjecture that there was in some cases even a transfer of inhabitants for the purpose of weakening national ties. Isocrates[9] states that the Spartans intentionally weakened the other Laconians by dispersing them over a great number of hamlets (μικροὶ τόποι), which they called cities (πόλεις), and which were situated in the most unproductive parts of the district, the best land of which they reserved for themselves. This last statement reminds us of the land-distribution of Laconia which Plutarch attributes to Lycurgus[10]—the assignment of thirty thousand allotments to the perioeci, of nine thousand

---

[1] Sir G. C. Lewis in the *Philological Museum* vol. ii. p. 54; Guirard (*La Propr. foncière* p. 164) leaves it an open question whether it was a capitation or a land-tax; he regards it as being the same as the βασιλικὸς φόρος (Plato *Alcib.* 18).
[2] *Panath.* § 181.
[3] Thyrea and Aethaea (Thuc. i, 101).
[4] Xen. *Hell.* iii. 3, 6. [5] Her. ix. 11.
[6] Xen. *Hell.* v. 3, 9.
[7] Thuc. viii. 6.
[8] *ib.* viii. 22, as ναύαρχος of an allied fleet from Chios in 412.
[9] *Panath.* p. 270.
[10] Plut. *Lyc.* 8.

equal lots to the Spartans. Both assignments have been thought with justice to be equally mythical.[1] But Isocrates' statement points to the fact that there was a distinction between the land of the Spartans and that of the perioeci; the former (the πολιτικὴ χώρα)[2] was in the rich plain of the interior, the latter on the coast and on the rugged territory round this plain.

But the perioeci did not tend naturally to an agricultural life, and there were many compensations in their position. They were not subjected to the rigorous discipline of the Spartans, and the trade and manufactures of the country were exclusively in their hands. They occupied the maritime towns of Laconia, many, if not most, of the hundred cities (Λακεδαίμων ἑκατόμπολις) lying on the coast; and the whole coast-line is sometimes called ἡ περιοικίς.[3] One of these towns was Gytheium, the port of Sparta itself; and Cythera, the nucleus of Lacedaemonian maritime trade, was also a perioecic settlement.[4] It is strange to reflect on the singularity of the position of the grim bands of Spartan warriors amidst the wealth and comfort of this subject people; in this case the dogs seem to have really guarded and not to have worried the sheep.

We have already noticed that the perioeci had none of the civic privileges of the central state—no voice, therefore, in the Spartan assembly. It is natural, however, to suppose that they enjoyed full civil rights in the communities to which they belonged; otherwise they would hardly have been called πόλεις. But, whatever degree of autonomy these cities possessed, we must remember that, when we are considering Sparta *as a state*, we must take no account of the perioeci at all; they are in public law members of distinct cities, not unprivileged members of a single city. The affairs of the perioecic cities seem to have been to some extent controlled by direct government from Sparta. We find a reference to twenty Spartan ἁρμοσταί, and epigraphic evidence seems to have verified the conjecture that these harmosts were governors of perioecic districts.[5] To Cythera we know that a magistrate was sent who bore the title Κυθηρο-

---

[1] Grote *Hist. of Greece* pt. ii. ch. vi.
[2] Polyb. vi. 45.
[3] Thuc. iii. 16.
[4] *ib.* iv. 53; vii. 57.
[5] The scholiast to Pind. *Ol.* vi. 154, in describing the σκυτάλη received by the harmosts, says ἦσαν δὲ ἁρμοσταὶ Λακεδαιμονίων εἴκοσιν. On an inscription from Cythera we find Μένανδρος ἁρμοστὴρ Τινδαρίδαι[ς] (Cauer n. 28).

δίκης.[1] In any case it is probable that, if governors were appointed from Sparta, they were governors not of the separate πόλεις, but of *districts*, amongst which these cities were distributed for administrative purposes. The internal administration of each separate πόλις might quite well have been in the hands of its perioecic inhabitants themselves. This status, once created, was applied by the Spartans to the organisation of their later conquests in Peloponnese. It has been noticed that some of the towns mentioned by Strabo as belonging to the Lacedaemonian ἑκατόμπολις were in Messenia,[2] and cannot, therefore, have been settled until after the conquest of that territory about the year 631; and later still the district of Cynuria, which was wrested from Argos about the middle of the sixth century, was organised as perioecic territory.

While the comparatively ample details which have been handed down about the Spartan perioeci give us a fair idea of the condition of the class of subject freemen, which is found as a result of conquest also in Elis and perhaps in some of the colonial settlements,[3] in the class that stands below them at Sparta, the Helots, we have a picture of predial slavery, also the result of conquest, of which the most striking parallels are found in the Penestae of Thessaly and in the Mariandynic inhabitants of the Pontic Heraclea. The origin of this servile class at Sparta is wholly uncertain. Modern inquirers favour the derivation which gives the word εἵλωτες the neutral sense of "captives," and thus a signification which throws no light upon the origin of the class; while, to explain the distinction in status between the perioeci and the helots, it has sometimes been supposed that the latter were a race which the Dorians found already a subject population when they invaded the Peloponnese. But there is no evidence to support this view, and Greek traditions know of no earlier slavery to the soil than that originating with the conquests which followed the migrations. In the condition of the helots we seem to find traces of a compact made between the Spartans and a con-

---

[1] Thuc. iv. 53.
[2] Schömann *Antiq. Juris publ. Graec.* iv. 1 § 5.
[3] The perioeci of Elis (Thuc. ii. 25) perhaps resembled the Spartan, and traces of a subject people are found in later Dorian foundations, such as Leucadia and Anactorium (Thuc. ii. 81, Arnold's note); but the word περίοικοι, as used, for instance, to describe the native populations surrounding Greek colonies like Cyrene (Her. iv. 159), may not be coincident with the status here described.

quered power; and, on the analogy of the Penestae, the inhabitants of Thessaly first subdued by the Thesprotians, it seems as though this condition may have originated in some community which submitted on terms, and may have been afterwards extended to peoples subsequently conquered, such as the Dorians of Messenia. The evidences for this origin are to be found in the status itself. The helots were in a certain sense public slaves, used by private individuals, but under the *dominium* of the state. The state assigned them certain localities for residence, and attached them to private individuals.[1] They could not be freed by their masters but only by the government, and they could not be sold out of the country.[2] The state too employed them for military service as light-armed troops, as rowers for the fleet, and even occasionally as hoplites. Again, they were under the protection of the state, or rather of the state religion; for, although they cultivated the lands of private individuals, they had to pay only a fixed proportion of the produce, which could not be increased under penalty of a curse.[3] Such a status could hardly have originated otherwise than in a compact which closed a war; the religious sanction is but the oath of the treaty perpetuated; and it does not seem impossible that a truth may be reflected in the traditional derivations which made them citizens of Helos, a town near the mouth of the Eurotas, or dwellers in the marshes (ἔλος) or fens about that river. Neither of these etymologies may be correct, but it is probable that we have in εἵλωτες a local designation which eventually became a class designation. The localities in which the helots are found in historical times throw no light upon their origin; they were settled as cultivators on the land owned by the Spartans, and Messenia, a later conquest, was for the most part helotised. In fact, most of the helots of Sparta were in historical times believed to be the conquered Messenians.[4]

[1] Ephorus ap. Strab. p. 365 τρόπον γάρ τινα δημοσίους δούλους εἶχον οἱ Λακεδαιμόνιοι τούτους, κατοικίας τινὰς αὐτοῖς ἀποδείξαντες καὶ λειτουργίας ἰδίας. Cf. Paus. iii. 20, 6.

[2] A precisely similar agreement—that they should not be sold out of the country—was made by the native Mariandyni with the citizens of the Pontic Heraclea (Poseidon ap. Athen. p. 263 d).

[3] Plut. *Inst. Lac.* 41 ἐπάρατον δ' ἦν πλείονός τινα μισθῶσαι κτλ.

[4] Thuc. i. 101; he adds ᾗ καὶ Μεσσήνιοι ἐκλήθησαν οἱ πάντες. Thus the revolt of the helots in 464 B.C. is sometimes spoken of as the Third Messenian War.

Our authorities often notice the difficulties which the Spartans experienced in controlling this large serf population. Aristotle[1] says that "the helots have often risen against the Lacedaemonians, for whose misfortunes they are always lying in wait"; and we have the still stronger expression of Thucydides[2]—which, even when applied to the military organisation of Sparta, seems exaggerated—that "most of the institutions of Lacedaemon were framed to guard against insurrections of the helots." One institution, at least, is recorded of which this was the specific object. This was the κρυπτεία or system of secret police, conducted by the ephors and entrusted to a select band of Spartan youths. Their object was to investigate and report, and, a credible tradition adds, to carry out the results of their investigations by a secret assassination of suspected helots. The state secrecy for which Sparta was so famed[3] might have concealed this last-mentioned element, as it has no doubt concealed many other ugly points in her administration, were it not revealed by the awkward religious scruple which made the ephors, after coming into office, declare war on the helots, that their death might be justified by religious law.[4] Externally the crypteia might seem simply a good police-training, inculcating hardihood and vigour on the young, and as such it is treated by Plato.[5] But the darkest of its ulterior objects seems demonstrated by the account given by Thucydides of how two thousand of the helots, of approved courage, disappeared (no one knew how) in the seventh year of the Peloponnesian War. We may well believe with Plutarch that organised assassination was not one of the original institutions of Sparta, but only originated after the great panic caused by the revolt of the helots in 464.

The two classes that we have considered, of perioeci and helots, however powerful their influence was in forming and perpetuating the military organisation of Sparta, and to this extent in determining the character of her political life, yet stood, strictly speaking, outside the state. Of the two the helot was more a part of it than the perioecus, for, besides being what Aristotle calls a "necessary condition" of the body politic, he was potentially at least a partial citizen, and might

---

[1] Pol. ii. 9. [2] iv. 80. [4] ὅπως εὐαγὲς ᾖ τὸ ἀνελεῖν, Plut. Lyc. 28.
[3] τῆς πολιτείας τὸ κρυπτόν, Thuc. v. 68. [5] Laws i. p. 633.

aspire to a position which the perioecus, the member of another city, could never fill. We will now consider two further classes which yet remain in this state of many grades. These are the νεοδαμώδεις and the μόθακες, classes which to some extent form a connecting link between the dependants and their rulers. Their existence shows a more liberal policy in the conferment of citizenship than that exhibited by many Greek cities, and, as admission in either case depended on ἀρετή, is an assertion of the profoundly aristocratic character of the admitting state.

The neodamodeis are briefly described by late authorities as "new citizens" and "emancipated helots."[1] But there is ground for thinking that this word signifies a second and not the first stage attained by a helot on enfranchisement. There is a stage of emancipation hinted at in some passages of Thucydides[2] which seems to precede the attainment of the position of the neodamodeis. The difference of status is unknown, but the conjecture[3] that the neodamodeis were enfranchised helots possibly of the second generation is rendered probable by the astonishing rapidity with which the class grows up during the later years of the Peloponnesian War. There is evidence that emancipation on a large scale went on from the beginning of this period, and this would explain the large numbers of this class that are found serving on foreign expeditions at its close.[4] Some of the rights of an emancipated helot we know to have been freedom from personal service and free choice of residence. In what the superiority of the neodamodeis consisted we do not know; but it is unlikely that they ever won active political rights, and it is probable that they merely enjoyed the passive rights of citizenship.

Of the μόθακες or μόθωνες Phylarchus, a writer of the close of the third century B.C., supplies us with a fairly complete definition. He says that they were freemen, but not Lacedaemonians, that they shared in the full Spartan training; and he implies that they might attain to full Spartan citizenship through merit.[5] Xenophon also describes a class of youths

---

[1] Hesychius (δαμώσεις = δημόται); Pollux iii. 83. Little can be made of the definition—perhaps a gloss—in Thuc. vii. 58 δύναται δὲ τὸ νεοδαμῶδες ἐλεύθερον ἤδη εἶναι.
[2] v. 34, 67.
[3] Müller *Dorier* ii. p. 45.
[4] One thousand are found serving in Asia with Thimbron (Xen. *Hell.* iii. 1, 4), and two thousand with Agesilaus (*ib.* iii. 4, 2).
[5] Phylarch. ap. Athen. i. p. 271 e.

admitted to the Spartan culture[1] which was composed partly of foreigners (ξένοι), partly of illegitimate sons of Spartan fathers (νόθοι), the mothers being, we may suspect, usually helot women. That it was possible for mothakes to become full citizens is proved by the great historic instances of Lysander, Callicratidas, and Gylippus: they were probably all of the mixed blood;[2] but it may have been equally possible for foreigners, such as the son whom Phocion sent to be educated at Sparta,[3] to graduate as well. We are not told the precise conditions requisite for admission to civic rights; but the evidence seems to show that the mothakes were half-burgesses who were permitted to share in the Lycurgean discipline, and then, if they showed a possession of the true Spartan ἀρετή, might be created citizens. If this was the case, it considerably modifies the view as to the exclusiveness of the Spartan state which we gather from Aristotle.[4] Even Athens, as a rule, insisted on free descent on both sides. It is, however, characteristic of the Spartan spirit that, if admission to the citizenship was to be made at all, it should be made only through a rigid observance of the Spartan ἀγωγή.

When we have ascended through these grades and reached the ruling class itself, the privileged circle of the true Spartiatae, we might expect such distinctions to disappear; but at the outset we are confronted with a twofold division within this circle—the result partly of a principle which insisted that other standards should join with free birth in being a necessary qualification for citizenship, partly of a conservatism which perpetuated some of the privileges of the original noble clans.

The first distinction is that between "peers" (ὅμοιοι) and "inferiors" (ὑπομείονες). All that we know for certain about the "peers" is that those only answered to the designation who had been brought up in the characteristic Spartan training;[5] but it is implied that another condition for this status was the continuance of the contribution which all citizens owed to the support of the public meals. Aristotle, at least, tells us that "the common meals were meant to be a

---

[1] Xen. *Hell.* v. 3, 9.
[2] Phylarch. *l.c.* Ael. *Var. Hist.* 12, 43. Lysander's father is said to have been a Heracleid (Plut. *Lys.* 2).
[3] Plut. *Phoc.* 20.
[4] *Pol.* ii. 9, 17.
[5] Xen. *Rep. Lac.* 10, 7; *Anab.* iv 6, 14.

popular institution, but the existing manner of regulating them is the reverse of popular. For the very poor can scarcely take part in them; and, according to ancient custom, those who cannot contribute are not allowed to retain their rights of citizenship."[1] We may conclude, therefore, that those Spartans were ὅμοιοι who satisfied both of two conditions, the obedience to all the regulations of the Spartan training, and the continuance of the contribution to the public meals—that the word was, in fact, a designation of *all* the full citizens of Sparta.[2] The ὑπομείονες, as a class distinct from the "peers," would be most naturally taken to be those who had not fulfilled either one or both of these conditions—who had, therefore, lost their political while still probably retaining their private rights as citizens.

It was very characteristic of Spartan institutions to designate *all* the Spartiatae, nobles and demos alike, as "peers"; for the reduction of the life of all the citizens to one level was a real basis of equality in the state. It was the Spartans, Thucydides tells us,[3] that first set the example of this equality in Greece, by their uniform simplicity in dress and enforced moderation in life. Their equality was the essential one of a common rule of manners; and, from this point of view, Sparta reminds us of those enlarged oligarchies of which Aristotle speaks,[4] in which the members of the privileged class formed, as it were, a democracy amongst themselves.

The most constant suggestion of this equality was contained in the membership of the common meals (συσσίτια) to which we have referred. Originally, perhaps, mere barrack-room messes for soldiers who had to be ever on their guard against the revolt of a subject district, they attained in time a more refined organisation which gave them a close resemblance to the ἑταιρείαι or unofficial clubs, half political, half social, of the rest of the Greek world. The syssitia were small dining clubs, consisting of about fifteen members each.[5] Admission was dependent on ballot and required the unanimous consent of the

---

[1] *Pol.* ii. 9 (Jowett).

[2] A final proof of this is furnished by the accounts of the conspiracy of Cinadon in 398. Aristotle says (*Pol.* v. 7 = p. 1306 b) that he conspired ἐπὶ τοὺς Σπαρτιάτας. Xenophon says (*Hell.* iii. 3, 5) that Cinadon himself was not one of the ὅμοιοι. As to the conspirators (§ 6), αὐτοὶ μέντοι πᾶσιν ἔφασαν συνειδέναι καὶ εἵλωσι καὶ νεοδαμώδεσι καὶ τοῖς ὑπομείοσι καὶ τοῖς περιοίκοις. The only classes left to be attacked were the ὅμοιοι and the Σπαρτιᾶται. They would apparently, therefore, have been identical.

[3] i. 6.

[4] *Pol.* v. 8 = p. 1308 a.

[5] Plut. *Lyc.* 12.

already elected members; no doubt the exclusion of a qualified citizen from all these societies was an impossible contingency, and no guarantee of admission was, therefore, needed from the state. A restricted public opinion, such as was encouraged by these clubs, though it gains strength from its very narrowness, and may promote bravery in the field and honour in private life, is not a happy thing to foster in a state, for it creates a character exclusive, proud, and cruel. Private debate in these societies, on the conclusions of which the utmost secrecy was enjoined, was some compensation for the lack of freedom of speech in the assembly; but it fostered the tendency of the Spartans to secrecy and intrigue, and gave them a *penchant* to the oligarchical club and a belief in the efficiency of narrow corporations which proved the ruin of the empire which they wrested from Athens in the Peloponnesian War. The principle of co-optation recognised in these clubs must have tended to emphasise such class distinctions as did exist in the state; but, since membership was certainly attainable by every one who had the means to pay his quota, an appearance of social equality between all the citizens was secured.

But, in spite of this apparent equality, we do find a distinction within the ὅμοιοι between the nobles (καλοὶ κἀγαθοί) and the commons (δῆμος). It was, apparently, a distinction between the members of the ancient clans and those who were not members, between the old and the new burgesses; and this distinction was of political importance, for apparently only the nobles were chosen for the γερουσία. How it came that a class which could be called the demos grew up at Sparta is not known. From the first there may have been a Dorian population outside the noble clans, but it was probably recruited by later accessions of inhabitants to the community. Legends of such later accessions are not wanting, and Aristotle tells us that "there was a tradition that, in the days of their ancient kings, the Spartans were in the habit of giving the rights of citizenship to strangers, and therefore, in spite of their long wars, no lack of population was experienced by them,"[1] and that at one time Sparta was said to have numbered ten thousand citizens. The Aegeidae, the non-Dorian tribe whose presence we have already noticed, may be the greatest of the instances of such later additions to the state.

[1] *Pol.* ii. 9.

We have already touched on a qualification for citizenship, which had such important results that it must now be considered more in detail. The mention of membership of the syssitia as a preliminary to the enjoyment of civic rights has prepared us for the fact that property and citizenship were indissolubly connected at Sparta. Aristotle[1] tells us that the decrease in the number of citizens was owing to the accumulation of property in a few hands—a statement which implies that the loss of property meant the loss of civic rights; and this fact has an important bearing on the much-disputed question of the tenure of land by the Spartans. Since all the wealth of the Spartiatae rested on land, trade being forbidden, and the contribution to the public meal was the basis of citizenship, we should expect to find some provision made for securing land-allotments to the citizens and for preserving this distribution. Some of our authorities assert that an equal allotment of all the available land was made[2]—a statement which cannot be accepted as literally correct, since evidences are found for a very early inequality of wealth amongst the Spartans, and this inequality of wealth must necessarily have meant inequality of landed possessions. But, as has often been pointed out,[3] this by no means shows the tradition of the distribution of equal κλῆροι amongst the citizens to have been a fiction. From the earliest times a distinction must have existed between the landed possessions of the nobility and of the demos. The nobility possessed large tracts of land, like the τεμένη of the Spartan kings, in the conquered territory, while the members of the demos had their separate κλῆροι allotted them, which were originally certainly inalienable and probably equal; for it by no means follows that, because some members of a state can be proved to be large proprietors, the others do not possess a minimum of land—such a minimum as was assigned to poorer citizens by Athens and Rome and other conquering states of the ancient world. The tenures of the ordinary land and of the minimum assigned by the state might naturally be different; and this seems to have been the case at Sparta, for a clear distinction was drawn between the ordinary landed possessions which an individual might acquire and the "ancient division" (ἀρχαῖα μοῖρα) or κλῆρος which had been

[1] *Pol.* ii. 9.
[2] Plut. *Lyc.* 8; Polyb. vi. 45.
[3] See especially Gilbert *Staatsalt.* i. p. 13; Guirard *La Propr. fon.* p. 41 ff.

assigned. It was the latter alone that could not be alienated;[1] and in the case of the extinction of the family this heritable and inalienable allotment must have lapsed to the state. The division was undertaken for political motives, and was gradual in the sense that it kept pace with conquest and the consequent acquisition of common land. Land once assigned was not thereafter touched by the state; for neither in Sparta nor in any community of early Greece is there any sign of collectivism or of periodical redistribution. The change in the tenure of land came with the law of the ephor Epitadeus, of unknown date, but which may with probability be placed soon after the Peloponnesian War,[2] the close of which marks the beginning of the social revolution in Sparta. This law permitted to every one free gift and free bequest of his house and land.[3] Even now *sale* was not permitted, and in later times it was still considered disgraceful, though not illegal, to sell one's property[4]— the last relic of the previous inalienability of land and a proof of the grounds on which it had been based.

This assignment of equal lots of land to the citizens, besides being the necessary completion of the Lycurgean system, was also more possible at Sparta than in any other state of the Greek world; for as long as she continued to be a conquering state there could be no difficulty in finding surplus land for distribution. When the period of conquest was closed the theory was still maintained that civic rights should be dependent on the possession of land, and no remedies could be adopted to make an impossible theory effective. So far from any check being placed on the increase of the citizens, the state had encouraged it by pronouncing the father of three sons exempt from garrison duty, the father of four free from all state burdens;[5] and the inconsistency noticed by Aristotle was committed, of attempting to limit the possession of land without regulating population. He thinks that a possible solution would have been to make the syssitia, as in Crete, depend on public land worked by public slaves; and perhaps it would have been better had Sparta pushed her theory of communism this one step further. The principle which was adhered to—that

---

[1] Heracleides Ponticus 2, 7 πωλεῖν δὲ γῆν Λακεδαιμονίοις αἰσχρὸν νενόμισται, τῆς δὲ ἀρχαίας μοίρας οὐδὲ ἔξεστιν. Cf. Plut. *Inst. Lac.* 22.
[2] Coulanges *Nouvelles Recherches* p. 60.
[3] Plut. *Agis* 5.
[4] Arist. *Pol.* ii. 9.
[5] *l.c.*

of the inalienability of the land—only increased the difficulty of the situation; for the minute subdivision of an allotment amongst many sons must often have meant that all of them were prevented from continuing the public training or contributing to the public meals. But the removal of this restriction had an unexpected result. Nearly two-fifths of the land came eventually, through inheritance, through dowry, and probably through voluntary transfer, to be possessed by the women [1]— a consequence which can only be explained by the exemption of women from the Lycurgean rules of trade, which prompted the Spartan to gain through his female relatives a use and enjoyment of capital from which he himself was debarred by law. As the land centred in fewer hands the population did not decrease, for the ὀλιγανθρωπία from which Sparta suffered was one of *privileged* citizens. Even at the beginning of the fourth century the number of the ὑπομείονες had enormously increased, as is shown by the conspiracy of Cinadon. This discontented element had thrown in its lot with the subject peoples, and Sparta was becoming a narrower oligarchy exposed to graver dangers.

§ 2 *The Political Constitution*

Sparta had no code of written laws, and the whole constitution was based on a few ῥῆτραι.[2] A rhetra was, according to Plutarch, an ordinance with a religious sanction. Another definition makes it a "contract."[3] But these two notions are not exclusive of one another: a rhetra is both an ordinance and a covenant. It was not, however, so much a covenant made between God and man as a compact between man and man dictated by a god, the ultimate sanction of which was an oath. Thus Xenophon[4] speaks of the covenant between the king and the people of Sparta instituted by Lycurgus, and this idea comes out very clearly in his account of the monthly oath interchanged between the king and the ephors.[5] The belief that compacts of this kind were dictated by a god was never lost,

---

[1] Arist. *Pol.* ii. 9.
[2] Plut. *Lyc.* 13.
[3] Hesychius ῥῆτραι· συνθῆκαι διὰ λόγων.
[4] *Resp. Lac.* 15, 1.
[5] *ib.* § 7. cf. p. 15. So *lex* at Rome meant a contract, as in *lex dicta, lex data*. A law was a covenant between magistrate and people, as "rhetra" here is a compact between king and people.

and even the rhetrae subsequent to Lycurgus were supposed to have had a divine origin.[1]

To the Greeks the constitution of Sparta seemed, almost in its entirety, to be the work of a master-mind, of the nature "half human, half divine"[2] of Lycurgus. But the legislator is only in a very limited sense a creator; he is at the mercy of circumstances, and the utmost that he can do is to codify the best tendencies of his time. The peculiarities of the Spartan constitution, in so far as they are exemplified by its communism and the mixed character of its institutions, may be explained as a normal development from certain primitive Dorian tendencies, which assumed a somewhat similar form in the cities of Crete, and, as realised there, furnished a parallel which appealed as strongly to the Spartans of Herodotus's day[3] as to Plato and Aristotle in later times. In so far as these peculiarities were exemplified in the purely military ideal and the strict military discipline of the state, they were the natural consequence of the environment of the Spartans, and the results of rules of life necessarily adopted by a handful of Dorian nobles set in the midst of a conquered and hostile territory. The attention of practical statesmen and philosophers was directed to Sparta, not because it was unique, but because it was the typical example of what the city-state should be. The statesman saw in it the realisation of his ideal of permanence, which it attained through the even balance of its different elements; the philosopher saw his dream of state-control fulfilled in the most perfect form—perfect because the control was not felt to be an infringement of individual liberty, since the ideal of the state and of the individual was the same. Yet, although the tendencies which led to this result may be explained by natural causes, the work associated with the name of Lycurgus seems to have been more comprehensive than that performed by any legislator of the ancient world. It bears, in fact, more resemblance to the constitution of a new state than to the reconstruction of an old. The tendency of modern inquiry is, as we saw, to bring the foundation of historic Sparta down to a comparatively late epoch, and it is possible that the political history of this Sparta begins with the constitution of Lycurgus. There was no doubt a Dorian settlement there from the date of the migration, but this was not the state created by the new conquest and amalga-

---

[1] Plut. *Lyc.* 6.   [2] Plato *Laws* p. 692.   [3] Her. i. 65.

mation. The reforms attributed to Lycurgus seem on examination to be the work of an οἰκιστής. In the account of him given by Herodotus he constitutes everything;[1] and the rhetra attributed to him, undoubtedly a genuine and probably an ancient document, contains the reconstruction of Sparta on a new basis. It is, in appearance, a charter of incorporation, and a detailed examination of its clauses will be our best guide to the primitive institutions of the state.[2]

The first ordinance has reference to worship, and enjoins the religious unity of the new state. A shrine is to be established to Zeus Hellanius and Athene Hellania. Zeus is recognised since he is the guardian god of the two Spartan kings; it is less certain why Athene appears; but their epithets "Hellanius"[3] and "Hellania" are easily understood when we remember the claim of the Dorians to be a branch of the original Hellenes of Thessaly and their close connection with the amphictyony of Delphi — that sacred union which, by accompanying their conquests southward, probably spread the name "Hellenic" over the whole of Greece.[4]

The people assembled in their ecclesia or ἀπέλλα are to meet within certain local boundaries, which are called respectively Babyce and Cnacion. The nature of these limits is not exactly known, but Cnacion is said to have been a river and Babyce a bridge,[5] and the boundaries here specified are doubtless the limits of the plain of Sparta itself, within which the four villages of Pitane, Limnae, Messoa, and Cynosura, that composed the commune, were situated. The meetings are to take place monthly; they are to be called "from full-moon to full-moon."

The people are to be divided into state-divisions called φυλαί and ὠβαί, and the latter are to be thirty in number. These thirty obes appear to be identical with certain subdivisions of the people which Herodotus attributes to Lycurgus and calls

[1] Her. i. 65 μετέστησε τὰ νόμιμα πάντα.

[2] The text of the rhetra is given by Plutarch (*Lyc.* 6) as follows:—Διὸς Σελλανίου καὶ Ἀθανᾶς Σελλανίας ἱερὸν ἱδρυσάμενον, φυλὰς φυλάξαντα καὶ ὠβὰς ὠβάξαντα τριάκοντα, γερουσίαν σὺν ἀρχαγέταις καταστήσαντα, ὥρας ἐξ ὥρας ἀπελλάζειν μεταξὺ Βαβύκας τε καὶ Κνακιῶνος, οὕτως εἰσφέρειν τε καὶ ἀφίστασθαι· δάμῳ δὲ τὰν κυρίαν ἦμεν καὶ κράτος.

[3] Σελλάνιος (for the unmeaning Συλλάνιος of the MSS.) is clearly equivalent to Ἑλλήνιος.

[4] See p. 51.

[5] Plut. *Lyc.* 6. Gilbert thinks that the Oenus and the Tiasa are meant.

τριηκάδες. This word τριακάς means apparently a division of thirty, and was at Athens applied to the clans (γένη), thirty of which went to form a phratry. Here too it probably denotes a similar division of a larger unit, in this case the whole state, between thirty clans; and consequently the obes, if identical with them, would appear as family divisions. Now it is certain that the obes of Sparta were local divisions,[1] and consequently we have, on this theory, to admit that the smaller local units were based on the clan.

A twofold character of a somewhat similar kind is found in the larger division of the tribe (φυλή). The tribes at Sparta were the Hylleis, Pamphyli, and Dymanes, with the separate "tribe" of the Aegeidae (if this was a φυλή in the sense of being a state-division). The first three are the tribe-names which appear in many, perhaps in most, states settled under Dorian influence. We find these names at Sicyon with the additional tribe-name of the Aegialeis, at Argos with the Hyrnathiae attached, and at Megara, where they continued up to Roman times, although other tribes were added. It is strange that, while the "tribe" of the Aegeidae is so distinct at Sparta, there should be no tribe-name recording an Achaean element in the population, the only trace of which was professedly represented by the royal house of the Agidae. The "Pamphyli," from its etymology, no doubt included the mixture of elements found in a Dorian state created by conquest, and possibly the Dorian tribe-names were imposed at a time when any small Achaean element that may have crept in was absorbed into the mass of Dorians. The Aegeidae are represented as having been a somewhat later accession, and it may have been for this reason that they preserved their tribe-name intact.

These tribe-names must originally have marked ethnic divisions of the people; but we have evidence which seems to show that the tribes, just like the obes, were local.[2] This combination of the ethnic and local nucleus is not an uncommon phenomenon in the Greek world. That the γένη at Athens, for instance, which were family, and sometimes ethnic divisions, were also to some extent local is proved by the fact that

---

[1] Hesych. s.v. ὠβαί—τόποι μεγαλομερεῖς. ἐν Σπάρτῃ. Hesychius can hardly mean that the tribe and the locality were distinct.

[2] Hesych. s.v. Δύμη—φυλὴ καὶ τόπος

in Cleisthenes' reforms the name of the clan not infrequently became the name of the deme. The combination does not imply that the ethnic or family and the local limits were identical, that the clan or the tribe sat circumscribed within certain local boundaries, but that the clan or tribe did tend to gather round a certain nucleus, the centre of the religious worship that bound its members together; and to this extent the ethnic or family divisions, the φυλαί and ὠβαί, were localised.

The tribes must have included all the citizens of Sparta; the obes, if we believe their "gentile" character to be established, must have consisted of close corporations of nobles, to each of which other citizens were possibly attached for religious purposes. That they were composed primarily of nobles seems shown by the analogy of other Greek clans, but chiefly by the correspondence of their number, thirty, with the thirty γέροντες or members of the council, for there is evidence that election to the γερουσία was based on the clan.[1] We should naturally expect the γέροντες to represent the clans, for they are the survival of the clan influence of the old Homeric council. The reform mentioned in this rhetra consists in making them represent thirty clans and no more. Two of these clans were the Agidae and Eurypontidae, represented by the kings in the council; and according to this theory these royal clans must themselves have been two of the thirty obes.[2]

The charter concludes by enacting that the people (δᾶμος) gathered in the Apella should have the "ratifying authority"—that is, that it should give its assent or dissent to proposals brought before it from the γερουσία, and that this decision of the Apella should be final.

There seems at first sight nothing very striking and very little that is "mixed" in this original constitution. It is the old Homeric *régime* of king, council, and people, rendered more determinate by a greater fixity of character being given to the council and more definite powers to the assembly. The precise powers of kings and council are not known to us until a later stage of Spartan history, when the growth of the ephoralty had impaired the importance of both; but the review of their functions on which we shall soon enter gives

[1] See p. 101.
[2] In Athenaeus (p. 141 f) we hear of twenty-seven phratries at Sparta. This is an isolated mention of an institution, neither the date nor the significance of which is known.

us an index to the unimpaired powers possessed by these bodies at an earlier period. The authority of the two kings was hardly less perhaps than that of the early consuls at Rome. They were generals and priests, and had the civil jurisdiction in their hands. They were also the centre of the administration, for it must have been they alone who presided at the meetings of council and people. The council possessed, with the king, the criminal jurisdiction, and it exercised all administrative authority subject to the limitation of asking the consent of the people to all important matters—such as peace, war, or alliance. Of legislative power there was none, for no change was contemplated in the constitution.

Even now this constitution is a balance, but one chiefly between kings and nobles, although in governments of this kind it is unsafe to ignore even the *nominal existence* of a third element, such as the ratifying power of the Apella. For, even when subject to control, the moral force of such an authority in the background is immense; it creates an uneasiness in the *de facto* sovereign, a necessity for shaping his views for other eyes, which is in itself a limitation of his power. How the structure of the state was changed by the introduction of a more definitely democratic element can best be seen by examining the powers of its different bodies as they existed in historical times.

The Spartan kings were called officially ἀρχαγέται and βαγοί, the former word, which is found in the rhetra of Lycurgus, being apparently the strict official title and perhaps denoting mainly their civil authority, while βαγοί ("leaders") lays more stress on their military powers. The traditional honour (τιμή)[1] of the two colleagues was not exactly equal. The Eurypontids were regarded as the "inferior house," and the Agids honoured more "in virtue of their older lineage"[2]— a preference that naturally attached to the house believed to be Achaean, which probably connected its traditions with those of the original rulers of the territory. The traditional and religious reverence for the kings was very great, and they were honoured more like heroes than like men;[3] their institution was greeted with choric dances and sacrifice,[4] their death received with an oriental excess of lamentation.[5] Their domains, which stretched

---

[1] For this idea cf. p. 16.
[2] κατὰ πρεσβυγενείην, Her. vi. 51.
[3] Xen. *Resp. Lac.* 15, 9.
[4] Thuc. v. 16.
[5] Her. vi. 59.

through many of the perioecic cities,[1] were of vast extent, and made them the richest individuals in the Greek world.[2] The monarchy was hereditary, but in a singular way, for the king was succeeded not by his eldest son, but by the eldest son born after his accession to the throne.[3] In the case of there being no direct heir the eldest agnate succeeded, and this relative acted as guardian (πρόδικος) to the infant king.

The military functions of the kings were so preponderant in historic times that Aristotle describes the Spartan monarchy as being merely an absolute and perpetual generalship.[4] Herodotus asserts that they had the power to "carry war"[5] against any country they pleased, and that no one could hinder the exercise of this power—a statement which may be true of the early Spartan monarchy, but was apparently not true of the monarchy of Herodotus's own day.[6] Against it we must place the distinct statement of Xenophon,[7] who only credits the king with the power of "leading an army whithersoever the *city* sends it out." By "the city" is meant the Ephors and the Apella. Yet passages have been pointed out where the monarch, even in later times, seems to make war at his own discretion.[8] But it is to be observed that in all these cases war had already commenced, and the power of the king here hardly exceeds that of a general of Rome on a foreign campaign. There the senate and people could alone declare war, but the *imperator* might use his armies in attacking a nation which had violated its neutrality by assisting the people with whom he was engaged. In later times we find two of the Ephors accompanying the king to the field,[9] not however to share the command—in this he is αὐτοκράτωρ—but for the purpose of assisting in negotiations after a victory or defeat. In the year 418 a commission of ten σύμβουλοι was appointed by the state to control the king's actions in diplomatic matters;[10] but this was apparently merely a temporary measure. After the year 510 the Spartan armies were divided between the two kings, and the command became still more absolute. Each had the power of life and death,[11]

---

[1] Xen. *op. cit.* 15, 3.
[2] Plato *Alcib.* p. 123.
[3] Her. vii. 3.   [4] *Pol.* iii. 14.
[5] πόλεμον ἐκφέρειν, Her. vi. 56.
[6] The expedition to Plataea, described in Her. ix. 9 ff. seems to be controlled by the Ephors.

[7] *Resp. Lac.* 15, 2.
[8] Thuc. viii. 5 : Xen. *Hell.* ii. 2, 7 ; iv. 7, 1 ; v. 1, 34 : Gilbert *Staatsalt* i. p. 49, note 2.
[9] Xen. *Hell.* ii. 4, 36 (403 B.C.).
[10] Thuc. v. 63.
[11] Arist. *Pol.* iii. 14, 4.

and was hampered in his actions only by the advisability of referring important matters to his council, which was in the fourth century composed of thirty commissioners (σύμβουλοι) selected by the king himself.[1]

In treating of the civil powers of the kings we are dealing with a mere relic of a once very extensive administrative and judicial control; for it is clear that all the civil powers which they retained[2] sprang from the religious presidency which they never lost. Thus they had the appointment of πρόξενοι, a duty connected with the old religious obligation of hospitality, the nomination of the Πύθιοι, the yearly envoys to Delphi, and, with the Pythii, the custody of the oracles—an important prerogative in a state swayed beyond all others by fear of the gods.[3] Their judicial functions were as closely connected with their religious character. The most important of these were the awarding of heiresses in marriage and jurisdiction in cases of adoption. Both these duties were connected with the preservation of the household, the continuity of the sacred rights of the clan, and at Sparta no doubt with the transmission of the inalienable allotments. The maintenance and the transmission of the family and of family worship were always sacred obligations in Greece and Rome, and in the exercise of these powers the Spartan king appears as the head of the religion of the state, as the *rex* was the head of the Roman religion. Herodotus adds to these a third judicial function—jurisdiction "about the public roads." This can only mean the settlement of disputes about the respective limits of public and private property: which may also be considered a function springing from the religious presidency of the king; for in the ancient world the boundary-stone (ὅρος) was sacred, and questions about the demarcation of property would depend largely on religious tradition.

Such was the archaic survival left by the encroaching power of the Ephors. But the actual influence of the kings, even within the city, cannot be estimated by these legal prerogatives. The words of men invested with a sanctity as great as that

---

[1] Xen. *Hell*. iii. 4, 2. In almost every particular the position of the Spartan king in the field bears a striking resemblance to that of the Roman *imperator*.

[2] Enumerated in Her. vi. 57.

[3] For the importance attached to oracles at Sparta see Her. v. 90, Thuc. v. 16. Even at Athens a collection of oracles had a political value. Her. vii. 6. Cf. Aristoph. *Eq*. 1003 ff.

which has ever encompassed a crowned head must have been of mighty force at the council-board. Deeds were a still surer ground of influence, and a king of military ability who was leading the Spartan armies on a successful career of conquest was certainly the most powerful *man* in the state, and might practically be its head.

The Council of Elders (γερουσία) was composed of the two kings and of twenty-eight members, probably chosen, as we have seen, from certain selected families of the state. The evidence of Aristotle and Polybius proves conclusively that only members of the nobility were eligible.[1] The other qualification was one of age: the γέροντες at Sparta were Elders in fact as well as in name, for no one under sixty years old might be chosen. But this limited qualification was accompanied by free election in the Apella. The aged candidates were led through the assembly one by one, and, as each passed, the people shouted. Judges locked up in a room near by listened to the cries, and the candidate who was welcomed with the loudest shout won the vacant seat.[2] This is the mode of election which Aristotle describes as "childish,"[3] but which was a sufficiently natural mode in an assembly that voted only by acclamation.[4]

The functions of the council were in the main twofold. In the first place it was a deliberative and administrative assembly, in the second a court of justice. In its deliberative capacity it was, at least in all important matters, merely a probouleutic assembly, deciding on every question before it went to the people. It appears as such in the rhetra of Lycurgus, and is found fulfilling this function in the later days of Spartan history.[5] In the last resort it might be partly a legislative assembly; for, although the introduction of new rhetrae was probably not contemplated in the constitution, and a rhetra was, as we saw, supposed to require the sanction of the gods, yet, if the constitution did require modification, the change rested in the first instance with the Elders.[6] These functions were apparently extended, the powers of the Gerousia increased,

---

[1] Arist. *Pol.* ii. 9; only καλοὶ κἀγαθοί were elected. Cf. v. 6 = p. 1306 a; In Polyb. vi. 10 they are κατ' ἐκλογὴν ἀριστίνδην κεκριμένοι. For ἀριστίνδην see p. 16.
[2] Plut. *Lyc.* 26.
[3] *Pol.* ii. 9.
[4] βοῇ καὶ οὐ ψήφῳ, Thuc. i. 87.
[5] Plut. *Agis* 11.
[6] *ib.*

and those of the Apella correspondingly diminished by the rhetra of the kings Polydorus and Theopompus (743-724), which enacted that "if the people decided crookedly, the Elders and kings might reverse their decision."[1] The result of this change was possibly the procedure described by Aristotle,[2] by which a negative decision of the people is final, a positive not final. The motive for this reaction is unknown; for the reason assigned by Plutarch—the reckless mode in which the assembly curtailed or amended bills sent down from the upper house—assumes a freedom of debate which probably never existed in the Apella. The change does not seem to have been permanent, since in the debate which decided the outbreak of the Peloponnesian War the Apella seems to have the final ratifying authority.[3] The growth of the ephoralty probably restored to the assembly the powers curtailed by Theopompus.

We have treated the Gerousia here as a probouleutic assembly; but undoubtedly most matters of routine administration were within its entire competence, partly in its own right, partly as the council-board of the Ephors. In its own right it seems to have exercised a censorial authority for the maintenance of the Lycurgean discipline,[4] although the actual enforcement of the alien acts ($\xi \epsilon \nu \eta \lambda a \sigma i a\iota$) which made Sparta so unpopular was in the hands of the Ephors.[5]

The council as a court of justice was concerned with criminal jurisdiction—a survival from the Homeric times, in which the heads of the clan, the $\gamma \epsilon \rho o \nu \tau \epsilon s$, meet for this purpose. In this sphere its control was absolute, and, as there was no written law at Sparta, its decisions were necessarily arbitrary, mere "dooms" or "ordinances" ($\theta \epsilon \mu \iota \sigma \tau \epsilon s$); but judgments pronounced by so large and experienced a body would doubtless be strictly modelled on the customary law. No office could have exempted from its jurisdiction, for the king or regent himself must appear before its tribunal,[6] and it could inflict the extremest penalties—such as death and disfranchisement.[7]

This combination of functions made the Gerousia very powerful, and we are not surprised to find that to the superficial observer it seemed the central government of the Spartan state. According to Isocrates it "presided over everything";

[1] Plut. *Lyc.* 6.   [2] *Pol.* iv. 14 = p. 1298 b.   [3] Thuc. i. 87.
[4] Gellius xviii. 3. He refers to Aeschines as his authority.
[5] Her. iii. 148.   [6] Paus. iii. 5, 2.   [7] Xen. *Resp. Lac.* 10, 2.

according to Dionysius it had the whole control of the community.[1] Aristotle[2] is more concerned with noticing its many defects, the "childish" mode of election, the committal of the most important judicial functions to old men holding office for life. He objects to their irresponsibility, and says that many of the Elders are known to have taken bribes.

The question of its general efficiency is answered by Spartan history; the question of its actual power depends to a large extent on our view of its procedure. How was it summoned, and who were its presidents? Originally, no doubt, it was summoned by the kings, and Schömann thinks that the presidency may have continued to belong to each king alternately.[3] But it has been noticed that Herodotus does not make the presidency of the council one of the privileges of the kings: they merely "sit as members";[4] and the only theory that can explain the *working* of the Spartan constitution is to suppose that the Ephors—who, we know, for certain purposes sat with the council[5]—also summoned and presided over it. It is at least necessary that there should have been a very close connection between the deliberative and administrative body on the one hand and the executive body on the other. The Ephors were the only officials capable of laying questions of foreign administration and information on foreign politics before this body. The Gerousia is thus the great deliberative, judicial, and administrative body of the state. But the power of a deliberative assembly is clearly limited by its dependence on some other authority for meeting, or at least for the transaction of its most important business. The council *may*, for certain purposes, have had stated times for meeting; but if it could only transact the usual official business on the summons of the Ephors, this fact largely explains the power of the latter body.

There is a conflict of evidence about the origin of these officials. Herodotus makes them a creation of Lycurgus; but

---

[1] Isocr. *Panath.* § 154; Dionys. ii. 14. Polybius (vi. 45) is more accurate, οἱ — γέροντες — δι' ὧν καὶ μεθ' ὧν πάντα χειρίζεται τὰ κατὰ τὴν πολιτείαν.

[2] *Pol.* ii. 9.

[3] *Antiquities* i. p. 213. From Thuc. i. 20 (μιᾷ ψήφῳ προστίθεσθαι) it has been concluded that the kings voted last. This may have been so, but would not prove them to have been the presidents. At Rome the presiding magistrate did not vote at all.

[4] παρίζειν, Her. vi. 57.

[5] When assembled as a criminal court, Paus. iii. 5, 2.

constitutional anomalies are not as a rule created, and the slightest knowledge of comparative politics would alone be sufficient to convince us that they were of later growth. The more credible account is that of Aristotle and Plutarch, who refer their origin to the reign of Theopompus.[1] Plato, too, speaks of the "third saviour" of the Spartan state who established the ephoralty;[2] and a final proof of this view is found in Pausanias' assertion that the state-seal used by all official boards bore on it the effigy of Polydorus, the colleague of this king.[3] The epoch of their institution must have been looked back on as the origin of the liberties of the city, for the Ephors are essentially city magistrates, as opposed to the kings and Elders who represent the nobility. In the oath of office interchanged between the king and the Ephors the king swears "on behalf of himself," the Ephors "on behalf of the city."[4] Even their number, five, has been thought to have a close connection with the local divisions of the city—the four villages and the central fort, the πόλις or ἀκρόπολις.[5]

The name itself (ἔφοροι) has been variously explained. It means "inspectors," "overseers," and some have supposed it to mean "inspectors of the market." Whether this be so or not, that they were from the first judicial magistrates seems shown by the fact that to the last almost their only *independent* function is that of civil jurisdiction. This gives a strong appearance of truth to the legend that the Ephors were originally representatives of the kings, nominated by them during the Messenian wars for the trial of judicial suits while the kings were absent in the field.[6] Thus they would have been from the first magistrates of the demos which had been growing up by the side of the old nobility. Their career bears a shadowy resemblance to that of the tribunes of the plebs at Rome, with whom they have often been compared. Like them, they grew from being the representatives of a part of the state to being the representatives of the whole state. We may compare the general guardianship of the laws which the Ephors had, as expressed in the oath which we have cited, with the similar

[1] Arist. *Pol.* v. 11 = p. 1313 a; Plut. *Cleom.* 10.
[2] *Laws* p. 692. The first saviour was the god who gave the Spartans two kings; the second the half-divine nature who instituted the γερουσία, *i.e.* Lycurgus.
[3] Paus. iii. 14, 8.　　[4] See p. 15.
[5] *Philolog. Museum* ii. pp. 50 ff.
[6] Plut. *Cleom.* 10.

functions of the tribunes, and both have an extraordinary power of enforcing their decrees (*coercitio*). But their origin was more modest than that of the tribunes, the growth of their powers greater, their final position even more important. Aristotle[1] admits that this representation of the demos may have been due to chance, and by "chance" he means that the final position of these officials in the state was not that contemplated at their institution.

The Ephors were probably at first little more than delegates of the kings, and hence they must have been nominated by the kings. Later on there was no doubt popular election to the office. Aristotle describes the election to the ephoralty, like that to the Gerousia, as "childish"; hence the mode of appointment to the two offices was probably the same. The essential difference lay in the qualification; to the ephoralty any Spartan was eligible, and hence it is regarded as *the* democratic element in the Spartan constitution.[2]

We do not know the successive steps by which the functions of the ephoralty were extended, but we are told that this extension was gradual. An epoch in its history is said to have been marked by the ephoralty of a certain Asteropus "many generations after" the institution of the office.[3] What the change here noticed consisted in can only be a matter of conjecture. Some think it refers to the transference of the appointment of the Ephors from the king to the people; others think that the powers thus gained were the right of summoning and presiding over the meetings of the popular assembly and the right of sitting at the council. That both these changes took place there is no doubt, but their epochs cannot be determined. The final result was that these popular magistrates came to supplant the kings as the executive of the state. The dual monarchy rendered united action on the part of the kings impossible, while the board of Elders was too large and perhaps too aged to be an active executive. Hence

---

[1] *Pol.* ii. 9.

[2] The Ephors are ἐξ ἁπάντων, ἐκ τοῦ δήμου, and οἱ τυχόντες (Arist. *Pol.* ii. 9). When Aristotle says (*Pol.* iv. 9 = p. 1294 b) that one of the democratic elements in the constitution is that the people "appoint to the Gerousia and share in the ephoralty," he by no means implies that the Ephors were not elected by the people.

[3] Plut. *l.c.* The name of Chilon (*circa* 550) seems also to be associated with some change (Diog. Laert. 1, 3, 68), though what this was cannot be made out.

the new power of the Ephors, which was so unlimited as to be described as a "tyrannis."[1] But it appears that, absolute as their authority might be while in power, they might yet be called to account when they had quitted office, and Aristotle seems to imply that this scrutiny was exercised by their successors.[2] One of the Ephors gave his name to the year, for the tenure of office was annual. The five formed a college, in which the ἐπώνυμος had probably an honorary precedence. But they decided all questions by a majority of votes.[3] How important these questions were may be seen by a rapid summary of their developed powers.

(1) They summon, and are apparently the only officials that can summon, the Apella, and they conduct the business in this assembly.[4]

(2) They sit with the council,[5] and either preside over, or at least bring all important business before it. As members of this body they also share in its criminal jurisdiction.[6] Almost their chief function, however, in connection with the Gerousia, must have been that of carrying out its decrees. It is this merely executive function which accounts for many of the apparently exceptional powers which the Ephors possess. When, for instance, we are told that they could summon the king before them on a charge of treason, and even imprison him, the reference is simply to a duty which they perform as officers of a criminal court.[7]

(3) Independently of other bodies they have the control of civil jurisdiction. Aristotle[8] says that "they determine suits about contracts, which they distribute amongst themselves." They act, therefore, in this respect not as a college, but individually.

(4) It may possibly have been amongst their duties to call all magistrates to account after their term of office had expired. In this they must have acted only as a court of first instance, for final jurisdiction belonged to the Gerousia.

But (5) their most important power was no doubt that of being the executive magistrates for foreign affairs—of being,

---

[1] Plato *Laws* p. 692.
[2] Arist. *Pol.* ii. 9 δόξειε δ' ἂν ἡ τῶν ἐφόρων ἀρχὴ πάσας εὐθύνειν τὰς ἀρχάς. But the words may refer only to their νομοφυλακία.
[3] Xen. *Hell.* ii. 3, 34.
[4] Thuc. i. 87.
[5] Her. v. 40.
[6] Paus. iii. 5, 2.
[7] Thuc. i. 131; cf. Her. vi. 82.
[8] *Pol.* iii. 1.

in fact, the foreign ministry of Sparta. They doubtless had the execution of the decrees of the Apella and the Gerousia, and from this power are no doubt often credited with actions the initiative in which belonged to these two assemblies [1]—the decision as to war and peace, for instance, which belonged undoubtedly to the Apella,[2] and the true formula for which ran: "It seemed good to the Ephors and the assembly." [3] But the Apella could not act without the Ephors, and hence in their hands lay the initiation as well as the final execution of the decree. Thus they received foreign envoys, negotiated with foreign states, and sent out the expedition when the Apella had declared for war.[4] Their executive relations with the council and the assembly may conveniently be summed up under three heads:—(i) They received the first information on foreign matters and brought it before the Gerousia. (ii) They brought the προβούλευμα of the Elders before the Apella. (iii) They executed the degrees both of the Gerousia and of the Apella. Their influence in determining the course of Spartan policy was therefore strongly marked;[5] but it was too wholly a personal influence, and the annual change of Ephors sometimes produced a change in foreign relations which was not advantageous to the state.[6]

The Ephors, as the chiefs of the foreign executive at Sparta, were necessarily also to a great extent the guiding spirits of the Peloponnesian confederacy. How this was the case may best be seen by anticipating one of the points in the procedure of the council of this league which we shall soon discuss. In the final debate on any matter before this council Sparta is the mover, and it undoubtedly rests with her either to make a proposition or not to do so. But by Sparta in this instance we mean the Ephors, who bring the matter before the Apella, which is largely under their control. The guidance of the confederacy was, in fact, the culminating point in the growth of the power of the college of Ephors.

Here we take leave of the last element in this complex state; for the Apella, or popular assembly composed of all the ὅμοιοι, does not require separate discussion, since incidentally we have touched on all its powers and on its relation to other

---

[1] Gilbert *Staatsalt.* i. p. 59.
[2] As early as 480 the Apella decided about treaties, Her. vii. 149.
[3] Xen. *Hell.* iv. 6, 3.
[4] Her. ix. 7, 9; Thuc. iv. 50.
[5] Thuc v 36. [6] *ib.* iv. 50.

bodies. What kind of state is it that we have described? Historically Sparta is a balance of the three numerical elements of sovereignty: the nobles limit the king, and the demos the nobility, and all three are found finally together in a condition of stable equilibrium. But analytically we should be inclined to recognise only two elements, and to pronounce the constitution a dynastic oligarchy of a mild type modified by a strong democratic element. The dynastic element is obvious; it is the power of the Gerousia. Its mildness consists in the fact that the members of this body were elected by the people. The democratic element is threefold: the social equality to some extent enforced by the state; in a higher degree the popular choice of the Elders and Ephors, and the popular ratification or refusal of the council's acts; in the highest degree the vast powers exercised by the freely-chosen magistrates of the city. It is true that the refinements of the Greek intellect would not have been satisfied with this analysis. In election as here displayed the Greeks would have seen an "aristocratic" element, and to Plato the Ephors are "tyrannical"; again, there was the shadow of the monarchy to be taken into account. But the real power is a balance between the city and the nobility, and from this point of view Sparta was a mixture of democratic with dynastic elements.

If we ask "Why did not Sparta go on in the course which she had begun, and become still more democratic?" the chief answer is again to be sought in the Peloponnesian confederacy. We shall find that one of the surest means which Sparta adopted for maintaining a union of political interests in the league was the support of governments in the various cities of a conservative, stable, and, on the whole, oligarchic type. This policy must necessarily have exercised a reactionary influence on the leading state. The continuity of her hegemony necessitated the permanence of her political institutions. However variable the policy of the Ephors might be in detail, they remained consistent in the application of this one principle of stability—a natural consistency, since the maintenance of this principle made them practically the heads of the greatest power in the Greek world. For this reason the Spartan constitution, which had grown and expanded for so many generations, suddenly crystallised and remained fixed and unchanged for centuries.

§ 3 *The Peloponnesian Confederacy*

We have given a sketch of the main factors of the Spartan constitution considered from an internal point of view, with a hint, however, that this internal point of view is by itself insufficient. Her institutions are closely connected with her career as a conquering state, and we have already treated her as the mistress of Laconia, Messenia, and Cynuria. Her western conquests were early consolidated, her eastern limit reached about the middle of the sixth century. In the early part of the seventh century her design seems to have been to conquer the whole of Peloponnese; but a great defeat inflicted by Argos at Hysiae, and the subsequent rise to power of that state, checked her progress and turned her thoughts into other channels. She now sought to make herself the centre of a powerful confederacy, the stages in the growth of which are unknown, but which is found existing in full vigour in the year 510. This confederacy was brought together by conquest as well as by alliance, and a vigorous display of force was sometimes required to maintain it;[1] but on the whole a common interest seems to have kept together this largest and most stable of the voluntary unions of the Greek world. In extent it was a union of all the Peloponnesian states with the exception of Argos and the district of Achaea,[2] which were divided from Sparta as much on political as on national grounds. The permanent hegemony of Sparta, in fact, did not extent beyond the limits of the Isthmus, Megara on the north-east being her most distant ally. It is true that in the Persian Wars it rose to be a hegemony of nearly all Greece for a special purpose, and that at the beginning of the Peloponnesian War Sparta claims a kind of indefinite leadership over Dorian states outside the Peloponnese, and requests contingents from the Dorian cities of Italy and Sicily;[3] but these are only instances of temporary union for a professed object, and the union disappeared when the object was attained.

We know little or nothing about the legal basis of the

---

[1] Two great attempts were made to shake off her hegemony between the Persian and the Peloponnesian Wars: the first by Tegea supported by Argos, the second by all the Arcadians except the Mantineans (Her. ix. 35).

[2] Thuc. ii. 9; Paus. vii. 6, 3. Pausanias (*l.c.*) says of the Achaeans διὰ τὸ ἔργον τὸ πρὸς Τροίαν Λακεδαιμονίους Δωριεῖς ἀπηξίουν σφίσιν ἡγεῖσθαι.

[3] Thuc. ii. 7; cf. iii. 86.

confederacy, but it seems probable that the supremacy of Sparta and the existence of the alliance were secured by a system of separate treaties with the separate states. It is difficult to imagine any other basis when we consider the different periods at which Sparta was brought into relation with the different communities. The relations between herself and Elis, for instance, had existed from the earliest times, but it was only in the middle of the sixth century that she concluded the unequal alliance which made Tegea her subject ally.[1] The confederacy was probably brought together in two ways—by the conquest of states to which she left autonomy, and which she reduced to the condition of subject allies, and by defensive treaties concluded with more powerful communities, such as Elis, Corinth, and Sicyon, which naturally gravitated to her as the most powerful state in Peloponnese. The league, therefore, included cities of very different degrees of power, but Sparta was wise enough to raise or reduce all to the same level. Every state possessed autonomy and an equal vote in the council, and hence there were but few discontented elements among them. But an absence of discontent does not necessarily imply active loyalty, and Sparta had a more effective means for securing allegiance. This was by maintaining oligarchies friendly to her own interests in the states which were within the sphere of her influence.[2] In early times she had posed as the opponent of *tyrannis*, as the liberating city which had resisted the individual despot, as she was afterwards to resist the tyrant state of Athens. But in crushing tyranny she also opposed the revolutionary force which tended towards democracy, she established the existing oligarchies, and she was everywhere regarded as the supporter of stable government and conservative institutions. Her working on the inner life of states was subtle and indirect: before the fall of Tegea in 550, there was a "laconising" party within the town;[3] and in most of the cities of the league she contented herself with this indirect influence. But sometimes she had more difficult material to deal with, and then she resorted to measures more stringent than diplomacy. The influence which strengthened the oligarchy at Sicyon in 418, after the battle of Mantinea, was backed by force;[4] the one attempt at democratic reaction

[1] Her. i. 66.
[2] Thuc. i. 19, 76, 144.
[3] Plut. *Quaest. Graecae* 5.
[4] Thuc. v. 81.

made by Phlius was sternly repressed;[1] and Mantineia, the discontented and ambitious town of Arcadia, was more than once the victim of armed interference. Arcadia was the northern neighbour of Sparta, and this dangerous proximity may account in some measure for the harsh manner in which her towns were treated. Sparta seems to have been unwilling that these communities should be walled cities at all; the πόλις was more defensible, and city life tended towards democracy. Hence she preferred that they should keep their old tribal and village organisation, and, when she felt herself strong enough, enforced this preference—as in 385, when she compelled the Mantineians to pull down their wall, and divided the city into its four original villages.[2] Thus, when indirect influence was not sufficient to keep up a government favourable to her interests, Sparta was very willing, where she could, to bring direct pressure to bear upon the states. Her methods varied with circumstances, and wisdom dictated that they should be, as a rule, pacific. Had Sparta's hegemony in Peloponnese rested, like Rome's in Italy, everywhere on conquest, the league might have developed into a protectorate, and the protectorate into an empire. But Sparta, incapable of incorporating even her immediate dependencies of Laconia, had powerful rivals in Elis and Corinth, even within the states of her confederacy. Hence the league retained its original character, and since its independence never sank under the weight of a too powerful leader, its organisation continued uniform.

The relations of the states to one another were clearly, though not minutely, defined. It was a condition of the league that they should be all independent, small and great alike;[3] it was consequently the duty of Sparta to interfere if one state conquered another, as she did interfere when Mantineia reduced the Parrhasians of Arcadia to subjection and attempted to establish a small ἀρχή during the Peloponnesian War.[4] The states also bound themselves by a defensive alliance to repel

---

[1] Xen. *Hell.* v. 2, 8 and 3, 10.
[2] *ib.* v. 2, 7. Xenophon goes on to say that this dwelling κατὰ κώμας was much more favourable to aristocracy, the owners of the soil having local influence in the villages.
[3] Thuc. v. 77; cf. 79 αὐτόνομοι καὶ αὐτοπόλεις.
[4] *ib.* v. 29, 33. It was also the ground of interference with Elis (*ib.* v. 31); yet this city had pursued a successful career of conquest in Triphylia during the fifth century (Her. iv, 148).

any invader coming against Peloponnese;[1] accordingly any city of the league had a right to demand the assistance of the others against a foreign invader, as the Epidaurians did in the year 419 when the Argives entered their territory.[2] In a treaty concluded in 418 between Sparta and Argos we find a clause providing that the allies should submit their differences to arbitration.[3] It is difficult to believe that this was a permanent condition of the alliance, for the states seem to have exercised, even if they did not formally retain, some independent power of settling their differences by the sword, at least during the quiescent periods of the league.[4] But a standing condition of the treaty was that, when a war had been undertaken by the confederacy, all dissensions between the allies should cease; otherwise Sparta was empowered to march against the dissentient state which had commenced the quarrel.[5]

The freedom exhibited in the international relations of these cities shows how slight an approach the league was to a real federal system. Such cohesion as it possessed was due to Sparta's position, partly perhaps guaranteed by treaty, but chiefly no doubt the growth of custom. As the head of the league she was vested with full powers for carrying out its military decrees, and, once war has been determined on, she acts as the commanding state. Thus she raises supplies and military contingents from the cities, and decides where the latter are to meet her; and she sends round commanders of her own ($\xi\epsilon\nu\alpha\gamma$οί) to lead these contingents from the allied communities.[6] The fullest contingent demanded from each of the allies for expeditions *en masse* was two-thirds of its fighting men;[7] in ordinary circumstances smaller levies were requisitioned, the council itself fixing the full complement which the troops were to reach, and the different cities making up this complement in proportion to their populations;[8] but we find that, when the army was summoned to muster in the territory of one of the allied communities, this community had to appear with its full fighting force.[9] After the rise of mercenary armies in Greece

---

[1] Thuc. v. 77.   [2] *ib.* v. 54.
[3] *ib.* v. 79.
[4] There was an appeal to arbitration in the differences between Elis and Lepraeum in 421 (Thuc. v. 31), an appeal to the sword in those between Mantineia and Tegea in 423 (Thuc. iv. 134).

[5] Xen. *Hell.* v. 4, 36, 37.
[6] Thuc. ii. 75; Xen. *Hell.* v. 2, 7. Yet the armies of the allied states have their own στρατηγοί (Thuc. ii. 10).
[7] Thuc. ii. 10, 47, iii. 15.
[8] Xen. *Hell.* v. 2, 20.
[9] πανστρατιᾷ (Thuc. v. 57).

we find the states allowed to send money instead of men. To Sparta was given the power of fining states that did not furnish contingents or their equivalent.[1] The allies paid no fixed tribute to the league or to Sparta,[2] but merely had to furnish the expenses of their own contingents, the amount of the supplies necessary depending entirely on the nature of the expedition. This liberal system, though often criticised and sometimes a source of weakness, possessed many advantages. It preserved an appearance of liberty in the cities, it prevented the influx of money into Sparta, and it was supposed to represent an elastic principle more effective than that of regular contribution in times of pressing need.[3]

Although Sparta was certainly something more than the mere executive head of this association, yet all important decisions appeared to be arrived at by the council composed of delegates from the states. The council had to be summoned for the purpose of declaring war, or of accepting a peace or an armistice, and the formal sovereignty of the states composing it was asserted by their swearing separately to a treaty concluded with a foreign power.[4] There was perfect equality of votes amongst the cities, irrespective of their size; the decision of the majority was binding upon all;[5] and the allies claimed and exercised the right of refusing to follow Sparta to a war which had not been decided on by the majority of the council.[6] But a glance at the procedure of this assembly shows that Sparta had a very decided power of influencing its resolutions. Sometimes the first proposal for joint action came from Sparta herself; then she summoned the allies and laid her measure before them.[7] But the first suggestion might come from any quarter. The accounts of three meetings have been preserved, which show, in one instance a member of the confederacy, in the two others foreign envoys advocating a course of action.[8] In this case, when a complaint was made by an ally or a request for help came from some quarter outside the league, the first step taken by Sparta was to summon the allies before her own

---

[1] Xen. *Hell.* v. 2, 21.
[2] Thuc. 1. 19.
[3] ὁ πόλεμος οὐ τεταγμένα ζητεῖ was the reply of Archidamus when the allies tried ὁρίσαι τὸν φόρον (Plut. *Apophth. Lac.* p. 268).
[4] Thuc. v. 18 ὤμοσαν κατὰ πόλεις.
[5] Thuc. i. 119, 125; v. 30.
[6] Her. v. 74-75. [7] *ib.* 91-95.
[8] Thuc. i. 67 ff.; Xen. *Hell.* v. 2, 11; vi. 3, 3. In these passages of Xenophon the debate in the Spartan assembly, after the allies had withdrawn, is omitted.

Apella. The complainants speak before this combined assembly, but a formal proposal can be made only by a member of the confederacy. The proposal made, the Spartans dismiss the allies and decide on the question in their own assembly. Then the allies are summoned a second time and the question put to the vote. The states have, therefore, the final ratifying decision; but two points in the procedure show the weight of the leading city. Sparta has the sole right of summoning the allies, and, although the first proposal may be made by any state of the confederacy, yet in the final debate Sparta is the sole mover, and it undoubtedly rests with her either to make a proposition or to let the matter drop. It is this great power of initiative that more than any other prerogative makes her position in the league a true hegemony.

Such was the organisation of the confederacy, military in appearance but political in essence, which long stemmed the tide of constitutional development in Greece. Its final overthrow by the Thebans, due to the issue of a single disastrous battle, does not necessarily exhibit defects in its organisation. A graver symptom was its near approach to dissolution during the Peloponnesian War. The behaviour of Corinth and Elis during that war showed that Sparta was not powerful enough to enforce obedience on some of the states of her confederacy, and that the conditions of the league, and even the resolutions of the council, could be neglected with impunity. The course of the war also showed the slenderness of the bond of common interest which united the states, and how Argos, the centre of democratic aspirations in the Peloponnese, might be a match for Sparta in diplomacy, if not in arms. If a democratic union was possible within the league—and the union of Elis and Mantineia with Argos in 420 proved it to be possible—Sparta's influence was gone, and could only be restored by a successful battle against her own allies, followed by armed interference with their domestic politics. But if her political influence was precarious within this limited sphere, how much less likely was she to push it further with success! The Peloponnesian War had early resolved itself into a struggle between oligarchy and democracy; and the close of that war brought empire to Sparta, the only possibility of controlling which, she thought, was to organise it on her favourite model, and to make of it a system of narrow oligarchies. As force could not be directly exercised on widely scattered maritime dependencies, and Sparta had no intention of devoting her energies to the sea, the only means of securing her ascendency was by working on the internal politics of the states. This form of state-craft, which applied to Athens resulted in the tyranny of the Thirty, had hardly less disastrous results in the states which had been Athenian dependencies. Lysander, an exaggerated type of the Spartan genius for intrigue, had, on his arrival to take the command in Asia Minor, identified himself and the government of Sparta (they were practically the same) with the oligarchic clubs of the Greek cities there, and, where he did not find them, he organised ἑταιρεῖαι of his own. The result was that, after Aegospotami, these clubs were used as the universal basis of government throughout the cities. The imperial idea contributed by Sparta to the history of the world was that of a harmost at the head of a board of ten (δεκαρχία), composed of adherents of a past oligarchic faction. The day of triumph had come, Greece was free, and the result was a worse slavery than her states had experienced even under Persian rule—a slavery to narrow cliques who were made "the sole fountains of honour and the sole sources of punishment."[1] The justification for the Athenian Empire was that its political *régime* harmonised with the political tendencies of the time, and furthered the political progress of the Eastern world. The imperial policy of Sparta was only a brief interruption to a normal development which finally won the recognition of Alexander, the true liberator of the Eastern Greeks.

Expanded conquest and empire produced an unfavourable effect on the Spartan polity, based as it was on social conditions for which a rigorous isolation from the events of the outer world would have been the fittest protection. The outlines of this social revolution have been already sketched. It was due largely to the introduction of a commercial spirit which fostered the accumulation of capital and led to the decrease, not indeed of the free population, but of the qualified citizens. Ceaseless efforts on the part of the state to retain, and subsequently to recover, its position increased the drain on the national life; while the loss of Messenia in 369, with the allotments of that district, reduced yet further the numbers of the landed class. But still the Spartan ideal of what a citizen should be persisted,

[1] Plut. *Lys.* 13.

and the privileged members of the state still held that the true πολίτης must be a man of leisure and an owner of land. Two kings of the third century, Agis IV. and Cleomenes III., taking the same view but interpreting the principle somewhat differently, attempted a renewed division of the land. But the projected revolution of Agis was resisted with success, the battle of Sellasia (222) put an end to the still more violent projects of Cleomenes, and the monarchy did not long survive the defeat of the royal reformers. In 211 the double kingship, and with it the constitution, came to an end. There are few states in the world which have literally perished through lack of citizens. Yet this is almost true of Sparta. The fall of the constitution was but the overthrow of a narrow oligarchy, and it fell to make room for a new state. The city tyrannised by Nabis and recognised as a *civitas foederata* by Rome is not the city whose constitution we have sketched.

§ 4 *The Cities of Crete*

There is a reason which might have determined an inquirer, who classifies constitutions according to their form, to place those of the Dorian cities of Crete before that of Sparta. The reason is that an analysis of Cretan institutions shows a more aristocratic character and a less mixed type. But there are considerations which justify the order which we have preferred. One is that to a certain extent Cretan institutions were derived from Sparta, that is, from the primitive Dorian type of unreformed Sparta; the other is that we are able, in the case of these Cretan cities, to mark the dissolution of a mixed government and its change to a democracy. Their treatment, therefore, forms a connecting link between the mixed constitutions of our present chapter and the democracies of our next.

The statement that the germ of Cretan institutions was derived from the Peloponnesian Dorians, may seem strange to one who remembers the fixed belief of the Spartan that his institutions came from Crete.[1] But that was a simple argument from analogy. Wherever the Greeks found parallelism they predicated borrowing, and as the Cretan polity was associated with the name of Minos son of Zeus, it was necessarily thought older than the work of the human legislator Lycurgus. The

[1] Her. i. 65.

most recent inquiry is on the whole inclined to reject the account which derives the Dorians of Crete from the primitive Dorians of Histiaeotis in Thessaly, and which makes Cnossus a Doric settlement earlier than the migration. Of the foundation of this ancient residence of Minos no traditional records were preserved. Its institutions did not give evidence of remote antiquity, for Ephorus tell us that the Dorian customs (νόμιμα) were retained in a more primitive form in Lyctus, Gortyn, and many of the smaller cities than in the more famous Cnossus.[1] This, it is true, might have been the result of the longer development of the most ancient settlement; but it may also be a sign that the town was less purely Dorian, and we have definite evidences of the belief that the settlement of most of the cities of Crete was the result of Argive and Lacedaemonian colonisation after the return of the Heracleidae,[2] and that Lyctus, a colony from Sparta, was the earliest of these foundations.[3] But this origin does not in the least imply that the close correspondence which we shall trace between Cretan and Spartan institutions was the result of conscious imitation; for these Argive and Spartan colonies date from the infancy of Dorian settlement. A common germ is planted in two soils, and, under somewhat similar conditions, grows into the same tree. The resemblances are close enough to make us believe in parallel development, not close enough to lead us to think of imitation.

Of the forty-three independent cities of Crete of which the names have been preserved,[4] three—Cnossus, Gortyn, and Cydonia—were sufficiently powerful to control the activity of the rest. When they agreed, they held all the others in subjection; when they differed, they divided the whole island against itself.[5] As a rule Cnossus and Gortyn were hostile, and Cydonia but a make-weight, and the normal condition of the Cretan cities was one of faction (στάσις). That writers use the term faction and not war to describe their mutual hostility [6] was due partly to the very real tie of their common nationality, partly to the close international relations of ἰσοπολιτεία, ἐπιγαμία, and the like which existed between them,[7]

---

[1] Strabo p. 481.   [2] Diod. v. 80.
[3] Arist. *Pol.* ii. 10 ; Polyb. iv. 54.
[4] A list has been collected by Gilbert *Staatsalt.* ii. p. 217.
[5] Strabo p. 476.
[6] *ib.*; Plut. *de frat. amore* 19, p. 594 Didot.
[7] p. 54.

but chiefly to their wonderful faculty for combining against an external foe. This temporary union in the face of danger was known as συγκρητισμός.[1] It may possibly have been connected with a common court of arbitration (τὸ κοινοδίκιον), which we know existed at times for the settlement of differences between certain towns,[2] and which, in these periods of occasional calm, may have been so composed as to be capable of adjusting the mutual claims of all the Cretan cities.

The settlers in Crete had betrayed a true Dorian incapacity for assimilating the conquered nationalities; and each city is a miniature Sparta in relation to its immediate neighbours. It is, however, doubtful whether we are to recognise in Crete two classes of subject peoples or only one. A Cretan historian represents the ὑπήκοοι of the island as περίοικοι, but the latter word is indeterminate, and Aristotle compares the ὑπήκοοι in more than one respect to the Spartan helots.[3] The great code of private law discovered at Gortyn does nothing to settle the vexed question;[4] but its silence on the perioeci is no argument against their existence, for if they existed they must have been inhabitants of subject towns, which were found by the settlers in Crete, and were probably of non-Dorian nationality. They were, therefore, as much outside the Cretan πολιτεία as the perioeci were outside the state of Sparta. The members of the serf population were not assigned wholly to the use of individual citizens as at Sparta, and the chief sign of that more rigorous communism which distinguished the Cretan cities was the existence of a class of slaves working for the state and helping to support all the citizens by their collective labour. These were called μνωῖται, and cultivated the public land. The other class of private serfs (ἀφαμιῶται or κλαρῶται),[5] if they are to be identified with the Ϝοικέες of the Gortyn code, exhibit the mildest form of slavery in Greece. They were householders with property of their own, they could apparently intermarry with free women, and they had a subsidiary right of inheritance to their masters' estates. They possessed, however, no legal personality of their own, and before a court and in other legal acts were represented by their masters. The revenue

---

[1] Plut. *l.c.*   [2] Cauer n. 119.
[3] *Pol.* ii. 10.
[4] The ἀπέταιροι of this code, sometimes identified with the perioeci, rather suggest a class within the state—perhaps "freedmen," as thought by Mr. Roby.
[5] Athenaeus i. p. 263 f.

paid by the serfs to the state or to their own lords must, as in the case of the helots, have been a fixed one.

Lastly we have the privileged class of freemen (πολιᾶται), divided into the Dorian tribes of the Hylleis, Pamphyli, and Dymanes. Within this class the noble clans (γένη) were distinguished from the commons by certain special political privileges. These clans as a whole were further subdivided into smaller groups, called σταρτοί, the nature of which is unknown. They may have been military, they may have been family divisions: perhaps both. But they played the same part in the state as the obes did at Sparta, for it was on them that election to the higher offices was based.[1] The military character of this ruling class, necessitated by the smallness of its numbers, was strongly marked, and a Cretan city has been compared, with as much justice as Sparta, to a camp.[2] The citizens met at public meals (ἀνδρεῖα), which were supported directly or indirectly by the state; for even where, as at Lyctus, each member paid a tithe of his produce, he was at least partly reimbursed by receipts from the public revenues.[3] The common tables, to which the young were admitted, had by no means merely a social character, for their organisation was directed to military training and to education of a general kind.[4] Associations were encouraged of a military, political, and exclusive character. The young formed themselves into bands (ἀγέλαι) for hunting and mimic combat, the older men into clubs (ἑταιρεῖαι), which dined together at the public tables,[5] possibly fought together in the field, formed the same party in the state, and doubtless fostered the factious life characteristic of the Cretan cities. A union of these clubs was often sufficiently powerful to impair the constitution, as is shown by the occasional abolition of the highest magistracy by the nobles who would not submit to justice.[6]

The political constitution consisted of magistrates, senate,

---

[1] Baunack (die Inschrift von Gortyn p. 128) thinks that they were military τάξεις into which the most distinguished of the conquering families were divided. But each of these divisions which had a collective name (e.g. ὁ Αἰθαλεὺς σταστός Gortyn Code v. 5) may have represented a clan.

[2] In Plato's Laws (i. p. 666) the Athenian says to the Cretan στρατο- πέδου γὰρ πολιτείαν ἔχετε. Cf. ib. p. 626.

[3] Arist. Pol. ii. 10; for Lyctus Dosiadas ap. Athenae. v. p. 143 a.

[4] Ephorus ap. Strab. p. 483. Each ἀνδρεῖον contained a παιδονόμος.

[5] Athenae. i. p. 263 f.

[6] This suspension of the Cosmi was known as ἀκοσμία, Arist. Pol. ii. 10.

and people. The highest magistrates were the κόσμοι,[1] ten in number, and chosen only from the noble clans.[2] They were apparently elected by the people, but the choice must have been exceedingly limited, for, as a particular σταρτός is mentioned in connection with the κόσμοι of a year,[3] it has been concluded that these aristocratic corporations held office in turn, and that the popular choice each year was limited to selecting ten members from a single σταρτός. The term of office, based as it was on a system of rotation, was probably annual. Aristotle and Ephorus[4] compare the Cosmi to the Spartan Ephors. One point of resemblance was probably the gradual growth of their powers and the usurpation of the functions of the kings. Their general position in the state is the same. Like the Ephors they co-operate with and preside over the council; they are the connecting link between the council and the people; and they possess civil jurisdiction. But the complete extinction of the monarchy in Crete had caused them to inherit the military duties of the king as well, and command in war was one of their most distinctive functions. This unity of administration was centred in the hands of a narrow class of nobles, and there was no democratic power in the state such as that represented by the Spartan ephoralty. The administrative functions of the Cosmi were shared with the council, which they consulted on the most important matters.[5] In the exercise of their judicial functions they probably decided the most important civil suits themselves, while sharing criminal jurisdiction with the council.[6]

The council (βωλά, perhaps too γερουσία) was elected by the people from those who had been Cosmi.[7] The numbers of this body and their precise mode of election are unknown. It does not appear that all the ex-Cosmi were admitted;[8] but if a principle of rotation was adopted, similar to that which characterised the election of the magistrates, the people could have had but little freedom in their choice of councillors. All

---

[1] Other forms are κοσμίοντες and κόσμιοι.

[2] Arist. l.c.

[3] Gortyn Code v. 5 αἶ δκ ὁ Αἰθαλεὺς (σ)ταστός, ἐκοσμίον οἱ σὺν Κύ(λ)λῳ. Baunack l.c.

[4] ap. Strab. p. 482.

[5] Strabo l.c.

[6] We are not told this, but the γερουσία, where preserved, seems to have been invariably a criminal court.

[7] Arist. Pol. ii. 10 τοὺς γέροντας (αἱροῦνται) ἐκ τῶν κεκοσμηκότων.

[8] Ephorus (ap. Strab. p. 482) says οἱ τῆς τῶν κόσμων ἀρχῆς ἠξιωμένοι καὶ τἆλλα δόκιμοι κρινόμενοι.

classes of freemen were members of the assembly (ἀγορά), but it had, besides its elective functions, only the power of ratifying the decrees of the magistrates and council.[1] According to the Gortyn code adoption and the renunciation of adoption took place before this assembly; but here it appears only as the witness of a public act.

We cannot piece together the fragments of this Cretan constitution with such success as those of the Spartan, for some of its most important factors—the modes of election of the Cosmi and Elders—are but imperfectly known. It is clearly a constitution of a much more oligarchical or dynastic type than Sparta. What we classed as the most democratic element in that state—the vast powers exercised by the freely-chosen magistrates of the city—is here lacking; its place is filled by officials, elected it is true, but only in the narrowest manner from the noble clans. In spite of the apparent division of power the council must have been the central point of the administration, for a gathering of ex-officials is of all bodies the most likely to control a recalcitrant magistrate. The working of the constitution, and indeed its structure, must in many points have borne a resemblance to that of early Rome— especially if we consider the council to have been recruited, like the Roman senate, in an automatic manner. Here, as in early Rome, the yearly magistrate is vested with a combination of functions, military, judicial, and administrative, such as those contained in the *imperium*. He is nominally the controller of, really the intermediary between, senate and people; in both states the assembly is equally dependent on the magistrate, and can express its opinion only by assent or dissent; in both the magistrate is controlled by a council of ex-officials, in whose hands the sovereignty practically resides. But in Crete the dynastic element gained a legal recognition that was not present even in patrician Rome. The balance of this mixed constitution was very much on the side of the nobility. But the democracy won in the long run. In Greece the absence of barriers is alone sufficient to account for such a change; in Crete this absence may be illustrated by the lack of a stable democratic element in the constitution itself, and by the lack of a strong external motive, such as we found present in Sparta, for preserving the antique forms. By the third century

[1] Arist. *Pol.* ii. 10.

democratic institutions prevailed in certain towns,[1] and seem rapidly to have become universal. The names of the old offices continued to exist, but their nature had entirely changed. Amongst offices ($ἀρχαί$) to which annual election was now the rule[2] the council was probably included. The Cosmi, who must now have been elected from all the citizens, still represent the state in foreign affairs and preside in the assembly. The voice of the freemen in this assembly ($ἁ πόλις$) is supreme.[3]

[1] *e.g.* at Hierapytna, Cauer n. 181 l. 69.
[2] Polyb. vi. 46.
[3] The usual formula of decrees is ἔδοξε τοῖς κόσμοις καὶ τᾷ πόλει (Gilbert ii. p. 227). Gilbert concludes from the usual absence of the $βωλά$ in documents its comparative unimportance. Its duty was probably chiefly to prepare business for the assembly.

CHAPTER VI

DEMOCRACY

IN the primitive Greek state there are three powers, king, council, and people: the two first real, the last but dimly discerned. The monarchy fades first from view, and the magistracy which takes over its functions is not much more permanent as an independent authority. Even in mixed governments the collegiate principle is recognised, and oligarchies of a simple type tend to subordinate the magistrate to the council. Then comes the turn of the assembly, which, controlling or absorbing the functions of magistrate and council, claims to direct the whole administration of the state, and, to do so effectually, evolves from itself the new growth of a popular judicature. It is this rule of the freeman ($\dot{\epsilon}\lambda\epsilon\dot{\upsilon}\theta\epsilon\rho o\varsigma$) through his assembly and his law-courts that the Greeks called democracy. The democratic principle in its extreme form is the assertion that the mere fact of free birth ($\dot{\epsilon}\lambda\epsilon\upsilon\theta\epsilon\rho\dot{\iota}\alpha$) is alone sufficient to constitute a claim to all offices. It is never the claim of a *majority* to rule, but it is the demand that every one, whether rich or poor, high- or low-born, shall be equally represented in the constitution. This is what Aristotle calls the principle of numerical equality. In itself it is the shallowest of claims unless it implies a belief in the fitness of the freeman to rule—that is, unless it is in some sense aristocratic. And indeed we find that current Greek thought made an attempt to supply an aristocratic basis for democracy. Athenagoras, the Syracusan demagogue of Thucydides, represents democracy as the "collective name for a state" in which each class finds its proper level, in which the rich are the guardians of its wealth, the wise are chosen as its advisers, and the masses only make the claim of being capable critics and judges of policy and conduct.[1] This belief in the κριτικὴ δύναμις which even Aristotle believes to reside in the masses, which in large assemblies of men eliminates the error of individuals and makes the collective judgment well-nigh infallible,[2] is a deeper analysis and a sounder defence than the assumed fact of numerical equality. But it is only sound because it is narrow, and the claim to equal representation in the state was not justified by the ground advanced. It shows that the principle of democracy was clearly one which admitted of degrees. These degrees might be determined by intention or by accident.

They are determined by intention when a democracy recognises that certain other principles shall prevail in the administration of certain duties. The statement of Athenagoras has no meaning as a legal maxim unless he implies that the different degrees of excellence shall be reflected in the institutions of the state—that appointment to offices requiring special skill shall not be made by lot, that the finance offices shall be closed to all who cannot show a certain census. But such a state is not, according to the strict definition, a pure democracy. If, on the other hand, he merely implies that the "general will" of the people will recognise these qualities and choose their possessors as leaders or advisers, the state may be a democracy and the conflict simply be one between legal theory and moral influence. But with moral influence constitutional law is not concerned. That state only is a pure democracy in which no other principle but that of equal representation claims legal recognition. As a matter of fact such a pure democracy did not exist in Greece. In all we see certain aristocratic or oligarchic elements preserved. Yet the state was democratic where the true character of such elements was modified by subordination to the popular will, which could criticise and punish all holders of office. This is indeed the practical meaning of democracy in the Greek world; it is a power of fearless criticism which can at any moment issue in action.

A modification of this form of government may be determined by accident, when the social conditions of a nation are not sufficiently favourable to enable it to realise its own political ideals. Democracy in Greece meant personal rule exercised by each individual citizen. This was only possible in great com-

[1] Thuc. vi. 39 ; cf. ii. 40.   [2] Arist. *Pol.* iii. 11.

mercial or imperial states; for personal government meant leisure and therefore wealth, and also implied a residence close to the centre of affairs. Thus poverty or an agricultural life might necessitate a strongly aristocratic element in a nominal democracy.

We need not linger here to classify states according as they illustrate these changes in the conception or practice of popular government. The long history of Athens which we shall sketch illustrates all these conditions and variations in turn. To this we shall add the outline of the constitutions of a few states, about whose internal history little is known, but which seem to illustrate certain particular democratic tendencies.

§ 1 *Athens—the Classes and the State-Divisions*

The foundation of Athens illustrates a process characteristic of early Greek societies—that of the amalgamation of many distinct centres of government into one city; as this amalgamation was conceivably accompanied by a corresponding union of many distinct nationalities, some consideration of the original elements of the population of Attica is necessary even from the point of view of constitutional history.

The population of Attica was generally considered to be typically Ionian. Herodotus calls it Pelasgian, which, in this context at least, is equivalent to Ionian,[1] and the Athenians claimed to be natives of the soil ($αὐτόχθονες$). But there were many legends in Attica which conflicted with this account of their origin by recalling memories of the immigration of large branches of the population. Amongst such legends we may cite that which assigns a Thracian origin to the Eumolpidae of Eleusis and a Phoenician origin to the Gephyraei;[2] while, according to Attic tradition, Theseus himself, the highest type of Ionism, was a wanderer from Troezen in Argolis, and the last line of kings, the Melanthidae or Medontidae, came from Pylus in Messenia. More tangible evidence of intermixture

---

[1] Her. i. 56.
[2] *ib.* v. 57, 62. Toepffer's discussion of both these legends (*Attische Genealogie* pp. 24 and 293) tends to undermine the belief in the Thracian origin of the one race or the Phoenician origin of the other.

is given by local and family cults, such as the Carian worship of the family of Isagoras and the Phoenician worship of Heracles, which was peculiarly cultivated in Attica, was found at Marathon,[1] and formed the bond of union of the "four villages" of the South.[2] A further trace of Eastern, possibly Hittite, worship which has been noticed is the worship of Artemis in Brauron and Munychia. These oriental influences were impressed on the latest strata of that ancient civilisation, the infancy and maturity of which may both be traced in the tombs of Spata, Menidi, and Thoricus; though some may have been borrowed, after Attica, in consequence of the migrations, had become a refuge for the dispossessed of other lands. There is, therefore, abundant evidence that Attica in early times was subjected to varied influences; and this to some extent helps to explain the state of its earliest political organisation, which was scattered, circumscribed, and local.

The early condition of Attica, as sketched by Thucydides, was the same as that of Elis prior to its $συνοικισμός$ in 471.[3] It was inhabited by a country population gathered round separate strongholds ($πόλεις$); and Thucydides rightly regards the local interests and habits of the Athenians of his own day as a survival from the times when these local divisions were independent organisations. He might have added a further proof from the permanence of local legends, which, as Pausanias tells us, did not always agree with the legends of the capital.[4] Attica, according to this view, was composed of a number of quite independent organisations, each $πόλις$ having its own court-house ($πρυτανεῖον$) and magistrates ($ἄρχοντες$), and only uniting under a central government in times of some pressing national danger. At times there was even war between these communes, as between the Eleusinians under Eumolpus and the Athenians under Erectheus;[5] and, since some of the small independent $πόλεις$ of early Greece subdued one another,[6] a part of the unity of Attica may have been the result of conquest. But the main bond of union seems to have been religion. The earliest groups of cities were associations for a religious purpose round a common centre. Some of these groups can be recovered, and

---

[1] Diodor. iv. 39; Paus. i. 15, 3.
[2] Pollux iv. 105.
[3] Thuc. ii. 14-17. It has been thought that this union of Elis, occurring in historical times, may have suggested the details of Thucydides' description.
[4] Paus. i. 14, 6.
[5] Thuc. *l.c.*; cf. Her. i. 30.
[6] Thuc. i. 8.

may be regarded as the starting-points of the union. Such were the τετράπολις of Marathon in the North (composed of Marathon, Oenoe, Probalinthus, and Tricorythus [1]), in the South the τετράκωμοι (two of which villages were Peiraeus and Phalerum), and a group known as the τρίκωμοι.[2] From inscriptions we learn the existence of the ἐπακρεῖς and μεσόγειοι, centres of worship in later times.[3]

But by the side of this isolated grouping we find an account of a division of Attica, made by Cecrops, into twelve states, the chief division before the time of Theseus. Philochorus,[4] our authority for this division, gives eleven names, Cecropia, Tetrapolis, Epacria, Deceleia, Eleusis, Aphidnae, Thoricus, Brauron, Cytherus, Sphettus, and Cephisia; it has been suggested that the twelfth was Phalerum. This enumeration is based on a division which constantly occurs in Ionian settlements. The δωδεκάπολις was found in Aegialis (the later Achaea) in Peloponnese and in the Ionian states of Asia Minor; and this may have been the reason why the same system was invented for Attica. Invented it clearly was, for the country could hardly have been united and then divided into twelve prior to its final union. The only importance of the list is to be found in the real local unions which it indicates in certain cases, especially in those of Cecropia (the original Athens), Tetrapolis, and Eleusis.

The next legendary epoch was marked by the συνοικισμός effected by Theseus, commemorated by the festival of the συνοίκια.[5] Athens was made the political centre of the whole of Attica; the people still dwelt in their old homes as before, but had now but one πόλις, one βουλευτήριον, and one πρυτανεῖον. Some points in the legends concerning Theseus throw light on this work, which is ascribed to him. To the Greek mind he was much more of a historical than a mythical figure, and belonged, it was felt, to a period of late development in politics. He came to be regarded in later times as the hero of the democracy, the first creator of popular government, and the first who broke down the local influence exercised by the noble

---

[1] Strabo p. 483.
[2] Pollux l.c.; Steph. Byz. s.v. Εὐπορίται.
[3] For the latter cf. Ath. Pol. 21 (ten of Cleisthenes's trittyes were τῆς μεσογείου).
[4] ap. Strab. p. 397.

[5] Thuc. ii. 15. Besides the συνοίκια Theseus is said to have made the Panathenaea a common festival (Plut. Thes. 24). It had existed before in the central state, its origin being attributed to Erichthonius.

clans in Attica.[1] How this great union was brought about we do not know. The legends of Theseus' many struggles may show that it was not effected without violence;[2] from the Ionian character of Athens after the union we may perhaps infer that immigrant bands of Ionians united the country and turned the scale in favour of an Ionian civilisation.

Attica as a united country is always represented as divided into four tribes (φυλαί). The final division into the four Ionic tribes of Geleontes (or Teleontes), Hopletes, Aegicoreis, and Argadeis lasted down to the time of Cleisthenes, and was the basis of much of the religious and political organisation of the state. It was believed, however, that these were by no means the earliest tribe-names in Attica, and there are no less than three lists which precede them. But these earlier lists are practically worthless; they show a cross-classification of eponymous and local names,[3] and may perhaps be regarded as a later creation of Attic chroniclers or legend. The final list is at least consistent; it was to the Greek mind a classification on a system, a division of the citizens according to βίοι or modes of life. The Hopletes are warriors, the Aegicoreis shepherds, the Argadeis artisans. Over Geleontes the learned stumbled. To Strabo they were priests, to Plutarch field-labourers. The first explanation is impossible, as no priestly caste ever existed in Attica, and both interpretations are obviously guesses.[4]

It is indeed difficult to see how these tribes could ever have denoted classes of the population. By the time of Solon at least they were of equal importance, for his council admitted an equal number of members from each. Again, by the side of this tribal division we have a cross-division that does denote class distinctions, that into Eupatridae, Geomori, and Demiurgi, which is attributed to Theseus;[5] and this distribution into ἔθνη or "classes" is not coincident with the division into tribes. The Eupatridae, for instance, and each of the other classes seem to have been distributed over all the tribes.

---

[1] Theophr. *Char.* viii. (xxvi.) περὶ ὀλιγαρχίας: Plut. *Thes.* 25.

[2] cf. Thuc. *l.c.* γενόμενος μετὰ τοῦ ξυνετοῦ καὶ δυνατός.

[3] *e.g.* the first (the division under Cecrops) is Κεκροπίς, Αὐτόχθων, Ἀκταία, Παραλία: the second (the division under Cranaos) is Κραναίς, Ἀτθίς, Μεσογαία, Διακρίς (Pollux viii. 109-111).

[4] Strabo p. 383; Plut. *Sol.* 23; cf. Plato *Timaeus* 24. Ζεὺς Γελεών is found in an Attic inscription (*C.I.A.* iii. 2); it has been thought that the word may mean "brilliant," "glancing."

[5] Plut. *Thes.* 25.

If we surrender the view that they were class distinctions, the most probable explanation of their origin is that they were introduced from abroad, and were arbitrarily applied as the divisions of the people of Attica at a time when the meanings of the names—if these ever signified βίοι—had been wholly lost. The names themselves are genuinely Ionic, and as persistently accompany Ionian settlement as the Hylleis, Pamphyli, and Dymanes accompany Dorian foundations. They are all found at Cyzicus, the Argadeis at Ephesus and Tomi, and the Geleontes at Teos. No time seems more suitable for their application to Attica than the period of the συνοικισμός. The country was united by immigrants from abroad, and the names were imposed as tribal divisions when Ionism finally prevailed. If these tribes were local, they were so only in the sense that, like the phratries and the clans, they had their local religious centres—for the tribe was inherited, not acquired by residence.

In fact, the division of the Athenian people into φρατρίαι and γένη, for the purposes of private life and private law, is indissolubly connected with these four Ionic tribes. Our authorities[1] represent a thoroughly systematic arrangement, each tribe being divided into three phratries, each phratry into thirty clans. The total number of clans would thus have been three hundred and sixty. But such a systematic division does not tally with the character of the clan, which was a natural unity or association based on family life. Such associations cannot be regulated numerically; and, if such a distribution was made at any period of Athenian history, it could have been at the utmost but a selection of those clans whose religious rites the state cared to recognise, and to which, therefore, it attached those members of the community who were outside the family circles.

The members of the Attic γένος appear under three names—γεννῆται, ὁμογάλακτες, and ὀργεῶνες. Of these words gennetae may have been used as the generic name including the other two; but strictly it is equivalent to homogalactes,[2] this word signifying those members who had traditions and what to them

---

[1] Pollux viii. 11; Schol. in Plat. Axioch. p. 465.

[2] In the Lexic. Demosth. (p. 152) it appears in a still narrower sense, of those thirty members of each clan ὧν αἱ ἱερωσύναι ἑκάστοις προσήκουσαι ἐκληροῦντο.

were proofs of common descent, who were therefore the only true members of the clan sharing in all its rights, amongst them the decisive family right of inheritance in the last resort. The orgeones were those who had no such traditions, who were not full members, and were only attached to a clan as participators in its sacred rites (ὄργια).[1] From this distinction it is evident that the clans at Athens were aristocratic institutions, and that all remained noble and exclusive. They never admitted new members except as mere participators in their rites—or rather in some of these, for it is not likely that an ὀργεών would have been allowed to share in the inner cultus of the clan. Every Athenian citizen was, therefore, in a certain sense a member of a γένος, but only a limited number were in the fullest sense γεννῆται. Thus the created citizens (δημοποίητοι) could never become full members, except possibly by adoption.

The φρατρίαι, on the other hand, were in historic times unions which included any and every Athenian citizen, for the juristic formula ran: "The members of the phratry must receive into their body both the homogalactes and the orgeones."[2] Every Athenian father had to bring his child for admission into the phratry at the Apaturia, and take the oath that it had been born of a citizen woman who was his wedded wife.[3] The φράτορες voted on the question, and an adverse vote meant a denial of the legitimacy of the child, and therefore a denial of its right to citizenship. The phratry is thus the connecting link between the family and the state, for membership of this body was the deciding point in the question of citizenship. The external sign of such membership was the right to participate in the two sacred cults of Apollo Patrous and Zeus Herceius, which were common to all of these associations.[4]

Does this account of family associations as they existed in later times throw any light on the status of those members of the old nobility who in early Athens were known as Εὐπατρίδαι? The fact that membership of the two phratric cults was the old test for admission to the archonship,[5] makes it possible that in early times the phratries with their worship were confined to the Eupatrids. This is equivalent to saying

[1] Photius s.v.
[2] Suidas s.v. ὀργεῶνες.
[3] Dem. c. Eubul. § 67 τὸν νόμιμον τοῖς φράτορσιν ὅρκον "ἀστὸν ἐξ ἀστῆς ἐγγυητῆς αὐτῷ γεγενημένον εἰδώς."
[4] Photius s.v. Ἑρκεῖος Ζεύς.
[5] The question asked of the candidates was εἰ Ἀπόλλων ἐστιν αὐτοῖς καὶ Ζεὺς Ἕρκιος (Pollux viii. 85).

that they were composed wholly of homogalactes, and that the class of orgeones was of later growth. With the growth of this class, participation in these cults, which was originally a condition of admissibility to the higher offices, became a condition of citizenship. If the Eupatrids were originally the only phrators, *a fortiori* they must have been the sole members of the clans, and the exclusive possession of both phratry and clan would have made them the only full citizens of Athens. The true members of the clan, the homogalactes, may have been from time to time recruited by adoption, and have swelled to large numbers without ever becoming merged in the orgeones, who always continued outside this exclusive and select circle. But with this change the term Εὐπατρίδης ceased eventually to mean "true member of a clan," and what it signified in later Athenian history cannot be precisely determined.[1] Yet, if the Eupatrids were the only citizens, the members of the demos were from the first freemen; Athens shows no trace of the clientship of Rome, and has no traditions of a gradual evolution of private and personal rights.

Although the phratries came to include individuals who were only partially members of the clans, yet the connection between the two forms of association continued unimpaired, and in many cases it was a *local* connection; the centre of worship of some important clan might be taken as that of a phratry, although in these cases the priests of the two associations were probably distinct. The number of the phratries is not known, but certainly seems to have been greater than the traditional number twelve. A chance of adding to them was offered to Cleisthenes when he enrolled a number of new citizens, who could not be made full members of the ancient clans, but had to be made members of the phratries. This might have been done either by attaching them as φράτορες to the existing divisions or by increasing the number of the latter. A statement of Aristotle, of rather vague import, has been quoted to show that he adopted the latter course;[2] but it is difficult to see how the phratries could be increased without either increasing the number of the clans, or disturbing the

---

[1] The term came to denote such a narrow class, that Toepffer (*Attische Genealogie* p. 175) thinks that there was a special genos of Eupatridae at Athens.

[2] Arist. *Pol.* vi. 4 = p. 1319 b. The passage in the *Ath. Pol.* (21) only states that Cleisthenes did not disturb the existing relations of individuals to the γένη and φρατρίαι.

existing connection between a particular phratry and a clan, and it is more probable that their original number remained unaltered.

As may be gathered from the position of the phratry in the state, citizenship at Athens was, as a rule, hereditary. It was, indeed, possible to increase the citizen body by a vote of the people, but the privilege was jealously guarded; rash proposals for admission were punished by the laws, and Solon laid down the conditions that no foreigners should be received but those who had been driven from their country into perpetual exile, or those who, for the sake of practising a trade, had transferred themselves and all their family to Athens.[1] But the hereditary principle itself admitted of variations, and in Greek states generally the particular qualification by birth depended partly on the nature of the constitution, partly on the numbers of the population.[2] At Athens it fluctuated considerably. The main principle adhered to was that the union from which the child was sprung must be one recognised by the state; this was usually legitimate marriage with a wife ($\gamma \upsilon \nu \acute{\eta}$), either through betrothal by a parent or guardian ($\dot{\epsilon} \gamma \gamma \acute{\upsilon} \eta \sigma \iota \varsigma$), or through assignment by a magistrate ($\dot{\epsilon} \pi \iota \delta \iota \kappa \alpha \sigma \acute{\iota} \alpha$);[3] but the quasi-polygamous customs of the fourth century placed on the same level legitimate cohabitation with a concubine ($\pi \alpha \lambda \lambda \alpha \kappa \acute{\iota} \varsigma$),[4] probably when it had been preceded by formal betrothal. Both these conditions are included in the oath for admission into the phratry, the primary condition of citizenship. The ancient formula also demands the possession of citizen rights by both parents. But the development which Aristotle traces began at an early period in Athens, assisted no doubt by the difficulties of preserving an accurate register in a large state; for it was not easy, in ancient communities where there were so many grades of political status and where birth, descent, and legal marriage had to be taken into account, to prevent the entrance of

---

[1] Plut. *Sol.* 24.

[2] Arist. *Pol.* iii. 5. In this passage it may be noticed that greater stress is laid on the citizenship of the mother than on that of the father. The child is regarded as belonging naturally to the mother; and where the condition of legitimate marriage was not taken into account, as it usually could not be if one parent was a foreigner, the maternity of the child was certain, its paternity might be doubtful.

[3] In the latter case, where the heiress was a ward in chancery, Gilbert remarks that formal $\dot{\epsilon} \gamma \gamma \acute{\upsilon} \eta \sigma \iota \varsigma$ must have taken place through the Archon, for the formula (p. 129) implies it.

[4] Isaeus *in her. Philoctem.* § 21; Dem. *c. Boeot.* § 40.

unqualified names. We find difficulties as early as the time of Peisistratus,[1] and the overthrow of the tyranny was followed by a scrutiny of the list. But the old conditions came again to be disregarded, and were revived by Pericles in 451.[2] He is said to have passed a measure limiting citizenship to those who were born of two Athenian parents, with the result that nearly five thousand citizens were disfranchised. This would have been a revolution had it been effected by a new law with retrospective force. It was probably a mere scrutiny of the list, permitted by a decree of the people, which resulted in the removal of names improperly registered. These renewed qualifications were again neglected, or dropped by legal enactment, during the Peloponnesian War, partly no doubt through the necessity of recruiting the population, partly perhaps through the influence of the Athenian Empire, which resulted in freer intercourse with other Greek states and a corresponding extension of the right of ἐπιγαμία. With the loss of empire the *raison d'être* of this extension disappeared. The old conditions were revived, at first with retrospective force, in the archonship of Eucleides (403). But the retrospective action of the law was felt to be too severe: this was removed, and it became simply prospective.[3] At the close of the fourth century the old conditions of citizenship were still in force.

The classes that stood outside the phratries had no part in the constitution; but without one of these classes the democratic constitution, at least in its final form, would not have been possible. The four hundred thousand Athenian slaves of the fifth and fourth centuries were the "necessary condition" of Athenian development. They were the "living instruments" of the household and the farm, they worked for the wealthy contractor in the mines, they manned the merchant fleet, and they sometimes formed a class of country tenants (οἱ χωρὶς οἰκοῦντες) who paid, like the helot, a fixed proportion of the produce to their leisured masters in the city. Socially they differed little from the poorer classes of citizens, and the democratic atmosphere of Athens had given them a freedom of demeanour and of speech which found few parallels in Greece.[4]

---

[1] *Ath. Pol.* 13. The Diacrii, Peisistratus' followers, were joined by οἱ τῷ γένει μὴ καθαροὶ διὰ τὸν φόβον.

[2] *ib.* 26; Plut. *Per.* 37.

[3] Carystius ap. Athenae. xi. p. 577 c.; Schol. in Aesch. *c. Timarch.* § 39.

[4] [Xen.] *Resp. Athen.* 1, 10 ff.

The state used their services for menial employments thought unfit for freemen; there was a Scythian police force, and we find public slaves of the mint. But the mass of Lydians, Paphlagonians, and Syrians that filled the Athenian slave-market could teach little to the Athenian citizen, and slave influence of the intellectual kind is not a factor to be reckoned with as at Rome. Yet the wealth and power of the aristocratic element, like the freedom of the citizen, depended on them, and the versatile activity of the Athenian statesman was largely due to these passive and nimble instruments. There is, however, another reason which forces the slave class at Athens on the attention of the constitutional historian; this is, that it is a class with rights. The master might not put his slave to death;[1] there is some evidence that his brutal treatment necessitated an enforced sale;[2] while an assault on a slave by a third party was an offence against the criminal law.[3] Here, as in Greek states generally, the theory that the slave as a chattel could not be the subject of rights was not rigorously pressed, and the state interfered with private ownership where the thing owned was also a person.

The large class of resident aliens, calculated as forty-five thousand for the fifth and fourth centuries, was the sign of the prosperity and liberalism of a great commercial state. It was composed partly of emancipated slaves (ἀπελεύθεροι or ἐξελεύθεροι), but chiefly of free strangers (ξένοι) residing in Attica. The slave might be freed in three ways—by the state, by his master, or by ransoming himself, although we do not know whether, in this last case, his master was obliged to free him if he presented the requisite money. After emancipation he owed certain duties to his former lord, whom he was obliged to take as patron (προστάτης). A failure to do this subjected him to the δίκη ἀποστασίου, defeat in which meant slavery, and victory freedom.[4] The stranger could not reside in Attica longer than a certain time without enrolling himself as a μέτοικος. In public and private law he was represented by a patron, a failure to choose one exposing him to the δίκη ἀπροστασίου,[5] the loss of which involved the confiscation of his property. The privileges

---

[1] Antiphon *de caed. Herod.* 8.
[2] Pollux viii. 13. The slave had, under certain conditions, the right πρᾶσιν αἰτεῖν.
[3] Hyper. ap. Athenae. p. 266 f.
[4] Harpocrat. *s.v.*
[5] *ib. s.v.* ᾑρεῖτο γὰρ ἕκαστος ἑαυτῷ τῶν πολιτῶν τινα προστησόμενον περὶ πάντων τῶν ἰδίων καὶ τῶν κοινῶν.

of residence possessed by the metoecs were sometimes extended by special grants, such as immunity from their special tax (ἀτέλεια), ownership of the soil in Attica, and access to the council and the ecclesia (πρόσοδος πρὸς τὴν βουλὴν καὶ τὸν δῆμον). But their burdens were greater than those of the citizens, for, besides the recurring pecuniary duties of the λειτουργίαι and the occasional εἰσφορά, they paid a special tax for their protection (μετοίκιον). Their military importance was due chiefly to their service on the fleet, but those of the requisite census had the privilege of serving as hoplites.

All these classes which we have considered are connected, by inclusion or exclusion, with the private law-divisions of the state, the phratries and the clans. A brief notice must now be given of certain divisions of the tribes which are said to have been, from the first, of political importance. These are the three τρίττυες and the twelve ναυκραρίαι into which each of the Ionic tribes was divided.

The full significance of the trittys is not known, but probably it always had some close connection with the military levy.[1] The old arrangement which connected it with the Ionic tribe disappeared before the reforms of Cleisthenes. The thirty τριττύες which he instituted, although primarily meant to serve a temporary purpose,[2] were probably permanent, and had a strictly local character, which is reflected in such names of these divisions as have been preserved.[3]

The naucraries, although known to us chiefly in connection with Solon's reforms, existed long before the date of that legislator, for their presidents (πρυτάνεις) are mentioned as taking part in the suppression of the conspiracy of Cylon (*circ.* 628).[4] How their distinctly local character was brought into relation with the four Ionic tribes we do not know; it is more easily understood after Cleisthenes had raised their number from forty-eight to fifty,[5] for the purpose of division amongst his ten local tribes. They were administrative centres found and utilised by two successive legislators. Solon employed them for purposes of taxation;[6] under Cleisthenes they still retained what was probably their

---

[1] τριττυαρχεῖν signifies some subordinate kind of military command (Plat. *Resp.* p. 415).
[2] *Ath. Pol.* 21.
[3] Such as Κεραμῆς, Ἐλεύσινοι, Μυρρινούσιοι, Ἐπακριεῖς. [4] Her. v. 71.
[5] Cleidemus ap. Phot. *s.v.*
[6] *Ath. Pol.* 8.

oldest function—the supply of a ship each to the Athenian navy.[1]

These state-divisions have little historical interest apart from their antiquity, for they are clearly the arbitrary creations of a central government. But the fact of this early centralisation is itself of some importance, and the naucraries with their presidents or ναύκραροι, officials partly financial, partly military, show an attempt at local administration which foreshadows the elaborate deme-organisation of later times.

§ 2 *The political Development of Athens—the Magistracy and the Council*

The early history of Attica consists mainly in the change from monarchy to aristocracy. Several lines of kings had held power in turn. First came monarchs of the Theseid family; then, about the time of the Dorian migration, these were replaced by an immigrant race of Pylians under Melanthus. For many generations these Melanthidae, Codridae, or Medontidae, as they are indifferently called from the first three successive names in the dynasty, continued to hold power until the inevitable change came, which tradition puts in the year 752. The monarchy was not abolished, as in many contemporary states of Greece, but was altered, we are told, into a presidency tenable for ten years.[2] This decennial kingship was still kept within the family of the Medontidae, and it is probable that these rulers still bore the title βασιλεῖς. But another juristic tradition, strangely interwoven with this, states that even in the time of the life-monarchy the power of the king had been limited by the introduction of the collegiate principle. At the outset of the rule of the Medontidae two other "first and highest offices"[3] were established to limit the power of the βασιλεύς. First a πολέμαρχος was appointed as the assessor of an unwarlike king. Then the civil office of ὁ ἄρχων was instituted; and these three functionaries continued to exist side by side—a life-

[1] Thus the Athenian fleet at the time of the war with Aegina consisted of fifty ships (Her. vi. 89).

[2] Paus. iv. 5, 10.

[3] *Ath. Pol.* 3 μέγισται καὶ πρῶται τῶν ἀρχῶν. Some traditions carried back the military assessor to the Erechtheid period (cf. Her. viii. 44); the office of ὁ ἄρχων was attributed by some to the reign of Medon, by others to that of his successor Acastus.

king without the shadow of power unwillingly assisted by two (apparently temporary) assessors. The office of Archon, originally the lowest of the three posts, in the course of years became the highest, and its holder the ἐπώνυμος of the year. The assessors are no doubt pictured as being also chosen from the royal clan. It was not until 712 that the supreme power was thrown open to all the Eupatrids. In the year 683 a double change occurred which completed the development: six θεσμοθέται[1] were added to the existing ἀρχαί, and the tenure of office became annual.

It is idle to speculate minutely on this tradition, especially on that part of it which deals with the limited life-kingship. We can only say that with some modifications (especially of date) it would show an historically possible and not unnatural development. It shows us the monarchy stripped first, unlike the Spartan, of its military powers, and later on divested of its civil authority, and remaining a mere religious presidency with powers of religious jurisdiction. It shows us further that, in the course of the secularisation of the state, the powers of the purely civil magistrate develop, as in the early history of the Ephors at Sparta, and "the Archon" becomes the highest magistrate of the city. When this stage was reached, the administrative functions of state were divided amongst a college of nine, although merely routine duties were originally assigned to the added six, and the civil, military, and religious presidency was still in the hands of the original three. The board is not properly a college, for functions are distributed among its members, and it is doubtful whether these magistrates bore a common official name.[2] The members of the board constituted in 683 were called officially by their special titles, and the title "Archon" was applied strictly only to the president.

The executive and judicial powers of this president must have been enormous at a time when Athens possessed but an ill-organised assembly (probably dependent on the summons of the magistrate), no executive council, no written law but a few recorded utterances until the time of Draco, and no audit from the popular courts. A guarantee against abuse of authority

---

[1] According to the *Ath. Pol.* (*l.c.*) they are not officials who give judgment, but who record and preserve judicial decisions (θέσμια).

[2] The existence of a πρυτανεῖον and πρυτανεῖα is no evidence that they were ever called πρυτάνεις.

was found in the separation of the military from the civil powers and in the existence of the council of Elders, which, though it did not interfere with the Archon's civil jurisdiction, must have held him responsible for his administrative acts.

But the importance of the office, even after Solon had limited its power, is illustrated by the incident of the attempted usurpation of Damasias. It was apparently an attempt to make the office perpetual; he was chosen Archon for two years in succession (probably in 586 and 585), and was then only deposed from office by violence. In consequence of this attempt a new principle of election to the archonship was introduced. It was enacted that ten Archons should be appointed, five to be chosen from the Eupatrids, three from the ἄγροικοι (*i.e.* the Geomori), and two from the Demiurgi. This change was of no importance in the development of the constitution, since it seems to have lasted but one year (584); but its details show something more than the result of a mere personal struggle for supremacy. The institution of ten Archons, chosen half from the Eupatrids or nobles and half from the two other non-noble classes, has been thought to show a compromise between the patrician and plebeian elements in the state.[1] Such a class struggle would explain the στάσις and the ἀναρχία which are mentioned as twice preventing election to the archonship before the attempt of Damasias.[2] The chief importance of the incident, as treated by the authority who hands it down to us, is that it shows the great and forgotten power which once centred in the person of "the Archon."

But the decline of the archonship was inherent in the constitution of Solon, for the popular courts which he instituted tended inevitably to lessen its power. The development of the jury system reduced the judicial functions of the board of nine to little more than those of mere preliminary investigation (ἀνάκρισις) and the mere formal guidance of the court (ἡγεμονία δικαστηρίου). Their administrative duties, with the exception of the military leadership of the Polemarch which for a time continued, became merely duties of routine, and the archonship ceased to be one of the great magistracies of the state.

We must now consider a question which in its ultimate

---

[1] H. Sidgwick in *Classical Review* vol. viii. n. 8.
[2] *Ath. Pol.* 13. For the possible combinations by which the date of Damasias has been variously fixed see Sandys' ed. of *Ath. Pol.* p. 49.

bearings is perhaps the most important in Athenian public law, although its treatment at this point will necessarily lead us to anticipate some of the reforms of Solon and Cleisthenes. The question is that of appointment to office. We are told that in the "ancient constitution" which existed before the time of Draco "they appointed the magistrates with reference to birth and wealth,"[1] which apparently means merely that officials were chosen from the Eupatrids who were the owners of the soil. We do not know whether this is meant to apply to the supposed assessors of the βασιλεύς either before or after the decennial limitation of the monarchy; the head of the state religion (the βασιλεύς himself) might have been selected by the sacred ceremony of the lot; but election is meant to be predicated of the archonship after 683. As to the electors of this period, the *Constitution of Athens* conjecturally assigns the appointment of magistrates at this time to the Areiopagus.[2] This body was, as we shall see, probably the only original council at Athens, and there is nothing strange in this power having been possessed by the aristocratic assembly of the state before the proper organisation of the ecclesia. If we decline to recognise the Draconian constitution embodied in this Aristotelian treatise,[3] this system may have continued to the time of Solon. Then a new principle was introduced—one that has sometimes been thought an anachronism, but that is really eminently characteristic of the whole Solonian system. It was a principle of direct election modified by the use of the lot, which was now perhaps becoming divested of its religious character and beginning to be applied as a mere political institution. Each of the tribes selected ten of its members, and from the whole forty the nine Archons were chosen by lot.[4] This is the mode of appointment which Aristotle describes as common to oligarchy and democracy,[5] one therefore eminently befitting the professedly mixed type of this constitution. Solon retained the elective principle previously existing,[6] but modified it in a way which combined a demand for fitness with an

---

[1] ἀριστίνδην καὶ πλουτίνδην, *Ath. Pol.* 3.
[2] *ib.* 8.
[3] *ib.* 4.
[4] *ib.* 8. A reminiscence of this mode of appointment is found in Isocr. *Panath.* § 145.
[5] *Pol.* ii. 6.
[6] Arist. *Pol.* ii. 12 ἔοικε δὲ Σόλων (this is probably Aristotle's own opinion) ἐκεῖνα μὲν ὑπάρχοντα πρότερον οὐ καταλῦσαι, τήν τε βουλὴν (*i.e.* the Areiopagus) καὶ τὴν τῶν ἀρχῶν αἵρεσιν.

assertion of partial equality between the members of the circle from which the Archons were chosen. An accidental consequence of this mixed system was that the two stages of election were still preserved even after the lot had become the sole principle of appointment in both.[1]

At this point we may naturally raise the question, "What is the meaning of this new element in political life which was destined to become almost the most characteristic feature of the Athenian and other democracies?" From the treatment of the lot by Plato and Aristotle we should be inclined to gather that it was a consciously adopted democratic institution,[2] that it was the final assertion of the numerical equality of all citizens and of the principle of equal representation. But to realise this character it must be accompanied by universal admission to office. We know, however, that the use of the lot preceded universal admission; we shall see, when we come to discuss the qualifications for office, that in early Athens it was an assertion of the equal fitness for rule of the members of only a narrow circle; and we are further informed that in some cases of its employment it had other meanings than that of an assertion of equality. It was sometimes adopted as the final solution of a difficulty—in the case, for instance, of equality of votes.[3] Here it is a mere appeal to chance, as in Homeric times it was an appeal to heaven. In the state of Heraea the lot was introduced as a means of avoiding the bribery and canvassing which accompanied direct election.[4] But, though it was a political expedient that might be applied with other objects, we must regard its use as being, on the whole, in the highest and purest sense democratic. A low view of democracy as the right of a majority to rule, such as had begun to be entertained at Athens in the fourth century, might justify Isocrates' assertion that the direct election of magistrates is more favourable to popular government than their selection by lot.[5] For under the former system the people choose their own representatives, under the latter chance will rule and the oligarchically minded sometimes slip into the government of the state. But true democracy is the assertion of the equal representation of all individuals, classes, and interests; and there is much to be said for the view that the effect of the lot

---

[1] *Ath. Pol. l.c.*
[2] The idea is as old as Herodotus (iii. 80).
[3] Arist. *Pol.* vi. 3 = p. 1318 a.
[4] *ib.* v. 3 = p. 1303 a.
[5] Isocr. *Areop.* § 23.

at Athens was the protection of the rights of minorities,[1] although we cannot admit that this was the primary motive for its introduction. There is abundant evidence that the lot existed at Athens before the constitution could be described as democratic;[2] but, in the developed democracy, its employment was a guarantee that all offices should not be swamped by the triumphant majority of the moment. It was a standing protest against that party government which the Greek thinker knew to be the deadliest enemy of liberty, and at which, as realised in the pseudo-democracies of America and England, the true Greek democrat would have stood aghast.

Next to the question of its meaning comes that of its justification as a working principle. We must here distinguish its employment as a mode of appointment to individual offices like the archonship, or to small corporations like the financial boards, on the one hand, and the faculty of admission it gave to large administrative bodies such as the council of five hundred on the other. In the former cases there seems a greater danger of lack of fitness or of maladministration. For in large bodies gifted with the power of discussion and debate the aristocracy of intellect is certain to prevail; the decisions of the council at Athens were often those of a Cleon or an Androcles; and its constitution does not need as its justification the modern thesis that "on general questions the votes of forty academicians are not better than the votes of an equal number of water-carriers,"[3] for the lot admitted men of every grade of intellect. In the case of smaller bodies at Athens the danger of the lack of the intellectual element was met by the routine nature of their duties and the constant direction of the ecclesia, of the lack of the moral element by the scrutiny before admission (δοκιμασία) and the rigorous examination of conduct after quitting office (εὔθυνα). This created an individual responsibility which was demanded even of members of as large a body as the council. Where special knowledge was required, as in the στρατηγία or the great finance offices of the fourth century, the lot was not employed. It was a misfortune that in one sphere at least where special knowledge would have been desirable, the law-courts, it was recognised as the

[1] Müller-Strübing *Aristophanes* p. 206.
[2] To the passages in the *Ath. Pol.* we may add Plut. *Arist.* 1, *Per.* 9.
[3] Le Bon *Psychologie des Foules*.

universal principle of admission. In these courts there was no debate, and therefore no intellectual guidance, and this is the weak point of the Athenian system.

Some details are given by the *Constitution of Athens* as to the steps by which this development was attained. The use of the lot seems to have ceased with the despotism of Peisistratus,[1] for it was inconsistent with his personal appointment to office, and it was not resumed by Cleisthenes. Under his constitution the Archons were directly elected, perhaps by the ecclesia. It was not until the year 487 that the lot was reinstituted after the Solonian model. The posts were now allotted amongst previously elected candidates (πρόκριτοι), five hundred in all (fifty from each of the ten Cleisthenean tribes), chosen by the members of the demes, a certain number being apparently elected from each deme.[2] We do not know when the lot pure and simple was introduced, but there finally grew up, probably in the middle of the fifth century, the practice which is described as existing in the fourth, the lot being applied first tribally and secondly to the candidates so selected from the tribes.

Almost equal in importance to the history of the mode of election would be that of the qualification for what long continued to be the highest office in the state. But unfortunately we have no credible information as to the conditions required for holding the archonship while it still remained a power. The little that is known of the prae-Solonian system has been already told. Solon's constitution recognised a timocratic qualification based on land, and the archonship was apparently restricted to the highest class in the census, that of the πεντακοσιομέδιμνοι, or possessors of land which produced an income of five hundred medimni.[3] It is not known how long this qualification continued in force, or whether the second class, the ἱππεῖς, were admitted before 479. But in this year the democratic fervour which was the result of the victory over the Persians induced a radical change, and the whole basis of the property-qualification was altered. A decree of the people, introduced

---

[1] *Ath. Pol.* 22 ; Thuc. vi. 54.

[2] *Ath. Pol.* 22. When in c. 62 it is said that originally the κληρωταὶ ἀρχαί associated with the archonship were ἐκ τῆς φυλῆς ὅλης κληρούμενοι, we may perhaps understand that in the allotment of office each of the ten tribes supplied one or more officials (*e.g.* the nine Archons and their secretary, the boards of ten or thirty).

[3] *ib.* 8.

by Aristeides, changed the land census into a census of all property.[1] The principle which Sparta cherished to the last—that the citizen should be a land-owner—was abolished for nearly every office of state;[2] the special privileges of the landed aristocracy were swept away; and the rich trader, who would previously have been relegated to the lowest rank of θῆτες could now perform the high ceremonial functions of the archonship. Yet poverty still continued to be a bar to office, and it was not until 457 that the third class of ζευγῖται, the possessors of an annual revenue worth two hundred drachmae, were admitted.[3] The lowest class of θῆτες, whose income was under this sum, were never legally qualified for the archonship at any period of Athenian history down to the close of the fourth century. This disability must have been a mere oversight of the constitution, for the thetes were admitted by the transparent legal fiction of never being expected to declare their own incapacity.[4] It is valuable to learn from this recorded fiction that even in a Greek state the practice sometimes outstripped the legal theory.

From the magistracy we pass to the council, a belief in whose early existence is expressed in the view that even the life-monarchy of the Medontidae was a "responsible" office.[5] Many different efforts have been made to find in our records a suitable body of Eupatrids. The council has been variously identified with the three hundred members of this class who tried the Alcmaeonidae at the time of the conspiracy of Cylon,[6] and with the "presidents of the naucraries" whose activity is mentioned in connection with the same event.[7] But the first-named body, although by a strange coincidence their number reappears in the three hundred partisans of Isagoras, the aristocratic opponent of Cleisthenes,[8] may have been but a temporary

[1] This hypothesis is the only mode of reconciling the statement of Plutarch (*Arist.* 22) that Aristeides made the πολιτεία "common" to all, and threw the archonship open to every citizen with the system of gradual admission described in the *Ath. Pol.*

[2] In later times an Athenian strategus had to own land in Attica, but this was a guarantee of good faith.

[3] The *Ath. Pol.* (c. 7) proves that this was the census of the zeugitae, as against the conclusion drawn by Böckh from Demosth. *c. Macart.* pp. 1067-8, that it was 150 medimni or (in terms of the post-Aristeidean assessment) drachmae.

[4] *Ath. Pol.* 7. On the question being put as to the candidate's census οὐδ' ἂν εἰς εἴποι θητικόν.

[5] Paus. iv. 5 ἀντὶ βασιλείας μετέστησεν ἐς ἀρχὴν ὑπεύθυνον.

[6] Plut. *Sol.* 12 τριακόσιοι ἀριστίνδην δικάζοντες.

[7] Her. v. 71.

[8] *ib.* v. 72.

board of judges ; the latter were apparently military officials to whom was entrusted the siege of the acropolis on the occasion of Cylon's *coup d'état*. A third tendency, which is probably correct, is to identify the council with the Areiopagus. A belief in the antiquity of this body is expressed in the tradition that the Messenians, before their first war with Sparta, offered to refer the question in dispute either to the amphictyony of Argos or to the Areiopagus at Athens.[1] One authority brings the partisans of Cylon before this body,[2] and the *Constitution of Athens* (doubtful as its evidence is for all prae-Solonian history) lends weight to the view that there was no other original council of Athens.

But before entering on the history of the Areiopagus it is necessary, for reasons which will be soon apparent, to touch on that of a body of equal, if not of greater antiquity, whose early existence as a corporate body is assured. This is the board of Ephetae (ἐφέται), the earliest mention of whom occurs in a law of Draco, a fragment of which has been preserved,[3] although it is not probable that they were first instituted by this legislator. They formed a board of fifty-one members, over fifty years of age and chosen from the Eupatrids.[4] Their name seems to be derived from their judicial function as "referees" in cases of homicide,[5] and may have been gained after their employment by Draco for what proved to be the most permanent of his reforms—the amendment of the law of homicide which was incorporated by Solon into his legislation. Previously to Draco the practice of private vengeance and of compensation had prevailed, and vast powers were permitted to the family associations to which the slain man had belonged, especially to the phratry, to which in the last resort belonged the duty of pursuing the slayer. In the case of involuntary homicide the phrators seem to have had the power of refusing satisfaction by compromise or of settling the terms of the compromise themselves. This power was lessened by the rule that "if the Ephetae decide that the homicide was involuntary, ten of the phrators shall be chosen, if they please, and with them the Ephetae shall compromise the matter.[6] But it is also

[1] Paus. iv. 5.
[2] Schol. Aristoph. *Equites* 1. 443.
[3] Hicks n. 59.
[4] Photius *s.v.*; Pollux viii. 125.
[5] Suggested by Photius and given by Pollux (*ll. cc.*) Lange and Gilbert derive the name from οἱ ἐπὶ ταῖς ἔταις, "those set over the clanbrethren."
[6] Hicks *l.c.*

possible that before Draco's time no distinction had been drawn between different kinds of slaying, between wilful murder and accidental or justifiable homicide. This distinction existed under Draco's legislation in connection with the various courts on which the Ephetae sat.[1] At the Palladium were adjudged cases of involuntary homicide; at the Delphinium were held the trials of persons declaring that the homicide they had committed was justifiable; at the Prytaneium inanimate objects which had slain a man were brought to justice; while at the Phreattys "exiles against whom a second charge was brought made their defence from shipboard to judges sitting on the land," in order to avoid the pollution of the soil. The fifth court for the trial of wilful murder was the Areiopagus, and, unless by this is meant merely the locality, it seems inevitable that we should to some extent identify the Ephetae with the council of that name. After Solon the two certainly became distinct, and it is true that in a retrospect contained in one of Solon's laws[2] the Areiopagus and the Ephetae are mentioned as two distinct bodies; but the opposition here is merely formal, the latter word standing for "the other courts," and the true conclusion may be that the Ephetae did form the bulk of the original Areiopagus.

This body appears, like the Spartan Gerousia, both as a council and as a court; and the name of its place of meeting, "the hill of curses" (ἀραί), is in harmony with its sombre functions of criminal jurisdiction. We can only guess at its original composition. One of the latest theories on the subject of its probable constitution, that of Lange and Gilbert, is a development of a hint given by the Attic historian Philochorus that the council was composed of the nine Archons and the fifty-one Ephetae.[3] That it was constituted through the archonship alone, and filled with present and past holders of that office—a theory favoured by the *Constitution of Athens*[4]—is far less probable; for it is not likely that even after 683 it so

---

[1] Paus. i. 28; *Ath. Pol.* 57.
[2] Plut. *Sol.* 19. Disfranchised persons were to be restored to their civic privileges πλὴν ὅσοι ἐξ Ἀρείου πάγου ἢ ὅσοι ἐκ τῶν ἐφετῶν . . . καταδικασθέντες . . . ἐπὶ φόνῳ ἢ σφαγαῖσιν . . . ἔφευγον ὅτε ὁ θεσμὸς ἐφάνη ὅδε. Sandys (*Aristotle's Const. of Athens* p. 214) thinks that φόνος refers to trials before the Areiopagus, σφαγαί to those before the Ephetae.

[3] Philochorus 58 (*Fragm. Hist. Graec.* i. 394). Both the constituent elements are here mentioned, but they are separated in time.

[4] *Ath. Pol.* 3.

immediately lost its independent character of a βουλὴ γερόντων. The college of nine may have always formed a portion of the body, but other members it must have had, and these may have been the Ephetae. When Solon is said to have "set the Areiopagus before the Ephetae," the meaning may be that he eliminated these additional members, composing the council exclusively of Archons and ex-Archons—a theory which explains Plutarch's apparent belief that it was Solon who first made the archonship a stepping-stone to the Areiopagus. His further statement that "most people"[1] attributed the very creation of this assembly to Solon is particularly valuable as showing that there could have been little evidence for its constitution or its powers before that time, even though its previous existence might be proved by its mention in one of Solon's laws. The attempt at reconstruction made by the author of the *Constitution of Athens* is characterised by greater boldness than success. The Areiopagus, as it was known at a somewhat later date, is carried back to a time for which there was no direct evidence; the account throws little light either on its original constitution or on the growth of its powers, and refers to a period earlier than Draco certain vaguely-defined prerogatives which Plutarch, following other authorities, refers to Solon.

The functions which tradition assigned to the early Areiopagus are as various as they are vague. Besides the elective powers which we have already noticed, it makes it the chief administrative body,[2] credits it with a guardianship of the ordinances of the state,[3] with an autocratic censorial authority over the lives of the citizens, and, after the time of Draco, with a power of enforcing, and apparently revising, the laws.[4] These powers reappear, almost in precisely the same forms, in the Solonian Areiopagus, that reformer either investing it with or allowing it to retain a general oversight of the whole state and the guardianship of the laws, together with censorial functions which extended to an inquisitorial examination into the means of livelihood of particular citizens. An added power, connected

---

[1] οἱ πλεῖστοι, *Sol.* 19.
[2] *Ath. Pol.* 3. Yet, at the time of the conspiracy of Cylon (*circ.* 628), Thucydides (i. 126) makes the nine Archons, Herodotus (v. 71) apparently the prytanies of the naucraries, the chief administrative power.
[3] *Ath. Pol.* 3 τὴν μὲν τάξιν εἶχε τοῦ διατηρεῖν τοὺς νόμους.
[4] *Ath. Pol.* 4 ἐξῆν δὲ τῷ ἀδικουμένῳ πρὸς τὴν τῶν Ἀρεοπαγιτῶν βουλὴν εἰσαγγέλλειν, ἀποφαίνοντι παρ' ὃν ἀδικεῖται νόμον.

with its guardianship of the laws but created by Solon, was that of protecting the constitution against traitors; and it not only took the initiatory steps, but originally exercised jurisdiction in such cases of treason.[1] Besides these functions we may safely attribute to the Areiopagus the powers which it is found to possess in later times, even after its authority had been curtailed. Its guardianship of the sacred olive groves, known from a speech of Lysias,[2] is probably but one instance of a general power of inspection over the *cultus* of the community; while even in the fourth century the choice of an advocate to plead a religious cause before the amphictyony of Delphi was entrusted to this body.[3] The criminal jurisdiction, which it still retained and never lost, covered cases of murder, wounding, poisoning, and arson.[4]

This summary is sufficient to show that the Areiopagus was a great power in the state, and the new mode of its constitution made it tend to become a still greater power. Nine Archons passed into it each year,[5] and it would thus become a large body, yet not so large as to be unwieldy. In the Areiopagus of the Solonian constitution we have a dignified self-existent council, charged with a great trust and gifted with exceptional powers, receiving annually the highest officials of the state, and capable, it seems, of rejecting unworthy members from its body.[6] The tenure of office was for life, and though at a later period we find that the Areiopagites could be called to account, like other Athenian magistrates, before the popular courts [7] (at what intervals of time we do not know), yet at this early period they may have been irresponsible. The power of the council and its dominant position in the state are shown by the fact that the struggle which ended in the full assertion of the Athenian democracy, is represented as a struggle between the authority of the Areiopagus and the rising power of the demos. Aristotle sums up the situation when he tells us that "the reputation gained by the Areiopagus in the Persian Wars seemed to tighten

---

[1] *Ath. Pol.* 8 καὶ τοὺς ἐπὶ καταλύσει τοῦ δήμου συνισταμένους ἔκρινεν, Σόλωνος θέντ[ος] νόμον (? εἰσαγγελίας) περὶ αὐτῶν.

[2] Lys. περὶ τοῦ σηκοῦ.

[3] Dem. *de Cor.* § 134.

[4] *Ath. Pol.* 57; Lysias *de caed. Eratosth.* § 30.

[5] It was composed of ex-Archons (Plut. *Sol.* 19), and according to one account, in the fourth century, of the Archons of the year as well (Lysias περὶ τοῦ σηκοῦ § 22).

[6] There is evidence of a special δοκιμασία of incoming members before the Areiopagus itself, even for the fourth century (Athenae. p. 566 f).

[7] Aesch. *c. Ctes.* § 20.

the reins of government, while on the other hand the victory of Salamis, which was gained by the common people who served in the fleet and won for the Athenians the empire of the sea, strengthened the democracy."[1] The more detailed narrative[2] informs us that, after the Persian Wars, the Areiopagus grew in strength and "governed the city," basing this supremacy on no "act of state" (δόγμα), but simply on the reputation it had gained by its conduct of affairs before the battle of Salamis, and that this hegemony lasted for seventeen years (479-462). A *de facto* hegemony of this kind possessed by a council is generally based on a moral control exercised over individual magistrates. The difficulty is to understand how this control was extended over the popular bodies, the ecclesia and the heliaea; for the entire dependence of the popular assemblies on the magistrates, which guaranteed the Senate's ascendency at Rome, seems to have been lacking in the Athens even of this period. The control exercised by the council must have been more direct and the vague powers, with which it is originally credited—the guardianship of the law and the direction of the magistrate—must now, strained to their uttermost, have seemed new prerogatives,[3] and have overshadowed every department of the state. The people might decide, but the Areiopagus might revoke its decision, or impede the magistrate in carrying it into effect. Yet, even in the very year when the council had gained its new power, Aristeides had carried the reform which undermined the influence of the landed aristocracy; and eminently suited as the government of this council was for the active imperial organisation of the next few years, it was doomed as soon as its efficiency came to be doubted or its necessity failed to be realised. The challenge came in 462 from Ephialtes "the incorruptible," the first great demagogue of Athens, who crowned a successful career of criticism and impeachment of Areiopagites and high officials with the destruction of the one barrier which impeded the free march of the demos. By his side stood Pericles, still a tiro in politics, but a recognised adherent of the party of progress.[4] The result of the revolution effected by

[1] *Pol.* v. 4 = p. 1304 a.
[2] *Ath. Pol.* 23, 25.
[3] They are spoken of as "acquired powers" (ἐπίθετα) (*Ath. Pol.* 25).
[4] Arist. *Pol.* ii. 12; Plut. *Per.* 7; *Ath. Pol.* 25, 27. Themistocles, introduced by the *Ath. Pol.* as the supporter of Ephialtes, has been eliminated from the narrative, in accordance with the usually accepted chronology of Thucydides (i. 136-137).

the two reformers was to force the Areiopagus from its unconstitutional position as the *de facto* head of the state, and to strip it of certain of its legal powers—its guardianship of the law, its control of the magistrates, and probably its censorial functions. The council still retained its criminal jurisdiction and its power of religious supervision. The protection of the state against treasonable designs, with which Solon had entrusted it, continued to be exercised in a modified form. The council had the right of making a revelation or statement (ἀπόφασις) to the people concerning some danger with which it believed the state to be threatened. Here its duty might end, and the case might be tried in one of the popular courts; but it is probable that the people sometimes entrusted the Areiopagus with the process.[1]

As a political power the council was dead, but its past was not wholly forgotten, and the very grimness of the associations connected with the ancient council which sat on the seat of the Furies and wiped out the stain of blood kept alive a reverence for it in the popular mind, of which party leaders like Demosthenes were not slow to avail themselves when it suited their political purposes. Throughout the latter part of the fifth century we scarcely hear of it; but with the more self-centred politics of the fourth century it again becomes something of a power. Social distinctions were then more keenly felt than they had been at the time when the whole state was straining every nerve to retain an empire. And the Areiopagus was a social power, composed as it was almost exclusively of distinguished and wealthy citizens; for the poorer classes did not often present themselves for the unremunerative office of Archon. In the last days of Athenian independence it throws in its weight with the propertied classes, who lean on Macedon, and opposes the irreconcilables, who clamour for war. The assembly, which in its prime had helped to save Greece from the Persians, recognised in its old age that resistance was useless, and that the independent city-state was a thing of the past.

Our account of the development of the original constituent elements of the state has left Athens with a magistracy almost annihilated and a council crushed. Let us now observe the

---

[1] The most extreme case is that of the traitor Antiphon, accused of a plot to burn the Athenian docks (Dem. *de Cor.* § 133). The Areiopagus also investigated the case of the bribery of Harpalus (Deinarch. *c. Demosth.* §§ 82 ff.), which it sent before a δικαστήριον.

processes which enabled the popular bodies to be a substitute for these vanished authorities.

§ 3 *Epochs of Constitutional Reform at Athens*

The earliest movements of the demos at Athens were prompted by two pressing dangers—the arbitrary character of the Eupatrid government and the economic distress of the time. It is difficult to say which of these evils pressed hardest; but the first was more easily met than the second, and reform was first mooted in the shape of a demand for the publication of a code; the rules according to which Eupatrid judges decided were to be known, and the penalties of the criminal law to be fixed. The demand was met by the publication of the laws by Draco (*circ.* 621)[1]—a mighty work, of which only a fragment, embodying a reform which we have already discussed, has been preserved. The elaborate civil code of Solon superseded this Eupatrid law, and what may have been Draco's sole change—the new law of homicide— alone survives to mark the work of the legislator. It is true that an almost certainly spurious record[2] attributes to Draco, and even partly to times preceding him, a constitution of a curiously artificial character—a timocracy which recognised the rule of the middle class, with a magistracy partly elected partly chosen by lot, with an assembly attendance at which was enforced by fines, and a council the members of which were chosen in rotation from the qualified citizens. But these prophetic anticipations of the political refinements of a later age have with justice been regarded as a political forgery, originating perhaps in the reforms contemplated at the close of the fifth century: the work of men who wished to get even behind Cleisthenes, the darling of the moderate oligarch, and by appealing to the name of Draco to enlist authority if not sympathy on the side of a partial subversion of the Athenian democracy.

The structure of a constitution, on a carefully-laid-out plan, is first found in the work of Solon (*circ.* 594). But the economic evils of the time were such that the ground had to be carefully prepared before the first stone of the structure

[1] Arist. *Pol.* ii. 12; *Ath. Pol.* 41.   [2] *Ath. Pol.* 4.

could be laid. Solon bears a double character. He was, in the first place, a "corrector" (διορθωτής) called on to abolish certain temporary evils, or, regarded as an intermediary between certain opposing classes of the population, he might, from this point of view, be spoken of as a "reconciler" (διαλλακτής). In the second place, he is the framer of a constitution (νομοθέτης).[1] It is with this second character that we are chiefly concerned, but his social reforms have such an important political bearing that they demand some notice. The agrarian question which he came to solve seems to have originated with the abuse of a system of *métayer* tenure, which worked ill in a country so little fitted by nature for a purely agricultural life as Attica. The land which was not the immediate domain of the Eupatrid families and worked by their slaves, was occupied by tenants who were in a position neither of clientship nor of serfdom, but whose dependence on a lord was marked by their payment to him of one-sixth of the produce of their farms;[2] otherwise these πελάται or ἐκτημόριοι were free, and their allotments were heritable within the clan, though not capable of alienation without it. But a bad harvest put the farmer at the mercy of his landlord, debts were incurred on the security of the persons of the debtor and of his family, the tenants became serfs or were sold out of the country, and mortgage-pillars (ὅροι) marking the debt sprang up everywhere on the farmers' lands. Solon seems to have found but one means of meeting the difficulty—the heroic measure of a cancelling of all debts (χρεῶν ἀποκοπή), whether owed to individuals or to the state, accompanied by a prohibition against lending on the security of the person.[3] This was the famous *seisachtheia*, which removed the burdens from the bodies of the masses, and was the first step in the establishment of a popular constitution in which their minds might have free play. The next preliminary was a work of amnesty, taking the form of a restoration of civic rights to classes of citizens who had lost them. Solon cancelled all decrees of ἀτιμία except in the case of those who had been condemned for murder, homicide, or an attempt at tyranny.[4]

[1] διορθωτὴν καὶ νομοθέτην (Plut. *Sol.* 16); διαλλακτὴν καὶ ἄρχοντα (*Ath. Pol.* 5).

[2] Another explanation makes the ἐκτημόριοι pay five-sixths; but that a family could have lived off one-sixth of the produce of its land in a country so barren as Attica is incredible.

[3] *Ath. Pol.* 6.

[4] p. 144, note 2.

The constitution which he then proceeded to frame cannot be defined in simple terms. It wore the external appearance of a landed timocracy, for, though it is doubtful whether Solon first instituted, or merely availed himself of, the division of the citizens into the four classes of pentacosiomedimni, hippeis, zeugitae, and thetes, he at any rate first made them the basis of political life by making membership of them a requisite condition for holding office. As the census was estimated wholly on landed property,[1] there is some justification for the statement that Solon wished to leave the offices of state "as they were," *i.e.* to the rich proprietors of the land;[2] but the preservation of a wide circle of holders of office may possibly be the meaning of the law mentioned by Aristotle,[3] "prohibiting an individual from possessing as much land as he pleased," for every fresh acquisition of land would mean a renewed exclusion of certain citizens from the higher classes, and a timocracy of this kind might, if indiscriminate acquisition were allowed, develop into a narrow oligarchy or δυναστεία—although no doubt this law was also directed to prevent a return to the economic conditions which preceded the seisachtheia. The permanence of these Solonian property-classes is remarkable; they survived the Cleisthenean reforms and continued down (with important bearings on public and private law) late into the fourth century. The census on which they were based was, as we saw,[4] altered, to meet the changing conditions of the time, from an estimate of land to one of all property; and the chief reason for their permanence was that, before the institution of the system of taxation by "symmories" in 378, the census of Solon became the basis for the collection of the extraordinary war-tax (εἰσφορά). When it became so is not known, and no date is assigned for the introduction of the ingenious sliding-scale of taxation by which pentacosiomedimni were assessed on an imaginary capital of a talent (*i.e.* twelve times their income), the hippeis on half a talent (ten times their income), the zeugitae on ten minae (five times their income), and the thetes remained untaxed.[5] But if this system be referred to Solon, it is clear that extraordinary taxation pressed only on land, and that the privileges

---

[1] "In dry and liquid measures," *Ath. Pol.* 7; Plut. *Sol.* 18.
[2] *ib.* 18.
[3] *Pol.* ii. 7.
[4] p. 142.
[5] Pollux viii. 129-130.

of the aristocracy of office were severely balanced by duties. We do indeed find the mention of εἰσφοραί in connection with Solon's system. They were local contributions for local purposes, collected in the naucraries and disbursed by the ναύκραροι, the local officials whom Solon retained for purposes of finance;[1] but whether these dues were akin to the later extraordinary property-tax we do not know.

Primarily, at least, the census was meant to form the basis for admission to office. All our authorities are agreed that only the three higher classes were admitted to ἀρχή, the thetes being admitted to no office but having only a share in the ecclesia and the popular courts;[2] and this word ἀρχή includes membership of the newly-created council, from which the lowest class was also excluded. The office that still stood highest in titular rank, and perhaps in real power, the archonship, was, as we saw, restricted to the pentacosiomedimni; the general result of the new arrangements being, we are told, to leave the chief magistracies in the hands of those who already possessed them, the γνώριμοι and the εὔποροι.[3]

A council of four hundred members was created, one hundred being chosen from each of the four Ionic tribes. We are not told how the appointment to this body was made; there is no anachronism in supposing election by the tribes, since this was employed for the preliminary stage in the selection of Archons; but the members were perhaps selected by lot from the qualified citizens in rotation.[4] The council was of a "probouleutic" character,[5] and its chief, perhaps its only, function was to prepare business for the assembly. We do not know whether it possessed independent powers as an administrative body or the limited jurisdiction of the later βουλή. Its existence seems to imply an extension of the deliberative powers of the ecclesia, which may not have been created, but which must have been increased, by Solon. The probouleutic council of this type is a new thing in Athenian, perhaps in Greek, politics. This permanent deliberative board secured constant and regular meetings for the ecclesia; it was

---

[1] *Ath. Pol.* 8.
[2] Arist. *Pol.* ii. 12; *Ath. Pol.* 7; Pollux viii. 130. Amongst offices the *Ath. Pol.* enumerates the nine Archons, the treasurers, the Poletae, the Eleven, the Colacretae, but does not state the special landed qualifications required for each.
[3] Arist. *Pol.* ii. 12; Plut. *Sol.* 18.
[4] The mode of appointment which the *Ath. Pol.* (4) assigns to the doubtful council of Draco.
[5] Plut. *Sol.* 19.

only a modification of the popular assembly, separated from it by no large gap and with only a slight restrictive qualification for its members. We do not know the nature of the co-operation between the two assemblies, or whether Solon instituted intermediary committees answering to the later πρυτάνεις: it is possible that the Archons, who still possessed considerable executive power, may have been the presidents of both assemblies.

But if the tendency of this reform is democratic, in the next democracy stares us in the face. A criticism preserved in Aristotle's *Politics* is to the effect that "Solon appears to have established the democracy by composing the jury courts (τὰ δικαστήρια) out of all the citizens,"[1] even though he did give what seemed the minimum of power to the people—the power of electing its magistrates and of calling them to account.[2] The function of the courts here characterised as democratic is that of the audit of magistrates, and the judgment is but an illustration of the maxim that the character of a constitution will never correspond to the character of its nominal executive, if judicial functions (including political jurisdiction) are given to another body; for the state will always be swayed by the classes represented in the judicial body. Now this popular judicature of Solon's was something distinct from every other department in the state; it was not even the ecclesia summoned for judicial business, for our authorities assert that Solon created separate courts, chosen from all the citizens and apparently chosen by lot.[3] This plurality need not imply the fixed and permanent panels of the later democracy; it rather suggests groups of citizens summoned and sworn to hear separate appeals from the magistrates. Before these courts the audit of magistrates was from the first conducted, if a special charge was made against their conduct while in office; and thus the procedure was originated for the practice of the later democracy, in which, after the examination of the magistrates' accounts by the λογισταί, and, if necessary, by the higher auditors (εὔθυνοι), the ultimate reference, whether on charges of malversation or abuse of power, was made to a δικαστήριον. If the essence of the "rule of law" is that magistrates are tried before the

---

[1] *Pol.* ii. 12. [2] *ib.* iii. 11.
[3] Arist. *Pol.* ii. 12 (κληρωτὸν ὄν); *Ath. Pol.* 7, 9; Plut. *Sol.* 18.

same courts as ordinary citizens,[1] this rule may be said to have been inaugurated at Athens by Solon. Democracy, as we saw, means, practically though not ideally, the power of criticism and punishment by the masses; this power was exercised at Athens through the popular courts, and by their institution Solon was (perhaps unwittingly) responsible for a startling democratic reform.

The collective aggregate of the people, which assembled in sections for purposes of jurisdiction, was known as the heliaea[2]; in organisation it differed wholly from the ecclesia, but was chiefly distinguished from it as a sworn from an unsworn body, the institution of the heliastic oath being itself referred to Solon.[3] In this respect the Athenian popular courts differed from the *judicia populi* of the Romans, with which they have been compared.[4] In Rome they were simply the ordinary legislative assemblies, the sovereign body gathered to listen to appeals and to exercise their right of pardon. In Athens they cannot be regarded even as committees of the ecclesia, for with the oath they assume a responsible character which makes their members guardians of the constitution even against possible decrees of the assembly, sworn, amongst other things, to preserve the democracy and never to revert to extreme social measures—such as a redivision of the land or the abolition of debts.

The final assertion of the exclusive judicial competence of the people was the result of gradual growth.[5] It sprang from the practice of hearing appeals from the magistrate, who passed in consequence from an independent court into a court of first instance, and finally into an official mainly engaged in conducting the mere preliminaries of a trial. The scope of Solon's reform made this development inevitable; for not only was the appeal applied to civil as well as to criminal cases, but the courts appealed to were apparently from the first interpreters not of the fact only but of the law, and the very obscurity of Solon's legislation was thought to have assisted

---

[1] Dicey *Law of the Constitution* p. 181.
[2] The word ἡλιαία occurs in a law of Solon's quoted by Lysias (κατὰ Θεομνήστου αʹ), the genuineness of which there seems no reason to doubt.
[3] Demosth. *c. Timocr.* pp. 746-47.

Although portions of this oath show a later origin, the very attribution of it to Solon expresses the belief that he constituted the sworn "heliaea."

[4] Plut. *Solonis et Poplicolae comp.* 2.
[5] Arist. *Pol.* ii. 12; *Ath. Pol.* 9; Plut. *Sol.* 18.

the increase of their power. But under his constitution the Archons probably retained considerable powers of independent jurisdiction, and it was some time before their functions degenerated into the mere formal duties of the ἀνάκρισις.[1]

The general verdict of the later Greek world on the Solonian constitution seems to have been that it was intended to be a mixed type of government. Athens for the moment seemed to be a harmonious mixture of oligarchic, aristocratic, and democratic elements; the first was represented by the hardly impaired power of the Areiopagus, the second by the magistracy, the third by the popular courts.[2] Without denying the justice of this general view, Aristotle in the passage of the *Politics* which we have cited finds it an easy task to show that the real tendency of Solon's reforms was in the direction of democracy. The most capable legislator that Greece ever saw found it impossible to frame a mixed constitution the balance of which should be permanent, for his liberalism almost outweighed his capacity. It is true that in the mixed governments of Greece generally the demos was to some extent represented directly or indirectly, yet it never had that singular power of judicial investigation and the scrutiny of public offices which rendered it inevitable that in the long run the other powers of the state should yield to that of the people. "The demos when it is master of the voting pebble becomes master of the constitution," was the verdict of a writer of the close of the fourth century,[3] to whom the retrospect showed the mode in which the democracy of his day had been made. But was this foreseen by Solon, or are we to accuse him of shortsightedness in laboriously building up a complex structure the ruin of which was assured by the disproportionate weight given to one of its component parts? Perhaps he was neither wholly prescient nor wholly blind. The critics of Solon are the critics of change. Greece had seen legislators who had established rigid systems of government which they meant to be permanent, and which they held to be practically, if not ideally, the best; while permanence itself, with the strength and reverence which grow out of the absence of change, was an object of mingled hope and

[1] Suidas *s.v.* ἄρχων. On this subject the *Ath. Pol.* (9) sensibly remarks οὐ γὰρ δίκαιον ἐκ τῶν νῦν γιγνομένων ἀλλ' ἐκ τῆς ἄλλης πολιτείας θεωρεῖν τὴν ἐκείνου βούλησιν.

[2] Plut. *Sol.* 18; Arist. *Pol.* ii. 12.

[3] *Ath. Pol.* 9 κύριος γὰρ ὢν ὁ δῆμος τῆς ψήφου κύριος γίγνεται τῆς πολιτείας.

admiration to the political speculators of Greece. Whether Solon can be called a legislator or a thinker of this type is at least an open question. He gave the people as much power as they could bear, but we have no right to say that, because certain elements in his constitution inevitably led to further political development, this development was wholly unforeseen. He himself represents his reforms as essentially measures of compromise: "I gave the people such power as is sufficient; I threw my strong shield over both parties."[1] Perhaps the power, even as he gave it, was a trifle more than "sufficient," for he was the most liberal legislator that Greece had yet seen. He set Athens politically in advance of other Greek states, while, in place of the restricted country life characteristic of the Athenians up to this time, he was by his commercial legislation the inaugurator of a brisker city life which was one of the chief sources of her further political development. He was, if not the creator of the Athenian democracy, at least the creator of the main conditions which rendered this democracy possible.

But meanwhile, though he had created a liberal government for which some degree of permanence might be hoped through its seemingly even balance of political claims, Solon had omitted to correct certain evils which threatened any constitution in Athens with constant danger. He had attempted by one of his laws[2] to create a national spirit and to do away with the political apathy characteristic of a demos unaccustomed to exert its powers—ineffectually, as was shown by the fact that it was this apathy which rendered the subsequent restoration of Peisistratus possible. But there were two disturbing causes which he had not banished. The first was to be found in the local feuds which existed before his legislation and continued after it. So far from attempting to break up these local unions, his legislation must have intensified their strength; for, while the "men of the plains" would have been for the most part pentacosiomedimni and hippeis, the "men of the hills" would probably have been in the main thetes, and thus the members of these local divisions, which were based to a large extent on distinctions of wealth, must have found themselves in different classes of the Solonian census. The second dis-

---

[1] Solon ap. *Ath. Pol.* 12.
[2] That which imposed the penalty of ἀτιμία on any one guilty of neutrality in a political στάσις (Plut. *Sol.* 20).

integrating influence was due to the power and separate interests of the clans, and Solon had kept the four Ionic tribes and the clan system which was an integral part of this distribution. Both these elements of disturbance soon showed themselves. The local feuds were the proximate cause of the usurpation of the Peisistratidae, and this despotism seems to have been the first power which succeeded in stamping them out entirely. The clan feuds reappear again immediately after the expulsion of the tyrants in the struggle between Cleisthenes, the leader of the dominant Alcmaeonids, and Isagoras, who headed a union of the other clans against him. But at this crisis the influence of Solon's constitution, and possibly also of the succeeding despotism, was felt in the important fact that the demos was a factor to be reckoned with and an element which had to be taken into account even in a dynastic feud. "Cleisthenes," Herodotus tells us, "took the demos into partnership," and with its help he inaugurated a new series of reforms.

It was in the year 508 that the firm foundations for the later democratic machinery were laid.[1] That Cleisthenes had learnt the lesson taught by the immediate past and the circumstances of his own rise to power, is shown by his change in the tribes. He abolished the four Ionic tribes and substituted ten new ones. Each tribe was composed of smaller units called "demes," which were not necessarily contiguous; and therefore each, though of a local character, was not representative of a local interest. Their names were derived from eponymous Attic heroes and drawn from Attic legends; such names as Aegeis, Pandionis, Cecropis,[2] preserving the memory of ancient kings of Attica, suggested of themselves a union of the whole people. Each tribe had its chapel and cultivated the worship of its eponymous hero, but as no local or peculiar traditions were associated with the names of these deified personalities, these separate worships could not interfere with the feeling of the unity of the state. To preserve this unity and to destroy the old clan influence by a complete divorce of state from family organisation, was the meaning of the redivision; it was typical

---

[1] The date of the Cleisthenean constitution, left doubtful by Herodotus (v. 66, 69), is fixed by the *Ath. Pol.* (21) as the archonship of Isagoras, in the fourth year after the expulsion of the Peisistratidae. The *Ath. Pol.* represents the reforms as not being (at least finally) completed until after the expulsion of Cleomenes and Isagoras.

[2] Aeantis was the only tribe called after a ξένος: but Aias had been a "neighbour and ally" (Her. v. 66).

of the reforms thought appropriate to a democratic legislator, whose object should be to make the people "mix as much as possible with one another, to destroy separate interests, and thus to create a common national spirit."[1] But, not content with fostering the tendencies that might make for democracy in the existing members of the state, Cleisthenes infused into Athens a fresh strain of plebeian blood and sentiment by conferring civic rights on a large number of individuals of foreign birth, or of the lowest origin. These were metoecs—either stranger residents or enfranchised slaves, doubtless engaged in mercantile callings and therefore of advanced and liberal views —whom he enrolled in his new tribes.[2] He necessarily gave them also membership of the phratry; for this had become the test of citizenship before the time of Cleisthenes, although it is, as we saw, improbable that he actually increased the number of these associations. The legislator often found in religion a potent means of healing the tendency to disintegration; and certain words of Aristotle, to the effect that legislators of this type should reduce the number of private cults ($ἴδια\ ἱερά$) and make them common to all the citizens,[3] may imply that Cleisthenes adopted the remedy of raising into public worships some that were originally private. This was possibly effected by making the "orgeones" participate to a greater extent than they had hitherto done in the worship of the clans. But the rights of the clan were not touched by his legislation, so far as these were based on natural family ties. Even its indirect influence on public life still continued, for membership of a powerful clan provided a leader with a ready following; but with Cleisthenes its direct political importance disappears.

This change in the tribes had an important influence both on military and civil offices, and some of these changes which were realised either immediately or after the lapse of a few years may be noticed here. Although we cannot attribute the institution of the ten $στρατηγοί$ to Cleisthenes, we are told that the number was fixed shortly after his reforms,[4] when the generals were brought into strict relations with the tribes. Each general was elected by the $φυλή$ which he commanded

[1] Arist. *Pol.* vi. 4 = p. 1319 b; *Ath. Pol.* 21.
[2] Arist. *Pol.* iii. 2 πολλοὺς γὰρ ἐφυλέτευσε ξένους καὶ δούλους μετοίκους. Others read καὶ μετοίκους, which represents Cleisthenes as making citizens of actual slaves.
[3] *ib.* vi. 4 = p. 1319 b.
[4] Ath. *Pol.* 22.

and to which he belonged, and at this period each was merely a tribal officer.[1] The Polemarch was commander-in-chief, and the army was drawn up in the order of the tribes.[2] The Athenian fleet was still supplied by the naucraries, which, as we saw, were now raised to fifty, and the duty of its upkeep by private individuals (the τριηραρχία) was in all probability still connected with these divisions.

When we turn to civil offices of state, we find that, in the developed Athenian constitution of the fifth and fourth centuries, the number ten or a multiple of ten forms throughout the basis of the official boards; but, although it was Cleisthenes who introduced this decimal system into Athenian public life, only one of these many boards can with any authority be attributed to him. This was the body of ten "receivers" (ἀποδέκται),[3] chosen by lot one from each tribe, as these corporations usually were. They were controllers and auditors of the Exchequer, receiving the revenues "before the senate in the senate-house"[4] and checking the receipts. As the chief financial officials they replaced the older board of the Colacretae,[5] but the primitive control of the latter over the domestic economy of the prytaneium was still continued and even in the course of time increased. They were still entrusted with the care of money spent on public dinners and on sacrifices, and after the jury-pay had been introduced they were its treasurers. For the δικαστικὸς μισθός was paid from the court fees (πρυτανεῖα), and was thus brought within the sphere of the financial officers of the prytaneium. In all their other duties they were replaced by the new board of apodectae, which was destined to be permanent.

But the greatest of all the creations dependent on the new state-divisions was the βουλή of five hundred, composed of fifty members from each of the ten tribes. What precise organisation Cleisthenes gave this council we are never told, but it appears from certain indications that it now became a more self-existent body than the parallel council of Solon. The connection of the

[1] Thus at Marathon Aristeides of Alopeke commanded the Antiochis, Themistocles the Phrearian the Leontis (Plut. *Arist.* 5).
[2] Her. vi. iii.
[3] Harpocrat. *s.v.*; Androtion stated that they were appointed by Cleisthenes in place of the Colacretae.
[4] *Ath. Pol.* 48.
[5] κωλακρέται is derived by Lange from κῶλα and κείρω. They were men who cut up joints for the dinners in the prytaneium. The alternative form κωλαγρέται would mean collectors of joints (ἀγείρω). Officials of this name were found also in Cyzicus.

apodectae with this corporation may point to new financial functions, while a few years later the bouleutic oath was instituted,[1] which looks as though its functions of administrative jurisdiction commenced about this time.

A system of local government—formerly imperfectly represented by the naucraries—was the completion of the legislator's scheme. Its basis was formed by the recognition of the δῆμοι, most of which had existed before as hamlets in Attica and were only rearranged by Cleisthenes in his new tribes. The demes belonging to the same tribe were not locally contiguous, this arrangement being made to break up local unions and to prevent tribal jealousies; the whole number was first divided up into thirty local aggregates called trittyes, and these larger unions were distributed by lot amongst the tribes, the effect of this distribution being that each tribe contained demes in different parts of Attica.[2] If the apparent statement of Herodotus, that the number of demes was originally a hundred, is correct, it must have been increased from time to time, for later evidences point to a number far in excess of this.[3] The deme-names were partly local, partly those of eponymous heroes. In later times we find an elaborate deme-organisation, and these unions became very perfect centres of local government. How much of this is attributable to Cleisthenes we do not know; he certainly instituted the δήμαρχοι, who exercised the kind of powers formerly possessed by the presidents of the naucraries, and this is equivalent to saying that the demes became the centres of local government in all questions connected with local taxation. The demarchs had also at this time the preservation of the state-register (ληξιαρκικὸν γραμματεῖον), the official designation of the Athenian citizen by his deme having now been introduced.[4]

The final institution connected with the name of Cleisthenes was the great precautionary measure of the ostracism,[5] afterwards imitated by the democracies of Argos and Syracuse, and found also at Megara and Miletus. It was a means of securing the absence

---

[1] *Ath. Pol.* 22.
[2] *ib.*
[3] Her. v. 69 δέκα δὲ (δεκα < χῆ > δὲ Lolling) καὶ τοὺς δήμους κατένειμε ἐς τὰς φυλάς. Polemo (of the end of the third or beginning of the second century) gave the number as 174 (Strabo p. 396). If we exclude duplicates (such as a "lower" corresponding to an "upper" Lamptrae), the number of known names is 168 (Gelzer in Hermann's *Staatsalt.* pp. 797 ff.).
[4] *Ath. Pol. l.c.*
[5] *ib.*

from the state for ten years of an unwelcome citizen by a decree of the people, which, however, did not entail the loss of honour, rights, or property. The primary motive for its introduction at Athens, as subsequently at Syracuse, was the avoidance of tyranny. It was, therefore, meant to be employed when one man's influence became so great as to threaten the existence of the constitution; it was an effectual way of showing that there was an overwhelming majority against him, and a mode of frustrating his possible designs without having to resort to violence and bloodshed. But it also served the important secondary purpose of producing a national consciousness and sustaining an interest in the government, as the careful nature of the procedure adopted forced the people to continuous reflection on the political situation. The ecclesia had first to determine whether a resort to ostracism was advisable, and on this occasion the whole political situation would necessarily be discussed. If the resolution was in the affirmative, the people met again and voted by tribes, under the presidency of the nine Archons and the council,[1] recording on tablets the names of the men whom they individually destined for exile. A bare majority was sufficient to effect it, but at this second stage six thousand votes had to be recorded in all.[2] Considering the frailty of Greek constitutional governments, and the recent experience of Athens in the time of Cleisthenes, the institution was a useful one; but it was evidently open to abuse. Ostracism might be worked by a powerful party to banish a legitimate constitutional leader. It was a combination of this kind—one resulting from the mutual fears of party leaders—that resulted in the banishment of the possibly objectionable but politically harmless Hyperbolus in 417;[3] and this abuse caused the downfall of the institution at Athens. Its abstract justification is hardly on a level with its utility, and Aristotle rightly treats ostracism as a "tyrannical" act, as an exercise of sheer force and a policy comparable to that pursued by imperial states, of crushing all likely opposition by force of arms; yet he admits that, on the presumption that the existing form of the state is worth maintaining, it is a necessary

---

[1] Append. Photii (Porson) p. 675.
[2] It is improbable that 6000 votes had to be recorded against a single man for ostracism to be effective. It was a principle of Attic law that 6000 votes had to be recorded in all in the cases of νόμοι ἐπ' ἀνδρί (*privilegia*), amongst which ostracism would fall.
[3] Thuc. viii. 73.

assertion of that community's principle of justice, a means of restoring symmetry to the state when it has become unsymmetrical through the abnormal growth of one of its members.[1]

It is somewhat easier to form a general estimate of Cleisthenes' work than it was of Solon's, for his aims were simpler. To ancient writers he sometimes appeared the creator of the democracy;[2] his restoration of popular government after the despotism of the Peisistratidae might have partly suggested the title,[3] but it is sometimes used with a deeper meaning which a general review of Cleisthenes' constitutional arrangements makes it at first sight hard to justify; for, so far as positive reforms went, they were no great advance on the Solonian. The Areiopagus still remained a power, the magistracy was still limited to the landed class, and we hear of no development of the popular judicature. Half a century later "the aristocracy of Cleisthenes" was on the lips of conservative statesmen who wished to stem the democratic reforms of Pericles;[4] and on the establishment of the oligarchy of 411, a proposal was mooted to examine into the laws of Cleisthenes as suited to the existing exigencies of the state.[5] His claim as a reformer rests on the abolition of certain conditions which were unfavourable to any form of established government. The break-up of the clan-organisation, the fresh local unions which banished old associations and substituted new ones in their place, and the introduction of ostracism, were all means of getting rid of disturbing causes. Thus the creations of Cleisthenes were permanent, and were the starting-point for all further development. The Cleisthenean constitution was the unalterable basis on which the future ultra-democratic changes rested, and in this sense, but in this sense only, Cleisthenes was the founder of the Athenian democracy. We will now see how this ultimate end was reached.

Between the times of Cleisthenes and Pericles, Athens had passed through the most eventful period of her history. The Persians had been fought and conquered, and the Athenian Empire had been created. The influence of the Persian War in raising the aspirations of the demos is dwelt on by Aristotle,[6]

---

[1] Arist. *Pol.* iii. 13.
[2] Her. v. 69; vi. 131.
[3] *Ath. Pol.* 20.
[4] Plut. *Cim.* 15.
[5] *Ath. Pol.* 29.
[6] *Pol.* v. 4 = p. 1304 a.

but the influence of the empire was equally great. From 454, when the treasury of the league was removed from Delos, Athens became a "tyrant city," and all Athenians came to feel an equal interest in the preservation of the empire which they had won and which was a source both of honour and of profit. The Periclean idea, as expressed by Thucydides, is that the citizens of Athens, resting on the empire as their material basis, should form an ideal of intellectual and political development for the Greek world, that the individual Athenian should be a type of intellectual many-sidedness and varied political activity. Such an ideal as this left no room for an aristocracy within Athens, and hence the tendency of political development within the state was necessarily democratic. The guidance of the Areiopagus had been swept away, and grave duties now devolved on the popular bodies. The ecclesia, which had of old pronounced on matters of foreign policy, on peace and war, had now to decide the most momentous questions of imperial administration. To the dicasteries had to be brought important cases from the subject allies, such cases as must come under the cognisance of an imperial state. This made their business infinitely larger, and rendered it necessary to increase the attendance at these courts and to properly subdivide their functions. When we take all this into consideration, it does not surprise us to learn that the chief change connected with the name of Pericles was the introduction of payment for state-services. Our authorities are inclined to regard this change made by Pericles as mere bribery—an effort to counteract the influence of his wealthier rival Cimon by "giving the masses their own property."[1] He taught the people, Greek critics said, to live off the state, which practically meant living off the temporary supremacy of Athens, instead of subsisting on their own industry. A possible element of truth in these charges is that the reforms of Pericles may to some extent have been directed by the necessities of his political position; but the question of payment admits of another explanation, which shows it to be necessarily connected with a political ideal such as that which he pursued. Payment for administrative services was clearly a necessity of a true democratic constitution, as ancient states understood democracy. A modern democracy may tolerate the expression of the people's will through representatives,

[1] διδόναι τοῖς πολλοῖς τὰ αὑτῶν (*Ath. Pol.* 27); cf. Plut. *Per.* 9.

who may be willing and able to perform their administrative duties gratuitously. But to the Greek such a government was aristocratic. Since popular government meant personal government on the part of the demos, and such personal government, which implied the political education of the masses, was part of the Periclean ideal, to secure services from the poorer citizens some compensation for the loss of time was necessary, and the numerical equality which democracy demands would have been a mere fiction had not these services been secured by pay. This is the extreme theory of the system of payment, the theory as expressed in the institutions of the period succeeding the Peloponnesian War. The system inaugurated by Pericles fell far short of this. He introduced pay only for the courts[1]—that is, only for a portion of the people engaged in an occupation which absorbed all their time and attention. Considering the circumstances of the time this was clearly a necessity, for the heliaea was now organised and subdivided and perhaps for the first time assumed the form of courts sitting permanently, and the increase of business, due to the formation of the empire, rendered an increase of attendance necessary. Again, the pay as given by Pericles was not a real compensation for services. The δικαστικὸς μισθός seems originally to have been only one obol per day,[2] and, though it was afterwards raised to three, the mention of the τριώβολον by Aristophanes in connection with Cleon's name[3] renders it probable that it was that statesman, the exaggerator of all Periclean tendencies, who was responsible for its introduction. Three obols was probably full compensation for services and as much as could be earned in an ordinary trade.[4] But the one obol introduced by Pericles must be looked on rather as an ἐφόδιον—a means of ensuring country people the power of getting to Athens and performing their services at all. The system as adopted by its first exponent was, therefore, a very mild one; its importance was due to its recognition of the true democratic principle,—that services could be expected from all the citizens only on the condition of the introduction of some such measure.[5] The council of five hundred came also to be

---

[1] Arist. *Pol.* ii. 12 ; *Ath. Pol.* 27.
[2] Aristoph. *Clouds* 863.
[3] *Knights* 255 ; cf. *Wasps* 595.
[4] It was the rate of pay for the fleet and half the rate for the Athenian hoplites on foreign service.
[5] In Plato's *Gorgias* (p. 515 E) we find that it was Pericles who first made the Athenians "idle and talkative" (ἀργοὶ καὶ λάλοι), which means (interpreted

paid—we do not know when, but probably at an early period,[1] —for this was a permanent body sitting all the year round, and it was as necessary for its members to receive payment as it was for the dicasts. The rate was a drachma a day for all days except festivals.[2]

The pay for attendance at the ecclesia ($\mu\iota\sigma\theta\grave{o}s$ $\dot{\epsilon}\kappa\kappa\lambda\eta\sigma\iota\alpha\sigma\tau\iota\kappa\acute{o}s$) was a much more sweeping measure. It was not introduced until after the Peloponnesian War by Agyrrhius, who became a prominent politician about the year 395. The amount was at first one obol, which was then raised by a certain Heracleides to two, and afterwards by Agyrrhius again to three obols.[3] This payment was a consequence of the loss of the empire and the consequent lack of interest in public business, for we are told that it was considered necessary to ensure a sufficient attendance of the masses, and a chance reference, dating probably from 392, informs us that the attendance became larger when the pay had been raised to three obols.[4] This payment for the ecclesia was much less necessary than that for the other bodies, for the assembly met less frequently and its sittings were less prolonged. There is, in fact, some absurdity involved in the idea of a whole people paying itself for attendance on public business, and the payment may have been in the nature of a fine, those present gaining what those who were absent lost. But the money may have been drawn largely from burdens laid upon the rich; the institution seems to have been a desperate effort to keep up the old traditions and retain the balance of classes, and this effort pushed up the rate at the close of the fourth century to a drachma a day.[5]

Other measures connected with the leaders of this period are so-called bribes in the shape of state-distributions to the people ($\delta\iota\alpha\nu o\mu\alpha\acute{\iota}$ or $\delta\iota\alpha\delta\acute{o}\sigma\epsilon\iota s$). This custom was established long before the time of Pericles, for the surplus revenue from the mines of Laurium had in early days been so divided.[6] The later distributions consisted of corn-doles, land-assignments in the form of

into Periclean language) that they had the $\sigma\chi o\lambda\acute{\eta}$ which became an imperial aristocracy, and that they gained the political insight ($\kappa\rho\iota\tau\iota\kappa\grave{\eta}$ $\delta\acute{\upsilon}\nu\alpha\mu\iota s$) which came from the free discussion of political questions.

[1] In *Ath. Pol.* (24) the five hundred are included in the number of citizens who lived off the empire. Thuc. (viii. 69) mentions this $\mu\iota\sigma\theta\acute{o}s$ for the year 411.

[2] Hesych. *s.v.* $\beta o\upsilon\lambda\hat{\eta}s$ $\lambda\alpha\chi\epsilon\hat{\iota}\nu$. According to *Ath. Pol.* (62) the members received five obols.

[3] *Ath. Pol.* 41.

[4] Aristoph. *Ecclesiaz.* 301.

[5] *Ath. Pol.* 62.

[6] Her. vii. 144.

cleruchies, and payments for festivals (θεωρικά). Probably none of these originated with Pericles, and the third abuse, which was to become the greatest, grew out of the payment of two obols for the theatre (διωβελία) which was introduced by Cleophon.[1] It is true that the system of distribution went on on a far larger scale during the presidency of Pericles and his immediate successors than had heretofore been possible. This was an inevitable consequence of the vast resources added to the state by the existence of the Athenian Empire, and accounts for the association of this practice with the name of the greatest of the democratic leaders, who may have exaggerated the system, and led to the enormous scale on which it was afterwards applied. But the principle of "distribution" was one inherent in the structure of a Greek democracy. It was due to the simple principle that the state was a κοινωνία, a joint-stock company, and hence that any surplus in "goods" which accrued to it should be distributed *viritim* amongst the citizens. Athens had now a great deal to distribute, but it was not all unearned increment. The profits of the empire were won by rigorous work which kept 20,000 Athenian citizens engaged in constant political, military, and naval service.[2] The great change which we have traced, the introduction of pay, was itself not a cause but a symptom. A people does not demand payment for political services until it is fit to rule. Even the vast slave population of Athens could not create the ideal democracy. It required an empire.

§ 4 *The Working of the democratic Constitution of Athens*

The apex of the constitution was the council of five hundred, which was open to all citizens over thirty years of age, and which continued to be chosen by lot, fifty members from each tribe, fifty more being selected as substitutes (οἱ ἐπιλαχόντες) to fill up possible gaps in the body. The office was not a burden imposed on the citizens; the candidates presented themselves voluntarily, and competition for membership was keen, since the functions of the post were dignified and important and the services well paid. The members had to pass a δοκιμασία before the previous council,[3] and, at the close of their functions, the

[1] *Ath. Pol.* 28.   [2] *ib.* 24.   [3] *ib.* 45.

theory of individual responsibility was enforced by submitting each councillor to a separate audit.[1] The board had certain definite officials connected with it for certain definite purposes; but it seems safest to regard the chief of these as not themselves members of the body, for the secretary of the city [2] was elected by the people even in the fourth century, and other officials had been formerly elected in this manner but were afterwards chosen by lot. Chief amongst such officials must have been the auditor of the council (ἀντιγραφεὺς τῆς βουλῆς), apparently an independent authority and an external check on its actions, who kept a record of its proceedings and an audit that was probably concerned mainly with finance.[3]

But the council was too large a body to perform its functions as an active executive efficiently without further subdivision of its members. It worked, therefore, through committees. Occasionally these were temporary, appointed for special purposes. But there were besides regular but changing committees known as πρυτάνεις, which brought the council into relation with the ecclesia. The council was divided by tribes into committees of fifty members each, each presiding tribe (φυλὴ πρυτανεύουσα) sitting in turn for a tenth part of the year, which was called a πρυτανεία. In the fifth century a narrower board of ten, chosen from this tribe and sitting for seven days, with a president (ἐπιστάτης) selected daily by lot from this narrower body, were the intermediaries between the council and the ecclesia and the presidents of both bodies.[4] A change subsequently introduced, not known earlier than the year 378 but probably dating back to the archonship of Eucleides (403), divorced the presidency of the council and popular assembly from the committee of the prytany. When the council or ecclesia was summoned, the epistates of the prytany selected by lot nine πρόεδροι, one from each tribe except the one presiding, and a second epistates from them, and it was this still more evanescent committee that laid business before the two assemblies.[5] The task of the latter was merely formal, for the preparation of business was of course made by the permanent board of

---

[1] Aesch. c. Ctes. 20; a psephism (C.I.A. ii. 114) recommends a councillor to be crowned "as soon as he shall have passed his audit."

[2] Ath. Pol. 54; Thuc. vii. 10.

[3] Pollux viii. 98; Harpocrat. s.v.; the title itself does not occur in Ath. Pol. (54), although Harpocration quotes Aristotle.

[4] Arg. ad Demosth. c. Androt. p. 590.

[5] Ath. Pol. 44; Suid. s.v. ἐπιστάτης.

prytaneis for the daily meetings of the whole body of five hundred, and from them, in all matters which the council was not competent to decide, the debate spread to the wide circle of the people. For the council had a double character. It was a probouleutic senate preparing business for the ecclesia, but it was also the chief administrative authority which carried out the resolutions of the assembly. Its administrative power was exercised by a general presidency over other officials, whom it could summon for the purpose of instructions, less frequently by commissioners appointed from its own body. A review of its executive functions shows that they were connected with almost every department of administration. The council had the peace control of the military arrangements of the state; it inspected the fleet and the wharfs, and saw to the upkeep of the cavalry ($ἱππεῖς$), and doubtless also of the hoplite force. It performed the routine duties connected with foreign policy, received embassies and brought them before the people, and swore to treaties with foreign states; the empire added new duties to its foreign control, and it was the council which prepared the schedules of tribute that were to be submitted to the people. In the domain of finance it had a real control over the details of expenditure, and perhaps the chief voice in the question of estimates. It was its duty to see how the necessary supplies for the year could be raised; it leased the taxes, receiving the returns with the apodectae; and it exacted debts to the state from private individuals. Lastly, it possessed jurisdiction, for special impeachments ($εἰσαγγελίαι$) were brought before the council. These were prosecutions for special crimes affecting the welfare of the community—such as conspiracy, treason, and bribery of certain kinds.[1] Usually (in later times almost invariably) it acted only as a court of first instance; but we are told that it originally had summary jurisdiction and could punish with fines, imprisonment, and even death. Subsequently these powers were taken away, and an appeal from its judgment was allowed to a dicastery.[2] The council had also, in the fourth century, the right of hearing, in the first instance, appeals against magistrates for not carrying out the laws. Its jurisdiction was therefore to a limited extent what we should call "administrative" (*i.e.* applying only to a certain class of offenders), but as a whole it was concurrent

---

[1] Hypereid. *pro Eux.* § 22. [2] *Ath. Pol.* 45.

with, where it was not merely preliminary to, that of the popular courts.

The ecclesia was nominally the whole body of free Athenian citizens over eighteen years of age; practically it was as many as could be got together, and even during the Peloponnesian War the maximum attendance did not exceed 5000.[1] For those legislative acts the validity of which nominally required ratification by the whole people, the number 6000 was taken to represent the state; and this quorum was demanded for acts of privilege (νόμοι ἐπ' ἀνδρί), such as the conferment of citizenship, of dispensation from the laws (ἄδεια), and probably for the ostracism.[2] The meetings of the ecclesia were of two kinds. It was the ordinary and regular meetings (αἱ τεταγμέναι ἐκ τῶν νόμων), of which there were four a prytany, which made the assembly the chief administrative body; for these meetings were independent of the special summons of a magistrate, and business was discussed in them according to a regular programme. But the great questions of the hour generally came up for discussion in the extraordinary assemblies (σύγκλητοι), which were specially convened by the prytaneis, usually at the request of a strategus. In both cases the business was prepared for the ecclesia by this committee of the council, and came before it in the form of a probouleuma. Sometimes the council takes on itself the duty of advice, and sends down a bill containing a definite proposal which it urges the assembly to accept; at other times it does not venture an opinion, but simply states a question in the bill handed down through the prytaneis, and asks the members of the lower house to come to some conclusion by themselves.[3] In the case of a proposal of the first kind debate in the ecclesia could be entirely avoided, at least in the fourth century, by a very effective system of closure known as the προχειροτονία, a preliminary vote being taken as to whether the assembly should accept the proposal of the council without debate or not.[4]

At first sight a very strict limitation on the powers of a deliberative assembly seems to be contained in the rule that no business could be debated in the ecclesia which had not first

[1] Thuc. viii. 72.
[2] Andoc. de Myst. § 87.
[3] In the first case the formula of decrees runs γνώμην δὲ (τοὺς προέδρους) συμβάλλεσθαι τῆς βουλῆς εἰς τὸν δῆμον, ὅτι δοκεῖ τῇ βουλῇ κτλ: in the second ὅτι δοκεῖ τῇ βουλῇ τὸν δῆμον . . . βουλεύεσθαι ὅ τι ἂν αὐτῷ δοκεῖ ἄριστον εἶναι.
[4] Harpocrat. s.v. προχειροτονία.

been prepared by the council. But at Athens this restriction was merely formal. The members of the ecclesia had an unlimited power of adding to bills, and inscriptions show numerous decrees in which riders have been appended to the original probouleuma. Again, though they were limited in debate to the matter brought forward by the council, they were not bound merely to accept or reject even a definite proposal of that body, but could come to a directly opposite or even alternative decision on the subject.[1] And lastly, the ecclesia gained an indirect power of originating business by suggesting that the council ought to bring forward a probouleuma of a certain kind.[2] We may imagine that this moral pressure was seldom disregarded.

The ecclesia was the sovereign administrative power in the state, but it was not a true legislative assembly. The idea of the full sovereignty of the people did not originate until late in Athenian history, and was probably never held quite thoroughly. The sovereign was the constitution, and the constitution was protected by the courts of law, not so much by the heliaea as a whole as by each separate panel of dicasts which had taken the heliastic oath, and which performed in the course of its ordinary jurisdiction the functions of a supreme court. In the year 409 we find the ecclesia denouncing the verdict of a jury which, on appeal, had declared the illegality of a decree in honour of one of the assassins of Phrynichus. It suggests that the jurors have been bribed, and desires that they shall be brought to trial.[3] But its energies are spent in the vote of censure; it cannot upset the decision of the court. The ecclesia could, in fact, only be the author of administrative decrees (ψηφίσματα), not laws (νόμοι), and, though it could originate legislation, it could not complete it. To support this theory some check on the action of individual members of the ecclesia was clearly necessary; otherwise the people might be betrayed into the committal of illegal acts. Hence the institution of the indictment for illegal proposals (γραφὴ παρανόμων), the efficiency of which as a safeguard to the constitution caused it finally to replace every other system of checks which had been devised. It might be levelled equally against the proposer

---

[1] An instance is found in Xen. *Hell.* vii. 1, 1-14.
[2] The formula runs δέδοχθαι (or ἐψηφίσθαι) τῷ δήμῳ προβουλεύσασαν τὴν βουλὴν ἐξενεγκεῖν ἐς τὸν δῆμον περὶ κτλ. [3] Hicks n. 56.

of a psephism or the initiator of a law, and the mover was liable to prosecution within the limit of a year, if his measure was invalid either in matter or in form. A psephism was invalid in form if it had not been submitted to the judgment of the council, or if it was one of those bills which, like the raising of a property-tax, required as a preliminary to its promulgation a decree of exemption (ἄδεια) which had not been gained; it was invalid in contents if it was in conflict with an existing law. The invalidity of laws rested chiefly on the question of form; neglect of proper promulgation or of the other rules which regulated the introduction of new laws might expose a would-be legislator to this indictment.[1] Attempts on the part of the ecclesia to assume a legislative power and on the part of individuals to tamper with the constitution were thus frustrated. Since there was no proper ministry at Athens holding office for a term of years and responsible for all important measures, the introduction of the γραφὴ παρανόμων was necessary to make the unofficial orator feel the responsibility of his position, and was the means by which the assembly protected itself from the appalling consequences that might follow the extreme freedom of initiative permitted in that body. It has, indeed, been thought that a law at least might be assailed "on the vague charge of inexpediency," and that the indictment lay against legislation which was not unconstitutional but which subsequent reflection proved to be bad.[2] It is not impossible that the ever-increasing danger threatened by the irresponsible adviser may have forced the Athenians even to this stage of iniquitous precaution, but it is unlikely that the principle found a place in the original theory of this indictment. There were, however, limits to the Graphe and precautions against its being used as a mere party weapon. After the expiration of a year the mover was free from criminal prosecution, and the law or psephism alone could be assailed, while the prosecutor who did not obtain one-fifth of the votes was fined and lost the right of bringing such indictments in the future.

There was therefore, properly speaking, no strictly legis-

---

[1] In one rare case we find a conflict of the contents of laws. Timocrates proposed a law of his own with retrospective action, without previously repealing a law which enacted that measures should come into operation from the day on which they were passed (Dem. c. Tim. §§ 43, 73). But this too is resolvable into a question of form.

[2] Wayte (Dem. c. Androt. and c. Timocr. p. xxxv.)

lative sovereign at Athens, no one body whose mandate had immediately the force of law; for the Athenian, like the Greek citizen generally, conceived himself to be living under the impersonal sovereignty of law itself. Yet, although progressive legislation was an idea which had little attraction for a Greek, revision and amendment were indispensable, and there was a means, at once safe, rapid, and scientific, of effecting a change in the laws at Athens. The procedure of early times is indeed lost to us, and we know the process of legislation only in its final stage. Two normal modes of correcting the laws were ultimately developed—one depending on the initiative of private individuals, the other on that of officials whose duty was revision. The first mode was initiated in the ecclesia. At annual intervals the question was put to the vote whether the laws should be confirmed as they stood or be revised, and for this purpose they were submitted in groups to the people.[1] If a revision of one or more groups was voted for, provision was taken for the appointment of $νομοθέται$ by the ecclesia. Meanwhile individuals who wished to suggest changes had to ensure the proper publication of their amendments, while the assembly appointed five public advocates ($συνήγοροι$) to argue in defence of the laws assailed. The nomothetae, the final ratifying authority to which the respective claims of the new and the old measures were to be submitted, were not a permanent body, but were on each occasion appointed by lot from the heliaea, their numbers varying from five hundred to a thousand, probably according to the importance of the laws under consideration. They were organised as a miniature ecclesia with an epistates and proedri of their own, and their vote, whether given in favour of the existing measure or of the new proposal, was final. The second mode (the $διόρθωσις\ τῶν\ νόμων$) differs from the first only in the respect that this machinery was set in motion by the thesmothetae of the year. It was their annual duty to examine the whole code of laws and to see if there were any which were contradictory or out of date.[2] Discoveries of this kind were published with amendments suggested by these officials, and the alternatives submitted, as in the former case, to the judgment of nomothetae appointed by the ecclesia.

Legislation, therefore, was a work of co-operation between the two great popular bodies, the ecclesia and the heliaea. But,

[1] Dem. c. Timocr. §§ 20 ff. [2] Aesch. c. Ctes. § 38.

though hampered in its legislative action, the administrative powers of the assembly were as wide as they well could be.[1] It declared war and made peace, received envoys introduced to it by the council, appointed ambassadors, and sanctioned commercial relations with foreign states. It had the supreme ratifying authority in all matters affecting revenues and the administration of finance, even venturing at times on such extreme measures as the creation of monopolies[2] and the depreciation of the coinage.[3] It professed to control the state religion and to sanction the admission of foreign gods into the Attic Pantheon, until the liberalism of the democracy, combined with the desire for divine protection of every kind, had made of Athens a very Egypt of strange divinities.[4] It conferred citizenship and the right of intermarriage on foreigners, immunity on states or kings, and rewards and honours, such as maintenance in the Prytaneium, on its benefactors. There is nothing surprising in the exercise of powers of a general or only occasionally recurring character by a body constituted like the Athenian ecclesia. What may surprise us is the minute attention it paid to the details of administration, typical instances of which may best be found in its control of the highest officials of the state in a department which a popular body has peculiar difficulty in administering—that of foreign policy. The ecclesia exercised a minute supervision over the conduct of generals engaged on a foreign campaign, and the free criticism of their actions by the assembly was often a prelude to prosecution before a court of law. The independent powers of commanders on foreign expeditions do not appear to have been very clearly defined, and the difficulty of the position of the strategi was due to the fact that no clear line was drawn between what they might and what they might not do. The jealous demos might even censure them for granting unauthorised terms to a town which they had captured;[5] and generals seem occasionally to have been convicted for carrying out the literal

---

[1] On these see Schömann *de Comitiis Atheniensium* pp. 281-338.
[2] [Arist.] *Oecon.* ii. 37.
[3] Aristoph. *Eccles.* 816 ff.
[4] Aristoph. ap. Athenæ. ix. p. 372 b. (*Fragm.* 476 Dindorf) Αἴγυπτον αὐτῶν τὴν πόλιν πεποίηκας ἀντ' Ἀθηνῶν. It was the ecclesia that deified Alexander (Ael. *Var. Hist.* 5, 12) and paid divine honours to Demetrius Poliorcetes (Plut. *Demetr.* 10).
[5] Thuc. ii. 70 (the surrender of Potidaea in the winter of 430) Ἀθηναῖοι τοὺς στρατηγοὺς ἐπῃτιάσαντο ὅτι ἄνευ αὐτῶν ξυνέβησαν.

instructions and not the implied wishes of the people.[1] For, though it was the courts that condemned, this condemnation was but the final expression of the criticism of the assembly. The supposed limitations of the ordinary commander are best illustrated by the fact that, for distant or important expeditions, generals were sometimes appointed with autocratic powers (στρατηγοὶ αὐτοκράτορες) who were *not* expected to refer the details of administration to the home government—that is, to the council and the ecclesia. If patriotism or strong political feeling prompted a general in the field to adopt an independent line of action, he was playing a somewhat uneven game. Success did not always mean condonation, for it might not coincide with the political views of the majority for the time, while failure meant treason and death. When the Thebans freed themselves from their Spartan garrison in 379, two generals co-operated with them from the Athenian frontier; they were successful but condemned. When Diopeithes, the Athenian general in the Chersonese, made a wanton and unauthorised attack in 342 on the Macedonian possession of Thrace, his action was justified by the people, and the war which ended with Chaeroneia was the result. A strong government can afford to be capricious. Its absence of principle does not render it assailable from within, and may enable it to accept the results of success from without.

The authority of the ecclesia, great as it was, would have been very incomplete had it not been supplemented by that of the parallel corporation of the heliaea. This ranks with the council as one of the sworn, responsible, and (for foreign purposes) representative bodies of the Athenian state.[2] It was composed nominally of all full Athenian citizens over thirty years of age; but, since service appears to have been voluntary, it would practically have consisted of those who, having taken the heliastic oath,[3] had given in their names to the nine Archons and been declared duly qualified for the service. Their number in the fifth century appears to have been unfixed, and the

---

[1] As *e.g.* in the condemnation of the generals of the Sicilian expedition of 425 (Thuc. iv. 65). These generals seem to have acted within their instructions (*ib.* iii. 115), but they had not accomplished the unexpressed object of conquering Sicily.

[2] *e.g.* the treaty with Chalcis (Hicks n. 28) begins Διόγνητος εἶπε· κατὰ τάδε τὸν ὅρκον ὁμόσαι Ἀθηναίων τὴν βουλὴν καὶ τοὺς δικαστάς.

[3] All Athenian citizens took the heliastic oath (Harpocrat. *s.v.* Ardettus).

traditional six thousand, if not an exaggeration,[1] was probably a nominal number. For the extreme improbability has been pointed out of so many duly-qualified citizens serving in the same year.[2] The list must have excluded the magistrates, the council of five hundred, and all citizens who did not wish to serve, since the duty was not compulsory. Aristophanes' references would lead us to suppose that the jurors were usually elderly, and indeed the post, though a convenient retiring pension for an old man, would not be a good investment for the energy of a young one. In the fourth century we find the heliasts divided into ten panels (the number having no connection with the tribes), and these panels, as well as their places of meeting, were called "dicasteries." It is generally supposed that they were composed of five hundred jurors each, with one thousand as an added and supplementary number. But, if the full number was not six thousand, different panels must have been partly composed, as Fränkel has shown, of the same individuals—a practice for which there is direct evidence.[3]

These dicasteries were numbered A to K, and each heliast was presented with a ticket which contained the number of his panel and his own name and deme. The court in which each section had to sit for the day was assigned by lot, but every case was not tried by a complete section. Some were heard before parts of sections, others before several sections combined, the numbers varying from 200 to 2500.[4] These panels may doubtless be dated back to the fifth century, and form the final development of the right of appeal which Solon gave to the people. As these appeals had been made indifferently in civil and criminal cases, so the final jurisdiction of the courts covered both. The distinction between the civil or private law and the criminal as a part of the public law, though not strongly marked in theory, was expressed by a difference of procedure and a difference of name. The characteristics of private suits (δίκαι ἴδιαι or δίκαι simply) were that they could be brought only by the interested party, that the compensation recovered belonged

---

[1] Aristophanes (*Wasps* 660) gives it as an approximate, the *Ath. Pol.* (24) as a round number.

[2] Fränkel *die Attische Geschworpengerichte*.

[3] Aristoph. *Plut.* 1166 οὐκ ἐτὸς ἅπαντες οἱ δικάζοντες θαμὰ σπεύδουσιν ἐν πολλοῖς γεγράφθαι γράμμασιν.

[4] Care was, however, taken that the number should always be an odd one, to avoid equality of votes.

to the plaintiff, that court fees ($\pi\rho\nu\tau\alpha\nu\epsilon\hat{\iota}\alpha$) were deposited as a surety, and that if the plaintiff threw up the action he was not punished for his retirement from the case. In public suits on the other hand ($\delta\acute{\iota}\kappa\alpha\iota$ $\delta\eta\mu\acute{o}\sigma\iota\alpha\iota$ or $\gamma\rho\alpha\phi\alpha\acute{\iota}$), which covered criminal cases, such as serious offences against the person and offences against the state, the charge could be brought by any full Athenian citizen and the compensation, if in money, belonged to, or, if it took the form of punishment, was inflicted by, the state. No court fees were deposited, and if the prosecutor gave up the charge or did not get one-fifth of the votes, he was fined a thousand drachmae and lost the power of bringing other similar charges in the future.

In the heliastic oath the jurors swore to give their decisions according to the laws and decrees in force;[1] but there was little guarantee that they knew the law, and the circumstances were adverse to their respecting it when known. It is true that Athens, as perhaps most Greek states, took care to simplify her law as much as possible by constant revision, and the process of codification and publication which was ever going on enabled her to dispense with a professional class of lawyers But the theory that every Athenian citizen knew the whole law was hardly a justifiable corollary from this practice, or a sufficient ground for dispensing with a class of skilled interpreters. The dicasts did not, like the Roman *judices* in criminal trials and like the modern jurymen, decide on questions of fact under the legal guidance of a judge. The only guidance they had was that of interested parties quoting the law on either side. Most of their verdicts must have been mere decisions in equity, on what seemed to them the merits of the case; and appeals to an Athenian jury must have been at the best appeals to abstract considerations of justice, at the worst to personal passions and prejudices. There was no power which could revise their sentences; a new trial might be granted by the legal fiction of false evidence having been tendered in the first ($\delta\acute{\iota}\kappa\eta$ $\psi\epsilon\nu\delta o\mu\alpha\rho\tau\nu\rho\iota\hat{\omega}\nu$), but most of the cases before these courts were of the nature of $\delta\acute{\iota}\kappa\alpha\iota$ $\alpha\mathring{\nu}\tau o\tau\epsilon\lambda\epsilon\hat{\iota}s$, final and irrevocable. If we add to all this the fact that the dicasts were the only irresponsible officials at Athens, the great powers which they wielded are manifest and must have been only too clearly felt

---

[1] Dem. *c. Timocr.* p. 746 $\psi\eta\phi\iota o\hat{\nu}\mu\alpha\iota$ $\kappa\alpha\tau\grave{\alpha}$ $\tau o\grave{\nu}s$ $\nu\acute{o}\mu o\nu s$ $\kappa\alpha\grave{\iota}$ $\tau\grave{\alpha}$ $\psi\eta\phi\acute{\iota}\sigma\mu\alpha\tau\alpha$ $\tauο\hat{\nu}$ $\delta\acute{\eta}\mu o\nu$ $\tauο\hat{\nu}$ $\mathrm{'}A\theta\eta\nu\alpha\acute{\iota}\omega\nu$ $\kappa\alpha\grave{\iota}$ $\tau\hat{\eta}s$ $\beta o\nu\lambda\hat{\eta}s$ $\tau\hat{\omega}\nu$ $\pi\epsilon\nu\tau\alpha\kappa o\sigma\acute{\iota}\omega\nu$.

by themselves. Their capacity may be gauged by the fact that they were composed of the classes who found it profitable to give up regular employment for the pittance of three obols a day. Their purity of administration does not seem to have been often tainted with direct bribery—a precaution against which was found in the provision that a dicast should not know until the very day of the trial in what court he was to sit. The two earliest cases of suspected bribery both date from the year 409,[1] but there is ample evidence that about this time a peculiarly shameless form of corruption had grown up in state trials. The juries were a professional class and lived off their pay; they were the poorest class and knew their advantage over the rich: consequently it was not uncommon for prosecutors to tell the jury that such was the state of the public finances, they could not hope to draw their pay if they did not convict the accused and confiscate his property.[2] This practice—hardly credible if not so well supported by first-hand evidence—was merely one of the phases of the free fight between rich and poor in which the Peloponnesian War resulted, and a sign of the evils which necessarily followed the ill-judged effort to maintain a political *régime* which the empire alone justified. But national feeling must have been almost as grave a source of wrong as party interest. The Athenian courts were composed of large masses of men, varying from two hundred to a thousand, and subject therefore to those waves of emotion which the Aristotelian theory of the infallibility of judgment of the gathered multitude ignores.[3] Arguing before such a court was like speaking before a political audience, and its decisions must to a large extent have been directed by the political prejudices of the moment. The history of the impeachment of Pericles and of many another statesman shows that not only was it a change in political sentiment which directed the prosecution, but that the same change decided the verdict. It was the policy of party leaders and their followers that was really on trial in these courts, and the collapse of almost every statesman and general who fell was determined by their sentences. For the fifth century we may cite the instances of Pericles, Paches, Laches and the other generals to Sicily; in the fourth the charges become more frequent as changes of policy become

---

[1] Hicks n. 56 § 3; *Ath. Pol.* 27. (*c. Nicom.*) § 22. Cf. Aristoph. *Eq.*
[2] Lysias 27 (*c. Epicr.*) §§ 1, 2; 30 1357.   [3] Arist. *Pol.* iii. 11.

more rapid. The peace of Antalcidas brought with it the prosecution of Agyrrhius and of almost every other prominent man whose influence seemed to have led up to it; Callistratus' long rule of oratory ended in exile and death; and after the battle of Chaeroneia, which was fought over again in the courts, many were found to have escaped the chances of war only to fall victims to the relentless oratory of Lycurgus. Yet this was perhaps the purest form of government that the Greek world saw, for even its tyranny was open and undisguised; and the judgment of a sober critic of the close of the fourth century, while it notes the absolutism of the demos, justifies it by its results. "The demos has made itself lord of everything, and manages all branches of the administration by its decrees in the ecclesia and by its judgments in the law-courts. In these it is the people which is the sovereign, for even the decisions of the council are brought before it. And the principle seems to be right. For the few are more corruptible than the many, more susceptible to bribery and to favour."[1]

But the assembly and the courts, although the main, were not the only channels through which popular energy was expended and political education won. The administrative offices held by individuals were particularly large in number, and were at least doubled when Athens became an imperial state and a new Athens grew up in the cleruchies and colonies beyond the sea. Many of these we have already mentioned, and many more will be treated when we come to deal with the organisation of the empire. It is sufficient to observe that the *Constitution of Athens*, in an attempt to estimate the numbers of the bureaucracy for the middle of the fifth century, makes the total reach the alarming proportions of fourteen hundred, of which half were "home" and half "foreign" offices.[2] As appointment to most of these was made by lot, the Athenian citizen was unfortunate who did not once in his lifetime get his share of individual rule. And even a year of such office implied an education of no mean order; even at home, where the duties were mainly those of routine, it meant an insight into the working of the hidden machinery of the state; abroad,

---

[1] *Ath. Pol.* 41; cf. Arist. *Pol.* iii. 15 "again the many are more incorruptible than the few; it is like water: the greater the volume the purer the stream."

[2] *Ath. Pol.* 24 ἀρχαὶ δ' ἔνδημοι μὲν εἰς ἑπτακοσίους ἄνδρας, ὑπερόριοι δ' εἰς ἑπτακοσίους.

in the cities of the empire and in the cleruchies, it gave a knowledge of how men must be guided, new contingencies faced, and unforeseen dangers overcome.

But, if democracy be taken to imply the levelling of individual eminence, that of Athens was a failure. Few states have ever been more completely under the sway of great personalities. It is a phase of national life which, on general grounds, should not create the least surprise; for it is one of the oldest lessons in history that, while oligarchy is the true leveller of merit, a democracy brings with it a hero-worship generally of an extravagant kind, and that the masses attain sufficient union for the exercise of power only through the worship of a supposed intellectual king. At Athens periods of long personal ascendency will be recalled by the bare mention of a few names. For the fifth century we need but cite those of Pericles, Cleon, Nicias, and Alcibiades; for the fourth those of Timotheus, Agyrrhius, Callistratus, Eubulus, Demosthenes, and Lycurgus. The types of power represented by these names, and those of others almost equally great, are very varied. Pericles holds a long and continued series of military commands; the influence of Nicias, Alcibiades, and Timotheus also rests mainly on the personal conduct of expeditions; Callistratus and Demosthenes sway the state almost exclusively by their oratory; Cleon, Agyrrhius, Eubulus, and Lycurgus are financial geniuses of a very high order. We are here only briefly characterising the *main* sources of the influence of these men. In many cases the various personal qualifications are combined, and the happy possessor of these versatile gifts assumes a position greater than that of a modern prime minister, for he combines a greater number of powers and exercises personally a greater variety of functions than the highest official of any modern state. Now the constitutional historian is hardly concerned at all with this phenomenon, if the personal ascendency which he observes is simply the result of a wholly informal personal influence, and can be proved to rest simply on public opinion. He need only note it as an effect of the practice and a violation of the spirit of the constitution. The ecclesia which will listen only to the voice of Pericles and Callistratus, and the courts which condemn at the nod of Cleon and Lycurgus, are still thoroughly democratic bodies. It is only when he observes traces of the fact that such personal power was, if not contemplated, at least allowed by the actual form of the constitution, that he feels it his duty to discuss those spheres of office which might have made their holders possible heads of the state.

The first office which attracts attention is that of the generals ($\sigma\tau\rho\alpha\tau\eta\gamma o\iota$), who formed, as we saw, a college of ten based on the ten Cleisthenean tribes. Their most distinctive right was that of procuring special meetings of the ecclesia,[1] debate in which seems to have been strictly limited to proposals put before them by the general; and no other meetings were allowed to take precedence of assemblies thus specially convened.[2] From this power of meeting the council and ecclesia was developed a series of financial functions, including the estimates of the military budget for the year and proposals for raising the requisite supplies. This was especially the case in the fifth century, when the great finance offices had not yet arisen: the separate state treasuries were in the hands of controlling boards, but the estimates for different departments could be made only by magistrates. The strategi were thus ministers of finance for foreign affairs,[3] and controlled the details of expenditure in their own departments, all the funds voted from the treasuries for military purposes passing through their hands.[4] Amongst their special military duties we may reckon, besides their actual leadership in war, the general command of the home forces and control of the home defences. They possessed jurisdiction in military matters, for the appeal against the levy ($\kappa\alpha\tau\acute{\alpha}\lambda o\gamma os$) was made to them, and they had the direction of the court in all offences against martial law, which they either undertook in person or remitted to the taxiarchs; while in the field they had the right of punishing summarily with death the most serious offences, such as treasonable negotiations with the enemy.[5] One of their chief responsibilities at home was the care of the corn supply of Athens.[6]

In the details of foreign administration their influence must also have been very great. It was they who introduced most of such business to the assembly and brought forward questions

[1] It was effected through the prytaneis, but it is unlikely that the permission was ever refused.
[2] Hicks n. 44, l. 59.
[3] As such they nominated to the trierarchy, and had the presidency of the court ($\dot{\eta}\gamma\epsilon\mu o\nu\acute{\iota}\alpha$ $\delta\iota\kappa\alpha\sigma\tau\eta\rho\acute{\iota}ov$) in suits arising from the trierarchy and the $\epsilon\iota\sigma\phi o\rho\acute{\alpha}$.
[4] Hicks n. 46.
[5] Lys. 13 (c. Agorat.), 67.
[6] $\tau\dot{\eta}\nu$ $\pi\alpha\rho\alpha\pi o\mu\pi\dot{\eta}\nu$ $\tau o\hat{v}$ $\sigma\acute{\iota}\tau ov$ (Böckh Seeurk. xiii. p. 423).

arising from treaties or from negotiations with foreign states. They officiated in treaties and were responsible for their formal execution, seeing that the oath was taken and that the proper sacrifices were offered on the occasion.[1] The existence of the Athenian Empire added to the sphere of their powers. They were the commanders-in-chief of the garrisons and of the captains of the guard (φρούραρχοι) whom we find in the subject states.[2] They saw to the exaction of the tribute when it was in arrears by commanding the "tribute-collecting ships,"[3] and probably had the levying of the contingents from the allies both in ships and men.

It will be seen from this enumeration of their functions that the Athenian generals were at once leaders in war, ministers of war, foreign ministers, and to a great extent ministers of finance. It is difficult to see how such powers could be exercised collectively by a college of ten. But the difficulty applies only to the greater part of the fifth century. In the earlier years of this century the polemarch was still commander-in-chief, the generals tribal officers. In the fourth century we find a complete differentiation of functions amongst the members of the college: each general has a title answering to his special competence, and is commander of the docks, the Peiraeus, the home defences, or the fleet, as the case may be; while in the early part of the third century the "general of the hoplites" appears to be the head of the board.[4] It would not therefore be a very extreme hypothesis to assume a similar presidency for the period when it is most needed—that of the Peloponnesian War, when Athens is *par excellence* a military state. And indeed, though direct evidence fails us, constructive evidence is strongly in favour of this view.[5] The college would only follow the analogy of other Athenian boards which are constructed of a president and colleagues (συνάρχοντες);[6] and if the president of the strategi could direct the actions of his colleagues, we have only to remember the duties of his office to realise what a power in the state he was.

---

[1] Hicks n. 28 ll. 19, 67.

[2] As in Erythrae (Hicks n. 23 l. 6). At the end of the charter of Chalcis we find also περὶ δὲ φυλακῆς Εὐβοίας τοὺς στρατηγοὺς ἐπιμέλεσθαι (Hicks n. 28 l. 77).

[3] Thuc. iv. 50.

[4] στρατηγὸς ὁ ἐπὶ τὰ ὅπλα, or ὁ ἐπὶ τοὺς ὁπλίτας (*Ath. Pol.* 61). He is χειροτονηθεὶς ἐπὶ τὰ ὅπλα πρῶτος ὑπὸ τοῦ δήμου, circa 272 B.C. (*C.I.A.* ii. n. 331).

[5] See Appendix.

[6] στρατηγοῖς Ἱπποκρατεῖ Χολαργεῖ καὶ συναρχοῦσιν (Hicks n. 46 l. 5).

He would have been the only magistrate at Athens in the fifth century who was in constant contact with the ecclesia; he at least, if not his colleagues, was elected by the whole people and no longer by a single tribe; and his tenure of power might be perpetual, for indefinite re-election to the strategia was allowed.[1] The president and his colleagues might be returned year after year by their supporters, or might, by a change of feeling, be turned out of office to be replaced by a body of an equally homogeneous character. The annual elections must in any case have been expressive of the political feeling of the time; but, if this theory of the presidency be valid, it is hardly an anachronism to speak of "party" in the sense of "ministerial" government when we are dealing with Athenian politics of the fifth century. There are, it is true, important differences between this accidental and imperfect and the modern contemplated and perfect form of responsible government. An Athenian ministry did not retire when defeated, and a general might be elected for military skill alone and be at political variance with his colleagues. But some such personal pre-eminence as that which we have described seems to be implied in the accounts of the position of Pericles during the last fourteen or fifteen years of his life. The only alternative is to suppose that he either strained to the utmost or violated the existing forms of the constitution.[2]

The strategia was, therefore, undoubtedly the highest office of the state, the most natural object of ambition, and the surest basis of power. It depended very much on the holder, and to a certain extent on the times, whether it became the real central point of the Athenian administration; but by the extent of the duties it involved, its special powers of initiative, and its continuity it offered opportunities of influence far above those presented by any other magistracy in the state. Yet it was the least democratic office at Athens. Direct election is often, if not generally, in favour of men of birth and rank, even when it is perfectly free. But election to the strategia was practically not free. The office was felt to demand a degree of military training and skill which was to be

---

[1] Phocion is said to have been general forty-five times (Plut. *Phoc.* 8).

[2] Plut. *Per.* 16; cf. Thuc. ii. 65 στρατηγὸν εἵλοντο καὶ πάντα τὰ πράγματα ἐπέτρεψαν. A similar position seems to have been held by Nicias in 425 (Thuc. iv. 28).

found only in the ranks of the constantly drilled and practised "knights," and not even amongst the hoplites; while the mere mob orator, whose strength was his irresponsibility, shrank from putting himself forward for a post which might necessitate his carrying out in the field with disastrous consequences to himself the suggestions he put forward in the ecclesia. Since this office was closed to the rabble, men of the lower classes, if they were ambitious of leadership, had to seek some other stepping-stone to power; and this was found in financial activity. But this activity was necessarily unofficial, since it is almost certain that no great finance office, which could be held by an individual, existed in the fifth century.[1] Finance during this period was managed by boards or by magistrates with other functions. It was partly in the hands of the central board of the apodectae working with the council, partly in those of the separate controlling boards of separate treasuries, such as the Hellenotamiae, the "treasurers of the sacred money of Athene," and the "treasurers of the other gods," which had no initiative but acted merely on the command of the council and the assembly; while separate departments had the control of their own expenditure, and of these the most important were the strategi. There is no evidence of any central individual authority directing the finances of the state as a whole before the year of reform marked by the archonship of Eucleides (403). But the references to Cleon in the *Knights* of Aristophanes exhibit a man of marvellous financial activity: which is not only shown in the criticism and prosecution of magistrates on their audit,[2] but has a positive connection with state contracts, with the sale of confiscated property, even with the imposition of such burdens as the trierarchy and the property-tax.[3] A portion of this influence may have been exercised by Cleon in a semi-official capacity, for there is evidence that he was at one time a member of the council;[4] a persuasive orator might easily sway the decisions of the Five Hundred, and the proposer of a measure in this body usually (perhaps invariably) carried it through in the ecclesia. But

---

[1] The evidence of the numerous official documents preserved in inscriptions seems to be decisive on this point, although Plutarch speaks of Aristeides as τῶν [δὲ] δημοσίων προσ- όδων αἱρεθεὶς ἐπιμελητής (*Arist.* 4).

[2] ll. 258 ff., 304 ff.

[3] ll. 103, 258, 912, 923, 1226, 1250.

[4] Aristoph. *Eq.* 774.

perhaps such influence was as often exercised by men who were merely private members of the assembly, by means of amendments to bills or alternative proposals on the measures before the house. The financial genius of the fifth century who was not a general had to content himself with this informal control. But the early part of the fourth century marks a period of complete reform in this department, and it is to this century that the names of the great chancellors and treasurers, Eubulus, Diophantus, Demosthenes, and Lycurgus, belong. The chief reason for this reform, and for the new specialisation in finance, was the loss of the empire with its abundant revenues. The rabble wanted as much, or rather more, in the way of festival-money ($\theta\epsilon\omega\rho\iota\kappa\acute{a}$) than they had got during the empire; the state was still often engaged in war; and how, with a greatly reduced income, to supply both these channels of expenditure was the aim of most practical statesmen. The burden could not now be laid so heavily on the richer classes as it had been by the old sliding-scale of the property-tax, and the older mode of imposing the burden of the upkeep of the fleet. Excessive taxation had in 411 prompted the richer classes to conspiracy, and degrees of wealth had been levelled by the long and disastrous war. This was the motive for the introduction of taxation by symmories ($\sigma\upsilon\mu\mu o\rho\acute{\iota}a\iota$), which was applied first to the property-tax and afterwards to the trierarchy—a system by which pecuniary burdens were made to fall mainly upon the upper middle class. This motive is particularly obvious in the organisation of the new trierarchic service introduced by Periander shortly after 358. A selection of twelve hundred of the richer members of the state was made, who were divided into twenty symmories, two to a tribe, of sixty members each.[1] We do not know how the maintenance and upkeep of ships of war was distributed amongst these symmories; the greater portion of the expense was supposed to fall on the three hundred wealthiest members, but the object and working of the law was clearly to extend the incidence of this pecuniary burden. Some twenty years earlier, in 378, a similar system, the details of which are still more imperfectly known to us, had been devised for the eisphora, which apparently made three hundred of the wealthiest citizens responsible for the immediate advance of this war-tax when required. These then recovered

[1] Dem. *de Symm.* § 182.

from a larger circle of less wealthy citizens the dues owed by the latter. Both changes meant a gain to society and to the state, for they took from the oligarchically minded their one ground of complaint, and provided (what in the absence of a reserve fund was now an essential) a rapid mode of furnishing supplies. But they emphasised still further the distinction between the propertied and unpropertied classes, between the lovers of peace and retrenchment and the irresponsible proletariat reckless about plunging into a war the burdens of which fell neither on their persons nor their purses, and careful only of the preservation of their city shows and of the public doles which enabled them to enjoy their holidays. The great financiers were those who could hold the balance between classes, show a full treasury whose demands were moderate, and yet distribute the theorikon with a lavish hand. No statesman has better achieved the apparently impossible in finance than Eubulus as president of the theoric fund (ὁ ἐπὶ τὸ θεωρικόν); but the later financier Lycurgus holds an honourable second place in his administration of a post somewhat resembling that of a chancellor of the exchequer (ὁ ἐπὶ τῇ διοικήσει). Of these two new offices the second is the higher in titular rank and in the sphere of its administrative duties, and the importance of the first is due chiefly to the nature of the fund which it controlled.[1] There was no regular hierarchy in the bureaucracy of Athens, and statesmen who managed relatively minor departments might be as powerful as the chancellor. Given a foothold in office, influence depended on the personality of the holder; Demosthenes, for instance, proposed his reform of the trierarchy as superintendent of the navy (ἐπιστάτης τοῦ ναυτικοῦ).

The head of the financial administration [2] was the channel through which most of the revenue flowed into the different departments for whose use it was destined. His function was that of a distributer, and when all other claims were satisfied he paid the surplus originally into the theoric fund, but, after Demosthenes had in 339 succeeded in persuading the people

---

[1] Gilbert (*Staatsalt.* i. p. 231) explains the apparently equal importance of the two offices by the supposition that the presidency of the theoric fund originated with Eubulus (*circa* 354), and that the office of ὁ ἐπὶ τῇ διοικήσει, which largely replaced it, was not instituted until 339.

[2] ὁ ἐπὶ τῇ διοικήσει is the official title in inscriptions, but we find ταμίας τῆς κοινῆς προσόδου in the decree in [Plut.] *Vit. X. Orat.* p. 852 b.

to use this surplus for military purposes, into the war-office under the control of the strategi. He was, therefore, in theory merely a paymaster acting on the command of the ecclesia and obeying its decrees, some of which were of permanent application, others only of an occasional character. But it is obvious what influence a man who knew every detail of revenue, every item of expenditure must have had in that assembly. He was not gifted, like a modern chancellor, with the sole right of initiating financial proposals: that right was possessed by every individual citizen; but something approaching a ministerial character and implying the sole right of initiative came to attach to an office the holder of which was directly elected, was hampered by no colleagues, and remained in power for four years consecutively; and the twelve years' presidency of Lycurgus teaches us how nearly the working of the institutions of Athens, where the two elements of responsible government, individual control and continuity of power, were recognised, might approximate to that of a modern state. The presidency of the theoric fund, perhaps created in the year 354 by its first great holder Eubulus, represented only a single department of the state; but that department was one which attracted so much popular interest and anxiety that the assumption of the office did in certain cases carry with it the leading position in the government.[1] The anxiety of the mob to see that the festival-money, supplied from the surplus revenue, was increased by care and retrenchment in other branches of the service, was no doubt the motive which led to this office encroaching on the duties of other financial departments. It gradually subsumed the duties of auditor, of apodectae, of the presidents of docks and arsenals, and in fact "almost the whole administration."[2] This development was largely due to the personal influence of the first great president, for the office would never have been assumed as a fitting basis for power had it not been thought capable of indefinite extension.

A review of the military and finance offices which we have discussed shows that constitutional history can supply some-

---

[1] Besides Eubulus we may instance Diophantus, Demosthenes after Chaeroneia, and Demades during the same period, as great holders of the office.

[2] Aesch. c. Ctes. § 25; through the confidence which Eubulus inspired οἱ ἐπὶ τὸ θεωρικὸν κεχειροτονημένοι—σχεδὸν τὴν ὅλην διοίκησιν εἶχον τῆς πόλεως.

thing approaching a legal basis for the exercise of great individual power at Athens. It can point to great offices which naturally fell to men who had won the confidence of the people; but it does not assert that all who had the confidence of the people at any given time were holders of these offices. This theory, which underlies modern party government, was never distinctly held as a principle of Athenian public life; and we cannot better conclude a discussion on the working of the Athenian constitution than by supplying that corrective to the ministerial theory of government which is presented by the popular orator at Athens, the so-called "champion of the people" (προστάτης τοῦ δήμου). His sphere of influence was twofold, and comprised both the ecclesia and the courts. In modern deliberative assemblies, the functions of which correspond to those of the Athenian ecclesia, positive proposals, especially those affecting great imperial interests, are usually put forward only by a responsible ministry, and the opposition is supposed to confine itself to criticism and to attempts at throwing out bills. But a popular demagogue at Athens might baffle the "ministry" at every turn, whether this ministry were represented by the generals or a great financial official acting in concert with the council. He might, by having a temporary majority on his side, succeed, as Cleon did in 427,[1] in getting a measure passed which ran entirely counter to the wishes of the government, and which this government, so far from retiring on defeat, had to put into execution. The shifting nature of the Athenian ecclesia rendered defeats of this kind not uncommon, for the house did not always represent the nation. If the majority of the opposition proved to be a lasting one, the results would no doubt be shown in the elections of the following year, and the demagogue might, like Cleon in 424, be forced to step forward into the hierarchy of the ministry. In this way we can to a limited extent trace the "ins" and "outs" of parties at Athens; but as a rule the demagogue shrank from office and its consequent responsibilities, and one of the weakest points of the Athenian system is that the magistrates are by no means always the men who have the fullest confidence of the people.

It was, indeed, the purely negative and criticising attitude

[1] Thuc. iii. 36.

of the popular leaders that mainly invested them with their proud title of "champions of the people." Their critical activity began in the ecclesia and ended in the law-courts. They were the self-constituted protectors of the people, and guardians of popular liberty against attacks, real or supposed, on the part of the chief magistrates in power or the richer classes backed up by the political clubs which they had at their disposal. A "rhetor" might excite suspicions by accusation or suggestion, and profess to ward off the imaginary danger of his own invention; he might practically close the mouths of moderate men by hinting that they were hostile to the constitution,[1] with the effect of excluding from political life, by the suspicions attached to their character and motives, those who were branded as oligarchs.[2] The "prostates" also assumed a guardianship of the poorer citizens, and posed as a champion of the oppressed.[3] But his favourite sphere of activity was the law-courts. His prosecution at the audit (εὐθύνη) was the phantom that dogged a general's steps on a foreign campaign.[4] He professed himself guardian of the constitution, and in this capacity attacked the "conspiracies" of the political clubs by impeachment before the council or a dicastery;[5] and as prosecutor he might have a semi-official position, for the ecclesia sometimes elected a public advocate (συνήγορος) to assist an accuser, and a prominent "rhetor" would readily be appointed to this post.

The powers of such a man are obvious, and not the least of these was his unassailability. Hence the undying hostility felt for the "sycophant" by the official classes; but the mental attitude such a career assumes is not one that is inconsistent with honesty of purpose. For a picture of this mental attitude we have only to turn to the dramatic portrayal of Athenagoras, "prostates" of the demos at Syracuse in 415, by the great analyst Thucydides.[6] There we find a man on the look-out for the slightest appearance of oligarchic proclivities on the part of magistrates chosen from the aristocracy. He suspects their every act, and tries to make the people equally suspicious; the very news of the Athenian armament which was then sailing against Syracuse he conceives to be only a deep plot meant

[1] Thuc. iii. 42.
[2] ib. viii. 68.
[3] Aristoph. Frogs 569.
[4] ib. Acharn. 938; Thuc. vii. 14.
[5] Aristoph. Knights 861.
[6] Thuc. vi. 35.

to induce the people to confer greater military power on the aristocratic leaders. The demagogue, as here portrayed, represents that atmosphere of doubt and suspicion, equally terrible whether valid or not, which clouds the brilliant picture of democracy in Greece. He may have been a necessary product of her unstable constitutions, but like many other necessary symptoms he was neither pleasant nor harmless.

§ 5 *The Athenian Empire*

The Athenian Empire was the chief product, basis, and perpetuator of democracy in Greece; through it the liberty of the citizen was secured at the temporary expense of the liberty of the state. We shall now proceed to show how it was that a democracy became a tyrant, and how this tyrant performed the not unusual tyrannical function of protecting the rights of man.

The basis of the Athenian Empire was laid in the year 478, when the command of the Greek fleet, which had been victorious over the Persians, was transferred to Athens with Sparta's consent.[1] The earliest constituents of this naval union were the Greeks of many of the Aegean islands and most of the helpless Hellenic cities of the Asiatic coast. Both groups of cities had been made members of the great league of the united Greeks formed in 479, the European portion of which now died a natural death, while the maritime division, and with it the defence of the Asiatic coast, which had not been formally incorporated with but only placed under the protection of the league,[2] fell to the lot of Athens. The fleet under the command of the Spartan Pausanias had also freed from the Persians the states of the Hellespont and Propontis, and these too were added as active or protected members to the new Athenian hegemony.[3] To this original nucleus two subsequent additions were soon made. Cimon's conquest of Eion in 476 freed the Thracian cities, and some ten years later (*circa* 466) the victory of the Eurymedon added the Carian quarter, composed of the towns of the Carian, Lycian, and

---

[1] Thuc. i. 95; *Ath. Pol.* 23.
[2] Herodotus (ix. 106) represents only the islanders (Samians, Chians, Lesbians, etc.) as having been incorporated into this league.
[3] Thuc. i. 95.

Pamphylian coast.[1] The greater part of the Aegean was now a united whole, and from the cities that either bridged or fringed it was formed the Confederacy of Delos under the leadership of Athens. The essential feature of this confederacy was that, while deliberative and judicial powers were exercised by the cities of the league, the chief executive authority was from the first placed in the hands of Athens. All the states were independent ($αὐτόνομοι$), and their delegates met in common assemblies at the temple of Apollo in the island of Delos.[2] These assemblies deliberated on all matters concerned with the interests of the league, and must have acted as a common court of justice, perhaps in punishing individual cases of treason committed against the whole body, but certainly in exacting the required obligations from the cities, and in adjudging those states to be guilty which did not perform their part of the duties for which the league was framed.[3] The common treasury was also at Delos controlled by officials, who bore the title Hellenotamiae. But these were from the first purely Athenian officials, and the complete executive control of Athens is shown also by the fact that it was she who fixed at the outset the mode in which the contributions to the league should be assessed.[4] Some of the states were to furnish ships of war, others money—a difference in burdens which may to some extent have corresponded to the distinction which we have noted as existing between the active and the protected members of the confederacy. Doubtless the states which furnished ships of war would have had a more potent voice at the council; but the principle was not yet established that the power of debate and of voting was confined to these, and that the cities which furnished money should be reduced to a condition of passive and silent obedience. In fact, some of the states may have furnished both ships and money;[5] but the tribute ($φόρος$) said to have been assessed by the Athenian Aristeides[6] included the money contributions alone.

A change in the character of the league is visible at an early period of its existence. Fresh cities were taken and

[1] Her. vii. 107 ; Thuc. i. 100.
[2] κοιναὶ ξύνοδοι, ib. i. 97.
[3] This judicial function of the league was employed by the Athenians as a means of strengthening their hegemony (Thuc. vi. 76).
[4] ib. i. 96.
[5] Plut. Cim. 11. This passage also implies that the cities which furnished ships supplied land contingents besides their crews (οὔτε τὰς ναῦς ἐπλήρουν οὔτ' ἄνδρας ἀπέστελλον).
[6] Ath. Pol. 23.

added against their will, and one of these, Scyros, became an Athenian cleruchy and was wholly appropriated by the leading state.[1] In these deeds of force Athens was no doubt actively assisted by her confederates. We have only to remember the object for which the league was formed, and the way in which the allies regarded this object, to understand the events immediately following. The professed object was to keep the Aegean clear of the Persians and their Phoenician fleet and to guarantee the independence not only of the islanders but of the helpless Greek cities of the Asiatic coast. To effect this object a permanent defensive force was necessary, and the allies had taxed themselves heavily in ships and money. They would naturally wish these burdens to be distributed as evenly as possible over the states benefited by their protection; for the wider the limits of the league, the lighter would be the strain on its individual members. Thus their hostility would naturally be directed against two classes of Aegean cities: those that stood aloof altogether, and those that had belonged to the confederacy but refused to continue their contributions; both were reaping the benefits while others were bearing the burdens. Hence when Naxos, one of the bulwarks of the league, revolted in 466, and refused any longer to supply ships or to pay its equivalent quota, Athens was assisted in its reduction by her allies, and its subjection was no doubt felt to be justified on grounds of equity. More dangerous was the principle which dictated that its enforced re-entrance into the league should be made only on certain terms. It was to pay tribute in the future, to be deprived of its vote—to become in fact a subject of the confederacy.[2] Meanwhile more general causes had been at work which profoundly modified the relations of the states to Athens. The efforts of the confederates could not keep pace with the restless activity of the leading state. A tribal inscription of this period records the names of Athenians who in the year 460 had fallen in Cyprus, Egypt, Phoenicia, Halieis, Aegina, and Megara.[3] But a career of active interference with the empires of the East was something more than the mere protection from aggression, which was all that the allies desired and all that the league was

---

[1] Thuc. i. 98.
[2] *ib.* πρώτη τε αὕτη πόλις ξυμμαχὶς παρὰ τὸ καθεστηκὸς ἐδουλώθη, ἔπειτα δὲ καὶ τῶν ἄλλων ὡς ἑκάστῃ ξυνέβη.
[3] Hicks n. 19.

intended to secure. They fell into arrears in money and ships, and the penalty was doubtless the loss of their votes; they offered a monetary payment in place of maritime contingents, and Athens accepted the compromise. Thus the allies tended to become a class of tributaries (ὑποτελεῖς), while Athens held a fleet kept in the fullest degree of efficiency by constant active service. Her increased power was shown by the ease with which she crushed the revolt of Thasos in 465, her intentions by her persistent efforts to occupy strategical positions in the neighbouring district of Thrace, which was to be the key of her future empire. It was now plain to the Greek world that Athens was not the head merely but the only power in the league, and even Sparta took the alarm. But no efforts could be made to stay the development of the confederacy into an empire, which was finally attained in the year 454, when the common treasury was transferred from Delos to Athens, and the first-fruits of the tribute (one-sixtieth of each state's assessment), which had formerly been paid to Apollo of Delos, were now presented to Athene of the Athenians.[1] At this time the only states whose autonomy was guaranteed by the supply of ships in place of tribute were apparently Samos, Lesbos, Chios, and the Euboean towns; and it is probable that tributary states had now been excluded from all direct influence in the league—that, in fact, the votes of the great congress had dwindled down to the votes of these four islands and the city of Athens. For a time victory on the mainland of Greece had kept pace with success on the seas. But the land hegemony of Athens, who between the years 457 and 447 had either conquered or entered into close alliance with Boeotia, Phocis, Opuntian Locris, Megara, Achaea, and Argos, was closed by the loss of Boeotia in 447 and the revolt of Megara in 445. To Pericles the loss of this supremacy by land mattered little: it was more burden than profit to maintain control over all this extent of territory, and diverted the state's attention from its main object—the strengthening of its maritime power. In 445 even this seemed threatened by the revolt of Euboea, the towns of which had up to this time been autonomous. But the conclusion of this revolt strengthened Athens' hands; Euboea was subdued, Histiaea became an Athenian cleruchy, and the remainder of

---

[1] The year 454 is the date at which the tribute lists commence. The first-fruits (ἀπαρχή) appear as "a mina in the talent" (μνᾶ ἀπὸ τοῦ ταλάντου).

the island was made tributary.[1] In 440 Samos revolted, and was subdued during the following year after a hard struggle, in which Athens was assisted by the only two remaining free allies—the Chians and Lesbians.[2] This island also ceased to be free and became tributary. Yet even after this it required open revolt to forfeit the condition of independent alliance. After the defection of the greater part of Lesbos and its reduction in 427, one of its towns, Methymna, still shared with Chios the honour of remaining a free city;[3] while Samos for good service to the democracy regained its autonomy in 412.[4] These autonomous allies were strictly speaking not under the dominion ($ἀρχή$) of Athens at all,[5] and their independence was defined as consisting in control of their own courts and of their own finances.[6] They brought neither suits nor tribute to Athens, and were perhaps bound only by the prescriptions of the old Delian league, but they were by no means free from the practical interference of the leading state, which stopped any procedure likely to lead to their revolt.[7] For a time indeed an effort seems to have been made to keep up the fiction of a council, its object being to give a shadow of legality and a show of independent support to the aggressions of Athens on her revolted subjects;[8] but it is scarcely possible that this fiction survived the outbreak of the Peloponnesian War. Yet the legal language of official documents still recognises the permanence of the confederacy, and claims no sovereignty of Athens over any of the states. What Greek historians call the empire appears there as the "symmachy" of the Athenians; what they call the subjects ($ὑπήκοοι$) appear under the colourless names of "the allies" or "the cities."[9]

There is little doubt that the legal basis of the Athenian Empire was formed by a system of separate agreements with the separate states, although we have no means of determining whether this basis was universal and whether all the states of the Delian league were brought into new relations with Athens

---

[1] Thuc. i. 114. [2] *ib.* i. 116.
[3] *ib.* vi. 81. [4] *ib.* viii. 21.
[5] The Mytileneans describe themselves as $οὐκ ἀρχόμενοι ὥσπερ οἱ ἄλλοι$ (*ib.* iii. 36).
[6] $αὐτόνομοι$ is explained by the words $αὐτοτελεῖς$ and $αὐτόδικοι$, *ib.* v. 18.

[7] Thus in 424 the Chians were made to pull down their new fortifications on suspicion of an intended revolt (*ib.* iv. 51).
[8] *ib.* iii. 11.
[9] $ἡ Ἀθηναίων ξυμμαχία$ (Hicks n. 23 l. 30). The allies are $οἱ σύμμαχοι$ or $αἱ πόλεις$.

by a series of documents dictated by the people. The one-sided character of these agreements makes them of the nature rather of charters than of treaties, although sometimes they are confirmed by the mutual oath of the contracting parties. The character of these documents can best be estimated by a brief review of the contents of the two fullest which have been preserved—a charter granted to Erythrae in Ionia between 455 and 450, and another to Chalcis in Euboea on the settlement of that island in 445.[1] The charter of Erythrae gives that state a constitution, and is a remarkable and no doubt exceptional instance of the detailed reorganisation of a city which, when it passed into the power of Athens, possessed no regular form of polity.[2] The constitution is closely modelled on that of Athens. The existence of an ecclesia being presumed, the chief attention is devoted to the establishment of a council of a hundred and twenty members, which is to be the chief deliberative and executive, and, in this case, probably the chief judicial body. The qualifications of the members,[3] their scrutiny on entrance, and their audit follow the rules at Athens. They are to be selected by lot by the "overseer" (ἐπίσκοπος) and the "captain of the guard" (φρούραρχος) for the current year—in subsequent years by the captain acting with the council. The civil official here mentioned was merely a temporary commissioner sent out for a special work of organisation, and retiring when it was completed,[4] for Athens had no harmosts in her cities. But the military official is meant to be permanent, and therefore we must conclude that an Athenian garrison (φρουρά) was to be kept in Erythrae. It was, however, unusual for Athens to garrison the cities of her empire, and it seems only to have been done where, as at Samos in 439, it was thought necessary to secure the allegiance of the state,[5] or where, as in Thrace, the cities were actually the seat of war.[6] The council of Erythrae takes an oath, in which, after expressing in general terms the fullest

---

[1] Hicks nn. 23 and 28; a valuable supplement to these is the decree of the people referring to Methone (Hicks n. 44).

[2] The document shows that Erythrae had been in the hands of τύραννοι.

[3] Even the rule that the same member may not be chosen again for four years may have existed at Athens. In later times more than one reappointment to the βουλή was forbidden (*Ath. Pol.* 62).

[4] His temporary character is proved both by the document itself and by the reference to the ἐπίσκοπος in Aristoph. *Birds* 1023.

[5] Thuc. i. 115.

[6] *ib.* iv. 7, 108; v. 39.

allegiance to Athens and to her other allies, it agrees to limit its jurisdiction by reserving for the Athenian courts all cases of treason involving capital punishment.

This document represents but one side of the compact—the relations of the subject state to Athens; the charter given to Chalcis represents the other side as well, and grants distinct privileges. It opens with an oath taken by the two sworn bodies at Athens—the council and the heliaea—to the effect that they will take no extreme measures against the citizens of Chalcis, nor inflict death or exile, apart from such jurisdiction as the ecclesia ordains,[1] that the prytaneis shall never put the question to the vote where a charge has been improperly brought, and that free access to the council and to the ecclesia shall be allowed to envoys from the state. The Chalcidians take a counter oath. It professes general allegiance to Athens, expresses a promise to pay such tribute as the two states may agree on, and gives an indefinite guarantee of service and obedience, especially in the form of personal assistance. For the payment of tribute by no means exhausted the duties of the allies to Athens; they were bound to furnish land contingents, and to follow her to war when called on to do so, whether by a special decree applicable to a special state or by a common decree (κοινὸν ψήφισμα) which applied to the whole empire.[2] The charter goes on to confer immunity from all taxation—and consequently from the tribute which was collected from the local dues—on strangers resident in Chalcis and on certain classes of the citizens themselves, in terms which show that Athens, like Rome, claimed the singular privilege of exempting individuals or classes in the allied communities not only from imperial but from local burdens.[3] The final clause enacts that the audit of the magistrates of Chalcis shall take place in their native state, except where the charge is a capital one involving exile, death, or disfranchisement. In such cases there shall be a remit to the Athenian courts "in accordance with the decree of the people"—probably that decree which regulated the jurisdiction of this particular state.

---

[1] This is the only intelligible meaning that can be given to the words ἄνευ τοῦ δήμου τοῦ Ἀθηναίων (l. 9).

[2] κοινὸν ψήφισμα . . . περὶ βοηθείας (Hicks n. 44 l. 44). For instances of this levy see Thuc. ii. 9; iv. 42; vi. 26, 43.

[3] Exemption from the φόρος alone would have been impossible, as there was probably no fixed mode for its assessment in the allied states.

The general duties of the allies to Athens may be easily gathered from these two charters. They consist in a promise of fealty, a promise to pay the required tribute and to furnish active assistance in case Athens required it, and, further, in an agreement to give up some of their autonomous rights, the chief of these rights surrendered being that of jurisdiction in exceptional cases, such as those of treason to the central state and to the empire. The return that Athens made for all this was her protection. She is irresponsible, a "tyrant city," and in the position of one who commands. If she makes concessions, they are in the nature of privileges. She might impose limits to her own irresponsible power, and she sometimes grants special favours—such as immunity to individuals or practical exemption from tribute to whole states, which she allows to pay only the sixtieth as first-fruits to the goddess. But these are acts of grace, and the exemption granted to states was perhaps as much intended to promote differences of interests as to cultivate the loyalty of important outposts.[1]

The chief burden was the tribute, but its variations show it to have been always on a moderate scale. The amount imposed at the formation of the league in 478 is said by Thucydides to have amounted to four hundred and sixty talents. By the beginning of the Peloponnesian War in 431 it had risen to only six hundred talents.[2] It has been thought that Thucydides, in his estimate of the original tribute, antedates a maximum which was only reached some years after the formation of the confederacy, when more states had been forced to join the league and many more had ceased to furnish naval contingents and had become tributary. For a time an effort seems to have been made to keep the maximum the same by lowering the individual assessments as fresh cities joined. But after the year 437 this principle was abandoned, the older and higher rate was reverted to,[3] and the tribute swelled to the maximum which it had reached in 431.[4] The remaining epochs in its history were due to the pressure of the Peloponnesian War. The assessment list for the year 425 shows such an increase in the payments of individual cities as to verify the statement that the tribute was doubled before

---

[1] Such as Methone, on which this exemption is conferred (Hicks n. 44).
[2] Thuc. i. 96; ii. 13.
[3] Probably the rate which is called the "Aristeidean assessment" in Thuc. v. 18.
[4] Kirchhoff in Hermes xi. p. 27 ff.

the close of this struggle.[1] Finally in 413, when the empire was falling to pieces, the φόρος was commuted for a tax of five per cent (εἰκοστή),[2] probably on all imports and exports of the allied communities. The moderation of the tribute is shown by the fact that this commutation could be made with the hope of increasing the total; but the tribute list, when the assessment is at its highest, tells the same tale. Paros paid thirty talents, Naxos and Andros fifteen each, Thera five, while little islands like Belbina and Cimolus contributed from three hundred to a thousand drachmae. This was the rating of the allies only three years after the date when Athens had in a single year collected a property-tax of two hundred talents from her own citizens.[3] The assessment of the tribute produced the only modification of the view that the Athenian Empire was an aggregate not of districts but of cities; for it was divided into larger areas for purposes of taxation. These areas were convenient geographical divisions and corresponded to the stages in the acquisition of the empire. The tribute lists earlier than the year 437 show a division of the territory ruled by Athens into Ionia, the Hellespont, Thrace, Caria, and the Islanders. After this date a change occurs. The Carian quarter as an independent unit disappears, possibly in consequence of the unrecorded loss of some of the cities in this district, and the Ionian and Carian cities are classed together, appearing first as Ionian and afterwards as Carian.[4] A revision of the tribute, for the purpose of renewed assessment, was generally undertaken every fifth year.[5] For this the council was mainly responsible, but to secure assistance and advice it was in the habit of appointing special commissioners (τάκται), eight of whom are found (two for each of the great divisions of the empire) in the assessment list for the year 425. The mode of taxation, which had no less than five stages, illustrates the genius of the Greeks for minute political organisation. First each city proposed the amount of its own tribute.[6] This

---

[1] Aeschin. *de fals. Leg.* p. 337.
[2] Thuc. vii. 28. Its collectors were εἰκοστολόγοι (Aristoph. *Frogs* 363).
[3] Thuc. iii. 19.
[4] In the quota list for 443 (Hicks n. 30) the Ionian and Carian tribute are both included; in that for 436 (n. 35) the Ionian is found, the Carian omitted. In the assessment for 425 (n. 47) the Ionian and Carian cities are classed together.
[5] [Xen.] *Resp. Ath.* 3, 5.
[6] Hence the expression in the oath of the Chalcidians (Hicks n. 28 l. 26) καὶ τὸν φόρον ὑποτελῶ Ἀθηναίοισιν ὃν ἂν πείθω Ἀθηναίους.

proposal might be accepted by the council, or this body might reject it and prefer instead the estimate given by the commissioners. The whole case then went before the ecclesia, which might either accept the assessment of the council or reject it in preference for an estimate proposed by some private individual member of its own body. Matters did not even end here; for there might be an appeal from the ecclesia to the law-courts, and according to their final verdict the new taxation might be confirmed or invalidated.[1] These modes of assessment give us the four classes of states which are found in our inscriptions; the division is into cities assessed (i) by themselves, (ii) by the commissioners, (iii) by private individuals (ἰδιῶται), (iv) by the council (or presumably any of the other initiating powers) and the five hundred heliasts. The mention of an additional impost (ἐπιφορά) is sometimes met with in the tribute lists, but on what grounds it was imposed we do not know. The payment of the tribute was made to the Hellenotamiae by the allied states themselves at the Great Dionysia,[2] the "money-collecting ships" (ἀργυρολόγοι νῆες) of which we hear so much in the historians being sent out only in exceptional cases to collect debts from states which were backward in their payment.[3] The official records of the tribute, of which many specimens have been preserved in inscriptions, were of two kinds. They were either the so-called "quota" lists, i.e. lists of cities with the sixtieth part of the tribute paid to Athene appended to their names, or "assessment" lists (τάξεις φόρου), which gave the full tribute imposed on each state opposite its name.[4] The practice of grouping states together for the purposes of assessment makes these lists unsafe guides for an estimate of the number of contributing cities, which Aristophanes (probably with some exaggeration) represents as reaching the total of a thousand.[5] For, although in such groups (συντελεῖς) taxation would be distributed over the cities in proportion to their size, yet the largest and most important would probably

---

[1] This right of appeal is stated in the assessment for 425 (Hicks n. 47 § h).

[2] Schol. Aristoph. Acharn. l. 504; he quotes Eupolis.

[3] They are first mentioned in 428, when the Athenians were hard pressed for money (Thuc. iii. 19), and were no doubt sent out as the result of such a κοινὸν ψήφισμα for collecting arrears of tribute (τὰ ὀφειλήματα) as that mentioned in the decree about Methone (Hicks n. 44 l. 13).

[4] The assessment for 425 will be found in Hicks n. 47; five quota lists in nn. 24, 30, 35, 48.

[5] Aristoph. Wasps l. 707.

be responsible for the payment, and as such would alone appear in the tribute list.

The jurisdiction of the Athenian courts was the second great limitation on the independence of the allied states. It was inevitable that an imperial state in the position of Athens should reserve many cases for her own courts; but the scantiness of our information makes it very difficult to discover general principles, especially in the regulation of civil jurisdiction, and perhaps the practice recognised in the different charters varied considerably. An approach to a principle regulating criminal jurisdiction can be discerned in clauses of the two charters which we have discussed. In that of Erythrae it is laid down that no citizen shall be capitally punished in defiance of the jurisdiction ordained by the ecclesia; in that of Chalcis jurisdiction is given to the local courts, "except in cases involving exile, death, or disfranchisement."[1] It is clear that capital charges, at least of certain kinds, had to be brought to Athens. In the charter of Erythrae revolt from the empire and Medism are mentioned in connection with this provision, while the clause in the charter of Chalcis refers to the audit of local magistrates. It seems, therefore, that most of the criminal cases brought to Athens would be capital charges of treason; and this conclusion is borne out by an adverse comment of the time, which states that the individuals condemned at Athens belonged to the oligarchical element in the allied states, and hints that their condemnation was due chiefly to political motives.[2] The assignment of criminal cases to special courts whether by general or particular decrees was entirely in the hands of the ecclesia, and in no other department of the state was the sovereignty of this body so clearly asserted as in the regulation of the jurisdiction of the empire.

Of civil jurisdiction we know nothing beyond certain ordinances affecting certain states. From an extremely mutilated fragment of an inscription recording a treaty between Athens and Miletus it has been gathered that private suits, where the question at issue involved a sum over a hundred drachmae, had to be brought to Athens.[3] But there is little to show that this stringent regulation was universal. An im-

---

[1] See p. 195.
[2] [Xen.] *Resp. Ath.* 1, 16 καὶ τοὺς μὲν τοῦ δήμου σώζουσι, τοὺς δ' ἐναντίους ἀπολλύουσι ἐν τοῖς δικαστηρίοις.
[3] *C.I.A.* iv. 22 a.

portant class of cases seem to have been the suits of private international law known as δίκαι ἀπὸ συμβολῶν—suits arising from contracts concluded either "between individuals in the respective states, or between individuals and the state, or between the state and individuals."[1] It has been supposed, from the analogy of the procedure adopted in such cases during the second Athenian confederacy, that the equitable principle was adopted of recognising the jurisdiction of the local courts when the contract had been concluded in the allied city, and of bringing the case to Athens only when the contract had been concluded there.[2]

Our ignorance of this civil jurisdiction is the more to be regretted as the commercial was one of the fairest aspects of the Athenian Empire. The Aegean must have benefited by the secure trade which was maintained by the lasting peace, and which it was the interest of Athens to encourage, since active commerce meant the security of her revenues. It is possible that she may herself have profited by the creation of monopolies,[3] but there is no hint even from the most adverse sources of injustice committed by her commercial regulations. The Athenian jurisdiction was regarded as a grievance, but the hardship consisted in the summons of the parties to Athens, and perhaps in the application of Athenian law to these dependencies. We are never told distinctly that even the criminal jurisdiction was abused, although it would seem so to one hostile to the democracy, since convictions of oligarchs who stirred up sedition in the allied states were frequent. The greater part of the tribute was used to keep up the Athenian fleet, and so far in the interest of the allies. The empire fulfilled the promise of the confederacy in keeping the Aegean clear of enemies; and it is almost certain that until its fall the Greeks of Asia paid no tribute to Persia. But the surplus was employed by Athens for public buildings and for the theoric fund, and land was annexed in the conquered districts for the establishment of cleruchies. The primary object of these settlements was to provide land for the poorer citizens of Athens; they seem

---

[1] Hicks n. 58 § 4. They are probably the ξυμβόλαιαι δίκαι of Thuc. i. 77.

[2] C.I.A. ii. 11. If with Gilbert we read κατ[ὰ τὰς πρὶν] ξυμβολάς and not κατ[ὰ τὰς Χίων] ξυμβολάς, the supposition becomes a certainty, since this treaty with Phaselis would refer back to the procedure of the earlier league.

[3] Such as that created in Ceos during the second confederacy (Hicks n. 108).

usually to have been settled on territory that had become the prize of war, and their advent came to be dreaded rather as a sign of military coercion than because they interfered with the rights of peaceful members of the league. For their strategic came to outweigh their social importance, and one of their main functions was to inspire fear into the allies and to serve as a guard against intended revolt.[1] They assumed the form of organised communities, and as such mark the last stage in the history of state-directed colonisation. The settlement was decreed by the people and the settlers chosen from the poorer citizens by lot. The cleruchs remained Athenian citizens; collectively they were but a fragment of the demos settled in a distant outpost,[2] individually they still bore the designations which marked them as members of the Attic tribes. These settlements present rather the theory of an extended local government than that of the possession of a twofold citizenship by the same individuals. In some respects they resembled the states of the empire, and their jurisdiction was limited by the provision that all important cases had to be brought to Athens. Their structure was that of the typical democracy, and decrees were voted by their council and assembly. But they paid no tribute, and, unlike the allied cities, received magistrates from Athens.[3]

These Athenian stations were no greater abuses of power than the Roman military colonies which they strikingly resemble, and must have been less invidious than the only other alternative—the quartering of permanent garrisons in cities whose position was important or whose loyalty was suspected. The sins of commission with which Athens can be charged being so few, we are not surprised that greater stress is laid on her sins of omission. She ought, the Emperor Claudius considered, to have extended political rights to her allies.[4] But, if we regard the bare fact of her empire as a political crime, we must remember that a crime of this sort is

[1] Plut. *Per.* 11. Where this motive was not present the cleruchs at times did not even go out to their allotments. Those to whom the forfeited lands of the Lesbians were assigned in 427 remained at Athens receiving an annual rent from the original occupiers (Thuc. iii. 50).

[2] Hence such titles as ὁ δῆμος ὁ ἐν Ἡφαιστίᾳ or Ἀθηναίων οἱ ἐν Ποτιδαίᾳ κατοικοῦντες.

[3] ἄρχοντες in Antiph. *de caed. Her.* § 47.

[4] Tac. *Ann.* xi. 24 *quid aliud exitio Lacedaemoniis et Atheniensibus fuit . . . nisi quod victos pro alienigenis arcebant?*

to be judged by the political conscience of the age in which it is committed. We have already noted the absence of general international principles in Greece, and the idea had not yet originated that the only justification for empire is that it should be a burden. Whether the theory of despotism so brutally stated in the pages of Thucydides[1] was really cultivated and expressed with this unblushing frankness by Pericles and his successors, we do not know. If it was, it was mainly the result of alarm at the irresponsible position into which Athens had been forced; and fear was the pretext, though it cannot be the justification, of her occasional acts of cruelty.[2] But Athens as a rule expended her insolence in words, and was on the whole a kind and just task-mistress. More she could not be, although a certain class of politicians—men of the moderate or middle party—seem even to have hinted at the possibility of Imperial Federation.[3] But this was after the Sicilian expedition, when the empire was rapidly falling to pieces; it was a last resort, and is well compared by Beloch with the similar proposals for unification which were made at Rome after the battle of Cannae.[4] The federal system was indeed the only alternative to direct rule, for the states would not have thanked Athens for the useless gift of her citizenship, and, even had representative government been dreamed of, the mere municipal life which it would have left to the cities would have been a poor exchange for the relics of autonomy which they possessed. The only actual unity assumed by the Athenian Empire was the merely religious unity characteristic of Greece. The states were regarded, from a religious point of view, in the light of Athenian colonies, and had like them to send to the Panathenaea sacred offerings which were not meant as burdens but as symbols of a sentimental allegiance.[5] In 426 Athens made a really great and definite attempt at a unification of part of her empire by the reinstitution of the Delian games and the revival of the amphictyony of Ionian islanders.[6] There are also indications that at least a partial admission to the franchise was granted to some states during the later period of the

[1] Thuc. v. 105; vi. 85.
[2] Such as the massacres at Scione and at Melos.
[3] Aristoph. *Lysistr.* 528 ff.
[4] Beloch *Attische Politik* p. 67 note 2.
[5] They are instructed to send an ox and two sheep, and to take part in the πομπή (Hicks n. 47); cf. the similar injunctions on the Athenian colonists to Brea (Hicks n. 29).
[6] p. 49.

empire,[1] a modification of the policy of exclusiveness inaugurated by Pericles, which aimed at keeping Athens as the privileged aristocracy with the empire as its material basis. Yet even this policy was tempered by the nobler aim of asserting individual liberty by the spread of the democratic ideal, and of raising the subject classes of Athens' subject states by freeing them from the government of restricted oligarchies. An empire governed by a democracy must needs be democratic; and community of political interests between the rulers and their subjects need not necessarily be destroyed by the absolutism of the former and the partial loss of independence by the latter. In the Athenian Empire the tie between the government of the central state and the masses in the allied communities seems to have been peculiarly strong. The whole point of Cleon's gibe that "a democracy cannot govern an empire" is that the demos at Athens was much too prone to regard with tolerance and to rule with mercy their counterparts in the states.[2] This government was "the champion of the masses, the enemy of dynasties, denying the right of the many to be at the mercy of the few."[3] But it did not assert this right in the tyrannical form of overthrowing established constitutions to make way for democracies. The statement of Isocrates[4] that Athens "did not create confusion in the cities by establishing counter-governments" is borne out by facts. Where she had to reconstitute a state afresh she naturally established a constitution of a democratic type, as at Erythrae; but the only certain instance of the subversion of an existing oligarchy—the change of government effected in 440 at Samos on the eve of its revolt—was a transitory attempt to meet a pressing danger, for she allowed the state to resume its narrow polity before the close of the Peloponnesian War.[5] She recognised that loyalty could not be created; but the proof that it was felt in most of the states of the empire is so clear from the whole history of the Peloponnesian War, that we hardly need the definite statement of the moderate Diodotus that "the democracy in all the states is loyal," or the still more valuable confession of the oligarch Phrynichus that the cities look on the demos of Athens as "their refuge and the chastisers of the so-called nobility.[6] But, though a democratic govern-

[1] p. 132. [2] Thuc. iii. 37. [5] Thuc. i. 115; viii. 21.
[3] Isocr. *Paneg.* p. 62. [4] *l.c.* [6] *ib.* iii. 47; viii. 48.

ment would feel its existence imperilled by defection from the empire, and interest as well as sympathy dictated loyalty, if we look at the opposite side of the picture we see nothing but baffled resistance and constraint. "The few" must have hated the rule of Athens; for it is probable that the burden of the tribute, collected on the basis of a property-tax, fell most heavily on them, and they found themselves deprived of all chance of personal distinction in their own cities and of a free hand in administration. In most of the states we may imagine a patriotic party generally in the minority, an Athenian party generally in the majority; and this majority proves the truth of Aristotle's dictum[1] that the masses will remain quiet if only they are decently treated. "The poor," it has been said, "have no passions, only wants." The average democracy seeks protection even more than power, and if it cannot defend its interests by the absolutism of a Pericles of its own, will be content to seek shelter under the wing of a great imperial state.

The final break-up of this vast organisation did not come from the empire itself; and it is doubtful whether any revolt would have been stirred had not the disaster in Sicily given courage and strength to the patriots abroad and a chance of reaction to the oligarchs at home which fatally weakened the bonds of democratic allegiance in the states. But the effects of the empire were permanent. It had for seventy years fostered popular government in the East, and inscriptions tell us with what result. The βουλὴ καὶ δῆμος appear as the governing power throughout the Aegean and in Asia Minor, at Samos, Chios, Paros, Mytilene, Halicarnassus, Rhodes, Byzantium, and many other cities. Crushed for a moment by Spartan despotism, many of these cities again sought Athens as a liberator, and to assert their freedom formed the alliance generally known as the Second Athenian Confederacy.

§ 6 *The Athenian Confederacy*

The origin of this confederacy is to be sought in the victory gained by the Athenian admiral Conon at Cnidus in 394. This victory brought Athens again into close relations with the

[1] *Pol.* vi. 4 = 1318 b.

cities of the Asiatic coast, and for the second time she appears as a liberator bent on establishing a naval supremacy in concert with the cities which she protects. The Chians expelled their Spartan garrison and entered into close alliance with Athens. Mytilene, Ephesus, and Erythrae followed; then ensued a general expulsion of harmosts from the states, and the maritime empire of Sparta was at an end.[1] But Athens did not form a definite confederacy until 378, when the open hostility of Sparta displayed by the condonation of Sphodrias' attack on the Peiraeus gave her a pretext for forming an association to resist further attacks on herself and other states. Chios, Mytilene, Methymna, Rhodes, Byzantium, and Thebes joined the defensive union, and in the next year an invitation to alliance was offered to all cities, whether Greek or barbarian, which (out of respect for the terms of the peace of Antalcidas) "did not belong to the Persian king."[2] This invitation met with a ready response, and the league finally reached the formidable total of seventy or seventy-five members.[3] Its professed object was still to secure the freedom and autonomy guaranteed by the peace of Antalcidas against Lacedaemonian attacks, but it is needless to say that the confederacy continued long after this terror had passed away. Any distrust of Athens' real intentions that the history of the first confederacy may have sown in the minds of cities eager to join seems to have been removed by the proclamation issued by the Athenian ecclesia in 377.[4] It declared that each ally should be free and autonomous, that it should enjoy any constitution it pleased, that it should never be compelled to receive an Athenian garrison or governor or to pay tribute. To remove the fear of Athenian cleruchies it was further declared unlawful for any Athenian citizen, either in a public or a private capacity, to possess land or house in the territory of the allies. The penalty was confiscation by the council of the confederates.

In form this was almost a revival of the confederacy of Delos, for Athens was not a simple member of the alliance, and furnished no delegate to the council. She was, like Sparta in her Peloponnesian confederacy, the head. Her position was

---

[1] Diod. xiv. 84, 94; cf. xv. 30.
[2] ὅσοι μὴ βασιλέως εἰσίν (Hicks n. 81 l. 15).
[3] Seventy in Diod. xv. 30; seventy-five in Aeschin. *de fals. Leg.* § 70.
[4] Hicks n. 81.

secured by a system of separate treaties with the particular cities. The details of organisation may have been arranged by Athens, and must have been committed to writing; but there is no evidence for any general charter, other than the above-mentioned manifesto, which regulated the relations of the allies to the leading state.

Athens stood to her allies as the executive to the deliberative power. The council was composed of delegates from the states (οἱ σύνεδροι τῶν συμμάχων), each of which had an equal vote. Its opinion was taken on all foreign relations; we find it framing decrees on war, peace, and alliance, and voting on the use of money contributed by the allies.[1] But, as was usual in Greek confederacies, the executive power had the final voice in deliberation, and in the last resort everything depended on the decision of the Athenian ecclesia. While in the Peloponnesian confederacy a conflict between Sparta and her allies was avoided by the simple device of making Sparta the sole mover and the allies the final ratifying authority, in the Athenian confederacy the opinion of the "synedrion" went either directly or through the council of Athens to the ecclesia,[2] and this latter body had the final voice. The council of the allies was therefore a probouleutic, and as such tended naturally to become a mere advising body. Community of interest may have been thought sufficient to secure absence of conflict, but the clumsy procedure did not; and we know that late in the history of the league, in 346, such a conflict did take place between the now attenuated synedrion and the Athenian assembly. The peace concluded in that year with Philip of Macedon ran counter to the first resolution (δόγμα) of the council of the league, and a tardy consent was unwillingly wrung from the allies.[3] The tendency of events was, as in the earlier confederacy, in favour of the increased supremacy of Athens. Even money contribu-

---

[1] Hicks n. 84; *C.I.A.* ii. 62. From a clause of the proclamation (Hicks n. 81 l. 51) that "whoever proposes anything contrary to this decree κρινέσθω ἐν Ἀθηναίοις καὶ τοῖς συμμάχοις," it has been concluded that the council sat as a court of justice. But the words may mean only "in Athens and in the cities of the allies."

[2] In the decree voting honours to Dionysius I. (Hicks n. 84) it is enacted περὶ μὲν τῶν γραμμάτων ὧν ἔπεμψεν Διονύσιος ... τοὺς συμμάχους δόγμα ἐξενεγκεῖν εἰς τὸν δῆμον. It was probably more usual for the δόγμα to pass through the council.

[3] Aesch. *de fals. Leg.* § 60; *c. Ctes.* § 69. The passages show that the allies finally consented to the peace without committing themselves to approval of its terms.

tions came in time to be imposed and exacted. It is probable that no contributions at all were contemplated when the league was first formed; but one of the causes which developed the former empire was still at work, and the smaller states were eager to compound for personal service by a money payment. The Athenian financier Callistratus, realising how much depends on names, avoided the hated word φόρος, and the colourless "contributions" (συντάξεις) fixed by the ecclesia were collected when in arrears by Athenian officials.[1]

But the basis of this league was insecure, and it had its weak points both in East and West. It admitted the great land power of Thebes, and the sphere of Athenian influence in Asia Minor did not extend far inland. The great period of Theban supremacy began with the battle of Leuctra in 371, and parted the state from the alliance; the Euboean towns followed the new leader, and were not recovered until 358. The naval expeditions of Epaminondas severed other allies from the confederacy; and in 357 came the breach with the chief Eastern states which led to the Social War. The intrigues of Mausolus, working on the fears of Chios, Byzantium, and Rhodes, led them to believe that Athens was plotting against their liberties;[2] and this feeling, assisted by the distrust inspired by new Athenian cleruchies planted at Samos and Potidaea, led to the revolt of the former states. They were freed by the peace of 355; but a diminished number of satellites of Athens still lingered round her until Chaeroneia put an end to the shadow of a league and the last relics of Athenian supremacy.[3]

The permanence of this confederacy would not have added much to the constitutional history of Greece. It had in its origin performed the service of restoring democracy to many of the cities of the Aegean, but Macedon, after enslaving Greece, took over the rôle of liberator of the Eastern cities from the Persians. The gift of the Athenian Empire was perpetuated, and a new epoch of Hellenistic civilisation, based on a free political life, begins, which gradually merges, without essential changes, into the period of the all-embracing protectorate of Rome.

[1] Harpocrat. s.v. σύνταξις. For the collection of these dues, C.I.A. ii. 62. See Gilbert Staatsalt. i. pp. 416, 417. [2] Dem. pro Rhod. 3. [3] Paus. i. 25.

§ 7 *Disturbances in the Athenian Constitution—the closing Scene*

In treating Athenian political life, both internally and externally, as first an unimpeded march and then a triumphant progress of democracy, we have wilfully shut our eyes to all violent disturbing causes which ended in revolution. Such revolution is but the occasional storm that disturbs even the calmest sea. At Athens oligarchic reaction never led to a violent counter-reaction except in the one case of the supremacy of the Areiopagus, which we have treated. The changes are subtle and gradual, and oligarchic plots, whether successful or otherwise, had little influence on the main course of political development.

But the pathology of Greek states, which Aristotle thought as important a branch of politics as their normal development, may be instructively illustrated by the occasional breaks in the democratic life of Athens. The democrats had two enemies to fear, the one a subtle friend, the other a secret foe. The first was represented by the party of moderates which had opposed the radical reforms of Pericles, which felt, though it rarely ventured to express, disbelief in the system of imperial administration which gave birth to the ultra-democracy, and which looked back with admiration on the golden days of Cleisthenes. This admiration was largely the fruit of ignorance, for Cleisthenes was no framer of a constitution; but the Athens of Solon, defended from internal attack by the protective measures of his successor, seemed a modified form of popular government which appealed irresistibly to men wearied and alarmed by what seemed to them the caprice and excesses of the mob. The moderation which they desired could best be secured by a slight restriction of the franchise, for merely protective measures seemed hopeless against the irresponsible ignorance and poverty of the masses. Twice they gained their point, and once in a moment of temporary weakness, once in the days of her decrepitude Athens became a timocracy. Separated by but a thin line from this party of conservative idealists was the faction of the oligarchs—men whose extreme views were prompted as much by the desire for protection as by the hope of advancement, and whose destructive power was greater than their reconstructive ability. Some among them were fanatics of the type of Antiphon, others political sceptics such as Phrynichus and Peisander; the bulk were wealthy men engaged solely in the effort to save their fast-diminishing properties from what seemed to them the plunder of the mob. For even in time of peace the distribution of wealth was effected by heavy pecuniary burdens laid on the rich for choruses, gymnastic shows, and festivals; while in time of war the demos acted rigidly on the principle that in case of need the wealth of the individual becomes the wealth of the state, and cheerfully increased the number of triremes to be equipped by the wealthy and the amount of the property-tax which they mainly defrayed. Conviction, disgust, ambition, necessity, all prompted oligarchic moves; but as the open proposal of a measure directly hostile to the constitution was treason at Athens, such moves had to be made in secret through the associations known at Athens as in other Greek states as ἑταιρεῖαι.

The hetaeria or band of associates was the usual caucus or nucleus of a party which, first invented by Themistocles to replace the clan-following of the older times,[1] had come by the time of the Peloponnesian War to be a source of political influence which could not be neglected by any statesman. Pericles boasted a large body of recognised personal supporters through whom he acted and through whom he even spoke; Cimon numbered a hundred comrades (ἑταῖροι) openly devoted to his cause;[2] and it is clear that these associations, when used in accordance with the constitution, were open and undisguised and were not looked on with jealousy by the demos. Even the oligarchical clubs had outwardly an innocent appearance. They were often on the surface mere social or even religious associations,[3] which had existed from very early times at Athens and were recognised by law. Even their political character had an external side, for they were employed for assistance in canvassing for office and for mutual support in the law-courts.[4] It was only when employed for unconstitutional purposes that their main working was necessarily secret and that inwardly they sought their peculiar political ends by secret

[1] Plut. *Arist.* 2.
[2] *id. Per.* 7; cf. 14; *Cim.* 17.
[3] θυσίας ἕνεκα καὶ συνουσίας, Arist. *Eth.* viii. 5.
[4] Thuc. viii. 54 ξυνωμοσίαι ἐπὶ δίκαις καὶ ἀρχαῖς: cf. Plato *Theaet.* p. 173.

wire-pulling and, if necessary, by the dagger of the assassin. They were called "conspiracies" (ξυνωμοσίαι) on account of the secret oath taken by the members, an oath which in some states, we are told, contained the promise "I will be an enemy to the people, and will devise all the harm against them which I can."[1] In the very infancy of the democracy there are one or two doubtful instances of oligarchic designs against the constitution which may have been the work of these clubs.[2] But otherwise the working of parties during this early period was open and undisguised, and for many years after the last suspected plot in 457 we hear nothing of secret machinations of the oligarchs. No severe pressure was as yet put on the opposition to induce it to resort to extreme measures, for the fiscal difficulties which came with the Peloponnesian War had not yet originated. Towards the close of this war the clubs became secret combinations on the part of the wealthier classes to protect themselves against the attacks of the tribe of sycophants, the "drones with stings," which the democracy fostered; and although hetaeriae as a rule acted independently of one another, yet combination was easy, for communications were kept up between the various oligarchic centres, not only in Athens but throughout the cities of the empire.[3] In 413 such a combination was rapidly effected, and moderate and oligarch competed for the realisation of their pet schemes; for the Sicilian disaster offered a chance such as might never occur again for an open protest against extreme democracy. The war party had disgraced itself and felt itself deservedly discredited; but moderate counsels at first prevailed. Advantage was taken of the strong feeling running through Athenian society, that some check must be placed on the freedom of initiative, to establish a provisional board of ten πρόβουλοι, elderly men who would deliberate on all matters to be submitted to the people.[4] But the time was ripe for oligarchic reaction, to which even moderates like Theramenes gave their sanction, and in the next year (412-411) a movement first suggested by Alcibiades was carried out through the clubs. The procedure adopted illustrates the difficulty of reforming a Greek state by constitutional means. No constituent assembly was

[1] Arist. *Pol.* v. 9 = p. 1310 a.
[2] The conspiracy in the camp at Plataea (Plut. *Arist.* 13), and that before the battle of Tanagra (Thuc. i. 107; Plut. *Cim.* 11).
[3] Thuc. viii. 48, 54.
[4] *ib.* viii. 1; the office Aristotle classes as oligarchic (*Pol.* iv. 14 = p. 1298 b).

contemplated in the constitution, and the ecclesia had now to be made into such a body. This could be done only by repealing all protective measures, and by a decree of the ecclesia that no one should resort to the γραφὴ παρανόμων under heavy penalties and that any Athenian could propose any measure he pleased.[1] A resolution was thereupon proposed and carried that five presidents (πρόεδροι) should be appointed, who should select a hundred men, and that each of the hundred so selected should choose three colleagues. Thus a narrow government of 400 was established, which was intended to be merely provisional. The professed object of the reformers was to entrust the administration ultimately to a larger body of 5000 selected citizens; but the selection was indefinitely adjourned, and before the elaborate paper-constitution drawn up by the provisional government could be applied in practice,[2] the rule of the 400 was brought to an abrupt conclusion by a split between the moderates and the extremists. But the reaction was not violent; the moderates now had their turn. Their ideal was realised for the moment by the framing of a constitution in which payment for state services was abolished and the government was entrusted to a class of citizens approximately resembling that which was to have been specified in the never published list. But careful selection was now dispensed with, and the test for admission to the new body of 5000 was capacity to furnish the arms of a hoplite.[3] Athens was now in the hands of the middle class, but it is doubtful whether she remained even for a single year under the guidance of this respectable body. The government lasted just so long as the shadow of fear hung over the state. With the splendid efforts made by Athens to repair her disasters and regain her maritime control the old feelings returned and the old government was restored. It fell with Aegospotami and the fall of Athens, and a violent effort was made, under Spartan influence, to weed out the supposed vices of democracy. A commission of thirty was appointed to revise the laws, so as to leave no hold for the professional informer and to cut down the authority of the law-courts.[4] The commission became a government which during

---

[1] Thuc. viii. 67. A meeting of 6000 members of the ecclesia was legally capable of passing such a decree of ἄδεια (see p. 169).

[2] *Ath. Pol.* 29 ff.
[3] Thuc. viii. 97.
[4] Xen. *Hell.* ii. 3, 2; *Ath. Pol.* 35.

its reign of terror (404-403) exhibited the worst vices of oligarchy and tyranny combined. A patriotic movement, passively countenanced by the moderate party in Sparta, secured its suppression; and the good sense and equity invariably displayed in times of sore trial by the masses at Athens, whose virtues were always dimmed by prosperity, completed the work of amnesty and pacification. The archonship of Eucleides (403), although marked by detailed reform with a strengthening and revision of the laws, introduced no essential change in the constitution.[1] There was a better pretext now than there had ever been for narrowing the constitution: for with the loss of the empire the services of all the citizens were not wanted, and could not be employed, in the work of administration, and extreme democracy now meant an idle city-mob. But the proposal of Phormisius to limit the citizenship to land-holders—a proposal which if carried would have disfranchised 5000 citizens—was rejected.[2] The ideal of the moderate man, the return to the Cleisthenean constitution, was attained only by the loss of Athenian independence. In 322, after the close of the Lamian War, all Athenians who did not possess property of the value of at least 2000 drachmae were deprived of their active rights; the number of citizens so disfranchised proved to be more than 12,000, and the state became a timocracy governed by a minority of its former members.[3] It is true that Athens again became a democracy, and a democracy she remained, with intervals of Macedonian occupation and tyrannical rule, until her absorption in Rome. It is possible that, in accordance with the usual Roman principle, the franchise was limited and the state once more a timocracy; but the magic of its name was alone sufficient to secure it from provincial rule. Revolts, which would have entailed the degradation of any other city, were winked at by Roman statesmen, who saw in Athens the source and the living embodiment of their acquired Hellenic culture; the young life which had taught the world what democracy might mean was succeeded by a long old age of dignified academic repose, and the state which had been one of the great powers of the Eastern world

[1] If we can trust the decree in Andoc. *de Myst.* § 83, the Areiopagus was again entrusted with the guardianship of the laws. But no further trace of this power appears.

[2] Argument to Lysias *de Antiq. Reip.*

[3] Diod. xviii. 18. The number of citizens left in power was about 9000.

continued to enjoy, as a quiet university town, the sovereign rights possessed by a "free and allied city" of Rome.

§ 8 *Other Democracies—Elis, Argos, Syracuse, Rhodes*

Athens through her long political history exhausts almost every phase through which a democracy can pass. She is the mother of democracies in Greece, and most of the distinctively popular institutions which we meet with elsewhere are but copies of the work of her mighty statesmen. But these considerations do not exempt us from the task of completing this sketch of the last phase of city development by tracing the outline of the constitutional life of some other cities of this kind. For parallels are valuable since they are never exact; and divergences from a kindred type or cases of arrested development are still more worthy of notice.

The constitutional history of ELIS presents us with a popular government of a moderate and stable type—a democracy consciously preserving aristocratic elements, and still more aristocratic in practice than in theory from the fact that it was based not on a close civic but on an open country life. The union of the country under its original monarchy was soon dissolved; for two generations only does royalty seem to have survived, and the supreme power then passed into the hands of a territorial aristocracy. Efforts had been made by legislation, as at Thebes, to preserve the numbers and importance of the landed class, for a "law of Oxylus" is quoted which forbade the incurring of debts on the security of territorial possessions.[1] An inscription, probably as early as the opening years of the sixth century, shows the importance of the phratry and the clan (πατριὰ καὶ γενεά);[2] and the local influence of this clan-nobility seems to have rendered the different communities of the country largely independent of one another.

With union came the impulse to popular government which usually accompanied it. Rarely did the Greek world in the historic period witness amalgamation on a larger scale than that effected by the συνοικισμός of Elis in 471. It recalled the work of Theseus of Athens, and had the same effect of merging the

---

[1] Arist. *Pol.* vi. 4 = p. 1319 a.
[2] Cauer n. 253. The "kings" (βασιλᾶες) mentioned in this document are probably religious officials.

loosely connected communes into a single capital, the town of Elis, which became the sole centre of political life.[1] This union must have involved some alteration in the original constitution, but when the latter assumed a form that could justly be described as popular we do not know. Further developments took place, for Phormio of Elis is compared as a reformer with Ephialtes of Athens,[2] and cut down the power of some dominant aristocratic council. An outline of the developed democratic constitution for the year 420 shows us a hierarchy of magistrates who bear, as in former times, the title οἱ τὰ τέλη ἔχοντες, a popular council of six hundred, and the still surviving δημιουργοί.[3] What powers were exercised by the "demiurgia" we are not told. In many states the title denoted an individual magistracy; but it is thought that at Elis the term may have been applied to a curious survival of the old aristocratic constitution. This was a council composed of ninety members holding office for life[4] (perhaps the very body whose powers were curtailed by Phormio), which appears to have been still retained, after the creation of the larger democratic council, as a narrower within a wider executive. The ecclesia held the supreme power, and that inevitable product of popular government, the "champion of the people," is sometimes its ruler.[5] But the state never developed an extreme democracy, for it had no intense city life. Elis was the garden of Greece, and most of its inhabitants preferred to live in the country; the capital remained unwalled,[6] and even in the time of Polybius there were families who had not been in the city for generations.[7] This democracy belonged to the class described by Aristotle, "where the husbandmen and those who have moderate fortunes hold the supreme power and the government is administered according to law"; and where "the citizens being compelled to live by labour have no leisure, and where therefore they set up the authority of the law and attend assemblies only when necessary."[8]

ARGOS in its later history is an isolated instance of a continuous democracy amongst the Dorian settlements of the Peloponnesus. It is credited from its first foundation with

---

[1] The original communes are called by Diodorus (xi. 54) πόλεις, by Strabo (p. 336) δῆμοι.
[2] Plut. Praec. ger. Reip. 10.
[3] Thuc. v. 47; cf. Cauer l.c.
[4] Arist. Pol. v. 6=p. 1306 a.
[5] Xen. Hell. iii. 2, 27.
[6] ib. l.c.
[7] Polyb. iv. 73.
[8] Arist. Pol. iv. 6=p. 1292 b.

democratic tendencies, and at a very early period limited the power of its kings [1]; and although these restrictions were for a time broken through by Pheidon, who raised the royal prerogative to its old height and is consequently classed as a tyrant, they were reimposed on his successors, and this limitation saved the office. A titular king with some military power at the time of the Persian Wars marks the conservatism of a Dorian state; and the constitution at this period may have been some moderate type of mixed government.[2] But social and political reasons combined to give it a popular tendency. Argos was a maritime state and subject to the progressive influences of a commercial life; and these influences were accentuated by the intermixture with the native population which followed the great defeat inflicted by the Spartans at Hebdome, in the early years of the fifth century. Six thousand Argives fell, the thinned ranks of the population had to be recruited by the reception into citizenship of members of the perioecic towns,[3] and necessity effected here what design accomplished at Athens. But her deadly hostility to Sparta would alone have prompted Argos to develop a polity the very opposite of that which was inculcated by the encroaching diplomacy of the friend of oligarchies; and the climax of her political history was reached when in 461 she entered into close alliance with Athens. It was then in all probability that the democracy, which we find existing in 421,[4] received its final touches, some of which seem to have been consciously borrowed from Athens. Ostracism was introduced, popular courts instituted,[5] and the highest magistracy was represented by a college of five strategi[6]—the normal type of executive in a democratic state frequently engaged in war. A mention of the larger administrative bodies as they existed in the years 420 to 418 shows a double council as at Elis,[7] "the eighty" which existed by the side of the larger democratic βουλή being in this case also probably a survival from the older constitution.

The Argive democracy was amongst the most permanent in

[1] Paus. ii. 19.
[2] A king and a council are mentioned in Her. vii. 148, 149.
[3] Arist. *Pol.* v. 3 = p. 1303 a; cf. Her. vii. 148. This disaster may perhaps be placed as late as the year 495.
[4] Thuc. v. 31.
[5] Called Ἁλιαία in Schol. ad Eur. *Orest.* 861; a curious court held outside the city for trying cases of martial law is mentioned by Thucydides (v. 60).
[6] Thuc. v. 59; cf. c. 37.
[7] *ib.* v. 47, 59.

Greece, and it yielded only once to a mistaken policy co-operating with external forces which the state could not control. A small standing army, which the misguided ambition of the demos had selected from the *élite* of the citizens and trained to meet the professional soldiers of Sparta, betrayed the government, weakened by the recent defeat at Mantineia, in 418. Sparta set up an oligarchy which was overthrown with violence in the next year.[1] Nor was this unfortunately the only occasion on which the demos asserted its rights with sword and bludgeon. In the early part of the fourth century it was responsible for one of the worst massacres in Greek history, in which from twelve to fifteen hundred suspected or declared oligarchs perished.[2] We cannot expect a government such as that of Argos—an oasis of democracy in a desert of oligarchy, ever beset by danger from without and treason from within—to behave with the gentleness which a sense of security gave to the Athenian mind. Where the nerves of a democracy are highly strung its acts become marked by a grim fanaticism, and even this best of Greek governments has its sombre side. But the faith which was sometimes too vividly expressed, kept Argos a free government until the close of the period of Greek independence, and restored her, again a democracy, to the bosom of the Achaean league.

In SYRACUSE, as in most states, tyranny gave birth to democracy, and the despotism which began with Gelo and ended with Thrasybulus in 466 was followed by the framing of a popular constitution which, however vigorously undertaken, was not for the moment successful. Syracuse, like the other cities in Sicily, had had no experience of self-government, the composite state founded by Gelo had never known a political life of its own, and the tyrants by their arbitrary bestowal or deprivation of rights had left a legacy of discontent behind them. Syracuse was attempting democracy without possessing a national life, and the result was nearly another lapse towards tyranny. The danger threatened by the demagogue Tyndarides, who attached the poorer classes to himself and was obviously aiming at tyranny, led to his own destruction and the intro-

---

[1] Thuc. v. 81, 82; Arist. *Pol.* v. 4 = p. 1304 a.
[2] The so-called "bludgeoning" (σκυταλισμός) of 370 B.C. Diodorus (xv. 57) describes the massacre as φόνος τοσοῦτος ὅσος παρ' ἑτέροις τῶν Ἑλλήνων οὐδέποτε μνημονεύεται γεγονέναι.

duction of Cleisthenes' great preventive measure for the avoidance of similar attempts in the future. But the πεταλισμός, as the ostracism was called at Syracuse, was frightfully abused by the suspicious and undisciplined demos. Every influential citizen, rather than take his chance of the five years' exile which prominence entailed, buried himself in the obscurity of private life, and evenly balanced demagogues of the lowest type played fast and loose with the constitution.[1] The abolition of the institution restored confidence, and the upper classes again took the lead in public affairs. The external relations of Syracuse now admirably fitted her for the development of an extreme democracy, for she drew a heavy tribute from the native Sicel tribes which she had subdued,[2] and political leisure was secured by wealth. Yet for the time the constitution remained a popular government of a moderate type. This moderation was probably a matter of practice rather than of theory, for a state which means to conquer, as Syracuse meant to conquer Sicily, must entrust its highest offices to men of rank and knowledge; and we are not surprised to find that at the time of the last Athenian expedition in 415 the representative of the lower classes is the critical "prostates" who is not in office.[3] But the victory in the Great Harbour brought with it the results that Salamis had brought to Athens.[4] The people were the victors and they meant to rule. Their demand was met not by a succession of measures as at Athens but by a recodification, which marks a later period of growth, and which would have been impossible but for the tentative steps taken by their late enemy and present model. Diocles, the originator and the head of a commission for reorganising the constitution, in 412 introduced the lot as a mode of appointment to office, and published a code which so completely bore the stamp of his own personality as to be called the "laws of Diocles," and attracted an admiration which caused it to be voluntarily and permanently adopted by many other Sicilian cities.[5] But the political creations of Diocles were of short duration, for the democracy came to an abrupt conclusion in 405. In Sicilian history the external pressure from the Carthaginians often disturbed the even current of the constitu-

---

[1] Diod. xi. 86, 87.
[2] ib. xii. 30.
[3] Thuc. vi. 35.
[4] Arist. Pol. v. 4 = p. 1304 a ἐκ πολιτείας εἰς δημοκρατίαν μετέβαλεν.
[5] Diod. xiii. 34, 35.

tional life of the cities, and it was the fear of invasion that, co-operating with social causes, raised Dionysius I. to power. The tyranny inherited by his son was disturbed by internal factions, and the pressure of the Carthaginians on the divided state was renewed. In this crisis Corinth, in the person of Timoleon, came to the help of her daughter city; but the democracy which Timoleon established after the expulsion of the second Dionysius,[1] was of short duration. It changed into an oligarchy, which was soon merged in the tyrannies (or "monarchies," as they were called from their legitimate recognition) of Agathocles and Hiero, until the state fell under Roman rule.

RHODES is the last of the great democracies of the Greek world. Its three cities, Lindus, Ialysus, and Camirus, experienced the usual changes of states, tossed about between the Athenian and the Spartan powers. In the Athenian empire they are democracies, under Sparta oligarchies. In the second Athenian confederacy the whole island forms a democracy, for now the three cities have become a single state; and the voluntary surrender of their independent rights in 408 to the central government established at the capital Rhodes was probably due to a sense of the weakness of division, and was the prelude to a long history of independence, and even, to some extent, of empire. The greatness of Rhodes, unlike that of most other Greek states, begins after the epoch of Macedonian conquest. The expulsion of the Macedonian garrison in 323 was followed by a career of successful diplomacy; but with the thalassocratia of Rhodes, her relations with Rome and other powers, and the foreign possessions on the mainland which these alliances guaranteed to her,[2] we have here no direct concern. The chief interest which the state affords to a constitutional historian is twofold: it illustrates the organisation of a stable democracy that governs dependencies, and it shows an adjustment of the relations of the three great cities to the central government under democratic rule.

This central government possesses the normal boule and ecclesia, but the πρυτάνεις, the chief executive officials, are real presidents of the state.[3] The authority that we saw

---

[1] Diod. xvi. 70. [2] Strabo p. 652.
[3] Plutarch (*Praec. ger. Reip.* 17, 3) classes the πρυτανεία at Rhodes with the Strategia at Athens and the office of Boeotarch at Thebes. For its functions cf. Diod. xx. 98. Polyb. xxix. 4.

merely shadowed at Athens exists to the full in Rhodes, and here we find a democracy with a real presidency uniting civil with military powers. The prytaneis preside over the council and the assembly, guide the foreign politics of the state, and even command its army. Below them stands a college of strategi, one of whom is in command of the possessions on the mainland.[1] The strength of the central executive in the capital was probably due in the first instance to the continuance of town life in the other parts of the island, which made popular government less direct than it was at Athens; and it was perpetuated by the importance of the foreign relations of the state.

The three towns still continue to possess some degree of municipal independence. By the side of ὁ σύμπας δᾶμος of Rhodes stands τὸ πλῆθος of the municipal community,[2] which passes decrees (ψαφίσματα), and has its council of μαστροί, with a college of ἐπιστάται.[3] How wide the competence of these municipal governments was we do not know; inscriptions show us merely the voting of money for sacral purposes, regulations for temple usages, and decrees of honour.

[1] Cauer n. 182 l. 25 (στραταγοὶ) ἐπὶ τὰν χώραν and ἐπὶ τὸ πέραν.
[2] *ib.* n. 185. [3] *ib.* nn. 177, 183.

CHAPTER VII

FEDERAL GOVERNMENTS

FEDERAL government marks an expansion of political life beyond the limits of the city-state. We have already found that such expansion is not unknown in the early history of Greece, where we have found evidence of the existence both of nations and of leagues. A federal association occupies an intermediate place between these two extremes. It is a political unit which is itself an aggregate of units; it is something less than a nation and something more than a league. But, although it may be possible to feel, it is not possible to express with scientific precision the stage at which a government ceases to be a league or confederacy and becomes a true federation; nor is the line that separates such a state from true national life easier to draw. A federation must be defined positively by the degree of union which it has, and negatively by the degree of union which it has not, attained. Positively a federation of cities or districts implies the theoretically complete surrender of all foreign activity and foreign policy to a central government, a single deliberative and elective body and a single executive for the discussion, control, and conduct of external affairs, a common court of justice for offences committed against the association, or at least a central control over the local courts when deciding such matters, a power of raising and maintaining common military contingents, and either a common power of taxation or at least some control over local supplies destined to support the common action of the federation. Negatively the states must be sovereign in all matters unconnected with the purposes of the federation; each state must possess a constitution, a citizenship, and civic privileges peculiarly its own, and the freedom of its public life must be something more than a mere municipal independence.

Judged by these criteria the Peloponnesian confederacy is not a federal government. The first and second Athenian leagues very nearly deserve this designation, the points in which they fail being the absence of a common magistracy and the too great preponderance given to the executive power of a single state. But they are distinct stages in the growth of such associations, and familiarised the Greek mind with the idea of a union which was one neither of conquest nor of absorption, and which reconciled the demand for close corporate action with the claims of individual sovereignty. They showed that the only means by which the city-state could protect itself against a great national power from without, or even at times from a great dynastic power from within, was the wholesale surrender of that side of its autonomous life which was concerned with foreign relations.

The surrender of this cherished activity by the developed city-state, which has enjoyed a long history of independence, is a wonderful instance of political conversion due to bitter experience. It does not, however, show its internal decline but merely its external helplessness in the struggle with great nations such as Persia, Macedon, or Rome. Often it is a struggle for constitutional independence, which would be wholly lost by isolation, and might be partially regained by union, a free life under limitations being better than no free life at all.

But sometimes a federal government has its origin in the very absence of developed city life. The canton or the village tends more naturally than the city to a wider form of union, as we learn from the instances of Acarnania, Arcadia, Aetolia, and Epirus. In such cases it is sometimes difficult to distinguish between a federal and a strictly national life; but something approaching a federation is an early stage of the undeveloped as it is a late stage of the developed political society. The first federal impulse is therefore easier in such cases, and the federal history of such states is longer and more continuous.

We cannot, however, classify federal governments as they fall under one or other of these two heads, for in the course of time the two classes became combined. In the case of the two nations which carried out the federal system most thoroughly and consistently, Aetolia and Achaea, an absence of city life in the one and of intense city life in the other was favourable to the early formation of these close unions; but this very tendency helped them subsequently to assimilate states that had enjoyed a brilliant and independent city life. Other developed cities, such as those of Thessaly and Boeotia, worked out the problem for themselves, sometimes voluntarily, sometimes under pressure from a leading state; while elsewhere, in the transitory Olynthian federation, the motive for union is resistance against a threatening barbarian power. Lycia stands alone, for the federal government which we find there is apparently a conscious imitation of a Greek system— an adaptation of the only mode in which the political civilisation of the Hellenes could be applied to the national feeling which early tribal association had perpetuated.

In the order of their development, as known to us from scattered records (and therefore not necessarily in the order of their actual birth), the chief federal governments of Greece are those of Thessaly, Boeotia, Acarnania, Olynthus, Arcadia, Aetolia, Achaea, and Lycia.

The earliest union of THESSALY was attained by the voluntary subjection of the aristocracies of her towns to a king of their own choosing. He was chosen from the Heracleidae, but not always from the same branch of this widely-diffused race, with which all the noble Thessalian families seem to have claimed connection, and several clans and states were in turn represented in the monarchy. Thessaly is found acting as a united whole in the year 511.[1] At the time of the Persian Wars she is still a monarchy, although the power of the Aleuadae, who then held sway,[2] is evidently weakened by a stubborn resistance to their rule, partly due perhaps to the hostility of local dynasties, partly to a growing democratic sentiment, which soon asserts itself in the downfall of the monarchy, a change in the constitution, and an alliance with Athens in 461. It is not probable that the monarchy long survived the Persian Wars; and the government that concluded the treaty with Athens, sent her assistance at the outbreak of the Peloponnesian War in 431, and tried to stop the march of Brasidas to Thrace in

[1] Her. v. 63.　　　　[2] *ib.* vii. 6.

424, was probably some kind of federal council,[1] the political sentiments of which were certainly democratic, and which was the first expression of the collective life of τὸ κοινὸν Θετταλῶν. As a primary assembly could not have permanently represented the interests of such an area as Thessaly, the council must have been composed of delegates from the states; and this unknown Thessalian synod furnishes the earliest instance of political representation on a large scale in Greece. But the new government was as powerless as the late monarchy had been to control the dynastic influence which guided the politics of the separate towns and introduced the disorder and confusion which we have elsewhere traced.[2] The rule of the feudal nobility continued until the close of the Peloponnesian War, when unity was sought by the new method of a partial revival of the monarchical power. This was represented by the office of ταγός, which, like the Roman dictatorship, was a temporary resumption of the military authority of the early kings for the purpose of uniting the independent states of Thessaly for some common purpose. The tagus was apparently elected by a majority of the states, and the whole military force of the country was placed under his command; while the subject tribes of Perrhaebi, Magnetes, and Achaeans, which seem ordinarily to have been dependent on particular towns,[3] were brought under the control of the new government, to which they paid tribute and furnished contingents.[4] An attempt had been made by Lycophron of Pherae to secure this position in 404, but his violent efforts to unite the whole of Thessaly under his sway gained no constitutional recognition; he died a "tyrant," and his successor Jason, whose position was recognised in 375, was the first and last tagus of united Thessaly.[5] His assassination five years later brought the government to a close; none of his successors was able to maintain the constitutional hegemony, and the attempt of one of them, Alexander of Pherae, at regaining it again called into existence a federal government of a republican type. Only the executive officials of this government are known; they show that, for the purposes of organisation, the four τετράδες of Thessaliotis, Pelasgiotis,

---

[1] Thuc. i. 102; ii. 22; iv. 78 (τὸ πάντων κοινόν). Yet in 454 mention is made of a son of a "King of the Thessalians" (Thuc. i. 111).
[2] p. 64.
[3] Thus the Perrhaebi were dependent on Larisa (Strabo p. 440).
[4] Xen. *Hell.* vi. 1, 8-12.
[5] *ib.* ii. 3, 4, vi. 1, 18; Diod. xiv. 82, xv. 60.

Histiaeotis, and Phthiotis formed an intermediate stage between the city and the whole country: for while an ἄρχων stands at the head of the league, each tetras has its own polemarch, with subordinate commanders for the infantry and the cavalry.[1] But this second attempt at a federal system was still more transitory than the first. It was powerless to resist the attempts at usurpation which were constantly being made by the would-be followers of Jason; the aristocracy called in the assistance of Philip of Macedon in 352, interference paved the way for conquest, and Thessaly became a dependency of Macedonia in 344. From this time it has no independent history, for from Macedonian it passed into Roman hands through the battle of Cynoscephalae in 197. Its autonomy was indeed restored, but its constitution was organised by Roman commissioners and it was henceforth within the sphere of Roman influence.

The federal system was perpetuated under both dominions, and was in fact the only one applicable to a country of the size, the traditions, and the ill-organised city life of Thessaly. But these adaptations of it, imposed and even borrowed in some of their details from without, have little historical interest. The Macedonians combined the federal divisions (especially those of the great "tetrades") with a close oligarchical government. It is not known whether the councils of ten (δεκαδαρχίαι)[2] which they established were at the head of the whole league or of each of the four divisions; but the idea of this government seems to have been adopted from the Spartan system of imperial rule. The executive officials of τὸ κοινὸν Θετταλῶν after Flamininus' victory as clearly resemble those of the Achaean league, although the democratic character of this latter organisation was not imitated. At the head of the state stood a strategus; and the "consilium" which met at Larisa[3] was doubtless elected by the states. But there was probably no general assembly, the structure of the government reflecting the new constitutions of the cities which, in accordance with the usual Roman principle, were organised on timocratic lines.[4]

In BOEOTIA the earliest impulse to national unity seems to have been manifested in religious association, and we have

---

[1] πέζαρχοι and ἵππαρχοι (*C.I.A.* ii. n. 88; Dittenberger n. 85).
[2] Dem. *Phil.* ii. § 24.
[3] Livy xxxv. 31; xlii. 38.
[4] *ib.* xxxiv. 51 (Flamininus) *a censu maxime et senatum et judices legit.*

already noticed that the amphictyony which met at Onchestus was probably the first form of union amongst its towns.[1] The memory of this religious origin of the federation was preserved in the titular headship of united Boeotia being vested in the person of a wholly non-political official called ὁ ἄρχων, who was doubtless the president of the association which still continued the cult of Poseidon at Onchestus;[2] the memory of the final union of the territory under a single government was still further fostered by a festival of incorporation, the "Pamboeotia," celebrated in the temple of Athene Itonia near Coroneia.[3] The union, thus accidentally begun, would never have developed into a permanent federal government had it not been for the activity of Thebes. Linked by interest with some powerful states, she coerces unwilling cities into joining the league; her own individuality is never merged in the political union which she holds together; sometimes she is but a powerful associate, sometimes the actual mistress of the other cities, but she has a political life of her own, while the history of the other cities of Boeotia is but the history of Thebes. We have already noticed how the internal politics of the leading state and its weaker partners interacted on one another;[4] the federation, in the days of its independence, passes through two stages, an oligarchic and a democratic, and in structure the former shows the far more perfect federal system of the two. In the year 424, when this structure is first revealed to us, we find seven independent towns, Thebes, Haliartus, Coroneia, Copae, Thespiae, Tanagra, and Orchomenus, the other localities in Boeotia, whether cities or villages, being incorporated into these federal units, to which they probably supplied contingents and money for the purposes of the league.[5] The supreme controlling power was vested in a large council, which was composed of four smaller βουλαί.[6] These minor councils were doubtless local, controlling four departments of Boeotia. We do not know the nature of this control, nor how far it affected the autonomy of the nominally independent states. Probably the councils existed wholly for federal purposes; and the difficulty of imagining a sudden combination of these local

---

[1] p. 50.   [2] p. 50.
[3] Strabo p. 411.
[4] p. 68.
[5] For these attached communities, forming συντέλειαι with the central cities, see Thuc. iv. 76, 93; Strabo p. 409.
[6] Thuc. v. 38.

bodies leads to the supposition that the votes on federal questions were taken separately in each, a majority of the four votes being decisive. The chief executive officials were the Βοιωτάρχαι, eleven or thirteen in number, of whom two were Theban, the rest being appointed by the other federal divisions, but on what principle is unknown.[1] During their year of office they were the guiding power of the league in matters political and military; they conducted negotiations for external alliances with greater discretionary power than that possessed by most foreign ministers of Greece, although the validity of the agreement was dependent on the final consent of the four councils; and they were the generals of the Boeotian army in the field, the supreme command circulating amongst the members of the college in turn.[2]

When we next catch a glimpse of this federal organisation Thebes is democratic, and the political character of the other states is in harmony with that of their leader. But no true democratic federation was formed. The origin of the league was unfavourable to such a result, for the hegemony which Thebes renewed in Boeotia after 379 was founded on conquest; and the league is a crushed and half-unwilling partner of the central state in the short but brilliant period of Theban ascendency. Formally the federal government was still continued, and the federal council which met at the capital was the κοινὴ σύνοδος τῶν Βοιωτῶν.[3] We may imagine an assembly of delegates resembling the synedrion of the second Athenian confederacy, the votes being taken, as at a much later period of the league's history,[4] by cities and not by heads. Practically it must have been a mere advising body, whose counsel was disregarded when out of accordance with the wishes of the Theban assembly. For this ἐκκλησία appears to have been supreme, and we find it initiating new lines of foreign policy for its city and for the league.[5] The chief executive power is still held by the annually elected Boeotarchs, and the other federal cities, if they had a share in the appointment of these officials, may still have exercised an indirect control over affairs. The Boeotarchs now form a college of seven, who decide by a

---

[1] Thuc. iv. 91 τῶν ἄλλων βοιωταρχῶν (i.e. other than the two Theban) οἵ εἰσιν ἔνδεκα.
[2] ib. v. 37, 38; iv. 91.
[3] Diod. xv. 80.
[4] Livy xxxiii. 2 (197 B.C.).
[5] Diod. xv. 78, 79.

majority of votes;[1] sometimes they command the army collectively, but a distant expedition, such as that of Pelopidas to Thessaly in 364, was sometimes led by a single Boeotarch, and in 369 we find the college delegating the command to Epaminondas and Pelopidas.[2]

The confederacy fell with the subjection of Thebes to Macedon in 338; but, like the Thessalian federation, it was resumed again under Macedonian and Roman rule. Its self-dissolution through fear of Rome in 171 was not its closing scene, for it is mentioned amongst the associations which Rome broke up on the formation of the province of Achaea in 146.[3]

ACARNANIA, little as we know about its history, is an instructive type of the form of government which we are illustrating, since it presents two distinct stages of federal organisation. It is first a union of tribes or villages, and afterwards a union of cities. During the latter part of the fifth century it was still one of the most backward of Greek communities. Its inhabitants dwelt in unwalled villages and lived by plunder.[4] Yet even at this time the nation possessed a kind of unity, for at Olpae, a strong fort on a hill, they had a common court of justice (κοινὸν δικαστήριον).[5] This court was probably established, like the κοινοδίκιον of Crete, for the settlement of international disputes between the tribes, and does not necessarily show a federal government. But such a government is known to have existed in the year 391, when we find a κοινὸν τῶν Ἀκαρνάνων meeting at Stratos.[6] At this time the tribe was still the highest political unit, and it was not until the year 314 that, on Cassander's advice, the Acarnanians began to form small cities. The federation was still continued, is found existing at the close of the third and in the second century, and was not disturbed by Rome. It possessed a council (βουλά)[7]—probably, as in most federal governments, composed of an equal number of representatives from each city—and a primary assembly (κοινόν) of such members of the cities as chose to attend. There is every reason to suppose that, as in the Aetolian and Achaean leagues, the votes were taken by cities after free deliberation, in which any member present might engage. The Acarnanian assembly,

[1] Diod. xv. 52, 53.
[2] Plut. *Pelop.* 26; Diod. xv. 62.
[3] Polyb. xxvii. 2; Paus. vii. 16.
[4] Thuc. i. 5.
[5] *ib.* iii. 105.
[6] Xen. *Hell.* iv. 6, 4.
[7] Cauer nn. 240, 241. The first of these inscriptions is thought, from internal evidence, to date from about the year 220.

besides deciding questions of foreign policy, possessed criminal jurisdiction and the power of deposing its own magistrates; on one occasion we find it condemning two of the leading citizens for treason and abrogating the command of its own στρατηγός.[1]

OLYNTHUS, which made the next effort at federation which Greek history has handed down to us, attempted to be to her Thracian and Macedonian neighbours what Thebes was to Boeotia. Her motives, if not wholly disinterested, were at least favourable to the political liberties of the states which she endeavoured to incorporate. Nowhere was a strong Greek barrier more necessary than on the frontier of Macedon, and the Thracian domain might again be coveted by the southern powers. Her policy of incorporation was marked by liberal views, but where persuasion was not sufficient, force was used; a stout resistance was offered by Acanthus and other Greek cities threatened, which failed to realise that "the half was better than the whole"; Spartan assistance was called in; the league begun in 382 was dissolved in 379, and the path to Greece lay open to the Macedonian kings.

The little that we learn of this federation comes from the lips of a political enemy,[2] who is more interested in its aggressions than in its organisation. From this vague account we gather that Olynthus had attempted to free some cities from the King of Macedon, and was already in possession of Pella; that she had induced towns to "use the same laws" as herself and to enter into the relation of συμπολιτεία; and that the incorporated states, which are represented as sharing in her "politeia," possessed the rights of intermarriage and of owning land with her and amongst themselves. It is unlikely that Olynthus contemplated full absorption, which would have involved the merging of her own identity in that of the other cities. Her proposal was apparently the interchange of full and not merely of partial citizenship between the towns, and a federal government of which Olynthus was, for the time at least, to be the head. The opposition to the scheme was perhaps intensified by the closeness of the relations (unnecessary to a federal government) which were suggested, and which seemed to leave little beyond municipal independence to the separate cities.

[1] Livy xxxiii. 16.
[2] Cleigenes, the Acanthian envoy at Sparta in 382 (Xen. *Hell.* v. 2, 11-19).

The federal union of ARCADIA was, unlike those which we have considered, the result neither of a spontaneous national movement nor of the ambition of a single Arcadian city. It was the result of external forces working on a nation already predisposed to such a form of organisation but unable by its own efforts to obtain it. We have seen how the iron hand of Sparta repressed all tendencies to union amongst the Arcadian tribes and cities, when efforts were made to found this union on conquest.[1] It is far from likely that she would have lent more encouragement to voluntary political association; and therefore we must conclude that the early national coinage stamped Ἀρκαδικόν is but the sign of a common temple-mint, and the evidence merely of a religious amphictyony, not of a political league. But Sparta's policy of dissociation was, as we saw, coupled with an objection to the growth of walled cities in the district;[2] and the encouragement which she thus gave to tribal life was itself favourable to a federal form of government at the moment when her direct pressure was removed.

This pressure was removed by the battle of Leuctra in 371. The Arcadians found themselves free, and ready, with the assistance of Thebes, to play their part in history as a nation. The immediate effect of the victory was the resuscitation of Mantineia, whose villages again became a town;[3] but the traditional rivalry between this city and Tegea, which had been the representatives respectively of the independent and the Laconising influences in Arcadia, unfitted either for being the capital of the new federation. A new city, with no traditions and from which nothing was to be feared, arose in Megalopolis, and this became the seat of the federal government. The supreme power of τὸ κοινὸν τῶν Ἀρκάδων was vested in a large assembly, which is generally spoken of as "the Ten Thousand" (οἱ μύριοι).[4] But it is difficult to believe that the assembly contained precisely this number of qualified citizens, still more that it represented precisely this number of votes. The votes were probably taken, as was usual in federal governments, by cities, and "the Ten Thousand" was in all likelihood merely a name for the vast primary assembly, at which every Arcadian could meet, listen, and discuss—the

[1] p. 110.
[2] p. 110.
[3] Xen. *Hell.* vi. 5, 3.
[4] *ib.* vii. 1, 38; 4, 35 and 38.

number of citizens present from any given state in no way determining the voting power of that state. We may assume that a nucleus of this large assembly was composed of the regularly appointed delegates of the states. This may have been the council which met in the βουλευτήριον known as the Thersilion;[1] and it may have had the threefold character which we shall see exhibited in the councils of the Aetolian and Achaean leagues, of a probouleutic, an executive, and a permanently representative body. This, however, can be regarded only as a probable conjecture; actual records confine themselves to exhibiting the exercise of sovereign power by the Ten Thousand. This body concludes alliances in the name of all Arcadia,[2] receives ambassadors from other states,[3] and even sits as a court exercising political jurisdiction and passing sentence on members guilty of offences against the league.[4] The federation had common magistrates (ἄρχοντες), whose functions and whose very titles are unknown;[5] they may have been elected by the assembly, and must have been the executive body which assisted the strategus who was at the head of the government.[6] The latter probably combined, as in most Greek democracies and in the federal governments modelled on them, civil with military duties; as commander-in-chief he was the head of the select standing army which the league supported.[7]

The league was for a time successful, but its capital, Megalopolis, never fulfilled its intended function of focusing and absorbing the political life of the other towns, and the rivalries of the older cities tended to destroy a union which, even in its best days, may never have comprehended the whole of Arcadia. Mantineia and Tegea again became hostile, with the result that the former quitted the league; but Megalopolis still remained the nominal centre of Arcadia, and the Ten Thousand survived to be addressed by Demosthenes. The

---

[1] Pausanias (viii. 32) calls it the βουλευτήριον ὃ τοῖς μυρίοις ἐπεποίητο Ἀρκάδων. A βουλή existed in the revived league of the third century (Cauer n. 444). The remains of the Thersilion, which measure 175 × 135 feet approximately (*Excavations in Megalopolis*, published by the Society for the Promotion of Hellenic Studies) show an accommodation for a general assembly of considerable size.

[2] Xen. *Hell.* vii. 4, 2.
[3] Dem. *de fals. Leg.* § 11.
[4] Xen. *Hell.* vii. 4, 33.
[5] *ib.* vii. 1, 24; 4, 33. They were perhaps the δαμιοργοί of the later league, who then appear as representatives of cities (Cauer *l.c.*).
[6] *ib.* vii. 3, 1.
[7] *ib.* vii. 4, 33 οἱ ἐπάριτοι was the name borne by this standing army.

federation was perhaps dissolved by Alexander in 324; but the federal traditions were strong enough to prompt the Arcadians eagerly to seek admission into the revived Achaean league of 280.[1] Yet late in the third century a formal revival of the old κοινόν is witnessed by an official document, which mentions the μύριοι, with a council as the supreme authority.[2]

The Aetolian and Achaean leagues, which we have next to consider, open up to us a new vista of Hellenic politics. Federalism has become the rule, and any state which does not attach itself to one of these two associations is an isolated unit, which must either live a life of political torpor or attach itself to one of the great foreign powers. In both cases federal government has its origin in national life, but in both it extends far beyond the limits of the nation. The forces which had been silently working for unity in the Greek world, but had hitherto found voluntary expression chiefly in religious association, now led, under the pressure of enemies from without or tyranny from within, to the acceptance of a political organisation which saved by infringing the independence of the city, and which, looked to as the last safeguard of Greek city life, was consciously thought out and carefully elaborated. But the highest political unity which Greece attained was still singularly incomplete. Even if we except the recalcitrants and the waverers, and neglect the stubborn resistance of Sparta and the proud isolation of Athens, we find that the history of the two leagues is one of conflict: that their method of conversion to the new political faith is persuasion tempered by annexation: that even Achaea is willing to spread her propaganda by the sword: that Aetolia is a shameless plunderer, ready to share her spoils with Macedon or Rome: and that finally the rivalries of both compel them to call in the assistance of foreign powers, whose alliance brings Greece into the vortex of the world-politics of Rome and submerges her with Macedon under the protectorate of the great Western power.

The AETOLIANS of the fifth century are described as a backward portion of the Hellenic race, still preserving some barbarous customs and living in unfortified villages.[3] They

---

[1] Paus. viii. 6 συνεδρίοι δὲ τῶν Ἀχαιῶν μετέσχον οἱ Ἀρκάδες προθυμότατα Ἑλλήνων.

[2] ἔδοξε τῇ βουλῇ τῶν Ἀρκάδων καὶ τοῖς μυρίοις (Cauer l.c.).

[3] Thuc. iii. 94.

are described as a nation (ἔθνος); but this word, which emphasises both the feeling of racial connection and the absence of its expression in city life, does not necessarily imply a form of political organisation closer than that of a federal government, although the federation which doubtless existed at this time between the different Aetolian tribes was necessarily more compact than one like the Achaean league, which was composed of an aggregate of cities. The canton tends to a closer form of union than the town, and it is difficult to determine what degree of independence was left, either in earlier or later times, to the different districts of Aetolia. But it is natural to believe that their independence was greater after the tribal league had expanded into a city federation, and that originally the cantons had a common political life of a closer kind than was usual in federal governments. The federation seems to have had a continuous and uninterrupted life up to the date of the reformation of the Achaean league in 280. United action of the whole nation in foreign politics is proved by the negotiations with Philip of Macedon with respect to the cession of Naupactus to Aetolia as a whole,[1] and by the embassy sent by τὸ κοινὸν τῶν Αἰτωλῶν to Demetrius in 305 or 304.[2] We have every reason, therefore, for believing that the federal organisation, such as we know it in later times, was in all its main outlines perfected at an early period, although it doubtless admitted of modifications as the league expanded to include cities such as Naupactus and Heracleia in Trachis, two of its earlier annexations, or Mantineia, Tegea, and Orchomenus, some of its later voluntary associates. The modes in which accretions were made to the original nucleus were very various; sometimes they were the result of voluntary alliance, sometimes of conquest, sometimes of agreements into which states were forced in order to protect themselves from the piratical exploits of the Aetolians. For the race retained to the last its character as a nest of plunderers and brigands; its history is one of wanton aggression for the annexation of new territory, and more than once the Aetolians entered into agree-

---

[1] Dem. *Phil.* iii. § 44 (338 B.C.). Yet Arrian (1, 10) speaks of the Aetolians sending ambassadors to Alexander in 335 κατὰ ἔθνη. Hence Gilbert concludes that the league was not formed until after Alexander's death (*Staatsalt.* ii. p. 22). But Freeman's view (*Hist. of Federal Govt.* p. 256), that they were ambassadors sent by the whole Aetolian nation, but one for each tribe, appears more probable.

[2] Diod. xx. 99; cf. xix. 66.

ment with foreign powers for the partitioning of Greek soil. They conspired with Antigonus Gonatas of Macedon to break up the Achaean league, and subsequently came to terms with Rome for conquests in Acarnania, the spoils of which were to be divided between the two powers.[1] It is no wonder that the mixed motives of hope and fear drew states into their net, that towns like Mantineia quitted the quieter sphere of the Achaean league to join this band of robbers, and that even cities across the sea such as Ceos and Teos were willing to make terms which would secure them immunity from plunder ($\dot{a}\sigma\nu\lambda\iota\alpha$).[2] We should naturally expect that the mode of annexation would have dictated the status of the acquired community; and geographical position might also have decided whether a state should be admitted a full member of the league or remain only its ally. But general principles of treatment are difficult to discover, and there is no clear evidence that the league ever assumed a distinctly imperial character. While it incorporated some states it exercised a vague protectorate over others; even those distant cities which paid tribute and were garrisoned as military outposts by Aetolian troops, may conceivably have returned representatives to the federal council.[3]

The constitution of the league was as thoroughly democratic as was consistent with federal institutions. Democracy pure and simple was a gift reserved for the city-state alone, and we can prove for Aetolia what we can only suggest for the other federations of the Greek world—the presence of representative institutions. But the system of representation was modified in a manner which makes the federal organisation as here elaborated a kind of mean between the popular government of a Greek city and that of a modern nation. The council of Aetolia was, like a modern parliament, the permanently representative body; for we know that the $\beta ov\lambda\epsilon v\tau a\iota$ were chosen by the states, and it is probable that, in accordance with the true federal principle which recognises the interests of every state, whether great or small, as being exactly equal, every commune furnished one senator and had but one

[1] Polyb. ii. 45; ix. 38.
[2] ib. ii. 57; Cauer nn. 237, 238; in the last-cited document (a treaty with Teos) $\dot{a}\sigma v\lambda\iota a$ is specially guaranteed.
[3] In Polybius (iv. 25) it is said that these towns $\dot{a}\kappa ov\sigma\iota\omega s$ $\mu\epsilon\tau\epsilon\chi\epsilon\iota\nu$ $\tau\hat{\eta}s$ $A\dot{\iota}\tau\omega\lambda\hat{\omega}\nu$ $\sigma v\mu\pi o\lambda\iota\tau\epsilon\iota as$. By these words are meant, I think, merely participation in the federal system. See Polyb. ii. 41 for a similar use of $\sigma v\mu\pi o\lambda\iota\tau\epsilon\iota a$, and cf. ii. 57.

vote.[1] But, though the voting capacity of the states was fixed, and their permanent representation was secured by the council, every individual citizen of the Aetolian league had the right to deliberate and to vote in the popular assembly (the παναιτωλικόν). The citizens from any particular city or commune who chose to attend, voted with the councillor from that state, the vote counting only as one but the majority of voices deciding its character. If no unofficial members presented themselves from a city, the councillor alone gave the vote for that city. The general assemblies of the Aetolians were therefore partly representative, partly primary; and by possessing this double character they secured the rights of minorities more effectively than a modern parliament, for the elected councillor would necessarily represent the majority of his town, while a large proportion of the unofficial members from the same state who were eager to appear in the assembly would probably be politicians of opposite views who were eager to outvote him. Yet even with this provision the federal- could not be as democratic as the city-state. The poorest class from distant cities or districts would not be able to attend the assemblies at all, and the real voting was in the hands of the aristocratic element; while the impossibility of the exercise of direct personal government by the masses rendered the permanent executive authority very powerful.

This executive authority may to a large extent have been represented by the council, which, in addition to its being the board of permanent representatives in the assembly, may have been also a probouleutic and executive body. The question whether it possessed administrative functions depends on the possibility of its identification with the board known as the ἀπόκλητοι. We find the apocleti summoning the assembly in concert with the general,[2] and they have large spheres of competence within which they may act in the nation's name without consulting the assembly.[3] The large numbers of the body, from which a committee of thirty could be chosen,[4]

---

[1] A decree (probably of the end of the third century B.C.) referring to the towns Melitaea and Peraea enacts that, if they should form two states, λαχόντες ἀποπορευέσθων βουλευτὰν ἕνα (Cauer n. 239, l. 19).

[2] Polyb. xx. 10.

[3] Livy xxxv. 34. They are there called "*sanctius concilium,*" which "*ex delectis constat viris,*" as opposed to the "*concilium universae gentis.*" The word σύνεδροι, sometimes found, seems also to designate the council.

[4] Polyb. xx. 1.

increase the probability suggested by the character of its functions that in the apocleti we have, not a separate federal executive, but the council under another name.

The general assembly, composed of the councillors and the chance attendants, had one regular meeting a year for the election of magistrates.[1] Other meetings were specially convened by the executive for the discussion of important affairs. At these the usual sovereign powers of a declaration of war and acceptance of peace, of the commissioning and reception of ambassadors, were exercised.

At the head of the league stood a $\sigma\tau\rho\alpha\tau\eta\gamma\acute{o}s$, annually elected and entering office on the day of his election.[2] He possessed the usual combination of military and civil powers, commanded in the field, and represented the state in negotiations. The peculiarity of the Aetolian general is his relation to the assembly. It shows a judicious attempt to keep the executive and the deliberative powers apart; for, although the general presided over the assembly, he was forbidden to give any opinion on questions of peace or war.[3] He was a president and not a minister; and this regulation must have been particularly valuable in a state like Aetolia, where some chief with all the predatory instincts of his race might have hurried the nation into a disastrous war.

A board of regularly appointed officials for the revision of the laws and the care of public documents completed the *personnel* of the league. It was one of the duties of these $\nu o\mu o\gamma\rho\acute{\alpha}\phi o\iota$ to insert in the public acts agreements with foreign states or with new members of the federation which had been entered into since the last revision.[4]

The history of the ACHAEAN league is more inspiring than that of any of its predecessors, for it marks the last glorious struggle for constitutional freedom against overwhelming force. Yet this last stand was made by a nation which, through all the most brilliant period of Greek history, had remained aloof from political rivalry, had kept its neutrality whenever it could while Sparta and Athens rent one another and Theban armies swept over the Peloponnese, and was content to retain its democratic independence in isolation from the events of the great world.

---

[1] Polyb. iv. 37.
[2] *ib.* ii. 3; iv. 67.
[3] Livy xxxv. 25 *bene comparatum apud Aetolos esse, ne praetor, quum de bello consuluisset, ipse sententiam diceret.* [4] Cauer n. 238.

But this independence was probably preserved by a very early union amongst the twelve Achaean cities. They seem to have been united by some kind of federal tie, which was rendered possible by the similarity of their governments, which were all apparently of a moderately democratic type. The Peloponnesian War created some slight disturbance in their relations, for Pellene is found on the side of Sparta and Patrae on that of Athens, and in 417 Spartan influence was brought to bear on their internal politics.[1] But in 391 "the Achaeans" are spoken of as a whole: they admit a state to their citizenship, they have a common army, and they despatch ambassadors on behalf of the whole nation to foreign powers.[2] The democratic federation seems to have existed until the Macedonian conquest; whether Alexander destroyed it we do not know; but his successors established garrisons in some of the cities, tyrants in others, with the result that the dissolution of the league had been completely effected by the time of Antigonus Gonatas. The rise of a new Macedonian power under this founder of the later Antigonid dynasty was marked by an effort to extend its sphere of influence over all Greek cities not directly subject to its rule. Everywhere this influence meant the death of the constitution, for the means of control chiefly cultivated by Antigonus was the rule of the local tyrant.[3] The struggle for constitutional liberty began with the almost immediate revival of the league in 280. The beginnings were modest. Of the original twelve cities but ten remained, Helice having been destroyed by an earthquake and Olenus having disappeared; of these ten cities four—Patrae, Dyme, Tritaea, and Pharae—formed a nucleus for the federation, which gradually spread to the other towns;[4] and for nearly thirty years (280-251) the national league grew up quietly, and, under the guidance of men like Margos and Iseas of Ceryneia, assumed a constitution which was already fully formed when the federation was extended beyond the geographical limits of Achaea. Its history as a union of the Peloponnese and as a Hellenic power falls into two distinct periods. The personal influence of men of genius played a large part in its extension as well as in its

---

[1] Thuc. ii. 9 ; v. 52, 82.
[2] Xen. *Hell.* iv. 6, 1. Yet traces of local oligarchies are found in the year 366 (*ib.* vii. 1, 42).
[3] Polyb. ii. 40, 41.
[4] The other six towns were Leontion, Aegira, Pellene, Aegion, Boura, and Ceryneia (Polyb. ii. 41).

formation; and the first period is associated with the name of Aratus, the second with the names of Philopoemen and Lycortas.[1] In 251 Sicyon was added by Aratus; in 243 Corinth, freed from the Macedonians, was attached; and she was soon followed by Megara, Troezen, and Epidaurus, and later by Heraea and Cleonae. In 234 or 233 Lydiades laid down the tyranny of Megalopolis and added his state to the league; Megalopolis was followed by nearly the whole of Arcadia, and after 229 Argos, Hermione, and Phlius were admitted as members of the federation. The league was at its greatest when it was still only a combination of the three districts of Achaea, Arcadia, and the Argolid; for its real independence practically ceases with the year 221, which marks the close of the war with Sparta and the extinction of their only rival in the Peloponnese. For to crush this rival power which had been joined by the counter-league of the Aetolians, the fatal mistake was made of seeking the aid of Macedon. The league is now but a member of an Hellenic alliance under the presidency of the Macedonian king, who garrisons some of its towns and dictates its policy.

A new period of its history begins with the guidance of Philopoemen (207), when the league, weaker in actual power, reaches its widest territorial extent and makes of the Peloponnese a single state;[2] for Sparta had now been forced to join, and Messenia and Elis were attached. But active interference was now felt from Rome; the league could only shift from one protectorate to another, and anything like an independent policy was impossible. The last attempt at an assertion of Hellenic freedom closed with the conquest of Corinth by Mummius in 146, and the federation was for a time dissolved. It was never again revived with a political meaning; but, as in the case of other kindred associations, its harmless forms were allowed to continue under Roman rule, and the κοινόν of the Achaeans still existed in the times of the Empire.[3]

The Achaean league possessed a constitution of a strictly federal character, the constituent states being sovereign in all matters distinct from the common purposes for which the federation was formed, and the central government exercising no interference with their internal laws or constitutions.

---

[1] Polybius (ii. 40) calls Aratus of Sicyon the ἀρχηγὸς καὶ καθηγεμών, Philopoemen of Megalopolis the ἀγωνιστὴς καὶ τελεσιουργός, and Lycortas the βεβαιωτής of the league.
[2] Polyb. ii. 37. [3] Dittenberger n. 272.

For, although the latter appear to have been all democratic, this was the result of a natural tendency, and was not a fixed condition of the union.[1] The whole league was spoken of, somewhat loosely, as forming a nation (ἔθνος), and there was probably some interchange of civic rights between the different communities, although of this there is no direct proof.[2] The sovereign powers of the cities in all foreign and diplomatic action were surrendered entirely to the league. Once indeed we find a dispensation granted to Megalopolis, which was in 224 allowed to send envoys to Macedonia;[3] but, as permission was accorded by the central government, this was really an embassy of the league; and a statement of the true federal principle was contained in a clause of the first treaty between Achaea and Rome (198 B.C.), by which it was agreed that no embassy should be sent to Rome by any particular Achaean city, but only by the common government.[4]

The strength of the league was also shown in its financial and military requisitions on the separate cities. We find the federal congress voting supplies,[5] and, as we hear of cities refusing to pay contributions to the common treasury, the government must have assessed each city at a fixed sum. It probably did not dictate the manner in which this amount was to be raised, but we find it on one occasion interfering to check a financial revolution at Sparta in order to secure its own interests.[6] The whole military force of the cities was at the disposal of the federal assembly, which either required particular cities to furnish particular contingents,[7] or raised mercenary armies to be paid from the common funds. All questions of international law were as a matter of course referred to the central government, and not, as in the looser Peloponnesian confederacy, to arbitration; and the government had the power not merely of arbitrating but of punishing.[8]

Polybius describes the constitution of the league as a type of the purest democracy;[9] but its democratic possibilities were,

---

[1] Further instances of uniformity are given by Polybius (ii. 37) in the common weights, measures, and money of the cities of the league.

[2] ἡ ἐθνικὴ συμπολιτεία in Polybius (ii. 44) is equivalent to ἡ κοινὴ πολιτεία (xxvi. 1), and simply means the federal government.

[3] Polyb. ii. 48.

[4] Paus. vii. 9.

[5] Polyb. v. 1.

[6] ib. xxv. 8.

[7] ib. v. 91; iv. 7.

[8] Thus we find a fine inflicted on the Spartans for offences against the people of Megalopolis (*Archaeolog. Zeitung* 1879 p. 127).

[9] Polyb. ii. 38.

as in the case of Aetolia, limited by its federal character. The vast primary assembly which was the nominal sovereign could, it is true, be attended by any citizen over thirty years of age from any state in the league; practically it was composed of those whose political enthusiasm or whose wealth urged or enabled them to attend. This assembly had to be summoned twice a year; its other extraordinary meetings were dependent on the discretion of the magistrates. But the comparative infrequency of these, combined with the constant pressure of important business, military and diplomatic, on the permanent officials, threw great responsibility on the shoulders of the magistrates, and often placed the duty of deciding great questions of the moment entirely in the hands of the regularly constituted βουλή, which was always at the centre of affairs.[1] We are told neither the numbers nor the mode of constitution of this council, but the fact that it could and often did act for the assembly leads us to suppose that, like that of Aetolia, it was composed of representatives appointed by the states. It was thus the nucleus of the assembly, the votes of which were always taken by cities and not by heads, and a permanent guarantee that the interests of each state should be fully represented, independently of the chance attendance of the masses (οἱ πολλοί, τὸ πλῆθος), who voted with the representatives of their several cities. It is probable that the councillors were appointed annually, and were real representatives and not mere delegates with fixed instructions. The split between the Argive members of the assembly in 198, on the momentous question of alliance with Rome, may point to a division of opinion either between the councillors and the chance attendance from Argos or between the councillors themselves.[2] It is not improbable that this council, as a permanent body, may have had probouleutic and executive functions, although the passages of Polybius[3] which are usually quoted to support this view are inconclusive and may simply show the representatives of the states acting in the name of the general assembly. The place of meeting for the ordinary assemblies was originally Aegium, while the extraordinary convocations were held at any time or

---

[1] Polybius (xxix. 9) speaks of a σύγκλητος (at Sicyon) ἐν ᾗ συνέβαινε μὴ μόνον συμπορεύεσθαι τὴν βουλὴν ἀλλὰ πάντας τοὺς ἀπὸ τριάκοντα ἐτῶν. In ii. 37 the βουλευταί are mentioned.
[2] Livy xxxii. 22.
[3] Polyb. ii. 46; iv. 26.

place that was convenient; but in 189 the unfairness to distant cities involved in having a fixed capital for a federal government—a defect which scarcely appeals to us, but which must have been seriously felt in the ancient world on account of the difficulties of communication—was remedied by a measure carried by Philopoemen, which obliged the assemblies to be held in every city of the league in turn.[1]

The chief executive officials were the στρατηγοί, who stood at the head of the government, and ten purely civil ministers called δημιουργοί, who assisted them in the work of administration. For the first twenty-five years of the renewed existence of the league it was guided by two generals, but in the year 255 the number was reduced to one;[2] and the influence of strong personalities, which is such a marked feature of the history of this federation, henceforth has free play. The general was commander-in-chief of the army, and had unrestricted power while it was in the field; he conducted negotiations with foreign states, and was expected to initiate all important decrees of the assembly. Unlike the Aetolian general, he was not merely a president but a member of this body; and his membership inevitably made him its leader, to whom all looked for an expression of opinion on any important business.[3] The infrequent meetings of the assembly and the fact that the general had no colleagues possessing this unity of civil and military authority, made his ministerial powers far greater than those of similar officials in a city democracy. He was held responsible after the expiry of his year of office, but during that year detailed control was impossible; and that the vast powers possessed by this first minister were fully appreciated and felt to be dangerous was shown by the rule prohibiting immediate re-election to the post. A general might, however, be elected in alternate years, and, if he retained the confidence of the people, might secure in the intermediate periods the election of one of his own adherents. This was the way in which Aratus secured the continuity of his rule.[4] The general had little to fear from the irresponsible demagogue. He flourished only in large assemblies which met frequently, and the aristocratic character of the thinly attended

---

[1] Livy xxxviii. 30. [2] Polyb. ii. 43.
[3] ib. xxviii. 7 ἐκάλει γὰρ τὰ πράγματα τὴν τοῦ στρατηγοῦ γνώμην. Cf. Livy xxxv. 25.

[4] Plut. *Arat.* 24 παρ' ἐνιαυτὸν αἱρεῖσθαι στρατηγὸν αὐτόν (τὸν Ἄρατον), ἔργῳ δὲ καὶ γνώμῃ διὰ παντὸς ἄρχειν.

meetings of the Achaean league gave little opportunity for this exhibition of democratic mistrust.

The relations of the demiurgi to the general were not unlike those existing between the prytaneis and the strategus at Athens. With him they summoned the extraordinary meetings of the assembly,[1] and they doubtless had the presidency of this body and the right of putting questions to the vote; but, unlike the Athenian prytaneis, they were a board of at least the same degree of permanence as the general himself, and it was of the highest importance to him to secure their co-operation. Whether the mode in which the demiurgi were appointed provided a guarantee that they were of the same political views as the strategus, we do not know. Their number ten seems to point to an original representation of the ten Achaean towns; but this number must have been a mere survival after the league expanded, and their mode of appointment may consequently have been changed. The ministerial character of the Achaean government must have been still more marked if we imagine that the members of this controlling board were chosen by the assembly at the annual elections. In this case the general and his civil colleagues must have represented the same political views, and would have formed a kind of cabinet.

The expanded democracy which we have discussed thus bears many resemblances to modern popular governments. Citizenship, as Aristotle defines that term, was for the masses in the Achaean league, as it is with us, a mere potentiality. The power of the central government increased the wider the limits of privilege were extended, and the exercise of this power involved a foreshadowing of the modern ministerial system.

The last federal government which we have to chronicle is a very perfect Hellenic system evolved by a non-Hellenic race. The LYCIAN league is the fairest product of that Hellenism, that mastery of the barbarian mind by Greek political thought, which took such strong root in Asia Minor. The origin of the league is unknown, and the period of its independence, when its assembly used to decide on war, peace, and alliance,[2] is a blank. Lycia appears in its later history first as a dependency

---

[1] Polyb. v. 1; here the ἄρχοντες are said to have summoned the assembly. Other names for the demiurgi are συνάρχοντες, συναρχίαι, προεστῶτες. Livy (xxxviii. 30) speaks of "*demiurgi civitatium*" as "*summus magistratus.*"

[2] Strabo p. 665.

of Rhodes (188–168), then after 168 as a free state under Roman protectorate, until its independence is taken away by the Emperor Claudius and it is made subject to provincial rule. Yet through all the changes that precede the closing scene it preserves its federal institutions, a description of which is given by Strabo[1] for his own time (*circa* 29 B.C.–18 A.D.).

From this description we learn that twenty-three Lycian cities met in a federal assembly (κοινὸν συνέδριον), the place of meeting being any city which was thought best suited to the immediate gathering. The voting power of the cities was regulated in proportion to their size: the greatest had three, the middle-sized two, the rest one vote. In the same proportion they paid war-taxes and shared in public burdens.[2] In the federal assembly the Lyciarch was chosen with the other magistrates of the league, and federal courts (δικαστήρια) were constituted by this body. But the principle of proportion was observed even here; for judges and magistrates were appointed from each city in accordance with the number of votes which it possessed.

The peculiarities of this government are twofold. The first striking feature—its non-possession of a capital—which it shared with the later Achaean league, was one of particular value, if we conceive the federal assembly to have been primary as well as representative. But its distinguishing—although perhaps not wholly unique[3]—characteristic was the proportioning of votes, executive powers, and burdens to the size of the cities. This idea, in the extreme form in which it is found in the Lycian league, exhibits a very perfect form of national, but not of federal, government. The Lycian league stood midway between the two, and ignored the principle of equal representation, which should be found somewhere in a true federal system, since it is the expression of the equal interest and of the equal sovereignty of the only true unit of such governments—the state.

In concluding this sketch of federal governments we need not dwell again on their political significance, and on the part they played in maintaining the last fragments of Hellenic inde-

---

[1] *l.c.*
[2] τὰς εἰσφορὰς εἰσφέρουσι καὶ τὰς ἄλλας λειτουργίας (Strabo *l.c.*).
[3] In the later Arcadian league the δαμιοργοί are apparently chosen in proportion to the size of the cities (Cauer n. 444).

pendence. But a final word may be said on the constitutional machinery which they adopted for this purpose. It has sometimes been denied that representative institutions for the purpose of political government were known to the ancient world. This denial cannot in any case apply to the area which forms the district of the city-state, for in Athens and elsewhere we have seen election to state offices based on such divisions as tribes and even families. An extension of this system to federal purposes is proved by the representative senate of the Aetolian league, and the probabilities are strongly in favour of all the later federations having possessed a board of regularly appointed delegates or representatives from the states which they comprised; for even if we disregard the probability of a common type of federation, as of democracy, having been evolved, it is almost inconceivable that this device should not have been adopted by nations familiar with the representative institutions of the amphictyonies. The Greeks in their application of this system recognised in the main the true federal principle that each state must be equally represented. But they were not so happy in the solution which they adopted as to how the claims of individual citizens were to be met. To satisfy these claims they combined primary assemblies with representative bodies; but the tendency of primary assemblies on a large scale, even as regards the expression of opinion, is, as we have pointed out, really aristocratic, and no means were adopted of regulating voting power by population—except in the Lycian league, which in attempting to secure this object disregarded the equal claims of states. This difficulty of balancing the claims of *states* and of *populations* in federal governments has first been solved in the modern world by a double system of representation—by the institution, for instance, of a senate which represents the votes of states and of a lower house which represents the votes of heads of the population. It is doubtful how far this system would have satisfied the Greek desire for personal rule; but its working is certainly more democratic than the solution which they adopted of primary assemblies, which were really not representative in character and whose voting power was strictly limited. Democracy in its purest form is to be found in the city-state alone. If we rise a stage above it, the modern world offers better instances of popular government than Greece.

CHAPTER VIII

HELLENISM AND THE FATE OF THE GREEK CONSTITUTIONS

It has always been an open question where the history of Greece should end. Some have taken Chaeroneia as the final scene; others have with greater justice recognised that there is a history of Greek independence down to the close of the struggle with Rome in 146. Both these dates are purely arbitrary; for, even if we admit that at one of these two periods the Greek states did lose their liberties, it is somewhat meaningless to identify the history of a nation with that of its political independence. A nation may perform its function in the economy of the world all the better for being in a state of bondage. It is, indeed, possible that conquest may mean denationalisation, the wholesale destruction of a people's most essential characteristics under the pressure of a foreign civilisation; and in this case the nation's history closes. But it has never been maintained that this is true of Greece, whether we think of the Hellenic peninsula or of its offshoots in West or East. On the contrary, the fact that has most powerfully impressed historians is that the period of the subjection of the Greeks is a period of Hellenic conquest, of triumphant progress over and absorption of barbarian nationalities. Greece strikes her roots still deeper and more widely in the East; and the oriental world, assisted by a new political civilisation, acquires the language, the culture, and the art which, on account of its derived character and its deflections from the primitive type, we are accustomed to call not Hellenic but Hellenistic—a word which does not necessarily convey any shade of depreciation, for the old and the new are incomparable. In the West and North the Greek influence is more subtle, more purely an intellectual suggestion; for some of these regions had been barely touched by Greek colonisation, and even where the Greek city-state existed, it finally came into conflict with another political civilisation—that of Rome. This was not a better civilisation, nor was it even stronger in its actual organisation (for beneath barbarian attacks the Roman *civitas* succumbed even more rapidly than the Greek πόλις); but it was one whose destiny was dictated by geographical considerations and the past history of the surrounding peoples, and fulfilled by the decree of Rome which enacted that the West should be united to her by the strong ties of a Latin civilisation, if the East was to be the prize of the Greeks.

The general historian must needs take account of this Hellenism, if his work is not to be a mere torso—a thing imperfect only because it is incomplete. The historian of Greek constitutions, although he cannot dwell on it, must at least mention it, for it is his sole justification for the claim that Greek constitutional history does not close with the conquest of Greece by Macedon or by Rome. Every atom of this civilisation, the permanence of Greek art, coinage, literature, and the new forms which they assume, are dependent on the existence of the Greek city and on the maintenance of its constitution. It is true that, with the exception of the leagues which we have already treated, the centuries following the Macedonian conquest show few attempts at political creation. Such as were made were, in the first instance, mainly attempts to bring the life of the Greek city into harmony with the bureaucratic system of administration, which accompanied the more highly organised of the monarchies held by the successors of Alexander; and at a much later period fresh products were evolved by the attempt at a strong centralisation of government made by the Roman Empire. But the continuance of the forms of the old city life is the only adequate explanation both of Hellenism and of the possibility of organised empire in the countries of the East.

The original extension of Greek political civilisation to the barbarian was, as we saw, due to the unconscious influence of colonisation. Where the Greek city was planted Hellenism took firm root; but the strange cessation of the impulse to emigration in the fifth century left many Western lands untouched by this influence, and there was no possibility of its extension to the far East until the Persian power was broken by Alexander. The new conqueror of the East fortunately did not mean to become a ruler of the oriental type. A permanent and organised empire, governed by a man who professed himself the typical representative of Hellenism, must have city-states as the administrative centres for its districts and provinces. The city, not the tribe, was meant to be the unit of empire; and thus a movement, perhaps undertaken in the first instance purely as a means to the maintenance of a central government, ultimately gave a common political organisation and a common Hellenic civilisation to the East. The universal empire of Macedon soon passed away, but the means were more permanent than the end. The successors of Alexander realised that the security of their rule over barbarian populations, often unsympathetic and refractory, depended on the cultivation and extension of the Greek πόλις. The lesson was learnt by Rome. She found the problem of government solved for her in those Eastern countries where the Greek city flourished; where it did not exist she followed in the footsteps of Alexander and his successors by consciously cultivating it; and the Roman Pompeius is an even mightier founder of cities than the Macedonian Alexander.

It was not, however, the whole of the inheritance left by the Macedonian conqueror that fell into the lap of Rome. Faint traces of Hellenism persisted in lands far beyond the limits of the Roman Empire, as a result of the transitory settlements effected by Alexander on the Jaxartes, beyond the Oxus, in the Punjaub, and on the Indus. The semi-Greek towns north of the Hindoo-Koosh were swamped by a Scythian invasion, and even those of the Cabul valley yielded to the Indo-Scythian Empire. But the dynasty of these Sacae, established in 78 A.D. and lasting down to the third century, employs the Greek letters and generally Greek legends on its coins. And Hellenism had flourished for a length of time sufficient to influence the art and coinage of the Indian kings of Maghada, Guzerat, and Cabul.[1]

If we next glance at what becomes the Parthian Empire of the first centuries of our era, we find that directly east of the Euphrates Mesopotamia is covered with Greek commonwealths,

---

[1] Gardner *New Chapters in Greek History* pp. 433 ff.; Mommsen *Provinces of the Roman Empire* ii. pp. 8 ff.

and that in Babylonia there is a great Greek city, Seleucia on the Tigris, with more than half a million inhabitants, with the Greek language and Greek customs, and governed by a βουλή of three hundred elected members. In these towns the Hellenes formed the dominant element, and by their side existed a mixed population of Syrians and Jews. The commercial value of cities such as Seleucia was so great that the Hellenic polity was almost entirely independent of the central power. These towns gave a coinage with Greek legends to the empire, a polite language to the court, and the plays of Athenian dramatists to delight the heart of the Great King, and to be quoted in triumph over a fallen Roman foe.

Across the Euphrates we are within the limits of the Roman Empire, and here we find the almost complete spread of Hellenism from West to East. In Asia Minor little remained for the Romans to do in the way of founding or developing cities. It is true that, as long as the Persian Empire lasted, the Greek towns had formed but a fringe along the coast of the Aegean. Although they had stamped out the native organisation and almost the native language in these districts, they had not penetrated far inland. But the Hellenism of the interior had been effected by the Macedonian successors of Alexander. Galatia, the home of the Gallo-Graeci (an offshoot of the great Gallic migration of 280 B.C.), was for a long time an exception to this political Hellenism; for here the Celtic canton flourished. But city life developed rapidly after it had been converted into a province in 25 B.C. and Greek had been made the official language.

The close of the Mithridatic War (63 B.C.) gave Rome the provinces of Pontus, Syria, and Cilicia, and a suzerainty over the dependent districts of Cappadocia, Commagene, and Palestine; and now the imperfect Hellenism of the countries from the Black Sea to Judaea was completed by the greatest of Roman organisers, Pompeius. Everywhere it was effected by the cultivation of urban life, by the restoration of old cities and the establishment of new. On the Propontis and the Euxine, Cyzicus, Heracleia, Sinope, and Amisus rose afresh; in Pontus the work of "synoecising" towns from villages went on, and the Great City (Megalopolis), the New City (Neapolis), and the City of Pompeius (Pompeiopolis) were formed. Another city in Paphlagonia bore the founder's name; and in Cappadocia, although as yet a dependent kingdom and not a province, eight towns were restored and given constitutions. But the greatest triumph of order was the housing of the piratical hordes of Cilicia in cities; the moral influence of the Greek "politeia" was still all that was needed to make a citizen of a bandit. Altogether thirty-nine towns in these newly acquired provinces are said to have owed their creation to Pompeius. This outburst of creative energy was not due to any passionate pursuit of the Hellenic ideal; all that the unimaginative Roman desired was order, and this could be secured only within the sphere of influence of the Greek city.

In old Greece a kind of weak Panhellenic spirit had long prevailed at the time when its government was taken over by Rome. This Panhellenism had in the first instance been forced on Greece after her conquest by Philip of Macedon, when he had himself recognised as the leader of an unwilling confederacy. It disappeared with the universal empire of Macedon, but an attempt at its revival was again made by Antigonus Gonatas and his successors, and this attempt was rendered partially successful by the internal conflicts which led the Achaean league to attach itself to the fortunes of that house. This union between the wholly and the partially Greek was recognised by Rome when in 146 she constituted Macedonia and Achaea a single province. But, probably before the close of the Republic, the two were parted into two separate provinces; and the leading motive for this change may have been, as Mommsen suggests,[1] that of "separating the purely Hellenic from what was half Hellenic." But the desire of extending the Hellenic system to the more backward portions of Western Greece is shown by Augustus' foundation of Nicopolis in Epirus. It was a thoroughly Greek city, the result of a συνοικισμός of Southern Epirus with portions of Acarnania and Aetolia and the island of Leucas; it celebrated the Actian as Elis the Olympic games, and it was evidently destined to become the capital of Western as the Roman colony of Corinth was of Eastern Greece. But, like Megalopolis and other such mushroom growths, it did not fulfil its promise, and, though it remained a large city, even the neighbouring Patrae, which became a Roman colony, was of greater commercial importance. In fact, charters of freedom were granted

[1] *Provinces of the Roman Empire* i. p. 256.

to the cities with such a lavish hand that there was little room
for a peculiarly privileged capital. Sparta and Athens were
free and allied communities (*civitates liberae et foederatae*); and
the grant of *libertas*, which meant free control of their local
courts, finances, and coinage, was possessed by towns in
Boeotia, Phocis, and Locris, besides the two Roman colonies
of Patrae and Corinth, and was conferred by Augustus on the
eighteen communities of the Free Laconians (Ἐλευθερολάκωνες),
which had been formerly perioecic dependencies on Sparta.
Once, indeed, during the Empire all the cites of Greece were
declared free; for Nero carried the exercise of his mimetic
tendencies so far as to personate a second Flamininus at the
Isthmian games. But the grant was withdrawn by Vespasian,
and provincial rule again asserted over the less favoured cities.
Yet care was taken not to make this rule repulsive, and the
forms at least of the old free life were maintained. The
leagues which were at first dissolved were afterwards restored,
retaining their sacral if not their political character, and
Augustus reconstituted the amphictyony of Delphi on a new
basis. The constitution of most of the states was probably of
a timocratic character, but the patiently wrought out structure
remained unimpaired. Here as elsewhere the Roman rule
established, and did not destroy, the most perfect work of the
nation.

To the north of the peninsula the two countries of Macedonia
and Thrace had been only partly hellenised politically. The
interior of Macedonia, occupied by a people partly Greek in
origin and in the rudiments of its political civilisation, which
recalled that of Homeric times, had scarcely been touched by
the influences of the city-state; but the Greek polities of
Southern Macedonia had been zealously cultivated by the
kings. This fringe of Hellenism Rome took care to preserve,
and one city at least, Thessalonica, now the capital of the
province, was made a free state. In the Roman colonies of
veterans, established at Dyrrachium on the West, and at
Dium, Pella, and Philippi on the East, the Latin replaced the
Greek organisation; but these settlements had little political
significance: the province retained its Greek character, but in
no higher degree than in the time of the kings; for no attempt
was made to cultivate the πόλις in the interior of Macedonia
or to disturb its tribal life. Thrace too had been only fringed

with Greek settlements on its three seas; but here the number of inland towns with Greek civic rights was increased by Trajan and Hadrian. North of Thrace came the genuinely barbarian world, and here Greek foundations such as Tyra and Olbia found it difficult to preserve their Hellenism or even their existence in the face of the Scythian and Sarmatian hordes. In the same wild regions, beyond the limits of direct imperial rule but within the sphere of Roman influence, two Greek states in the Crimea—Chersonnesus, a republic, and Panticapaeum, a monarchy—maintained for centuries an almost complete independence, until the former was merged by subsequent conquest in the Eastern Empire of Justinian, and the latter was swamped by the invading Huns. Alliance with Rome meant here what dependence on her meant elsewhere— the protection of Hellenism against the barbarian.

When we turn to the Western world we find a very different picture. The city here is also the unit of empire and the basis of government; but, though it sometimes starts by being the Greek πόλις, it becomes in time the Latin *civitas*. The influence of Rome on the organisation of the Greek cities of Southern Italy is easily understood. They were from an early time amongst the immediate allies (*socii*) of Rome, and political necessities dictated that they should be brought into very close legal relations with her; hence the old juristic term *togati* (the wearers of the toga) grows into the wider term *Italici*, which includes the Greek wearers of the pallium in the South. The history of Sicily is more remarkable, for here we find the conscious alteration of a deeply-rooted Greek into a Latin political civilisation. The Greek cities, which in the Peloponnesian War formed only a fringe round the coast and left four other distinguishable nationalities in the territory, had by Cicero's time so thoroughly hellenised the island that there was no longer any distinction between Sicel and Greek; and it is difficult to believe that this absorption of the native populations was unassisted by the Roman government. But the dictator Caesar conferred Latin rights on Sicily, and henceforth its states are *municipia*, not πόλεις. Latin is the official language, and Roman law replaces the ordinances of Diocles. The political organisation of Africa was directed by the same considerations as that of Sicily. The nucleus of Hellenic civilisation created by Cyrene might have spread indefinitely under the fostering care of Rome; but the government willed it otherwise, and the history of the more important native towns of Africa is that of a Phoenician civilisation which gradually becomes Latin. In Spain and Gaul there was little chance for Hellenism, for they had been only touched by Greek colonisation; and this accident, while it made the organisation of these provinces the most difficult problem which the Romans had to face, dictated that this organisation when completed should be either purely Latin, as in Spain, or a blending of the Latin polity with the native canton system, as in Gaul. Even in Southern Gaul, where Massilia had spread her hellenising influence over the surrounding territory, symmetry enjoined that the Greek civilisation should be secondary to the Roman. Massilia still remains a Greek university, a centre for the spread of Hellenic culture and learning, but political influence centres in the Roman colonies of Narbo and Arelate.

Thus the political civilisation of the West is Italian, that of the East is Greek. And hence, when the huge empire parted asunder and Byzantium became a second Rome, this partition was but the natural fulfilment of a policy which had begun with the close of the Republic and had been actively carried out by the imperial rulers, who, while they could manipulate the barbarism of the West and even turn the sparse Greek tendencies found there into Latin channels, were themselves the slaves of the triumph of the Hellenic civilisation of the East.

But the law which the Eastern emperors took with them was Roman law, and it was their application of this system— as a system not merely of *private* but of *administrative* law—to their dependencies that finally caused the death of the Greek constitutions. During the existence of the Roman Republic there had been but little interference with the internal constitutions of the cities under its control. Some favoured states were entirely exempted from provincial jurisdiction; these were either free (*liberae*) or free and allied communities (*liberae et foederatae civitates*), the two classes differing not in the rights they enjoyed but in the legal basis on which these rights rested. Both the free and the allied communities possessed self-government, immunity from tribute, and exemption from the quartering of troops; but while the former could boast only of a charter (*lex data*) revocable by Rome, the latter had their rights guaranteed by a sworn treaty (*foedus*). But, even outside this select circle of privileged states, the practical independence enjoyed by the communities directly under provincial rule was considerable. It was an autonomy which, so far as it was not enjoyed by the charter of the province (*lex provinciae*), was permitted by the governor; but the permission was inevitable, for the very object of the cultivation of urban life in the provinces was to render a minute bureaucratic organisation avoidable. The provincial governor seldom usurped the criminal jurisdiction of the towns, which was theoretically entirely under his control; and, although it was his duty to exercise a general inspection over the financial affairs of the cities, he left the collection of local taxes and the defraying of local expenditure entirely to the native corporations. The provincial *civitates* or πόλεις of the Republic are in fact still true *states*, not mere municipal towns; centralisation, the force that can alone annihilate a nation's best intellectual gifts and turn its thoughts into vulgar channels, had not spread beyond the limits of Italy. The very beginning of the Principate heralds a change. The era of paternal government begins, and the military despot at Rome comes eventually to be consulted by meddling governors about trivialities which might be left to the subordinate officials of the meanest municipal corporation. The theory of provincial life is completely altered. In place of the view that the political energy of each state contributes to that of the empire, we find the new view that any energy which it may exercise flows directly from the centre of affairs. With the accession of Trajan this suicidal policy, which permanently weakened the strength of the empire and rendered it incapable of taking any action in its own defence against barbarian aggressions, gathered fresh strength, and it was elaborated by emperors and lawyers of the second and third centuries. The creation of the Eastern empire only strengthened this autocratic rule by tinging it with a colour of oriental despotism; and the Greek cities of this empire are now mere municipal towns subject to the most crushing system of central government that perhaps the world has ever seen.

APPENDIX

(*Note to p.* 182)

THE PRESIDENT OF THE COLLEGE OF STRATEGI

IN an article on the word "Strategus," written in 1890 for Smith's *Dictionary of Greek and Roman Antiquities* (3rd ed.), I attempted to give a summary of the views which have been held as to the possible presidency of the college and the modes in which it may have been exercised, together with a brief statement of the indirect evidence on which this theory of a presidency is based. Since the article was written the Aristotelian treatise on the *Constitution of Athens* has been discovered; but, though it gives us a clearer picture of the functions of the strategi in the latter part of the fourth century, it throws, as might be expected, little light on the position which they held in the state during the fifth. The only statement which bears directly on this question—*i.e.* that the generals were formerly chosen one from each tribe, but were, in the writer's time, elected from all the citizens (ἐξ ἁπάντων, *Ath. Pol.* 61)—contains a verification of what had been previously an almost certain conjecture. Yet even this assertion does not prove that *all* the generals were so chosen in the fifth century. It was a mode of appointment naturally resorted to when there was a complete differentiation of functions between the members of the college, but it may not have existed at a time when there appears to have been no assignment of functions to the different generals at their election.

It is possible that during the period of the Peloponnesian War we see a transition stage between the method of tribal and the method of popular appointment. It is known that at the close of the fifth century generals still offered themselves as representatives of special tribes (Xen. *Memor.* iii. 4, 1), although why they should have continued to represent phylae at a time when the taxiarch and not the strategus was the tribal commander, is not clear. It is also known that more than one general might belong to the same tribe. [Instances in Beloch *Attische Politik* p. 276.] A combination of these two factors has given rise to three alternative views of their appointment.

(i) The view of Droysen (*Hermes* ix. p. 8), that the generals were elected for each tribe from all Athenians and by the whole people.

(ii) That of Beloch (*l.c.*), who thinks that a president was elected by all out of all, but his nine colleagues each by his own tribe, one of the ten tribes each year giving up its right of election. This theory receives strong support from external evidence. On Beloch's system "when two generals are found to belong to the same phyle one of them must be the prytanis" (*l.c.*); and he has shown that "between the years 441–0 and 356–5 there are nine certain instances of two generals, but no certain instance of more than two, belonging to the same tribe in the same year; this occurs twice when Pericles, once when Laches is general, and one of the names is usually of sufficient eminence for us to consider its bearer a possible president of the college" (*Dict. of Antiq.* ii. p. 719). See, however, for 432–1, Mr. H. S. Jones in *Philologus*, vol iv.

(iii) A possible alternative is that the generals were elected out of all the Athenian people by the special tribes and for the special tribes —a system resembling the modern representation of constituencies. The reader may decide for himself which of these three views is the most probable.

I shall content myself in conclusion with supplementing the account of the στρατηγία which is given in the text by a very brief statement of the evidence from ancient sources on which the hypothesis of a "president of the generals" rests.

(i) We have general statements or indications which may point to such an office. It is said of Pericles that in 430 the Athenians στρατηγὸν εἵλοντο καὶ πάντα τὰ πράγματα ἐπέτρεψαν (Thuc. ii. 65). In 431 Pericles had power to prevent the ecclesia from assembling (a power which would have been uselessly exercised had it prevented only the specially convened meetings, and must therefore have affected the regular assemblies as well), and also exercised his authority to prohibit any informal gathering from being summoned (Thuc. ii. 22 ἐκκλησίαν τε οὐκ ἐποίει αὐτῶν οὐδὲ ξύλλογον οὐδένα). He could have exercised this power only as commander-in-chief over the whole body of Athenians regarded as an army. In 408 Alcibiades was appointed ἁπάντων ἡγεμὼν αὐτοκράτωρ (Xen. *Hell.* i. 4, 20). A slighter evidence is found in the position of Nicias in 425 (Thuc. iv. 28), when, in transferring the command to Cleon, he at least acts as spokesman for the whole college.

(ii) We find two technical expressions descriptive of the position of the strategi which suggest a leadership of the college.

(a) στρατηγοῖς Ἱπποκράτει Χολαργεῖ καὶ ξυνάρχουσιν is found in a financial decree of the year 426–5 (Hicks n. 46). The expression οἱ συνάρχοντες here clearly denotes that the nine generals are in an inferior position to Hippocrates. But as the generals may have taken the presidency of the board by agreement, by lot, or in rotation, the evidence is not conclusive for a permanent head.

(b) στρατηγὸς δέκατος αὐτός. The numeral adjectives πέμπτος, τέταρτος added to a general's name clearly imply some superiority of the general mentioned over the four or three colleagues who are suggested. On this analogy δέκατος αὐτός should imply supremacy over nine colleagues (whether strategi or not), who accompany on an expedition the individual general whose name is given. But in one of the two passages where the expression is applied to Pericles (Thuc. ii. 13) there is no question of an expedition; Περικλῆς ὁ Ξανθίππου στρατηγὸς ὢν Ἀθηναίων δέκατος αὐτός simply describes *his position at Athens* in 431. It may, therefore, have been a technical expression employed to designate the head of the college; and this may be its meaning in Thuc. i. 116, where it is applied to Pericles at the siege of Samos. In any case it is not likely that the Athenians often *sent out* ten generals at once on a single expedition, leaving no commanders of the home defences and no foreign ministry in the city.

If we believe in a president of the generals, it is by no means necessary to suppose that he was always a στρατηγὸς αὐτοκράτωρ. "Autocratic" power, which implied freedom of action on a foreign campaign, if conferred on a *single* general, would naturally be conferred on the head of the college, and this would still more naturally be the case if it was conferred at his election [Plutarch (*Arist.* 8) speaks of Aristeides as χειροτονηθεὶς στρατηγὸς αὐτοκράτωρ before the battle of Plataea]. But, usually at least, it was conferred after the elections with reference to a special service, and might be granted to several commanders, as it was to the three generals of the great Sicilian expedition (Thuc. vi. 26).

If we do not believe in a regular head of the college, yet the grant of autocratic power to *one* of the generals would place him in a position superior to that of his colleagues, at least of those who accompanied him to the field.

INDEX OF SUBJECTS

(The references are to the pages; "n." signifies the note on a page)

Abdera, 37
Abydos, 37
Acanthus, 228
Acarnania, 39, 248; constitution of, 227
Acastus, 135 n. 3
Accidents in history, 57
Achaea, Roman province of, 248
Achaean league, 71; constitution of, 235
Achaeans (of Peloponnese), 108, 126, 192
Achaeans (of Phthiotis), 51 n. 1, 223
Actian games, 248
Administrative jurisdiction, 168
Adoption, laws of, 67
Adrastus, the hero, 32
Aeaces, 37
Aegeidae, 80, 89
Aegialeis, 95
Aegialis, 126
Aegicoreis, 127
Aegina, 50, 58
Aegira, 236 n. 4
Aegium, 236 n. 4, 239
Aegon, 18
Aegospotami, battle of, 114, 211
Aethaea, 81 n. 3
Aetolia, 12, 248; federal government of, 231
Africa, 250
Agathocles, 218
Agidae, 79, 96, 97
Agis IV. of Sparta, 77, 115
Agrigentum, 30
Agyrrhius, 165, 178, 179
Alalia, 37 n. 1

Alcibiades, 34, 179, 210
Alcmaeonidae, 142
Aleuadae, 19, 63, 222
Alexander of Macedon, 114, 231, 236, 246
Alexander of Pherae, 223
Alienation of land forbidden, 42, 65, 91
Alliances between states, 55
Amasis, 39
Amisus, 247
Amphictyonies, 48
Amphipolis, 40
Amyclae, 79
Anactorium, 83 n. 3
Anaxilas, 45
Androcles, 140
Andros, 197
Antalcidas, peace of, 68, 178, 205
Antigonid dynasty, 236
Antigonus Gonatas, 233, 236, 248
Antiphon, the orator, 209
Antiphon condemned for treason by the Areiopagus, 148 n. 1
Apella at Sparta, 96, 97, 98, 100, 101, 106, 113
Aphidnae, 126
Apocleti, 234
Apodectae, 159, 183, 186
Apollo Archegetes, 40 n. 4, 43; Patrous, 129; of Delos, 192
Aratus, 71, 237, 240
Arbitration between states, 55
Arcadia, 12, 110; constitution of united, 229
Arcesine, 20
Archias, 25

S

Archon of Onchestus, 50, 225; archons at Athens, 136, 141, 146, 153
Areiopagus, 138; history of, 144
Arelate, 251
Argadeis, 127, 128
Argos, 18, 49, 57, 70, 72, 108, 113, 192; united with Corinth, 73; amphictyonies of, 50, 143; constitution of, 214
Aristagoras of Cumae, 37
Aristeidean assessment, 196 n. 3
Aristeides, 142, 147, 159 n. 1, 190
Aristeus, 47 n. 3
Aristocracies, early, 20, 62
Aristocratic element in oligarchy, 61
Aristodemus of Cumae, 30
Aristodemus of Sparta, 79
Asia Minor, Greek cities of, 17, 19, 23, 37, 38, 114, 126, 189, 247
Assembly, 122; at amphictyony of Delphi, 53; at Sparta (*see* Apella); at Crete, 120; at Athens, 152, 163, 165, 199, 206, 207; organisation and character of, at Athens, 169, 173; at Athens, acting as a constituent assembly, 211; at Elis, 214; at Rhodes, 218; at Thebes, 226; of Acarnanian league, 227; of Aetolian league, 234; of Achaean league, 239
Asteropus, 104
Athenagoras, 122, 123, 188
Athene, Hellania, 94; of Athens, 192; Itonia, 225; treasurers of at Athens, 183
Athens, 17, 20, 25, 29, 31, 37, 50, 57, 58; constitution of, 124
Atreidae, 80
Audit of magistrates, 153, 183; of councillors, 167; of officials at Chalcis, 195
Auditor of the council at Athens, 167
Augustus, 248, 249
Autonomous allies of Athens, 193

BABYCE, 94
Babylonia, 247
Bacchiadae, 19, 31
Basileidae, 20, 24
Belbina, 197
Boeae, 79 n. 4
Boeotarchs, 226
Boeotia, 51 n. 1, 192, 249; federal government of, 224

Boura, 236 n. 4
Brauron, 125, 126
Brea, 39; charter of, 41, 202 n. 5
Byzantium, 44, 58, 204, 205, 207, 251

CABINET in England, 77
Cadmeia, 68
Caesar, 250
Calauria, amphictyony of, 50
Callistratus, 178, 179, 207
Camirus, 218
Cappadocia, 247, 248
Carian worship, 125; relics, 125; quarter of Athenian Empire, 189, 197
Cassander, 227
Catana, 45
Cavalry in Thessaly, 63
Cecropia, 126
Cecrops, 126
Censorial authority of Spartan Gerousia, 101; of Areiopagus, 145
Census of Solon, 151
Central government of Roman Empire, 252
Ceos, 233
Cephisia, 126
Cerasus, 43
Ceryces, 33
Ceryneia, 236 n. 4
Chaeroneia, battle of, 68, 174, 178, 207, 244
Chalcis, charter of, 194, 195, 199
Chaleion, 47 n. 2, 66
Charondas, 17, 45
Charters of Athenian Empire, 194
Chersonesus (Tauric), 250
Chilon, 104 n. 3
Chios, 39 n. 1, 58, 192, 193, 204, 205, 207
Cilicia, 247, 248
Cimolus, 197
Cimon, 189, 209
Cinadon, 81, 88 n. 2, 92
Citizenship, 7; phratric conception of, 8; at Athens, 131
Clans in Greece, 13, 19, 20; in Thessaly, 63; in Opuntian Locris, 65; in Attica, 95, 128; in Crete, 118; in Elis, 213
Claudius, 242
Cleigenes, 228 n. 2

INDEX OF SUBJECTS

Cleisthenes of Athens, 20, 130, 134, 141, 149, 157, 208; constitution of, 157
Cleisthenes of Sicyon, 32, 33, 71
Cleomenes III. of Sparta, 115
Cleon, 140, 164, 179, 183, 187, 203
Cleonae, 49, 237
Cleophon, 166
Cleruchies, 40, 200
Clubs, political, 188; *see* Hetaeriae
Cnacion, 94
Cnidus, 39 n. 1; battle of, 204
Cnossus, 116
Codification at Athens, 176
Codridae, 135
Colacretae, 152 n. 2, 159
Colonisation, causes of, 24, 36; political characteristics of, 36; effects of, 245
Colophon, 23
Commagene, 247
Commerce in relation to colonisation, 38
Commercial treaties, 54
Committees of council at Athens, 167
Confederacy of Athens, 204
Conon, 204
Consilium of Thessaly, 224
Constitution, conception of, 4
Constitutional compared with general history, 4
Copae, 225
Corinth, 19, 26, 29, 31, 39, 44, 49, 70, 109, 110, 113, 237, 249; united with Argos, 73; constitution of, 71
Coroneia, 225; battle of, 67
Council of Elders, 13, 72; at Athens, 137, 142, 145
Council of Corinth, 72; of Erythrae, 194; of Sparta, 96, 97, 100; of Peloponnesian confederacy, 112; of Delian confederacy, 190, 193; of later Athenian confederacy, 206; of four hundred at Athens, 152; of five hundred at Athens, 159, 164, 183; structure and powers of council of five hundred at Athens, 166; of ninety at Elis, 214; of six hundred at Elis, 214; of eighty at Argos, 215; of Rhodes, 218; of Thessaly, 63, 223; of Arcadian league, 230; of Aetolian league, 234; of Achaean league, 239; of Seleucia, 247; four councils of Boeotia, 225
Cranon, 19, 63
Creondae, 19, 63
Cresphontes, 19
Crete, 9, 77, 91, 93; constitution of cities of, 115
Croton, 23, 44, 45
Cumae, 31
Cydonia, 116
Cylon, 31, 134, 142
Cyme, 18, 23, 27 n. 4
Cynoscephalae, battle of, 224
Cynosura, 94
Cynuria, 80, 83, 108
Cypselidae, 33
Cypselus, 29, 30, 31
Cyrene, 44 n. 1, 83 n. 3, 250
Cythera, 82
Cyzicus, 127, 159 n. 5, 247

DAMASIAS, 137
Daphnis of Abydos, 37
Deceleia, 126
Delos, amphictyony of, 48, 49, 202; confederacy of, 190, 192
Delphi, oracle of, 40; amphictyony of, 48 n. 5, 49, 94, 249; constitution of Delphic amphictyony, 51
Delphinium, 144
Demades, 186 n. 1
Demarchs, 160
Demes, 13, 141, 160
Demetrius, 232
Democracy, 122; the ideal, 7; tendency to, 7, 57; forms of, 58; in Crete, 120
Demosthenes, 148, 179, 184, 185, 186 n. 1
Depreciation of coinage, 173
Diacrii, 26, 132 n. 1
Dictatorship in Greece, 27
Diodotus, 203
Dionysiac worship cultivated by tyrants, 33; democratic character of, 33
Dionysius I. of Syracuse, 29, 218
Dionysius II. of Syracuse, 34, 218
Diopeithes, 174
Diophantus, 184, 186 n. 1
Dipaea, 108
Dium, 249
Dolopes, 51 n. 1
Dorieus, 42 n. 5

Doris, 51 n. 1, 52, 59 n. 2
Draco, 17, 23 n. 1, 143, 145, 149; constitution of, 138, 149
Dymanes, 95
Dyme, 236
Dynastic governments, 63
Dyrrachium, 249

Eion, 189
Eleusis, 33, 124, 125, 126
Elis, 12, 21, 49, 79, 83, 109, 110, 113, 125, 237; constitution of, 213
Emancipation at Athens, 133; at Sparta, 86
Empire of Sparta, 113; of Athens, 60, 114, 132, 162, 166, 181; organisation and character of Athenian Empire, 189
Emporium becoming a state, 38
English constitution as a mixed government, 76
Epacria, 126
Epaminondas, 207, 227
Ephesus, 18, 20, 128, 205
Ephetae, 143
Ephialtes, 147, 214
Ephors at Sparta, 77, 85, 92, 98, 101, 102, 107
Epidaurus, 50, 65, 111, 237
Epirus, 39, 248
Epitadeus, 91
Eponymous ancestor, 13, 20
Erectheus, 125
Ericthonius, 126 n. 5
Erythrae, 20, 205; charter of, 194, 199; constitution of, 194
Euboea, 52, 192, 207
Eubulus, 179, 184, 185, 186
Eucleides, archonship of, 132, 167, 183, 212
Eumolpidae, 21, 33, 124
Eumolpus, 125
Euphron, 71
Eurymedon, battle of, 189
Eurypontidae, 79, 96, 97

Faction, influence of on colonisation, 38
Family, influence of on state, 8, 143
Family worship, 16, 21, 99, 128; claims preserved by colonists, 44
Federal character of amphictyony of Delphi, 53; government, 59; characteristics of federal government, 220
Festivals instituted by tyrants, 33
Finance at Athens, 168, 173, 180, 183
Fine paid to temple, 54 n. 1
First-fruits of tribute, 192
Five Thousand at Athens, 211
Flamininus, 224 n. 4, 249
Foedus, 252
Four Hundred at Athens, 62 (cf. 162); establishment of, 211
Free Laconians, 249
Free or free and allied states of Rome, 251
Freedom, charters of granted by Rome, 249

Galatia, 247
Gallo-Graeci, 247
Games attached to religious associations, 49
Gaul, 250
Gela, 26
Geleontes, 127, 128
Gelo, 31, 32, 216
General tendencies in Greek history, 57
Geomori, 127, 137
Gephyraei, 21, 124
Germanic monarchy, 15
Geronthrae, 79
Gortyn, 116; code of, 117, 120
Gylippus, 87
Gytheium, 82

Hadranus, worship of, 41 n. 4
Hadrian, 250
Haliartus, 225
Halicarnassus, 39 n. 1, 204
Harpalus, 148 n. 1
Hebdome, battle of, 215
Heliaea, 154, 164, 172; organisation and powers of, 174
Helice, 236
Hellas, 45
Hellenes of Thessaly, 94
Hellenic name, spread of, 51, 94
Hellenism, 244
Hellenotamiae, 183, 190
Hellespont, 197
Helos, 84
Helots, 83
Heracleia (on the Euxine), 83, 247

INDEX OF SUBJECTS 261

Heracleia (in Trachis), 40, 44 n. 2, 232
Heracleidae, 19, 222
Heracleides of Athens, 165
Heracles, the Phoenician, 125
Heraea, 12, 139, 237
Herald, sanctity of, 47
Heredity, 15
Hermione, 50, 237
Hetaeriae at Athens, 209
Hierapytna, 54 n. 2, 121 n. 1
Hiero, 218
Himera, battle of, 32
Hippocrates of Athens, 255
Histiaea, 192
Histiaeotis, 116, 224
Hittite worship, 125
Homeric recitals suppressed at Sicyon, 32
Homicide, 143
Hopletes, 127
Hylleis, 95
Hyperbolus, 161
Hyrnathiae, 95
Hysiae, battle of, 108

Ialysus, 218
Iamidae, 21
Illyria, 39
Imperial Federation suggested at Athens, 202
Indian settlements of Alexander, 246
Indo-Scythian Empire, 246
International custom, 41; law, 45; relations, 54
Ionia, 197
Ionians, 51 n. 1, 52
Isagoras, 125, 142, 157
Iseas, 236
Islanders in Athenian Empire, 197
Italian Greeks subject to Rome, 250
Italici, 250

Jason of Pherae, 223
Jurisdiction in Athenian Empire, 199
Jury-pay, 159

Kings of Sparta, 79, 92, 97; at Elis, 213 n. 2; king at Argos, 215; see Monarchy
Knights, aristocracy of, 22; in Asia Minor, 23; in Athens, 182; see ἱππεῖς

Laches, 177, 254
Laconia, 78, 79, 81, 108
Lamian War, 212
Landed aristocracies, 65, 67
Land-distribution at Sparta, 81, 90
Language as a source of unity, 46
Larisa, 19, 63, 64, 224
Latin civilisation in the West, 250
Laurium, revenue from mines at, 165
Law in Greece, 8; public and private, 9; civil and criminal, 175; a covenant, 10; unwritten, 10; customary, 17; at Sparta, 92
Law-courts at Athens, 140, 153, 163, 174
Law-giver in Greece, 2, 56, 155; early law-givers, 17
Legislative authority, division of, 75; at Sparta, 97, 100; at Athens, 170, 172
Leontini, 23, 26
Leontion, 236 n. 4
Leros, 40 n. 2
Lesbos, 18, 192, 193, 201 n. 1
Leucadia, 83 n. 3, 248
Leuctra, battle of, 207, 229
Lex data, 251
Lex provinciae, 252
Limnae, 94
Lindus, 218
Local feuds at Athens, 156; government at Athens, 160
Locrians, 51 n. 1
Locri Epizephyrii, 23, 27, 42, 44, 45
Locris (Opuntian), 39, 192; constitution of, 65
Locris (Ozolian), 12, 59 n. 2; constitution of, 66
Lot, appointment by, 138, 166; meaning and use of, 139
Lycia, 189
Lycian league, 241
Lyciarch, 242
Lycophron of Pherae, 223
Lycortas, 237
Lyctus, 116, 118
Lycurgus (of Sparta), 92; constitution of, 93
Lycurgus (of Athens), 178, 179, 184, 185, 186
Lydiades, 237
Lygdamis, 30
Lysander, 87, 114

MACEDONIA, 62, 148, 207, 246, 248, 249; Roman province of, 248
Magistracy, conception of, 7, 122
Magnesia on the Maeander, 23
Magnetes, 51 n. 1, 223
Malians, 51 n. 1; constitution of, 64
Mantineia, 108 n. 1, 110, 113, 229, 230, 232, 233; battle of, 57, 71, 109, 216
Marathon, 125, 126
Margos, 236
Mariandyni, 83, 84 n. 2
Massilia, 43, 251
Mausolus, 207
Medon, 135 n. 3
Medontidae, 124, 135
Megalopolis (in Arcadia), 229, 230, 237, 238
Megalopolis (in Pontus), 247
Megara, 27 n. 4, 44, 95, 108, 160, 192, 237; constitution of, 68
Melanthidae, 17, 124, 135
Melanthus, 135
Melitaea, 234 n. 1
Menidi, 125
Mercenaries of tyrants, 30
Mesembria, 37 n. 1
Mesopotamia, 246
Messenia, 18, 19, 79, 84, 108, 114, 237
Messoa, 94
Métayer tenure in Attica, 150
Methone, 196 n. 1
Methymna, 193, 205
Miletus, 30, 37, 160, 199; colonies of, 38, 40 n. 2, 44 n. 1
Military colonies, 39; service as a claim to rule, 62, 64
Ministerial government, approaches to in Greece, 182, 186, 241
Ministry, absence of a true at Athens, 171, 182, 187
Minos, 10, 115, 116
Minyans, 80
Mithridatic War, 247
Mixed governments, 6, 10, 60, 74; Athens after Solon as a mixed government, 155
Moderates at Athens, 208
Molossians, 15
Monarchy, origin of, 14; heroic, 14; downfall of, 18; at Sparta, 97; at Athens, 135; in Thessaly, 222
Monopolies, creation of, 173, 200

Mummius, 237
Municipal autonomy, 65; at Rhodes, 219
Municipia, 250
Munychia, 125
Mutilation, 47 n. 5
Mycale, amphictyony of, 48, 49
Mycenae, 16
Mytilene, 19, 27, 38 n. 1, 193 n. 5, 204, 205

NARBO, 251
National characteristics, 58
Naucraries, 134, 159
Naucratis, 39
Naupactus, 39, 232; charter of, 43, 44, 55 n. 4
Nauplia, 50
Naxos, 27 n. 4, 30, 191, 197
Neapolis (in Pontus), 247
Neodamodeis, 86
Nero, 249
Nicias, 179, 182 n. 2
Nicopolis (in Epirus), 248
Nobles, growth of power of, 18; rule of the, 21
Nomothetae at Athens, 172

OATH of king, 15, 92, 103; in international law, 48, 54, 55, 194; of jurors at Athens, 154, 170, 174, 176; of council at Athens, 160; of political clubs, 210
Obes, 94, 95, 96
Oeanthia, 47 n. 2, 66
Oenophyta, battle of, 67
Oenus (town), 79 n. 4; (river) 94 n. 5
Oetaeans, 51 n. 1
Olbia, 250
Olenus, 236
Oligarchic constitutions, characteristics of, 73
Oligarchs at Athens, 208
Oligarchy, 60
Olpae, 227
Olympic games, 248; see Games
Olynthus, 228; constitution of Olynthian league, 228
Onchestus, amphictyony of, 48, 50, 225
Opus, 65
Oracle in colonisation, 40; political value of oracles, 99 n. 3

INDEX OF SUBJECTS

Orchomenus (in Boeotia), 50, 80, 225, 232
Orthagoras, 29
Orthagoridae, 33
Ostracism, 160, 169, 215, 217
Oxylus, law of, 213

Paches, 177
Palestine, Hellenic civilisation in, 247
Palladium, 144
Pamboeotia, 225
Pamphyli, 95
Panathenaea, 33, 126
Panhellenism, 248
Panionium, 49
Panticapaeum, 250
Paphlagonia, 247
Paros, 197, 204
Parrhasians, 110
Partheniae, 25
Parthian Empire, 246
Patrae, 236, 248, 249
Payment for state services, 163
Peiraeus, 126
Peisander, 209
Peisistratidae, rule of, 29, 31, 32, 34, 157
Peisistratus, 26, 28, 29, 30, 31, 33, 132, 141
Pelasgi, 124
Pelasgiotis, 223
Pella, 228, 249
Pellene, 236
Pelopidas, 227
Peloponnesian confederacy, 60, 62, 70, 72, 106, 107, 221; constitution of, 108
Peloponnesian War, 61, 68, 69, 86, 91, 108, 113, 132, 169, 177, 181, 236
Penestae, 63, 83, 84
Peraea, 234 n. 1
Periander (of Corinth), 28 n. 1, 33
Periander (of Athens), 184
Pericles, 132, 147, 177, 179, 182, 192, 209, 254; reforms of, 162
Perioeci (of Sparta), 19, 78, 249; (of Argos), 215
Phalaris, 30
Phalerum, 126
Pharae, 236
Pharis, 79
Pharsalus, 19, 63

Phaselis, 39 n. 1
Pheidon of Argos, 215
Pherae, 64, 223
Philip of Macedon, 53, 64, 224, 232, 248
Philippi, 249
Philolaus, 67
Philopoemen, 237, 240
Phlius, 110, 237
Phocaea, 39 n. 1, 43
Phocians, 51 n. 1
Phocion, 87, 182 n. 1
Phocis, 59 n. 2, 192, 249
Phoenicians, 124, 125; of Carthage, 76; Phoenician civilisation in Africa, 251
Phormio of Elis, 214
Phormisius, 212
Phratry at Athens, 129, 143, 158; at Elis, 213
Phreattys, 144
Phrynichus, 170, 203, 209
Phthiotis, 224
Piracy in international law, 54
Pisatans, 49
Pitane, 94
Pittacus, 27
Pleistoanax, 20 n. 6
Polemarch at Athens, 137, 159, 181; polemarchs of Thessaly, 224
Poletae at Athens, 152 n. 2
Polity as a form of government, 60, 64
Polycrates of Samos, 30
Polydorus, 101, 103
Pompeiopolis, 247
Pompeius, 246, 247
Pontus, 247
Poseidon at Eleusis, 33; Samios, 50; at Onchestus, 225
Potidaea, 207
Prasiae, 50
Priansius, 54 n. 2
Priesthood in Greece, 16, 21
Prisoners, treatment of, 47
Probalinthus, 126
Probouleuma, form of at Athens, 169
Proportional representation, 242
Prytaneis, 168, 169, 180 n. 1
Prytaneium, 159; court of the, 144
Psephism, 171
Public meals at Sparta, 87; in Crete, 91, 118

Public opinion as a support of government, 58
Pylus, 124
Pythagoreans, 45
Pythian games, 48

RANSOM of prisoners, 47
Religion as a source of unity, 46; control of by state at Athens, 173
Representation in federal governments, 52, 243; in Thessaly, 223; in Aetolia, 233
Revolution, 6; in the colonies, 45; in mixed governments, 77; at Athens, 208
Rhegium, 23, 26, 44, 45
Rhodes, 39 n. 1, 204, 205, 207, 242; constitution of, 218
Roman Empire and Greece, 38, 115; law applied to Greece, 251; organisation of provinces, 246; institutions compared with Greek, 7, 20, 21, 31, 44 n. 4, 76, 77, 78, 90, 97, 98, 99 n. 1, 102, 103, 120, 176, 195, 202, 223

SACAE, 246
Sacred wars, 52
Salamis, battle of, 57, 147
Samos, 23, 30, 192, 193, 194, 203, 204, 207
Sciritae, 80
Scopadae, 19, 63
Scyros, 191
Secretary of the city at Athens, 167
Seisactheia, 150
Seleucia on the Tigris, 247
Sellasia, battle of, 115
Senate of Rome, 13, 77
Sicans, 41
Sicels, 41, 217
Sicilian expedition, effects of, 210, 217
Sicily, 26, 38, 250; *see* Syracuse
Sicyon, 26, 29, 70, 95, 109, 237; constitution of, 71
Sinope, 43, 247
Slain, duties to, 47
Slaves, 7; to the soil, 83; in Crete, 117; at Athens, 132
Social War, 207
Socii, 250
Solon, 3, 11, 27, 31, 127, 131, 134, 137, 138, 145, 149; constitution of, 149
Sovereignty, conception of in Greece, 75; at Athens, 170
Spain, 251
Sparta, 9, 13, 14, 15, 18, 19, 21, 34, 44, 237; constitution of, 77
Spartiatae, 80, 87
Spata, 125
Sphettus, 126
Stenyclerus, 79
Strategi of Athens, 173, 180, 252; of Argos, 215; of Rhodes, 219
Strategus of Thessaly, 224; of Acarnania, 228; of Arcadia, 230; of Aetolian league, 235; of Achaean league, 240
Stratos, 227
Sybaris, 44, 45
Sycophant, 188, 210
Synedrion in Athenian confederacy, 206
Syracuse, 23, 25, 29, 31, 34, 44, 45, 57, 161, 188; constitution of, 216

TAGUS of Thessaly, 223
Talthybiadae, 21
Talthybius, 47 n. 4
Tanagra, 225
Tarentum, 25, 44, 58, 72
Taxiarchs, 180, 253
Tegea, 108 n. 1, 109, 229, 230, 232
Tellidae, 21
Telys, 45
Tenedos, 58
Ten Thousand in Arcadia, 229
Teos, 27 n. 4, 39 n. 1, 128, 200 n. 3, 233
Territorial sovereignty, 43, 80
Tetrapolis, 126
Thasos, 192
Theagenes, 29, 69
Thebes, 205, 225; constitution of, 66
Themistocles, 147 n. 4, 159 n. 1, 209
Theopompus, King of Sparta, 101, 103
Thera, 197
Theramenes of Athens, 210
Thermopylae, 51, 52
Thersilion, 236
Theseus, 124, 126, 127, 213
Thesprotians, 84
Thessaliotis, 223

Thessalonica, 249
Thessaly, 14, 19, 51 n. 1, 84; constitution of cities of, 62; federal government of, 222
Thetes, 41
Thirty at Athens, 114, 211
Thoricus, 126
Thrace, 33, 192, 194, 197, 249
Thrasybulus of Syracuse, 34, 216
Thurii, 43, 44 n. 2
Thyrea, 81 n. 3
Tiasa, 94 n. 5
Timocracy, 44 (cf. 23), 69, 151; at Athens, 212; in Thessaly, 224
Timocrates, 171 n. 1
Timoleon, 218
Timotheus, 179
Tiryns, 16
Togati, 250
Tomi, 128
Trade debarring from office, 67; see βαναυσία
Trajan, 250, 252
Trapezus, 43
Treasurers at Athens, 152 n. 2
Tribal unions, 12, 59, 65
Tribe, 13
Tribe-names, Dorian, 71, 95, 128; Ionian, 127, 128; of Cleisthenes of Athens, 157
Tribute of Athenian Empire, 196

Tricorythus, 126
Trierarchy, 159, 183, 184
Triopium, amphictyony of, 48, 50
Triphylia, 110 n. 4; amphictyony of, 50
Tritaea, 236
Trittys, 134, 160
Troezen, 124, 237
Tyndarides, 216
Tyra, 250
Tyranny, 25, 45; conception of, 27, 34; downfall of early, 34
Tyrants of Asia Minor, 37; established by Macedon, 236

VELIA, 37 n. 1
Vespasian, 249

WAR, laws of, 47
Wealth as an element in government, 22, 37, 60

XENAGI, 111

ZALEUCUS, 17, 23, 27, 45
Zeugitae, 41
Zeus Areius, 15; Lacedaemon and Uranius, 20; Hellanius, 94; Geleon, 127 n. 4; Herceius, 129

INDEX OF GREEK WORDS

(The references are to the pages; "n." signifies the note on a page)

ἀγέλαι, 118
ἀγορά, 120
ἄγροικοι, 137
ἀγωγή, 87
ἀγῶνες, 48
ἄδεια, 169, 171, 211 n. 1
αἰσυμνήτης, 27
ἀκοσμία, 77, 118 n. 6
ἁλιαία, 215 n. 5
ἀμφικτίονες or ἀμφικτύονες, 48 n. 3
ἀνάκρισις, 137, 155
ἀνδρεία, 118
ἀντιγραφεὺς τῆς βουλῆς 167
ἀπαρχή, 192 n. 1
ἀπελεύθεροι, 133
ἀπέταιροι, 117 n. 4
ἀποδέκται, 159
ἀποικία, 39
ἀποίκια, 41
ἀπόκλητοί, 234
ἀπόφασις, 148
ἀρετή, 15, 21, 75, 86, 87
ἀργυρολόγοι νῆες, 198 (cf. 181)
ἀριστίνδην, 16, 100, 138 n. 1
ἄριστοι, οἱ, 21
Ἀρκαδικόν, 229
ἁρμοσταί, 82
ἁρμοστήρ, 82 n. 5
ἀρχαγέται, 14, 97
ἀρχαί, 6, 121, 136; κληρωταί, 141 n. 3
ἀρχαῖα μοῖρα, 90
ἀρχή, 6, 110, 152, 193
ἄρχοντες, 125
ἄρχων, 64, 224, 225; μεσίδιος, 64
ἀσυλία, 233
ἀτέλεια, 134
ἀτιμία, 150, 156 n. 2

αὐτόδικοι, 193 n. 6
αὐτοκράτωρ, 98
αὐτόνομοι, 110, 190, 193 n. 3
αὐτοπόλεις, 110
αὐτοτελεῖς, 193 n. 6
αὐτόχθονες, 124

βαγοί, 14, 97
βαναυσία, 21, 72
βάρβαρος, 47 n. 5
βασιλᾶες, 213 n. 2
βασιλεῖς, 16, 135
Βασιλεῖται, 20
βασιλεύς, 14, 138
βασιλικὸς φόρος, 81 n. 1
βοιωτάρχαι, 226
βουλά, 227; βουλὰ καὶ δᾶμος, 70 n. 2
βουλαί, 225
βουλή, 152, 230, n. 1, 239, 247; βουλὴ καὶ δῆμος, 204
βουλευταί, 233, 239 n. 1
βουλευτήριον, 126, 230
βωλά, 119, 121 n. 2

γαμόροι or γεωμόροι, 23 (cf. 42 and 45)
γενεά, 213
γένη, 95, 118, 128
γένος, 13, 20, 80 n. 1
γεννῆται, 20, 128
γέροντες, 13, 17 n. 4, 96, 100
γερουσία, 13, 18, 72, 89, 96, 100, 101, 119
γεωνόμοι, 42
γνώριμοι, 61
γραφαί, 176
γραφὴ παρανόμων, 170, 171, 211
γυνή, 131

INDEX OF GREEK WORDS

δαμιοργοί, 230 n. 5, 242 n. 3
δᾶμος, 96 ; ὁ σύμπας δᾶμος, 219
δεκαδαρχία, 224
δεκαρχία, 114
δέκατος αὐτός, 255
δήμαρχοι, 160
δημιουργοί, 64, 214, 240
δῆμοι, 12, 160
δημοποίητοι, 129
δῆμος, 16, 17, 89
διαδόσεις, 165
διαλλακτής, 150
διανυμμί, 165
δίκαι, 175 ; ἴδιαι, 175 ; δημόσιαι, 176 ; αὐτοτελεῖς, 176 ; ἀπὸ συμβολῶν, 54, 200
δικασπόλοι, 17
δικαστήρια, 153 (cf. 175), 242
δίκη, 17 ; ἀποστασίου, 133 ; ἀπροστασίου, 133
διοικήσει, ὁ ἐπὶ τῇ, 185
διόρθωσις τῶν νόμων, 172
διορθωτής, 150
διωβελία, 166
δόγμα, 147 ; τῶν συμμάχων, 206
δοκιμασία, 140, 166
δυναστεία, 18, 24, 67, 151
δωδεκάπολις, 126

ἐγγύησις, 131
ἔγκτησις γῆς καὶ οἰκίας, 54
ἐθελοπρόξενος, 46 n. 2
ἔθνη, 51, 127
ἔθνος, 232, 238
εἶδος τῆς πόλεως, 5
εἰκοστή, 197
εἵλωτες, 83
εἰσαγγελίαι, 168
εἰσφορά, 134, 151, 180 n. 3 (cf. 183 and 184)
εἰσφοραί, 80, 152
ἑκατόμπολις, 82, 83
ἐκεχειρία, 49
ἔκκλητος πόλις, 54
ἐκτημόριοι, 150
ἐλευθερία, 122
Ἐλευθερολάκωνες, 249
ἐλεύθερος, 123
Ἐλευσίνοι, 134 n. 3
ἐξελεύθεροι, 133
Ἐπακρεῖς or Ἐπακριεῖς, 126, 134 n. 3
ἐπάριτοι, 230 n. 7
ἐπιγαμία, 54, 116, 132
ἐπιδημιουργοί, 39

ἐπιδικασία, 131
ἐπιλαχόντες, 166
ἐπιμελητής, δημοσίων προσόδων, 183 n. 1
ἐπίσκοπος, 194
ἐπιστάται, 219
ἐπιστάτης, 167 (cf. 172) ; τοῦ ναυτικοῦ, 185
ἐπιφορά, 198
ἐπώνυμος, 105, 136
ἑταιρεῖαι, 88, 114, 118, 209
ἑταῖροι, 15, 209
εὐγένεια, 15 n. 5, 61
εὐθύνη, 140, 188
εὔθυνοι, 153
εὐπατρίδαι, 129
ἐφέται, 143
ἐφόδιον, 42, 164
ἔφοροι, 103

ζευγῖται, 142

ἡγεμονία δικαστηρίου, 137, 180 n. 3
ἡλιαία, 154 n. 2

θέμιστες, 17, 101
θέσμια, 136 n. 1
θεσμοθέται, 136 (cf. 172)
θεωρικά, 166, 184
θεωρικόν, ὁ ἐπὶ τό, 185
θῆτες, 142

ἱερά, ἴδια, 158
ἱεραὶ σπονδαί, 49
ἱερατικαὶ θυσίαι, 17
ἱερομνήμονες, 52, 53 n. 1
ἱερὸς πόλεμος, 52
ἵππαρχοι, 224 n. 1
ἱππεῖς, 22 n. 3, 141, 168
ἱπποβόται, 22
ἰσοπολιτεία, 54, 116
ἵστωρ, 17 n. 4

καλοὶ κἀγαθοί, 61, 81, 89
κατάλογος, 180
Κεραμῆς, 134 n. 3
κλαρῶται, 117
κλῆροι, 67, 90
κληρουχία, 40 (cf. 200)
κοινὴ σύνοδος τῶν Βοιωτῶν, 226
κοινοδίκιον, 117
κοινόν, 65, 227 ; τῶν Λοκρῶν τῶν Ἡοίων, 65 ; Θετταλῶν, 223 ; τῶν

268   OUTLINES OF GREEK CONSTITUTIONAL HISTORY

Ἀκαρνάνων, 227; τῶν Ἀρκάδων, 229; τῶν Αἰτωλῶν, 232
κοινὸν δικαστήριον, 227; συνέδριον, 242
κοινωνία, 166
κόσμιοι, 119 n. 1
κοσμίοντες, 119 n. 1
κόσμοι, 119
κριτικὴ δύναμις, 123, 164 n. 5
κρυπτεία, 85
κυθηροδίκης, 82
κύριον, τό, 75
κωλαγρέται or κωλακρέται, 159 n. 5
κώμη, 13

Λακεδαιμόνιοι, 78
λειτουργίαι, 134
ληξιαρχικὸν γραμματεῖον, 160
λογισταί, 153

μαστροί, 219
μεσόγειοι, 126
μέσος πολίτης, 64
μεταβολή, 76
μετοίκιον, 134
μέτοικοι, 8, 47, 133
μισθός, δικαστικός, 159, 164; ἐκκλησιαστικός, 165
μνᾶ ἀπὸ τοῦ ταλάντου, 192 n. 1
μνωῖται, 117
μόθακες or μόθωνες, 86
μύριοι, οἱ, 229
Μυρρινούσιοι, 134 n. 3

ναύαρχος, 81 n. 8
ναυκραρίαι, 134
ναύκραροι, 135, 152
νεοδαμώδεις, 86
νοθοί, 87
νόμιμα, 116
νομογράφοι, 235
νομοθέται, 172
νομοθέτης, 9, 150
νόμοι, 170; θετικοί, 67; ἐπ' ἀνδρί, 161 n. 2, 169
νόμος, 17; κοινός and ἴδιος, 9; τοῖς Ἕλλησι, 47 n. 8

ξεναγοί, 111
ξενηλασίαι, 101
ξενία, 46
ξένοι, 87, 133
ξύνοδοι, κοιναί, 190
ξυνωμοσίαι, 210

Ϝοικέες, 117
οἰκία, 13
οἰκιστής, 39, 40, 42 n. 7, 94
οἰκοῦντες, οἱ χωρίς, 132
ὁμογάλακτες, 128
ὅμοιοι, 87, 106
ὁπλῖται, 22 n. 3
ὀργεῶνες, 128 (cf. 158)
ὄργια, 129
ὅροι, 150
ὄρος, 60, 99

παιδονόμος, 118 n. 4
παλλακίς, 131
παναιτωλικόν, 234
πατριά, 213
πέζαρχοι, 224 n. 1
πελάται, 150
πεντακοσιομέδιμνοι, 141
περικτίονες, 48 n. 3
περιοικίς, 82
περίοικοι, 83 n. 3, 117
πεταλισμός, 217
πλεονέκτης, 61
πλεονεξία, 34
πλῆθος, τό, 219
πόλεις, 14, 82, 125
πολέμαρχος, 135
πολιᾶται, 118
πόλις, 4, 7, 12, 39, 59, 103, 125, 126
πολῖται, 7
πολίτης, 8
πολιτεία, 4, 62; ὀρθή, 76; μικτή, 75
πολίτευμα, 5
πολιτικὴ χώρα, 82
πολιτοφύλακες, 64
πονηροί, 61
πρᾶσιν αἰτεῖν, 133 n. 2
προβούλευμα, 106
πρόβουλοι, 72, 210
πρόδικος, 98
πρόεδροι, 167 (cf. 172), 211
προεστῶτες, 241 n. 1
πρόκριτοι, 141
προξενία, 46
πρόξενος, 46 n. 2, 99
πρόσοδος πρὸς τὴν βουλὴν καὶ τὸν δῆμον, 134
προστάται τοῦ ἐμπορίου, 39 n. 1
προστάτης, 8 n. 1, 47, 133; τοῦ δήμου, 28, 187
πρυτανεία, 167
πρυτανεῖα, 159, 176
πρυτανεῖον, 125, 126

INDEX OF GREEK WORDS

πρυτάνεις, 134, 153, 167, 218
πρυτανεύουσα φυλή, 167
πρύτανις, 30
Πύθιοι, 99
πυθόχρηστοι νόμοι, 10
πυλαγόραι, 52 (cf. 53 n. 1)

Σελλάνιος, 94 n. 3
σκυτάλη, 82 n. 5
σκυταλισμός, 216
Σπαρτιᾶται, 79
στάσις, 116
στρατηγία, 140
στρατηγοί, 111 n. 6, 158, 240; αὐτοκράτορες, 174, 255
σύγκλητοι ἐκκλησίαι, 169
σύγκλητος, 239 n. 1
συγκρητισμός, 117
συλᾶν, 54
σύμβολα, 54
συμβόλαιαι δίκαι, 200 n. 1
σύμβουλοι, 98
συμμορίαι, 184, 193 n. 9
συμπολιτεία, 54, 228, 233 n. 3; ἐθνικὴ συμπολιτεία, 238 n. 2
συνάρχοντες, 181
σύνεδροι, 206
συνοίκια, 126
συνοίκισις, 14
συνοικισμός, 78, 80, 125, 126, 128, 213
συντέλειαι, 225 n. 5
συντέλεις, 198
συντάξεις, 207
συσσίτια, 88

ταγός, 14, 223
τάκται, 197
ταμίας τῆς κοινῆς προσόδου, 185

τάξεις φόρου, 198
τάξις, 5
τέλη : οἱ τὰ τέλη ἔχοντες, 214
τεμένη, 18, 41, 90
τετράδες, 223
τετράκωμοι, 126
τετράπολις, 126
τιμή, 16, 97
τιμοῦχοι, 39 n. 1
τριακάς, 95
τριηκάδες, 95
τριηραρχία, 159
τρίκωμοι, 126
τριττυαρχεῖν, 134
τριττύες, 134
τριώβολον, 164
τυραννίς, 3
τύραννος, 27

ὑπήκοοι, 117, 193
ὑπομείονες, 87, 92
ὑποτελεῖς, 192

φόρος, 190, 207
φράτορες, 129, 130
φρατρία, 80 n. 1, 128, 129
φρουρά, 194
φρούραρχος, 181, 194

χειροτέχναι, 8 n. 1
χίλιοι, οἱ, 23
χρεῶν ἀποκοπή, 150

ψαφίσματα, 219
ψηφίσματα, 170
ψήφισμα : κοινὸν ψήφισμα, 195, 198 n. 3

ὠβαί, 94

INDEX OF AUTHORS CITED

I. Greek Authors

Aelian
Variae Historiae

	PAGE
i. 19	26
v. 12	173
ix. 25	32
xii. 43	87

Aeschines
contra Timarchum

§ 13 . . . 9

de falsa Legatione

§ 60 . . . 206
§ 70 . . . 205
§ 115 . . . 57

in Ctesiphontem

§ 20 . . 146, 167
§ 25 . . . 186
§ 38 . . . 172
§ 69 . . . 206
§ 124 . . . 53

Andocides
de Mysteriis

§ 83 . . . 212
§ 87 . . . 169

Antiphon
de caede Herodis

§ 8 . . . 133
§ 40 . . . 201

Aristophanes
Acharnenses

l. 938 . . . 188

Equites

	PAGE
ll. 103, 258, 304, 774, 912, 923, 1226, 1250	183
l. 255	164
l. 861	188
l. 1003	99
l. 1357	177

Nubes

l. 863 . . . 164

Vespae

l. 595 . . . 164
l. 660 . . . 175
l. 707 . . . 198

Aves

l. 1023 . . . 194

Lysistrata

l. 528 . . . 202

Ranae

ll. 363, 569 . . . 188

Ecclesiazusae

l. 301 . . . 165
l. 816 . . . 173

Plutus

l. 1166 . . . 175

Aristotle
Ethics

v. 7 . . . 47

	PAGE
viii. 5	209
10	28

Politics

i. 2	7, 13, 14
ii. 6	138
7	3, 42, 65, 151
8	10
9	80, 85, 87, 88, 89, 90, 91, 92, 100, 102, 104, 105
10	116, 117, 118, 119, 120
12	7, 45, 57, 67, 138, 147, 149, 152, 153, 154, 155, 164
iii. 1	7, 8, 105
2	64, 158
3	1, 5
4	15
5	67, 131
6	5, 11
7	28, 58
11	123, 153, 177
13	61, 162
14	14, 17, 27, 98
15	27, 57, 178
16	10
p. 1289 a	5
1289 b	22, 58, 64
1290 a	60
1290 b	58
1291 b	58, 60, 61
1292 a	11
1292 b	22, 24, 214
1293 b	61

INDEX OF GREEK AUTHORS

	PAGE		PAGE		PAGE
p. 1294 a	. . 15	12 156		*de Corona*	
1294 b	. . 104	13 . . . 132, 137		§ 133 . . . 148	
1295 a	. 27, 57	16 . . . 31, 32		§ 134 . . . 146	
1295 b	. . 5	20 162		*de falsa Legatione*	
1296 a	. . 75	21 . 126, 130, 134, 157,			
1296 b	. . 58	158		§ 11 . . . 230	
1297 b	22, 57, 64	22 . . 14, 158, 160		*contra Aristocratem*	
1298 b	. 101, 210	23 . . 147, 189, 190			
1300 a	. . 69	24 . 165, 166, 175, 178		§ 238 . . . 63	
1301 b	. . 15	25 147		*contra Timocratem*	
1302 b	. . 67	26 132			
1303 a	. 139, 215	27 . 147, 163, 164, 177		§§ 20 ff . . . 172	
1304 a	57, 147, 162,	28 166		§§ 43, 73 . . . 171	
	216, 217	29 . . . 162, 211		§ 148 . . 154, 176	
1304 b	. . 69	35 211		§ 149 . . . 154	
1305 a	26, 29, 30	41 . . 149, 165, 178		*contra Aristogeitonem*	
1305 b	20, 30, 64	44 167			
1306 a	27, 100, 214	45 . . . 166, 168		§ 16 . . . 10	
1308 a	. . 88	48 159		*adversus Boeotum*	
1310 a	. . 210	54 167			
1310 b	. 28, 30	57 . . . 144, 146		§ 40 . . . 131	
1311 a	. . 30	61 . . . 181, 254		*adversus Macartatum*	
1312 b	. . 34	62 . . 141, 165, 193			
1313 a	. . 103	ARRIAN		§ 54 . . . 142	
1313 b	. 28, 32	*Anabasis*		*contra Eubulidem*	
1315 b	. 30, 31				
1317 b	. . 7	i. 10 . . . 232		§ 67 . . . 129	
1318 a	. . 139				
1318 b	. . 204	ATHENAEUS		DEINARCHUS	
1319 a	. . 213	*Deipnosophistae*		*contra Demosthenem*	
1319 b	. 130, 158	p. 141 f . . . 96		§§ 82 ff . . . 148	
1320 b	. . 72	143 a . . . 113		DIODORUS SICULUS	
1322 b	. . 14	263 d . . . 86			
1324 a	. . 22	263 f . . 117, 118		iv. 39 . . . 125	
1326 a	. . 10	266 f . . . 134		v. 80 . . . 116	
1332 b	. . 7	271 e . . . 88		viii. 24 . . . 29	
1341 a	. . 57	372 b . . . 173		xi. 26 . . . 32	
Rhetoric		566 f . . . 146		54 . . . 214	
		577 c . . . 132		68 . . . 34	
i. 10	. . 9	DEMOSTHENES		86, 87 . . 217	
Oeconomics		*in Philippum*		xii. 9 . . . 45	
ii. 37 . . . 173		ii. § 24 . . . 224		10 . . 43, 44	
Constitution of Athens		iii. § 44 . . . 232		30 . . . 217	
3 . 135, 138, 144, 145		*de Chersoneso*		xiii. 34, 35 . . 217	
4 . 23, 138, 145, 149,				xiv. 82 . . . 223	
	152	Argt. . . . 42		84, 94 . . 205	
5 150		*de Symmoriis*		92 . . . 72	
6 150				xv. 30 . . . 205	
7 . 142, 151, 152, 153		§ 182 . . . 184		40 . . . 70	
8 . 134, 138, 141, 146,		*pro Rhodiorum libertate*		52, 53 . . 227	
	152			57 . . . 216	
9 . . 153, 154, 155		§ 3 . . . 207		60 . . . 223	
				61 . . . 63	

xv. 62	.	. 227
78, 79, 80	.	. 226
xvi. 14	.	. 63
65	.	. 72
70	.	. 218
82	.	. 34
xviii. 18	.	. 212
xix. 66	.	. 232
xx. 98	.	. 218
99	.	. 232

Diogenes Laertius

i. 3, 68	. . . 104

Dionysius Halicarnassensis
Antiquitates Romanae

ii. 14	.	. . 102
iv. 25	.	. . 48
vi. 60	.	. . 28
vii. 2-11	.	. . 31

Heracleides Ponticus
Fragm.

2	.	.	. 91
7	.	.	. 91
25	.	.	. 23

Herodotus

i. 23	.	.	. 33
30	.	.	. 125
56	.	.	. 124
59	.	.	26, 31
61	.	.	. 30
65	.	93, 94, 115
66	.	.	. 109
144	.	.	48, 50
146	.	.	37, 44
148	.	.	48, 49
167, 168	.	.	. 37
ii. 143	.	.	. 20
167	.	.	22, 72
178	.	.	. 39
iii. 19	.	.	. 43
48	.	.	. 72
52	.	.	. 26
80	.	28, 32, 139
120	.	.	. 30
148	.	.	. 101
iv. 98	.	.	. 47
138	.	.	. 37
148	.	50, 80, 110
149	.	.	. 80

iv. 159	.	. 83
v. 40	.	. 105
44	.	21, 45
52	.	. 42
57	.	21, 124
62	.	. 124
63	.	. 64
65	.	. 30
66	20, 29, 157
67	.	. 33
68	.	26, 71
69	.	160, 162
71	31, 134, 142, 145
72	.	79, 142
74-75	.	. 112
77	.	22, 47
90	.	. 99
91-95	.	. 112
92	19, 30, 31, 32, 34, 72
vi. 3	.	. 159
7	.	. 50
38	.	. 42
43	.	. 38
51	.	. 97
56	.	. 98
57	.	99, 102
59	.	. 97
67, 68	.	. 32
79	.	. 47
82	.	. 105
89	.	. 135
92	.	. 50
103	.	. 31
127	.	. 63
131	.	. 162
vii. 3	.	. 98
6	.	63, 99
134	.	21, 47
144	.	. 165
148	.	48, 215
149	18, 106, 215
153	.	. 13
155	.	. 45
157	.	. 31
161	.	. 32
163	.	. 31
viii. 22	.	. 43
44	.	. 135
73	.	. 80
107	.	. 190
144	.	. 46

ix. 7	. . . 106
9	. . 98, 106
11	. . . 81
33	. . . 21
35	. . . 108
37	. . . 21
58	. . . 63
79	. . . 47
106	. . . 189

Homer
Iliad

i. 238	.	. 17
337	.	. 20
ii. 206	.	. 17
402 ff	.	. 16
404	.	. 13
iv. 266, 267	.	. 15
344	.	. 13
xi. 823	.	. 20
xvi. 269 ff	.	. 15
xviii. 497	.	. 17

Odyssey

| iv. 63 | . | . 20 |
| xiii. 181 | . | . 16 |

Isaeus
de Philoctemonis hereditate

| § 21 | . . . 131 |

Isocrates
Areopagiticus

| § 14 | . . . 1 |
| § 23 | . . . 139 |

Panathenaicus

§ 105	. . . 203
§ 145	. . . 138
§ 154	. . . 102
§ 170	. . . 81
§ 178	. . . 78
§ 181	. . . 81

Panegyricus

| p. 62 | . . . 203 |

Lycurgus
contra Leocratem

| § 4 | . . . 9 |

INDEX OF GREEK AUTHORS

Lysias

περὶ τοῦ Σηκοῦ

	PAGE
§ 22	146

de caede Eratosthenis

§ 30	146

contra Epicratem

§§ 1, 2	177

contra Nicomachum

§ 22	177

contra Agoratum

§ 67	180

Pausanias

i. 14, 15	125
25	207
28	144
ii. 19	215
iii. 2	79
5	101, 102, 105
14	103
20	84
iv. 5	135, 142, 143
vii. 6	108
9	238
16	227
viii. 6	231
32	230
x. 10	25

Pindar

Olympia

13, 6 ff	72

Pythia

10 ad fin.	63

Plato

Alcibiades

p. 123	98

Cratylus

p. 394 a	15

Gorgias

p. 515 c	164

Laws

	PAGE
p. 626	118
633	85
666	118
680 a	17
691 e	18
692	93, 103, 105
708	45
754	42
859 a	10

Republic

p. 415	134
565 d	28
580	28

Theaetetus

p. 173	209

Timaeus

24	127

Plutarch

Agis

5	91
11	100

Aratus

2	71
24	240

Aristeides

1	140
2	209
4	183
5	159
8	255
13	210
22	142

Cimon

11	190, 210
15	162
17	209

Cleomenes

10	103

Demetrius

10	173

Lycurgus

6	93, 94, 101

	PAGE
7	18
8	81, 90
12	88
13	92
26	100
28	85

Lysander

2	87
13	114

Pelopidas

26	227

Pericles

7	147
7-14	209
9	140, 163
11	201
16	182
37	132

Phocion

8	182
20	87

Pyrrhus

5	15

Solon

10	55
12	16, 142
16	150
18	151, 152, 153, 154, 155
19	144, 145, 146, 152
20	156
23	127
24	131

Theseus

24	126
25	19, 127

Amatoriae Narrationes

p. 944	25

Apophthegmata Laconica

p. 268	112

de fraterno Amore

p. 594	116

Praecepta gerendae Reipublicae

	PAGE
10	214
17, 3	48

Quaestiones Graecae

1	65
5	109
18	65

Vitae decem Oratorum

p. 852 b . . . 185

POLLUX

iii. 83	86
iv. 105	125
viii. 11	128
13	133
98	167
109-111	127
125	143
129, 130	151
130	152

POLYBIUS

ii. 3	235
37	237, 238, 239
38	238
40	236, 237
41	233, 236
43	240
44	238
45	233
46	239
48	238
57	233
iv. 7	238
25	233
26	239
37	235
54	116
67	235
73	214
v. 1, 91	238
vi. 10	100
45	90, 102
46	121
ix. 38	233
xii. 5	65
16	23
xx. 1, 10	234
xxv. 8	238
xxvi. 1	238
xxvii. 2	227
xxviii. 7	240
xxix. 4	218
9	239

STRABO

p. 63	20
260	45
325	26
336	214
343	50
346	80
354, 361	79
364	78, 80
365	84
374	50
382	26
396	160
401	80
409, 411	225
412	50
426	25
440	223
447	22
476, 481	116
482	119
483	126
635	40
652	218
665	241

THEOPHRASTUS
Characteres

viii. (xxvi.) . . 127

THUCYDIDES

i. 2	12
5	227
6	88
8	125
13	15, 25
17	31
18	34
19	109, 112
20	102
24	40
27	44
28	55
34	43
56	39
67	112
76	109
87	100, 101, 105
95	37, 189
i. 96	190, 196
97	190
98	191
100	190
101	84
102	223
107	210
111	223
112	52
114	193
115	55, 194, 203
116	193, 255
119, 125	112
126	31, 145
131	105
136, 137	147
144	109
ii. 5	48
7	108
9	108, 195, 236
13	196, 255
14-17	125
15	126
22	63, 203, 254
25	83
40	123
65	182, 254
67	47
70	173
81	83
iii. 11	193
19	197, 198
36	193
37	203
42	188
43	123
47	203
50	201
58	47
62	67
86	108, 187
92	40, 44
94	12, 231
101, 102	12
104	48, 49
105	227
114	55
115	174
iv. 7	194
28	182, 254
42	195
50	106, 181
51	193

INDEX OF LATIN AUTHORS

iv. 53	. . . 83	vi. 43	. . . 195	iv. 6, 4	. . . 227
65	. . . 174	54	. 31, 32, 141	7, 1	. . . 98
74	. . . 69	81	. . . 193	v. 1, 34	. . . 98
76	. . . 225	85	. . . 202	1, 36	. . . 72
78	. . . 223	vii. 14	. . . 188	2, 7 ; 2, 8	. 110
80	. . . 85	28	. . . 197	2, 11 ; 2, 21	. 112
91	. . . 226	58	. . . 86	2, 11-19	. . 228
93	. . . 225	viii. 5	. . . 98	3, 9	. 81, 87
108	. . . 194	6	. . . 81	3, 10	. . 110
v. 11	. . . 42	21	. . 193, 203	4, 46	. . 68
16	. 20, 97, 99	22	. . . 81	vi. 1, 8	. . 63
18	. 55, 193, 196	48	. . 203, 210	1, 8-12 ; 1, 18	. 223
29	. . . 110	54	. . 209, 210	3, 3	. . 112
30	. . . 112	67	. . . 211	5, 3	. . 229
31	. . 110, 215	68	. . . 188	vii. 1, 1-14	. . 170
33	. . . 110	72	. . . 169	1, 24	. . 230
34	. . . 86	73	. . . 161	1, 38	. . 229
36	. . . 106	97	. . 22, 211	1, 42	. . 236
37	. . 215, 226			1, 44	. . 71
38	. . 225, 226	XENOPHON		3, 1	. . 230
39	. . . 194	*Anabasis*		3, 4	. . 71
41	. . . 55	iv. 6, 14	. . . 87	4, 2 ; 4, 33	. 230
47	. 55, 214, 215	v. 5, 10	. . . 43	4, 35 ; 4, 38	. 229
52	. . . 236	*Hellenica*		*Respublica Lacedae-*
53	. . . 50	i. 4, 20	. . . 254	*moniorum*
59	. . . 215	ii. 2, 7	. . . 98	10, 2	. . . 101
63	. . . 98	3, 2	. . . 211	10, 7	. . . 87
67	. . . 86	3, 4	. . . 223	15, 1	. . . 92
68	. . . 85	3, 34	. . . 105	15, 2 ; 15, 3	. 98
77	. . . 110	4, 36	. . . 98	15, 7	. . 15, 92
79	. . . 55	iii. 1, 4	. . . 86	15, 9	. . . 97
81	. 71, 109, 216	2, 27	. . . 214	*Respublica Atheniensium*
82	. . 216, 236	3, 6	. . . 81		
105	. . . 202	4, 2	. . 86, 99		
vi. 3	. . . 25	iv. 4, 6	. . . 72	1, 10	. . . 132
26	. . 195, 255	6, 1	. . . 236	1, 16	. . . 199
35	. . . 217	6, 3	. . . 106	3, 5	. . . 197
39	. . . 123				

II. LATIN AUTHORS

CICERO		LIVY		xxxviii. 30	. 240, 241
de Republica		xxxii. 22	. . 239	xlii. 38	. . . 224
ii. 4, 9	. . . 38	xxxiii. 2	. . 226		
de Divinatione		16	. . 228	TACITUS	
i. 1, 3	. . . 40	xxxiv. 51	. . 224	*Annales*	
		xxxv. 25	. 235, 240		
GELLIUS		31	. . 224	iv. 33	. . . 71
xviii. 3	. . 101	34	. . 234	xi. 24	. . . 206

III. INSCRIPTIONS

Corpus Inscriptionum Graecarum

	PAGE
no. 1171	. . 53
3438	. . 27

Corpus Inscriptionum Atticarum

ii. no. 11	. . 200
62	. 206, 207
88	. . 224
114	. . 167
331	. . 181
814	. . 49
iv. no. 22 a	. . 199

CAUER

Dilectus Inscriptionum Graecarum

no. 108	. . . 70
119	. . 54, 117
177, 182, 183,	
185	. . 219
181, l. 69	. 121
237, 238	. . 233
238	. . . 235
239, l. 19	. 234

	PAGE
no. 240, 241	. . 227
253	. . . 213
444	. . 230, 242

DITTENBERGER

Sylloge Inscriptionum Graecarum

no. 85	. . 55, 224
272	. . . 237

GORTYN CODE

v. 5	. . 118, 116

HICKS

Manual of Greek Historical Inscriptions

no. 8	. . 12, 54
19	. . . 191
23	. . . 194
23, l. 6	. . 181
23, l. 30	. . 193
24	. . . 198
28	. . 174, 194
28, ll. 19, 67,	
77	. . 181

	PAGE
no. 28, l. 26	. . 197
29	. . 39, 202
29 A, ll. 8, 9	. 41
30	. . 197, 198
31, l. 8	. . 47
31, l. 15	. . 66
35	. . 197, 198
44	. 194, 195, 196
44, l. 44	. . 195
44, l. 59	. . 180
46	. . 180, 255
46, l. 5	. . 181
47	. 197, 198, 202
48	. . . 198
56	. . . 170
56 § 3	. . 177
58 § 4	. . 200
59	. . 16, 143
63	. 39, 55, 65
63, i. A	. . 43
63 AFH	. . 44
63 z	. . . 47
81	. . . 205
81, l. 51	. . 206
82	. . . 49
84	. . . 206
176, l. 35 ff	. 54

THE END

Printed in Great Britain by R. & R. CLARK, LIMITED, *Edinburgh.*

HANDBOOKS OF
ARCHAEOLOGY & ANTIQUITIES

EDITED BY

Professor PERCY GARDNER, Litt.D., of the University of Oxford, and Professor FRANCIS W. KELSEY, of the University of Michigan.

Extra Crown 8vo.

GREEK SCULPTURE. By Prof. ERNEST A. GARDNER, M.A. Second Edition. Illustrated. Complete in one vol. 12s. 6d. net.

THE ROMAN FESTIVALS OF THE PERIOD OF THE REPUBLIC. By W. WARDE FOWLER, M.A. 7s. 6d. net.

A HANDBOOK OF GREEK CONSTITUTIONAL HISTORY. By A. H. J. GREENIDGE, M.A. With Map. 6s. 6d. net.

ROMAN PUBLIC LIFE. By A. H. J. GREENIDGE, M.A. 12s. 6d. net.

THE PRINCIPLES OF GREEK ART. By Professor PERCY GARDNER, Litt.D. Illustrated. 15s. net.

LIFE IN ANCIENT ATHENS. The Social and Public Life of a Classical Athenian from Day to Day. By Prof. T. G. TUCKER, Litt.D. Illustrated. 6s. 6d. net.

THE MONUMENTS OF CHRISTIAN ROME FROM CONSTANTINE TO THE RENAISSANCE. By Professor ARTHUR L. FROTHINGHAM. Illustrated. 12s. 6d. net.

ATHENS AND ITS MONUMENTS. By Prof. CHARLES H. WELLER. Illustrated. 10s. 6d. net.

MACMILLAN AND CO., LTD., LONDON.

WORKS ON
GREEK HISTORY AND ARCHAEOLOGY

A History of Greece from the Earliest Times to the Death of Alexander the Great. By J. B. BURY, M.A., LL.D., Litt.D., Regius Professor of Modern History in the University of Cambridge. *Second Edition.* Illustrated. Crown 8vo. 10s. net.

Hellenic History. By G. W. BOTSFORD, Ph.D. Illustrated. 8vo. 18s. net.

The City-State of the Greeks and Romans. By W. WARDE FOWLER, M.A., late Fellow and Sub-Rector of Lincoln College, Oxford. Crown 8vo. 6s.

The Great War between Athens and Sparta: A Companion to the Military History of Thucydides. By Bernard W. HENDERSON, M.A., D.Litt. With Maps. 8vo. 18s. net.

Hellenistic Athens. An Historical Essay. By Prof. WILLIAM SCOTT FERGUSON. 8vo. 15s. net.

Problems in Greek History. By J. P. MAHAFFY, M.A., D.D. Crown 8vo. 7s. 6d. net.

Social Life in Greece from Homer to Menander. By J. P. MAHAFFY, M.A., D.D. Crown 8vo. 8s. 6d. net.

Rambles and Studies in Greece. By J. P. MAHAFFY, M.A., D.D. Globe 8vo. 6s. 6d. net.

Our Hellenic Heritage. By H. R. JAMES, M.A. 2 vols. Illustrated. Crown 8vo.

    Vol. I. Part I. The Great Epics. Part II. The Struggle with Persia. 3s. each. Complete, 5s. net.

    Vol. II. Part III. Athens: Her Splendour and Her Fall. 4s. Part IV. The Abiding Splendour. 3s. 6d. Complete, 6s. net.

MACMILLAN AND CO., LTD., LONDON.

WORKS ON
GREEK HISTORY AND ARCHAEOLOGY

Ancient Athens. By ERNEST ARTHUR GARDNER, M.A., Yates Professor of Archaeology in University College, London. Illustrated. 8vo. 21s. net.

Schools of Hellas. An Essay on the Practice and Theory of Ancient Greek Education, 600 to 300 B.C. By KENNETH J. FREEMAN. Edited by M. J. RENDALL. With a Preface by A. W. VERRALL, Litt.D. *Third Edition.* Illustrated. 8vo. 7s. 6d. net.

Pausanias's Description of Greece. Translated by Sir J. G. FRAZER, O.M., D.C.L., Fellow of Trinity College, Cambridge. With Commentary, Illustrations, and Maps. *Second Edition.* 6 vols. 8vo. 126s. net.

Studies in Greek Scenery, Legend, and History. Selected from his Commentary on Pausanias by Sir J. G. FRAZER, O.M., D.C.L. Globe 8vo. 3s. 6d. net.

Troy : A Study in Homeric Geography. By WALTER LEAF, Litt.D. Illustrated. 8vo. 15s. net.

Homer and History. By WALTER LEAF, Litt.D. 8vo. 15s. net.

MACMILLAN AND CO., LTD., LONDON.